REPUBLICAN PAPERS

REPUBLICAN PAPERS

EDITED,
WITH AN INTRODUCTION BY,
Representative Melvin R. Laird

ANCHOR BOOKS
DOUBLEDAY & COMPANY, INC.
GARDEN CITY, NEW YORK
1968

The Anchor Books edition is the first
publication of *Republican Papers*

Anchor Books edition: 1968

Also available in a hardcover edition
from Frederick A. Praeger, Inc.

CONTENTS

Introduction *by Rep. Melvin R. Laird*   ix

1. Strengthening the Federal System   1

Perspectives on Federal Grants-in-Aid
   by Deil S. Wright   1
The Case for Revenue Sharing
   by Rep. Melvin R. Laird   60

2. Crime in America   85

Criminal Justice in the United States 1967: A
   Survey *by G. Robert Blakey*   85
A Report and Critique of the Current Efforts of
   the Federal Government to Control and Combat
   Crime in America *by Rep. Richard H. Poff*   101

3. Poverty, Welfare, and Jobs   129

Where Liberals Went Wrong
   by Daniel P. Moynihan   129
The Untruth of the Obvious *by Yale Brozen*   143
Poverty in America *by Rep. Charles E. Goodell and*
   Rep. Albert H. Quie   160
The Republican Opportunity Crusade as an Alter-
   native to the Anti-Poverty Program
   by Rep. Charles E. Goodell and
   Rep. Albert H. Quie   171
The Case for the Republican Human Investment
   Act *by Rep. Thomas B. Curtis*   191
The Case for the Negative Income Tax
   by Milton Friedman   202
Appendix to Chapter 3 *by Rep. Melvin R. Laird*   221

4. Civil Rights   227

Man Was Born to Be Free: Toward Fulfillment of
   the Dream *by Rep. William M. McCulloch*   227
Human Relations: The Challenge of Today and
   Tomorrow *by Rep. Clark MacGregor*   245

5. Toward Better Housing   253

Housing, A Social Paradox: Facing a Twin Challenge *by John M. Dickerman*   253
A Republican Program for Housing
   by Rep. William B. Widnall   276

6. The Future of Agriculture   289

Agriculture in Midpassage *by Don Paarlberg*   289
Farm Prices . . . And Food for a Hungry World
   by Rep. Odin Langen   305

7. Strengthening Social Security   325

Social Security: The Past Thirty Years
   by Colin D. Campbell   325
Social Security: The Next Thirty Years
   by Rep. James F. Battin   338

8. Full Employment and Economic Stability   355

The Employment Act Objectives: Retrospect and
   Prospect *by Henry C. Wallich*   355
Economic Policy and the Lessons of Experience
   by Paul W. McCracken   372
Essential Ingredients of Future Policy
   by Rep. John B. Anderson   391

9. Budgetary Problems   405

The Need for Budgetary Reform
   by Murray L. Weidenbaum   405
The Federal Budget *by Rep. Frank T. Bow*   419

10. Monetary Reform: National and International   429

The United States Balance of Payments
  by Gottfried Haberler   429
A Monetary and Fiscal Strategy for the 1970s
  by Raymond J. Saulnier   454
The Need for Balance *by Rep. Robert H. Michel*   468

11. Oversight and the Need for Congressional Reform   477

Congress' Neglected Function *by John F. Bibby*   477
The Need for Reform *by Rep. Marvin L. Esch*   489

INTRODUCTION

Republican Papers is a volume of discussion papers on the domestic crises facing today's America. They were prepared by recognized scholars and experts and by Republican members of Congress.

Republican Papers is not the Republican Party's platform of 1968. It is not a partisan campaign document designed for use by precinct captains and campaign workers in the political contests this year. It is not even a document necessarily subscribed to in all its particulars by the 187 members of the House Republican Conference.

We who were involved in the preparation of this volume do not disavow a hope that it will be useful to Republican candidates and to those who shape our party's platform in this crucial year, but that was not the primary motivation behind this effort.

What then is *Republican Papers* and what prompted its compilation? Why the specific title *"Republican" Papers*, and why at this particular time?

In the summer and fall of 1967, two emerging patterns were discernible. One seemed well advanced while the other was in its early stages. Both, however, cast their long shadow on America's future.

First, in a very real sense, American society seemed to be coming apart. Old and tired institutions were responding to old and tired solutions hardly at all. The search for scapegoats was on in earnest. Each level of government and each layer of authority within those levels seemed bent on blaming the other power centers, never themselves. A sense of leadership and direction, whether from elected officials, appointed administrators, or leaders of thought, seemed everywhere absent.

Amid all this, a second pattern—a more hopeful one—seemed also to be emerging. Whereas the disarray apparent all around us seemed in advanced stages, there were early signs of a new coalition forming. Not a political or ideological or interest-group coalition in the traditional sense, but a meeting of minds among men who heretofore had not found any common ground among them for discussion. The "hope" lay in the possibility that such a coalition, properly nurtured, could contribute significantly to reversing present trends and moving America forward once again.

It was against the backdrop of these conditions—to stem the one and nurture the other—that *Republican Papers* was conceived.

The title was suggested by two facts. First, that free societies are governed by politicians and political parties, that in the American political system with its two major parties, political leadership goes to that party which convinces a majority of its countrymen that it can provide better leadership and direction than its opponent.

Second, that the kind of analysis offered and the type of solution proposed in this volume are more readily identifiable with general Republican philosophy than with that of our Democratic counterparts. Many of the proposals contained herein, such as Revenue Sharing and the Human Investment Act, have been adopted officially by the Republican Party's highest policymaking body, the Republican Coordinating Committee.

Republican Papers are "discussion" papers because in some cases, no formal Party position has yet been taken. Indeed, the papers in this volume, except those by members of Congress, are not necessarily written by Republicans. The most notable exception, of course, is Daniel P. Moynihan who, together with another contributor, G. Robert Blakey, identifies himself as a Liberal Democrat.

The timing was suggested by a sense of urgency both with respect to the 1968 elections and to the need for new directions in America. We, of course, believe that these represent two sides of the same coin.

There has always been disagreement among men of good will concerning both the nature of a society's problems and the best means of correcting them.

In recent years, we have suffered through a period where motives have been questioned, where true dialogue has been stifled by demagogic charges that the "other side" is unconcerned with the poor and the poorly educated, the handicapped and the sick, the minority group and the ghetto resident.

The emerging coalition we hope to nurture is one composed of men willing to face past mistakes, men not wedded necessarily to old commitments, men sincerely and *primarily* interested in finding viable and practical solutions no matter where they originate.

Such a coalition—which at the moment may be small in numbers—consists of men who are at last prepared to set aside the irrational argument as to who is most aware of the problems in our society and to turn instead to the more relevant questions of what to do about them.

Daniel Moynihan is included in *Republican Papers* because he is considered such a man. His analysis not only in this volume but at other times and in other places commends itself to thoughtful men who seek meaningful answers to thorny problems. His "solutions" may not necessarily be our solutions but his questing search for true causes makes dialogue possible and welcome.

Milton Friedman, one of whose "solutions," the Negative Income Tax, is explored in this volume, falls into the same mold from the opposite end of the political spectrum. Both Friedman and Moynihan and others like them have something important to say to all policymakers in their analysis of the effects of past public decisions.

This fact—that before viable solutions can be effectively adopted there must come a hard evaluation of what is wrong with present approaches—dictated in part the format of *Re-*

publican Papers. The urgent need for better solutions suggested the other half of that format.

The scope and structure of *Republican Papers* stemmed from the strong conviction that all of our problems are interrelated, that really to accomplish something effective in dealing with them, we must at the national level step outside the specific problem of urban renewal or air pollution or unemployment or crime, and attempt to view the fabric whole.

Taken as a "whole," this volume is an attempt to do that with most of the major domestic problems that face our country. Each chapter is divided into two major sections: The first section focuses on the nature of the problems, with emphasis on our record to date in coping with them; the second section seeks to set forth viable solutions.

There are obvious omissions in the subjects covered. This was partly dictated by limited space. In some cases, it was obviated by recent publication of book-length discussions undertaken by other Republican members of the House. In the last Congress, for example, one such volume appeared on Congressional Reform and in this session another appeared on the Draft. Such vitally important topics as education, health, environmental pollution, economic development, play a prominent part implicitly and explicitly in such discussions as Revenue Sharing (Chapter I), job creation (Chapter III), and the several chapters on economics.

If there is a general theme that runs through *Republican Papers,* it consists of two parts: first, that thirty years of experimentation with New Deal, Fair Deal, New Frontier, and Great Society programs have not produced the desired result nor fulfilled the great promise ascribed to them; second, that the sheer complexity and diversity of our manifold ills require arrangements different from those attempted in the past, arrangements that will unleash all of the forces within our society, public and private, that are capable of contributing to the solutions we all seek.

In the latter connection, it should be stressed that legislation and "public" programs are only one facet of the monumental task that lies ahead. Perhaps more than any other ingredient, a steady sense of direction is required from our leaders at all levels of society—including government, the church, and private individuals.

One example of what could have been done without legislation in the wake of last summer's riots was outlined in a letter to President Johnson last August. It ties in quite closely to Representative Curtis' discussion of the Human Investment Act in Chapter III and is therefore included as an appendix to that chapter.

Republican Papers was an ambitious undertaking, dictated by urgency and executed in the hope that it will make a significant contribution to the growing rational dialogue on the future of our society. It is our intention in a later volume to discuss the equally grave international problems facing America in the final third of the twentieth century.

A special note of thanks is due all the contributors who so graciously and promptly responded to my appeals. Their willingness to set aside extremely busy schedules and other demands to produce *Republican Papers* is testimony to the importance each of them attaches to such an undertaking in these critical times.

Credit for coordination, staff work, and general compilation of the volume must go to my legislative assistant, William J. Baroody, Jr.

Melvin R. Laird

January 1, 1968
Washington, D.C.

REPUBLICAN PAPERS

Chapter 1

STRENGTHENING THE FEDERAL SYSTEM

PERSPECTIVES ON FEDERAL GRANTS-IN-AID
by Deil S. Wright

DEIL S. WRIGHT is Professor of Political Science at the
University of North Carolina (Chapel Hill). He has
previously taught at Wayne State University, the University of
Iowa, and the University of California (Berkeley).
He has published several books and numerous articles
in the areas of state and local government, public administration,
intergovernmental relations, and public
finances. In addition, he has served as a consultant to
various state and local governmental units.

INTRODUCTION

Three major aspects of federal grants-in-aid will be discussed
in this paper: (a) historical development; (b) fiscal
trends; and (c) views of participants in the grant-in-aid
process. Circumstances require that this be a brief and unavoidably
sketchy survey of a highly complex field. A more
complete analysis of the topic may be found in the author's
study, *Federal Grants-in-Aid: Perspectives and Alternatives.**

This essay does no more than delineate certain aspects and
problems currently associated with the federal grant-in-aid
technique. Some or many of these problems could be mitigated
by alternative devices and actions at the federal level
to alter what has become in recent decades the traditional
American response to domestic problems: the categorical
grant-in-aid.

It should be stressed at the outset that federal grants-in-aid

* Washington: American Enterprise Institute, 1968 © 1968,
American Enterprise Institute.

have a firm legal basis, provided mainly by three sets of landmark decisions by the Supreme Court.

A) *Massachusetts* v. *Mellon* and *Frothingham* v. *Mellon.* The Sheppard-Towner "Maternity Act" of 1921 was challenged by the State of Massachusetts and Mrs. Frothingham of that state. The net effect of the Court's decision was to negate the ability of anyone to challenge directly the expenditure of funds for federal grants.

B) *U.S.* v. *Butler.* Decided in 1935, this case produced, among other things, the holding that Congress' power to authorize expenditures of public monies for public purposes is not limited by the direct grants of legislative power found in the Constitution.

C) *Carmichael* v. *Southern Coal and Coke Company, Helvering* v. *Davis,* and others. These cases, decided in March 1937, and including the Social Security Act cases, upheld broad interpretations of the "general welfare" clause as it related to the purposes for which the national government might spend money.

Two prominent conclusions may be drawn from these decisions. First, there is no serious question or doubt about the legal and Court-approved foundation for federal grants-in-aid. Furthermore, barring an unexpected revolution in Court attitudes, we see few if any restraints that the Supreme Court is likely to interpose in the spending field. Indeed, the Massachusetts and Frothingham cases indicate the difficulty of gaining status to challenge national spending measures.

Second, where matters of spending and federal grants are involved, the role of the courts in federal-state relations is that of a spectator rather than arbiter or umpire.

Based on the Court's past decisions, there is general agreement that the present and future character of federalism in the United States will be settled largely by the executive and legislative branches of the national government rather than by the courts.

HISTORICAL DEVELOPMENT

Perhaps the first monetary "grant" from the federal government to the states appeared in 1836 with the distribution of the Treasury surplus. While the surplus technically was apportioned as loans, there was no expectation of repayment. Although the Morrill Act of 1862 to establish and maintain land-grant colleges was funded by the proceeds of land sales, its provisions set several precedents for later grant-type programs. For example, the objectives of the act were carefully spelled out, restrictions were placed on the use of revenues from the granted lands, and annual reports were required. In 1887 the first regular annual money grant was authorized to assist the states in establishing agricultural experiment stations. Prior to 1900 most federal assistance to the states was in the form of land grants, chiefly for educational purposes, or through technical assistance and services in kind.

In the nineteenth century the federal government was land rich and cash poor. Although tariff revenues occasionally did provide embarrassing surpluses, the greatest wealth of the national government consisted of its vast holdings. It was only natural and logical that the federal government, to achieve the aims of education and economic (national) development, should allocate this resource not only to the States but to private enterprises (railroads) and individuals (homesteading). Table 1 indicates the disposition of the public domain and indicates that the states were second only to individuals (homesteaders) in benefiting from land grants.

The passing of the nation's land frontier early in the twentieth century coincided with what may be termed the "revolution" in federal finance. In 1913 the 16th Amendment (income tax) became effective. The subsequent availability of federal monetary resources in conjunction with several other influences led to the establishment of several significant grant-in-aid programs between 1914 and 1921. The impact

TABLE 1
DISPOSITION OF THE PUBLIC DOMAIN OF
THE U. S. GOVERNMENT

Recipient	Acres received
State Governments	230,000,000
Homesteads	274,000,000
Railroads	94,200,000
Cash Sales and Miscellaneous	418,000,000
Total	1,016,200,000

SOURCE: Council of State Governments, *Federal Grants-in-Aid* (Chicago: 1949), p. 3.

of the federal income tax on intergovernmental relations generally and federal-state relations specifically can hardly be over-estimated.

The passage in 1914 of the Smith Lever Act for cooperative agricultural extension is usually designated as the beginning of the modern grant period. This legislation incorporated at least three new features that were to become standard components of most subsequent grant programs. These were:

(1) an apportionment formula for fund distribution among the states,

(2) state matching requirements (on a dollar for dollar basis), and

(3) advance federal approval of state plans.

Only two years later, in 1916, a much larger grant program for highway construction was passed with the inclusion of similar provisions.

A few other grant programs such as vocational education, vocational rehabilitation and maternal and child health were established from 1916 to 1921. But no programs were enacted from 1921 until the Great Depression when approximately a dozen major programs were passed between 1933 and 1938. The most notable of these were the categorical public assistance programs (aged, blind, and dependent children), health services (general, maternal, and child welfare), employment security, and public housing. The notable features of these grant programs were twofold:

(1) the extensive amount of federal administrative supervision provided for, if not required, and

(2) the conditions (subsequently attached to the Social Security Act of 1935) that state and local personnel employed to administer these programs be covered by merit systems.

One additional feature of the public welfare grant programs was the "open-ended" characteristic of federal financial participation. The states were given some leeway in defining eligibility requirements and setting upper limits on payments. Once eligibility and benefits were determined, the federal government's share of the costs was determined by fixed percentages of the benefits in successive benefit brackets, e.g., $\frac{5}{6}$ of the first $30; $\frac{2}{3}$ of the next $15, etc. This novel but unwieldy and problem-laden arrangement has not been applied to other grant programs to date. These open-ended categorical grant welfare programs represented major departures from the formula grant concept of fund allocation to the states.

The period since World War II has seen a number of significant developments in the federal grant field. Without discussing particular characteristics of specific programs, or tallying the number of programs and dollar amounts involved, it is possible to offer a few generalizations about what has occurred in the past two decades:

(1) There has been an extensive proliferation in the number and variety of grant programs. Only the 82nd Congress (1951–52) failed to establish at least one new grant program and the 89th Congress (1965–66) probably broke all records by enacting more than two dozen identifiable new grant-in-aid programs.

(2) There has been a significant tendency toward the establishment of programs that either "bypass" the

states or involve only minimal participation by state governments, e.g., the passage of enabling legislation. Some components of grant programs, most notably under the Poverty Program even bypass local governments.

(3) In the distribution of grant monies among the States the allocation formulas in the past twenty years have included a recognition of the differing state fiscal capacities. Under these formula provisions some equalization occurs since the federal government assumes more of the financial burden in the lower-income states than in the wealthier ones.

(4) There has been a notable shift in emphasis brought about by the number and size of the new programs. The focus of this emphasis is on urban-type or urban-oriented grant programs.

(5) Finally, grants ostensibly and primarily for state and local governments have permitted voluntary non-profit groups performing a public function to qualify for granted funds. The program areas where this notable development has occurred are in education, hospitals, and economic opportunity.

In the nineteenth century it was rural strength in the Congress that pressed for and obtained grants. In the 1910–20 period it was the force of the Progressive Movement. Originating in the New Deal and extending through most of the post World War II period it has been the urban-oriented interests that have applied the pressure and carried the banner for federal grants.

Why have "cities gone to Washington" with their problems and why has the federal government responded favorably? Aside from (a) the elasticity of the federal budget and (b) the legal breadth of the federal spending power, cities have found the national government receptive on representational grounds. Until reapportionment in recent years the U. S. Congress was often more urban-oriented than many state legislatures. This is particularly true of the Senate in contrast to the House of Representatives. But more significant from the interests of urban areas is the extent of their influence, through the unique institution of the Electoral College, in the election of the President. Since the Congress, by and large, looks to the President for leadership, the representational function has cast the chief executive in the role of advancing the extension of federal grants. The position of former President Eisenhower was instructive in this respect. He was personally and ideologically reluctant to foster deeper federal involvement in state-local affairs. Despite this reluctance, he approved several executive and congressionally initiated federal grant programs of which the massive federal-aid highway program was perhaps the most prominent.

What has been the nature and extent of recent developments in the grant-in-aid field? In particular what has happened to grants under the impact of "creative federalism"? For a tabular view of recent expansions in the grant field we may refer to Table 2. The two columns under the grants-in-aid heading are of primary interest. The grant authorizations have been subdivided into grants that are apportioned on a formula basis as contrasted to those authorizing project grants. The twenty-seven new formula grants authorized between 1964 and 1966 is a substantial increase in both absolute and proportionate terms since sixty-four formula grants were in effect in the former year. A major shift in the nature of federal grants, however, is denoted by the data on project grant authorizations. A net increase of one hundred project grant authorizations was recorded in two years. It seems clear from these data that the character of recent federal grant activity constitutes a substantially different thrust and emphasis from past patterns. Some observers interpret the extension of project grants as the hallmark of President Johnson's "creative federalism." The descriptions and rationale of creative federalism remain imprecise, however. A more apt term for the trend might be "projectitis." While project grants have the advantage of precision in dealing with specific problems they have some distinct disadvantages. Among these are the difficulties of coordination with other programs

TABLE 2
Classification of Federal Aid Authorizations by Types of Aid Made Available Under Laws in Effect at Specified Dates in 1964, 1965, and 1966.

Date and source	Grants-in-aid Apportioned formula grants	Project grants	Loans, or loan guarantees or insurance	Technical assistance	Miscellaneous cooperative programs	Shared revenues	Gross total	Less[2] multiple classifications	Net total of separate authorizations
1964, April 1 (original Catalog)— revised count	64	126	26	35	47	9	307	68	239
1965, Jan. 4 (first Supplement)[1]	76	151	28	40	55	9	359	76	283
1966, Jan. 10 (second Supplement)[1]	91	226	31	48	74	9	479	80	399

[1] The net change from the preceding line reflects expiration or repeal of earlier authorizations as well as addition of new authorizations.

[2] Some authorizations make available more than one type of Federal aid—e.g., a single statutory provision may cover both apportioned formula and project grants, or grants and technical assistance, or project grants and project loans. The authorization is counted for each available type of aid in those preceding columns which are applicable, and duplications are eliminated by the deductions shown in this column.

SOURCE: "Number of Authorizations for Federal Assistance to State and Local Governments Under Laws in Force at Selected Dates During 1964–66," by I. M. Labovitz (Washington, D.C.: The Library of Congress, Legislative Reference Service, July 5, 1966), p. 13.

and activities, the tendency toward bypassing the states and/
or local units, and the greatly increased administrative discretion available in determining their allocation.

Another comment is worth mentioning in connection with
Table 2. Despite increases in all other types of federal aid
authorizations there was no change in the number of shared
revenue programs. The number remained at nine, a rough
indication of the submerged role and significance of this type
of aid in both past and contemporary federal-state relations.
It is likewise indicative of the restricted role of shared revenues in intergovernmental relations that all nine shared revenue programs are in the functional field of natural resources.

An additional significant observation should be added from
the Total column in Table 2. The totals for 1964 and 1966
reveal an increase in the number of separate grant authorizations of 160 in two years. Comparable data for years prior
to 1964 are not available to document longer historical trends.
However, the peaking and proliferation of federal aids during the 88th and 89th Congresses is cast in sharp relief when
the two-year increase of 160 is contrasted to the 239 created
in all the years prior to 1964.

How are federal grant-in-aid authorizations distributed
throughout the federal administrative establishment? What
departments and agencies conduct this array of programs?
Table 3 furnishes the most current information on these
questions.

The Department of Health, Education, and Welfare
(HEW) is the chief channel for federal aid programs. This
observation will surprise no one familiar with intergovernmental relations. The data reveal that nearly one-half of all
the aid authorizations are administered by HEW. Within
HEW the Public Health Service and the Office of Education
are responsible for nearly an equal number. These two agencies enjoy the dubious distinction of being the most proliferated aid agencies. As if to remove the opprobrium of this
designation, but for other and sounder reasons, the Public
Health Service has moved to consolidate several of its detailed categorical health grant authorizations and programs

TABLE 3
NUMBER OF SEPARATE AUTHORIZATIONS OR SUBCATEGORIES OF
PROGRAMS OF FEDERAL AID TO STATE AND LOCAL GOVERNMENTS,
BY FEDERAL DEPARTMENT OR AGENCY UNDER LAWS
IN EFFECT JANUARY, 1966

Department or agency	January, 1966
Department of Health, Education, and Welfare:	
Public Health Service	69
Office of Education	68
Welfare Administration	25
Other	22
Total, Department of Health, Education, and Welfare	184
Department of the Interior	35
Department of Agriculture	28
Department of Housing and Urban Development	33
Department of Defense: Department of the Army	15
Department of Commerce	25
Department of Labor	9
Department of State	1
Department of the Treasury	3
Appalachian Regional Commission	13
Atomic Energy Commission	5
Executive Office of the President:	
Office of Emergency Planning	3
Office of Economic Opportunity	15
Federal Aviation Agency	2
Federal Power Commission	1
General Services Administration	8
Interstate Commerce Commission	1
National Foundation for Arts and Humanities	2
National Science Foundation	4
St. Lawrence Seaway Development Corporation	1
Small Business Administration	3
Tennessee Valley Authority	1
Veterans' Administration	3
Water Resources Council	2
General authorizations	2
Total	399

SOURCE: "Number of Authorizations for Federal Assistance to State and Local Governments Under Laws in Force at Selected Dates During 1964–66," by I. M. Labovitz (Washington, D.C.: The Library of Congress, Legislative Reference Service, July 5, 1966), pp. 10–11.

into a single large grant program. The Congress passed necessary legislation during 1966 to eliminate numerous specific grants and replace them with a single grant to foster comprehensive state health planning and public health services. The effect of this change remains to be observed and evaluated. In principle it appears to be a much-needed step toward a bloc or consolidated grant approach, a reform that has previously enjoyed considerable support and discussion.

Of eleven cabinet-rank departments, nine, as of 1966, administered one or more federal aid programs. Only Justice and the Post Office were omitted. Four departments have six or fewer programs with two of these, State and Treasury, having only one each. In addition to the nine departments, twelve other agencies have assigned responsibility for federal aid programs. Both the number of agencies and the number of programs reveal how extensive, diverse, and proliferated the federal aid field has become. Furthermore, approximately 125 federal bureaus and divisions currently administer these manifold programs in what one observer has labeled "The Administrative Abyss."

The hundreds of federal aid authorizations present a partial perspective on the national government's increased role and current level of domestic activity in the intergovernmental relations sphere. In some respects the perspective is somewhat biased by the use of "separate authorizations" data. Instead of citing 399 aid authorizations in effect as of January 1966, we could have identified "only" 162 major aid programs or groups of programs then functioning. This smaller figure results from a consolidation of the more detailed authorizations into broader program groupings.

In other words, it is possible to play the "numbers game" with federal aids. However, the existence of 399 aid authorizations or 162 programs (plus others added by the Congress in 1966 and 1967) constitutes no game for the recipients or beneficiaries of federal aids. These numbers pose heavy hazards over and above the potential benefits for government at all levels in our federal system. Perhaps the most significant one at the federal level, apart from sheer size, is that of co-

TABLE 4

FEDERAL GRANTS-IN-AID TO STATE AND LOCAL GOVERNMENTS, 1902-68
(MILLIONS OF DOLLARS)

Year	Veterans services, benefits (1)	Health, welfare, labor (2)	Education and general research (3)	Agriculture and agricultural resources (4)	Other natural resources (5)	Commerce, housing, transportation (6)	Total[a] (7)
1902	1.0	0.0	1.2	0.8	0.0	0.0	3.0
1912	1.2	0.0	2.5	1.6	0.0	0.0	5.3
1920	1.1	1.8	4.6	5.9	0.0	20.5	33.9
1925	0.7	1.5	8.5	7.3	0.3	95.4	113.7
1929	0.6	1.5	9.4	11.0	1.1	86.0	109.6
1930	0.6	0.7	10.0	11.9	1.3	79.8	104.3
1931	0.5	21.2	10.6	13.0	1.6	138.1	185.0
1932	0.8	59.9	11.1	13.0	1.7	132.0	218.5
1933	0.8	63.1	10.3	13.0	1.5	104.2[b]	192.9
1934	0.5	1,817.4	9.6	12.7	1.5	0.4[b]	1,842.1
1935	0.5	2,243.7	12.6	12.7	1.5	0.3[b]	2,271.3
1936	0.6	2,248.2	13.1	21.7	1.5	27.6[b]	2,312.7
1937	0.6	2,546.8	13.8	22.0	1.5	79.2[b]	2,663.9
1938	0.7	1,972.4	24.2	32.9	1.5	143.1	2,174.8
1939	0.7	2,622.5	24.7	92.4	2.5	161.3	2,904.1
1940	1.4	2,066.4	24.4	143.1	6.4	153.5	2,395.2
1941	1.4	1,771.3	25.2	110.1	4.1	170.6	2,082.7
1942	1.4	1,506.5	25.5	77.5	4.5	204.1	1,819.5
1943	1.2	902.6	26.1	47.7	9.0	299.8	1,286.4
1944	1.2	616.2	25.5	66.3	7.4	286.7	1,003.3
1945	1.2	570.2	25.0	81.9	7.5	218.2	904.0
1946	20.2	567.9	25.3	92.4	8.3	180.5	894.6

1947	59.2	902.1	32.2	65.1	9.8	601.9	1,670.3
1948	85.0	1,024.5	37.2	70.9	11.5	387.5	1,616.6
1949	31.6	1,231.5	36.9	86.6	14.0	442.2	1,842.8
1950	15.3	1,562.3	38.6	106.3	17.0	475.0	2,214.5
1951	9.0	1,637.2	48.8	98.3	17.7	434.0	2,245.0
1952	6.7	1,662.0	122.2	83.9	17.7	481.7	2,376.3
1953	6.3	1,811.1	231.0	97.3	19.8	594.4	2,762.9
1954	6.9	1,890.4	203.2	213.2	22.8	630.3	2,968.9
1955	7.7	1,854.2	239.3	247.7	24.9	723.6	3,098.4
1956	8.1	2,109.3	208.7	389.3	25.9	873.7	3,615.7
1957	8.2	2,178.9	204.6	381.8	26.6	1,016.4	3,816.5
1958	8.3	2,523.4	165.9ᶜ	278.2	26.6	1,723.9	4,731.0
1959	8.3	2,777.2	296.7ᶜ	322.5	31.3	2,877.8	6,317.0
1960	7.9	2,923.6	363.6ᶜ	275.3	34.5	3,241.6	6,847.3
1961ᵃ	9.0	3,133.8	378.2ᶜ	398.2	35.3	3,355.9	7,308.4
1962ᵃ	6.5	3,540.0	405.2ᶜ	537.8	33.3	3,195.6	7,719.8
1963ᵃ	8.2	3,813.4	465.2ᶜ	521.4	34.7	3,492.8	8,354.9
1964ᵃ	7.6	4,259.1	479.4	656.0	53.9	4,430.7	9,877.7
1965ᵃ	8.1	4,477.4	610.3	517.6	44.9	4,945.2	10,654.7
1966ᵃ	8.9	5,781.3	1,524.7	368.7	107.1	4,785.9	12,696.4
1967ᵃ (est.)	11.4	7,012.4	2,228.5	525.1	226.9	5,024.5	15,063.2
1968ᵃ (est.)	15.0	8,042.0	2,497.9	559.0	261.3	5,588.1	17,107.3

ᵃ Data in this table are drawn from tabulations made in prior years by the Labor and Welfare Division, Bureau of the Budget and for more recent years from special analyses dealing with grants-in-aid and accompanying the President's Budget. Figures shown do not tally precisely with other figures used in the text since Budget Bureau classifications encompass a few additional items not falling within the definition of grant-in-aid. These differences in no way affect the orders of magnitude or trends of Federal grants-in-aid. Shared revenues, loans, and repayable advances are excluded from these totals.

ᵇ Federal aid highway program financed for these years out of emergency relief funds.

ᶜ $5–7 million for services to Indians embracing both education and welfare functions.

ᵈ Calculated from U. S. Budget, "Special Analysis; Federal Aid to State and Local Governments," 1963–68.

ORIGINAL SOURCE: Advisory Commission on Intergovernmental Relations Periodic Congressional Reassessment of Federal Grants-In-Aid to State and Local Governments (Washington; June, 1961, A-8), p. 12–13.

ordinating these multifarious activities among and between different agencies. At the State and local level the difficulties are not only coordination (with the federal government and between grants) but also the problem of comprehension. A substantial information gap appears to have developed around the availability, purpose, and requirements of the numerous aid programs. As one Bureau of the Budget official expressed it, "Great increases in the number, complexity, and cost of federal grant-in-aid programs creates an urgent need for improved information management within and among the various levels of government involved."

FISCAL TRENDS

Total federal grants in 1902 were reported to total only $3 million. (See Table 4.) The impact of what one writer has called "Progressive Agrarianism" raised this initial sum elevenfold by 1920. Despite "normalcy," federal expenditure retrenchment, and no new grant programs, grant expenditures more than tripled between 1920 and 1930. Grants hovered near $200 million from 1931–33 before experiencing a meteoric tenfold rise in 1934. Grants remained in the neighborhood of $2 billion from 1934 through the depression years and into the early war years of 1941 and 1942. A high point of $2.9 billion was reached in 1939 but this fell sharply during the war years, reaching a low around $900 million in 1945 and 1946. Beginning in 1948 an uninterrupted series of increases has raised federal grants from $1.6 billion to an estimated $17.1 billion in fiscal 1968. Over the past two decades, then, grants have recorded more than a tenfold increase. Within the past decade grant sums increased from $4.7 billion to the currently estimated figure. In relative terms, this recent fourfold increase is about the same as that experienced in the 1920–30 decade. In absolute terms, however, the dollar increase in the most recent decade exceeded $12 billion; in the former decade the dollar increase was around $70 million.

Recent year-to-year increases in federal grants reveal a highly variable pattern and the annual percentage changes also show considerable fluctuation. Time series data from 1949 from both these change components appear in Table 5.

TABLE 5
ANNUAL CHANGES IN FEDERAL GRANTS-IN-AID
FROM 1949 TO 1968

Grant-in-Aid Increases over the Prior Year

Year	Dollars (Millions)	Percentage
1949	226.2	14.0
1950	371.7	20.2
1951	30.5	1.4
1952	131.3	5.8
1953	386.6	16.3
1954	206.0	7.5
1955	129.5	4.4
1956	517.3	16.7
1957	200.8	5.6
1958	914.5	24.0
1959	1,586.0	33.5
1960	530.3	8.4
1961	461.1	6.7
1962	411.4	5.6
1963	635.1	8.2
1964	1,522.8	18.2
1965	777.0	7.2
1966	2,041.7	19.2
1967 (Estimate)	2,366.8	18.6
1968 (Estimate)	2,044.1	13.6

SOURCE: Calculated from Table 4.

The largest grant increases in dollar terms have occurred in two periods during the two decades, 1958–60 and 1964–68. The increases during the former period, ranging from half to one-and-one-half billion dollars, can be explained largely by the rapid expansion of the highway grant program beginning in 1956. The second period of great expansion is less traceable to a single program than to the myriad of new grants under the panoply of the Great Society programs. Since

1963 federal grants have grown by more than a half-billion dollars each year and the 1966, 1967, and 1968 increases each topped two billion.

In proportional terms federal grants have risen annually by 10 percent or more in exactly half of the two decades of continuous increases. For the entire twenty year period the average annual increase in federal grants was 12.8 percent (obtained by averaging the percentage increases in Table 5).

These financial totals and the aforementioned increases in the number of grants, document the extensive expansion of federal action via the grant technique.

Grant Trends by Functional Outlay. The functional components of federal grant outlays present varied patterns. Little would be gained by extensive commentary on the detailed figures for each function. Rather, a few general observations will be offered about long-term trends for each function on the basis of Table 4.

Veterans Benefits: With the exception of the years immediately following World War II (1946–50) grants to the states for veterans services have seldom exceeded $10 million. It is evident from these figures that the national government has not used the grant mechanism for significant action in this field. Instead, the federal government has assumed direct and nearly complete responsibility for veterans benefits and services as witnessed by the $5.6 billion spent directly for veterans benefits and services in 1966.

Health, Welfare, Labor: Major expenditures for grant programs in this field were incurred throughout the depression. After a post-war low these amounts gradually and steadily increased until they approached $4.0 billion in 1963. Under the combined impact of expanded economic opportunity and public assistance outlays these health-welfare expenditures have soared to an estimated $8.0 billion in fiscal 1968.

Education and General Research: Federal grants for educational purposes remained at modest and comparatively insignificant levels up to 1951. They first exceeded $100 million in 1952 as a consequence of 1950 legislation authorizing construction and operating grants to schools in federally "impacted" areas. The second notable rise in education grants followed the National Defense Education Act of 1958. Federal grants reached nearly $300 million in 1959 and doubled to $600 million by 1965. Passage of the Elementary and Secondary Education Act of 1965 produced immediate and revolutionary fiscal results. Estimated educational grant outlays for 1968 approached $2.5 billion, a fourfold increase in three years.

Agriculture and Agricultural Resources: Grants to states and local governments seldom exceeded $100 million before 1954. In that year grants rose above $200 million for the first time and subsequently have fluctuated rather inconsistently between $200 million and $650 million. The chief variant in these grant outlays is the value of donated surplus agricultural commodities. This donable program in value terms constitutes from three-fifths to three-fourths of the grant amounts for agriculture.

Other Natural Resources: Federal grants for natural resources were, with one exception, less than $50 million as recently as 1964. In the short span of four years a tenfold expansion in outlays has been recorded. This rapid increase can be traced to new and expanded programs in two program areas. These are water pollution control and land and water conservation. Between 1964 and 1966 no less than twenty-one new grant authorizations were enacted in the natural resources field. Both the number and dollar amounts confirm the recent activity in this functional area. An additional dimension of federal impact in the resources field via shared revenues should be acknowledged. Shared revenue programs are currently (1968 estimate) producing over $200 million for the states. These aids have likewise experienced notable increases in recent years, e.g., from $100 million in 1964.

Commerce, Housing and Transportation: Federal grants for the numerous programs encompassed by the commerce-housing-transportation category were less than $600 million, except in 1947, until 1954. Beginning in this latter year, and especially following 1956, the financial totals reflect the combined impact of expanded highway and urban renewal pro-

TABLE 6

FEDERAL GRANTS-IN-AID TO STATE AND LOCAL GOVERNMENTS, 1902–68
(PERCENTS)

Year	Veterans service and benefits (1)	Health welfare and labor (2)	Education and general research (3)	Agriculture and agricultural resources (4)	Other natural resources (5)	Commerce, housing, Transportation (6)	Total[a] (7)	Total (billions of dollars) (8)
1902	33.3	–	40.0	26.7	–	–	100	b
1912	22.6	–	47.2	30.2	–	–	100	b
1920	3.2	5.3	13.6	17.4	–	60.5	100	b
1925	.6	1.3	7.5	6.4	.3	84.0	100	.1
1929	.5	1.4	8.6	10.0	1.0	78.5	100	.1
1930	.6	.7	9.6	11.4	1.2	76.5	100	.1
1931	.3	11.5	5.7	7.0	.9	74.6	100	.2
1932	.4	27.4	5.1	5.9	.8	60.4	100	.2
1933	.4	32.7	5.3	6.7	.8	54.0	100	.2
1934	.0	98.7	.5	.7	.1	.0	100	1.8
1935	.0	98.8	.6	.6	.1	.0	100	2.3
1936	.0	97.2	.6	.9	.1	1.2	100	2.3
1937	.0	95.6	.5	.8	.1	3.0	100	2.7
1938	.0	90.7	1.1	1.5	.1	6.6	100	2.2
1939	.0	90.3	.9	3.2	.1	5.6	100	2.9
1940	.1	86.3	1.0	6.0	.3	6.4	100	2.4
1941	.1	85.0	1.2	5.3	.2	8.2	100	2.1
1942	.1	82.8	1.4	4.3	.2	11.2	100	1.8
1943	.1	70.2	2.0	3.7	.7	23.3	100	1.3

1944	.1	61.4	2.5	6.6	.7	28.6	100	1.0
1945	.1	63.1	2.8	9.1	.8	24.1	100	.9
1946	2.3	63.5	2.8	10.3	.9	20.2	100	.9
1947	3.5	54.0	1.9	3.9	.6	36.0	100	1.7
1948	5.3	63.4	2.3	4.4	.7	24.0	100	1.6
1949	1.7	66.8	2.0	4.7	.8	24.0	100	1.8
1950	.7	70.5	1.7	4.8	.8	21.4	100	2.2
1951	.4	72.9	2.2	4.4	.8	19.3	100	2.2
1952	.3	69.9	5.1	3.5	.8	20.3	100	2.4
1953	.2	65.6	8.4	3.5	.8	21.5	100	2.8
1954	.2	63.7	6.8	7.2	.8	21.2	100	3.0
1955	.2	59.8	7.7	8.0	.8	23.4	100	3.1
1956	.2	58.3	5.8	10.8	.7	24.2	100	3.6
1957	.2	57.1	5.4	10.0	.7	26.6	100	3.8
1958	.2	53.3	3.5	5.9	.7	36.4	100	4.7
1959	.1	44.0	4.7	5.1	.5	45.6	100	6.3
1960	.1	42.7	5.3	4.0	.5	47.3	100	6.8
1961	.1	42.9	5.2	5.4	.5	45.9	100	7.3
1962	.1	45.9	5.2	7.0	.4	41.4	100	7.7
1963	.1	45.6	5.6	6.2	.6	41.8	100	8.4
1964	.1	43.1	4.9	6.6	.5	44.9	100	9.9
1965	.1	42.0	5.7	4.9	1.0	46.4	100	10.7
1966	.1	45.5	12.0	2.9	1.8	37.7	100	12.7
1967 (estimate)	.1	46.6	14.8	3.5	1.7	33.4	100	15.1
1968 (estimate)	.1	47.0	14.6	3.3	2.4	32.7	100	17.1

a Detail may not add to 100 because of rounding.
b Less than .05 billion.
SOURCE: Calculated from Table 5.

grams. In 1957 expenditures for this functional category stood at approximately $1.0 billion. Projected outlays for fiscal 1968 are nearly $5.6 billion. Of this latter amount $3.8 billion is the estimated expenditure for the federal aid highway program (from the highway trust fund). Housing and community development expenditures are planned for about $1.3 billion. This figure includes approximately $450 million for urban renewal and $275 million for low-rent public housing. Transportation (highways) remains the dominant program but recent rapid increases have been recorded in the housing and community development category. From 1964 to 1968 outlays have tripled in this area while the number of new grant authorizations doubled from 17 to 32 between 1964 and 1966.

The percentage distribution in Table 6 provides the basis for considering the changing functional emphases among grants over time.

Prior to 1932 the dominant portion of federal grants, more than 60 percent was spent on commerce-transportation-housing functions. Federal response to the depression drastically altered the functional focus in the grant-in-aid field. From 1934 to 1946 more than 60 percent of all grants were spent on health-welfare purposes. During the depression and New Deal years health-welfare outlays were more than 90 percent of total federal grants.

The decade from 1950 to 1960 produced a consistent decline in the proportion of grants to the health-welfare function. The decline is partially explained by moderate increases in the proportions of grants to agriculture. The chief cause of the decline, however, came from the rising percentages of grants going to commerce-transportation-housing functions. In 1950, 21 percent of all federal grants went for these purposes. By 1960, the proportion slightly exceeded 47 percent. Since 1960 the relative position of this functional area has declined to about one-third of all grants. The displacement is the result of recent and rapid expansions in education grants. The latter function accounted for 5 percent of grants in 1960. In 1968 its estimated share will be about 15 percent.

From an original concentration on commerce-transportation-housing functions federal grants have altered to emphasize, in varying degrees, the health-welfare functions. More recently, the function of education has assumed a greater relative importance. The fact remains, however, that nearly half of all present federal grants are for health-welfare activities. About one-third support transportation-housing activities with education commanding about one-seventh of all grant funds.

Federal Grants Relative to Other Financial Trends. How do the increases in grants compare with what is occurring in other sectors of federal, state, and local finance? Are federal grants an increasing, constant, or decreasing proportion of state and local revenues? How do grants compare as a proportion of state and state-local expenditures? With regard to federal outlays, are grants increasing as a percentage of cash payments to the public?

Federal grants in the past two decades have become an increasing proportion of revenue and expenditure aggregates at the state and local level. (See Table 7.) Their relative impact is pronounced on both the revenue and expenditure sides of the ledger. In 1946 grants were less than 8 percent of state-local general revenue. By 1965 the proportionate reliance on grants had more than doubled and approached 17 percent. The intervening percentages show a clear though inconsistent trend upward. A similar overall trend can be observed for state and state-local general expenditures. The divergence between the 1946 and 1965 state-local expenditure proportions is approximately the same as for revenues. For state expenditures, with local outlays excluded, a similar secular trend upward is evident although the percentage for 1965 is not double the 1946 proportion. The dominant feature of this time series, however, is major reliance of states on federal grants. More than one-third of state financed general expenditures is derived from federal grants. Currently the state-local sector is receiving more and spending more in proportionate terms from federal grants than at any time since

TABLE 7
FEDERAL GRANTS-IN-AID AS A PERCENTAGE OF
STATE AND LOCAL FISCAL AGGREGATES
1946–65

		Grants as a Percentage of	
Year	State-Local general revenue from own sources	State-Local general expenditures less intergovernmental revenue	State general expenditures less intergovernmental revenue
1946	7.8	8.8	20.4
1948	10.5	10.2	20.9
1950	12.0	10.9	22.5
1952	10.5	10.1	21.2
1953	11.3	11.0	23.2
1954	11.4	10.7	23.0
1955	11.1	10.1	21.8
1956	11.5	10.8	23.2
1957	11.1	10.4	22.2
1958	13.0	11.8	25.2
1959	16.2	14.9	32.0
1960	15.7	15.2	33.4
1961	15.6	14.9	32.7
1962	15.3	14.8	32.4
1963	15.4	14.9	32.0
1964	16.9	16.7	35.6
1965	16.8	16.7	35.5

SOURCES: Federal grant data from Table 5; state-local fiscal data from U. S. Bureau of the Census, from *Historical Statistics on Governmental Finances and Employment,* Vol. 4, No. 4, *Census of Governments: 1962* (Washington: 1964) and, since 1962, from *Governmental Finances* (annual), Series GF-No. 6.

NOTE: The percentages in this table are slightly and uniformly higher than comparable ones for similar aggregates appearing in *U. S. Budget* and *Special Analysis* Tabular presentations. These divergences result from the exclusion of intergovernmental revenues from these state and local fiscal aggregates but not from those on which Budget Bureau computations are based.

the end of World War II. The gist and conclusion of this analysis is simple and direct: federal grants are increasing at a more rapid rate than state and local revenues or expenditures.

If increasing proportions are the rule for federal grants in relation to state and local fiscal aggregates, what is the pattern at the national level? Are federal grants a growing part of cash payments to the public? Here the limits of the available data require us to restrict our time perspective to the years since 1955. We also have to deal with financial totals that encompass all federal aids—loans and shared revenues as well as standard grants. (See the column headings of Table 2 for grant and non-grant categories included under the broad concept of "federal aids.")

A glance at the percentages in both columns of Table 8 shows that federal aids are becoming a large proportion of federal cash payment outlays including or excluding military-related outlays. In both instances the proportions have about doubled in the fourteen fiscal years. In other words, aids to state and local governments have about doubled in relation to federal fiscal aggregates, in a fashion almost identical to their changing relation to state-local finance except that the former has occurred in a shorter time than the latter. The impact of Vietnam outlays will no doubt deter somewhat the subsequent figures in the first column of Table 8. Current proportions channeled into federal aids constitute one-tenth of all federal cash outlays and one-fifth of domestic federal outlays.

The persistent and predominant theme of this section is clear and has been documented in different ways by a variety of measures. Whether measured in number of programs, aggregate or functional outlays, or by grants (or aids) as a proportion of state-local or federal finances, federal grants have increased significantly in the past two decades, substantially in the past single decade, and very sharply in the past three to four years. In light of these trends it is relevant to consider the attitudes that grants have engendered among public officials responsible for their enactment and administration.

TABLE 8

TOTAL EXPENDITURES FOR AID TO STATE AND LOCAL GOVERNMENTS
(BUDGET AND TRUST ACCOUNTS) AS A PERCENTAGE OF
CASH PAYMENTS TO THE PUBLIC

| | Federal Aids as a Percentage of | |
Year	Total cash payments to the public	Domestic cash payments to the public[a]
1955	4.6	11.9
1956	5.1	12.7
1957	5.0	12.5
1958	5.9	14.2
1959	7.0	15.0
1960	7.5	15.6
1961	7.1	15.0
1962	7.3	15.6
1963	7.6	16.1
1964	8.4	17.5
1965	8.9	17.7
1966	9.4	18.8
1967	9.6	19.5
1968	10.1	20.4

[a] Excluding payments for national defense, space, and international affairs and finance.

SOURCE: *Special Analyses, Budget of the United States, Fiscal Year 1968* (Washington: n.d.) p. 148.

PARTICIPANTS' PERSPECTIVES

The purpose of this section is to examine the views of participants involved in federal grant and federal aid programs. Most of the information presented and discussed was gathered and analyzed by standardized objective procedures that would afford a basis for supportable generalizations about participants' attitudes. In addition to this systematic data we also draw on interpretative and qualitative data to point up some of the friction points with respect to federal grants. There is an acknowledged element of bias in this selectivity since a major focus is on the problematic aspects of grants.

Unless these points of tension are recognized, however, there is a tendency to overvalue the aims and achievements of grants with lesser regard for the problems and difficulties associated with the grant device.

We will examine the perspectives of several grant-in-aid participants starting with Congress. Subsequently we will turn in order to: federal administrators, governors, state administrators, and local officials.

Congress and Grants. What is the attitude of Congress toward grants-in-aid? Roll call votes in both sessions of the 86th (1959–60) and 87th (1961–62) Congresses provide an interesting sample. The former Congress was Democratically controlled in the House (282–154) and Senate (64–34) while the White House was occupied by Republican President Eisenhower. This Congress featured many attempts by liberal Democrats to push through social and economic legislation on the heels of major victories at the polls in November 1958. The 87th Congress was also controlled by the Democrats with majorities of 263–174 in the House and 65–35 in the Senate. Contrasted with the 86th Congress, however, the Executive Branch featured the expansion-oriented New Frontier programs of President John F. Kennedy.

From both of these Congresses we selected for analysis all roll call (recorded) votes on grant-in-aid programs. The chief criterion for the selection and use of a roll call was that the issue voted on directly posed either of two questions: (1) instituting a new federal grant-in-aid program, or (2) expanding or otherwise enlarging an existing grant program.

The number of roll call votes on grants eventually selected in both Congresses by chamber were:

86th Congress:
    House—12 roll calls
    Senate—18 roll calls
87th Congress:
    House—21 roll calls
    Senate—23 roll calls.

The larger number of roll calls recorded in the House in the 87th Congress may be attributed in part to the expansion of the House Rules Committee in 1961. This enlargement was aimed at bringing more legislation to a vote on the floor of the House and it apparently succeeded in the case of grants-in-aid.*

These roll calls, by Congress and by chamber were analyzed quantitatively by means of an attitude ordering technique known as cumulative scaling. This method permitted us to place each legislator on a continuum from least to most favorable toward more and expanded grants-in-aid. This continuum we designated as the lesser-larger federal role scale.

Our analysis of the 74 roll call votes produced seven separate but highly interrelated attitude scales: one for the House in the 86th Congress and two each for Senate in the 86th and for both chambers in the 87th. The economies of space require us to limit our data presentation. (More complete analysis and presentation appear in the author's previously mentioned book. See p. 1.) However, the similarity of substantive results that persist throughout the larger analysis make the following tabulations and discussion fully representative.

What is the relationship between the positioning of House and Senate members on lesser-larger federal role scales and their party affiliation? The results of cross-tabulating political party and two grant-in-aid attitude scales for the 86th Con-

---

* The program fields in which each of the grant-in-aid votes occurred, together with the number of roll calls (in parentheses) were:

86th Congress:
    House: Education (3), Water Pollution (3), Airports (4), and Area Redevelopment (2).
    Senate: Education (6), Airports (5), Area Redevelopment (6), and Water Pollution (1).
87th Congress:
    House: Education (7), Public Assistance (3), Unemployment Compensation (2), Depressed Areas (2), Highways (1), Housing (3), Public Works (1), and Water Pollution (2).
    Senate: Education (12), Depressed Areas (6), and Public Works (5).

gress appear in Tables 9 and 10. What observations may be drawn on the basis of these illustrative analyses?

First, it is clear that party identification is a critical variable sharply dividing members of both chambers in their outlook (and voting behavior) on federal grants. In Table 9 for example only 8 percent of the Democrats but 81 percent of the Republicans voted at the "high" end of the lesser federal role scale. At the opposite end of the scale, 60 percent of the

TABLE 9

CONGRESSIONAL ROLL CALL VOTING ON LESSER FEDERAL ROLE ISSUES
(FEDERAL GRANTS-IN-AID) FOR 12-ITEM SCALE BY PARTY,
U. S. HOUSE OF REPRESENTATIVES, 86TH CONGRESS (1959–60)

Lesser Federal Role	Party	
	Democrat	Republican
	(percentages)	
High[a]	8	81
Medium[b]	32	16
Low[c]	60	3
	100%	100%
N =	267	147

SCALE COEFFICIENTS: CR = .92; CS = .48
[a] Voted in favor of a lesser Federal role on 9 to 12 of the 12 items.
[b] Voted in favor of a lesser Federal role on 1 to 8 of the 12 items.
[c] Voted in favor of a lesser Federal role on none of the 12 items.

TABLE 10

CONGRESSIONAL ROLL CALL VOTING ON LESSER FEDERAL ROLE ISSUES
(FEDERAL GRANTS-IN-AID) FOR EDUCATION SCALE (6 ITEMS)
BY PARTY, U. S. SENATE, 86TH CONGRESS, (1959–60)

Lesser Federal Role	Party	
	Democrat	Republican
	(percentages)	
High[a]	9	65
Medium[b]	20	20
Low[c]	71	15
	100%	100%
N =	65	34

SCALE COEFFICIENTS: CR = .89; CS = .65
[a] Voted for lesser Federal role on 4 to 6 of the 6 items.
[b] Voted for lesser Federal role on 1 to 3 of the 6 items.
[c] Voted for lesser Federal role on none of the 6 items.

Democrats voted in favor of a larger federal role on grants in every instance on the twelve roll call items that constituted the scale. Only 3 percent of the House Republicans were found at that end of this particular grant scale.

Second, a majority of all Democrats in both the House and Senate invariably fall in the "low" category so far as a lesser federal role is concerned. Stated conversely, they would rank in the "high" category so far as a larger federal role through grants-in-aid. Generally the scale positioning of the Democrats put a majority of them in favor of a larger federal role on *every* roll call item in the scale. This polarization and uniformity was nowhere matched by the Republicans. In no instances did a majority of Republicans vote uniformly at a single scale position on the lesser-larger federal role continuum.

While the percentages in the tables are artifacts of the collapsing among the scale categories, it is possible to discern some inter-scale as well as inter-party contrasts and similarities. We have already noted that Republican voting is less polarized than the voting behavior of Democrats. It is also apparent that Republicans in the Senate for both Congresses are not as strongly disposed toward a lesser federal role as their brethren in the House. For the Democrats the same pattern holds. Higher proportions of Democrats in the Senate than in the House appear in the low category for a lesser federal role. In other words, the Democrats in the Senate are far more favorably disposed toward grants than their counterparts in the House. Thus, for both parties, Democrat and Republican, we find less favorable dispositions toward a lesser federal role than in the House. This finding, persisting across party lines, suggests a different institutional outlook toward the federal system in the Senate. It is apparently indicative of the broader, more urban, and varied constituencies to which Senators respond. The difference may also reflect the more immediate electoral proximity of the House members to the voters by virtue of their two-year terms.

This House-Senate contrast suggests an irony about the role of the Senate in the federal system. The framers of the Constitution and writers of *The Federalist* papers thought of the Senate as a guardian of the states' interests. Not only did the guardian role not develop historically but currently there is more favorable sentiment for federal involvement via grants in the Senate than in the House of Representatives.

One overriding conclusion thrusts itself to the forefront. We traditionally hear about the absence of noticeable differences between parties in the United States. This analysis of roll call votes on grants-in-aid reveals that party membership is a powerful and significant variable in explaining Congressional stands on the lesser-larger federal role continuum. Furthermore, the association persists across chambers and across congresses confronting Presidents of different political persuasions.

Federal Administrators and Grants. A systematic survey of federal administrators of grant programs was conducted by the Senate Subcommittee on Intergovernmental Relations in 1965 and published (as a Committee Print) under the title *The Federal System as Seen by Federal Aid Officials.* It is not possible in the short space available to do justice to the scope, complexity, and richness of the findings disclosed by the Committee survey. We will attempt to convey some of the major results in a few paragraphs that rely heavily on the Committee's work.

A 77-item questionnaire was distributed under Committee auspices to over a hundred federal administrators responsible for one or more aid programs. Of the 100-plus officials responding 48 were specifically identified as directors of major grant-in-aid programs. The others' responsibilities were more limited in scope, e.g., directing shared revenue or loan programs.

How can we sum up the attitudinal perspectives of federal aid administrators? Four perceptual themes seem to persist among the managers of federal aid programs: (1) functionalism, (2) professionalism, (3) protectionism, and (4) indifference.

The functional focus of these administrators was to be expected. What was not anticipated was the excessive preoccupation with program politics and a consequent insensitivity to

the complexities and the nuances of intergovernmental relationships. Functionalism produced a one-track-mind approach
within this crucial set of grant program participants. Single-
mindedness, while occasionally laudable, has severe shortcomings in dealing with political complexity.

Professionalism reinforced the functional outlook of the
administrators. There was a deep and commendable commitment to professional ethical standards, specialized competence,
the merit system, and the upgrading of program performance at all levels of government. But this attitude syndrome
also produced a distrust of any partisan policy influences on
the grant program and a special dislike for "meddling" gen-
eralist administrators seeking to keep grant programs in phase
and coordinated with other ongoing activities. Especially disconcerting to the attitudinal frame of reference of these
administrators were the efforts of state and local policy gen-
eralists to assert the importance of intergovernmental coordination. The aid administrators saw intergovernmental
coordination only in a single program sense. They preferred
to deal with their functional counterparts at other levels. Even
in this latter instance a note of disdain was struck. The federal officials were conscious of their senior role and specialized competence through which they hoped to upgrade their
state and local counterparts.

A distinctly conservative and protective note characterized
the outlook of the administrators when questions of changed
procedures, altered administrative practices, and policy innovations were presented to the respondents. Administrative in-
clinations toward stability and continuity are well known and
certainly necessary to some extent. But these grant administrators exhibited these tendencies in an unusual degree,
rejecting as ill-considered several possible changes in grant
procedures that would alleviate friction from the state and
local governments' standpoints.

The indifference of the aid administrators to intergovernmental matters was reflected throughout their questionnaire
responses. This indifference was partly attributable to the preceding attitudes of functionalism, professionalism, and protec-

tionism. But the simple fact of ignorance also contributed to the indifferent outlook of these administrators toward intergovernmental relations. Grant administrators' "tunnel vision" seems to stem from the security of the positions they hold, from the needed expertise they furnish to the programs they administer, and from their view that many major questions and problems involving intergovernmental relations are the responsibility of others. Let George do it!

The significance of grant administrators' perspectives deserves emphasis. These administrators constitute more than just one of three legs in the "triple alliance" of Congressional committee, interest group, and administrative bureau support of grant enactments. They are also one of the prime sources from which ideas for program changes originate and develop. It is not inaccurate to say that administrators' views often make the critical difference in legislative decisions on pending legislation. Congressmen also look to administrators for new and innovative ideas in policy areas. The prime lesson from the opinion survey of administrators is that the Congress cannot obtain the necessary breadth of advice about intergovernmental problems from federal administrators.

Perhaps none of the existing and traditional channels of information input to the legislative process are adequate. Congress' current informants are heavily biased. In the grant-in-aid field this means a bias toward more specialized categorical grants. Important alternative approaches are obscured or not raised and even marginal adjustments (such as program coordination mechanisms) are quashed in pursuit of programmatic professionalism.

The brunt of the blame cannot be legitimately laid at the feet of federal administrators. Grant programs cannot be created and expanded without the continuing assent of the Congress. The recent and long-term expansions of grants-in-aid by the Congress have been revealed by the roll call analysis and the fiscal and numerical trend data. The roll call data demonstrate important lessons about the politics of categorical grants. Republican opposition to grants, while general and substantial, has not been as uniform and consistent as the

Democratic position favoring categorical grants. Republican opposition, however, appeared to have had anti-spending as its mainspring rather than utilizing what might be termed "the strategy of the constructive alternative."

The results of party polarization on grants can easily be seen from the twenty-twenty vision that hindsight provides. The Democratic party has controlled both houses of Congress since 1946 with the exception of the 80th (1947–49) and 83rd (1953–55) Congresses. The "predictable" results have been clearly documented in a number of ways. There appear to be only two ways to break the lock-step approach into which we have fallen on the grant device. First, significant numbers of the majority party will have to realize or be convinced that the cumulative consequences of categorical aids cry out for revision. A second avenue is for the minority party to become the majority party and in the process commit itself to the pursuit of sensible alternatives to categorical grants. Whichever political solution is arrived at, it will be necessary for the Congress to obtain, on a more regular and systematic basis, the broader perspectives on intergovernmental relations necessary to intelligent legislation. Important contributors to these broader viewpoints will be state and local officials. We obtain some indications of these officials' current perspectives in the following sections.

Governors and Grants: The position of a governor in relation to the "new federalism" of grant-in-aid programs is anomalous, ambiguous, and ambivalent. Grants supply a major portion of state budgets. Politically and programmatically it would border on electoral suicide flatly to oppose or refuse to accept grants. Indeed, there are positive political payoffs from the governor's standpoint in knowing about and obtaining as much federal aid as possible. Federal aid does assist in meeting some demands for services and, perhaps more importantly from the governor's position, grants are believed to keep state taxes down. In this latter respect grants may be especially revered by governors as a means of forestalling political defeat at the hands of an angry tax-conscious electorate.

But grants have disadvantages. From the gubernatorial perspective these are both political and administrative in character. Politically, grants from a national perspective restrict the range of policy choices open to the state's chief executive not only between programs but also within aided programs where several detailed categories of grants may exist or where statutory and administrative policies may sharply limit flexible and effective use (from the governors' viewpoint) of grant funds.

An additional dimension of policy restraint on the governor comes from pressure groups. Highways is one example. The locus of policy determination seldom rests with governors. It usually lies with reinforcing alliances of highway engineers at all levels and highway construction contractors.

Grants-in-aid assuredly foster and contribute to the hazards and headaches experienced by governors in the performance of their political and administrative leadership roles. One student of the governorship, Coleman Ransone, has succinctly summarized the cross-pressures faced by state chief executives in the contemporary intergovernmental context: "The New Federalism—Bane or Boon?" In his book *The Office of Governor in the United States* he suggests two summary observations (p. 249–50) regarding the political and administrative roles of the governor vis-à-vis grants: (a) "In practice, therefore, the governor finds that his policy decisions are conditioned by the policy decisions which have been made in Washington," and (b) "The governor, to a considerable extent, is by-passed in the line of communication and finds that his control over both policy and management of the agencies which administer these (grant) programs at the state level is weakened considerably."

How do the governors themselves express their views regarding several aspects of grant programs? We draw on exceptionally limited data. We are not aware, for example, of the frequency and regularity with which governors are called upon to testify before Congressional committees. Governors' meetings with the President are sufficiently noteworthy to produce newspaper coverage but we still lack any systematic analysis of the frequency and substantive nature of president-governor interactions.

Very few efforts have been made to solicit reactions from governors to questions on grants-in-aid. Probably the most productive of these was sponsored by the House Subcommittee on Intergovernmental Relations in 1957. The number of governors responding to the battery of questions posed varied from twenty to more than thirty. Detailed questions were posed in four functional areas: employment security, highways, public health, and welfare. Although some reservation exists about the extent to which the responses represented directly the views of the governors rather than some of the governors' program officials, it appears that all the responses to the Committee's inquiry were cleared through the governors. These responses are presented for the four major functions in Table 11.

There was predominant if not majority sentiment favoring expansion in all four program areas. Clear majorities were satisfied with federal supervision but a notable minority indicated some dissatisfaction. There was also a substantial minority of the governors favoring some transfers of responsibility in the programs, mainly in the direction of a greater state role. The last two areas probed by the survey pointedly demonstrated the dissonance present among governors—with respect to grant programs. With only incidental exceptions the governors were single-minded in noting that federal legislation was "urgently needed" and that administrative actions and improvements were needed at the federal level. Their positions on these items stand in contrast to their prior expansionist policy positions and their general satisfaction with program responsibilities and federal supervision. These response patterns, although dated and admittedly limited in scope and representativeness, nevertheless document the problematic status of the governor under the "new federalism." If space permitted we could speculate at length on the impact of "creative federalism" on the governor's position. Suffice it to say that the proliferation of grants by number, type,

TABLE 11

NUMBER OF STATE GOVERNORS REPLYING TO SELECTED QUESTIONS FOR FOUR MAJOR GRANT PROGRAMS, 1957

Program	Total[1]	Transfer responsibility Yes, to				Adequacy of program				Legislation urgently needed			Federal supervision		Administrative measures needed		
		Federal	State	Local	No	Adequate	Expand	Reduce	Eliminate	Yes Federal	State	No	Satisfactory	Unsatisfactory	Yes Federal	State	No
Public welfare	32	2	7	0	19	9	17	1	1	24	0	1	21	6	20	3	2
Highways	26	0	8	1	10	1	15	0	0	12	0	3	19	1	9	3	2
Public health	22	0	4	3	7	7	10	0	0	17	0	2	15	5	14	3	2
Employment security	21	1	9	0	10	6	8	0	0	14	1	0	13	4	13	2	1

[1] Replies to individual questions may not add to total for program because respondents did not answer all questions in every case.

SOURCE: *Replies From State and Local Governments to Questionnaire on Intergovernmental Relations* Sixth Report by the Committee on Government Operations, U. S. House of Representatives, 85th Congress, 1st Session, House Report No. 575 (June 17, 1957), p. 4.

and dollar amounts have undoubtedly added to the complexities and strains on his position.

Generally speaking, then, governors acknowledge the political and programmatic advantages accruing from grants but are quick to find fault with the financial and administrative problems that almost invariably accompany grants. In this connection it seems appropriate to illustrate some of the specific complaints that governors see as concomitants of grants. Three excerpts will exemplify the depth and breadth of problems encountered.

The first involves the "single agency" requirement present in many grant stipulations. This provision specifies that a state receiving a particular grant must agree that the program will be administered by one state agency with sole responsibility for the activity. The difficulties posed by the single-state-agency concept are well illustrated in the following sketch of a case study arising from Oregon's effort to institute a state reorganization plan for health, education, and welfare activities.

> The Oregon plan contemplated a state agency similar in program responsibilities to the federal Department of Health, Education and Welfare. The Governor would appoint the Director of Social Services who would appoint division heads responsible for administration of health, mental health, public assistance, veterans' affairs and vocational rehabilitation programs. The plan also provided that administrative decisions of the respective divisions would be reviewed by the Director of Social Services.
>
> The proposed reorganization plan was questioned (by federal officials) on three grounds: (1) that it interposed between the Governor and the administrators of aided programs the Director of the Department of Social Services; (2) that it provided for appointment of administrators of aided programs outside the merit system; and (3) that administrative authority would be subject to review beyond that of the respective divisions. An additional

obstacle presented itself in the case of vocational rehabilitation in that the federal law specifies that, to be eligible for federal assistance, the general vocational rehabilitation program must be administered or supervised by the vocational education agency or an agency primarily concerned with vocational rehabilitation. No cure appears feasible here other than amendment of the federal law.

In brief the barrier that the Oregon reorganization plan met was the "single state agency" concept. Departmental concern was expressed that the Oregon approach failed to lodge final administrative responsibility in the several administrative units of divisions of the Department of Social Services as required by the Social Security Act's public assistance and child welfare provisions and the Public Health Services Act's venereal disease control, tuberculosis control and general health services provisions and its hospital construction provisions.

This example, from *State Government Organization and Federal Grant-In-Aid Requirements* (p. 16–17), is one of several included in a special report to the governors conference in 1962 by the Council of State Governments. That study, which noted the single agency rule as the chief federal deterrent to state administrative reorganization, was authorized by the 1961 Governors' Conference where a resolution was passed deploring "the tendency of federal agencies to dictate the organizational form and structure through which the states carry out federally supported programs."

A second group of objections from a governor's point of view centers around the lack of consistency among grant programs in allocation formulas and matching requirements. Illustrative of problems present in these areas is the testimony of Rhode Island Governor John H. Chafee.

Let us take the case of a 15-year-old boy on aid to dependent children who has a hearing problem that can be corrected. My natural response, as I am sure yours is too, would be "correct his hearing." However, confusion arises when one considers whether he should be referred

to the public assistance medical care program administered by the Department of Social Welfare, the Division
of Vocational Rehabilitation administered by the Department of Education, or to the crippled children's program
administered by the Department of Health. Under such
conditions there is the temptation—and I must say this
is a very real one—to refer such a patient not to the program which is best organized to meet his particular need,
but to the program in which the State obtains the best
financial advantage. The Federal Government will pay
50 percent of the cost when the care is provided by the
Crippled Children's Division; it will pay 56 percent under
title XIX since he is on aid to dependent children; and,
if he is cared for by vocational rehabilitation, the Federal Government will soon pay 75 percent of the bill.
Each of these programs has some variations in standards
for eligibility but nonetheless the differences in Federal
reimbursement seem extremely puzzling. (*Investigation
of HEW,* Hearings, Committee on Interstate and Foreign
Commerce, House, 89th Congress, 2nd Session, p. 4)

The range of gubernatorial objections and exasperations
vary considerably. Consider as a third example the following
portions of a governor's speech at the 1958 Governors' Conference.

What is needed is the redirection of our energies away
from the theoretical arguments over a separation of State
and Federal activity to a consideration of the deficiencies
in the mechanism as it now operates. There are many
deficiencies in Federal-State relations. We should seek to
identify them and to develop sensible recommendations
for their correction.
    We should in other words, analyze what Professor
Grodzins has called the "squeak" points in intergovernmental relations and how they impair the operation of the Federal-State mechanism. We should examine such conditions and problems as the following:
    (1) Because Federal appropriations are voted on an

annual basis and many States operate on biennial budgets, the States experience great difficulty in planning their programs involving Federal aid. They do not know how much will be available until Congress has acted.

(2) The large numbers of separate Federal aid programs introduces a chaotic note in State budgeting, tending to impair the maintenance of the executive budget. Some kind of coordinated activity at the Federal level would enable the States to participate in Federal aid programs on a more planned and more integrated basis.

(3) Federal aid programs tend to skew State financial programs in favor of those activities that have Federal support. When a State can, in effect, obtain $2 by the expenditure of $1, such programs obviously will be given preferential treatment. This makes it important to assess at some point the total impact of all Federal aids upon the State's overall financial program.

(4) Another skewing effect results from the tendency of some Federal aids to favor certain groups of citizens. For example, in the welfare field persons who qualify for Federal aid categories, such as aid to the blind or aid to dependent children, almost everywhere have a favored position over those who qualify for only general relief.

(5) Some of the worst features of bureaucratic control are manifest in Federal aid programs. Some administrative forms are so complex that they make administration unnecessarily unwieldy. Often great amounts of irrelevant information are required. States frequently experience troublesome delays in obtaining needed decisions from regional and national offices. Sometimes authority to act on behalf of Federal agencies is not clearly spelled out; at times Federal agents will be too indecisive, at other times too arbitrary.

(6) The many Federal aid programs are conceived, established, and managed independently of each other. No central or single mechanism coordinates programs which often affect each other. The Joint Action Com-

mittee might very well consider establishment of an administrative mechanism at the national level that would be responsible for bringing the numerous aid programs into balance with each other and for helping States maximize their participation in the aid programs.

(7) A top level reviewing mechanism would prevent the sudden springing of a new Federal aid program without full preparation on the part of both the States and the Federal administering agencies. In 1956 when Congress approved $5 million for aid to rural libraries the Department of Health, Education, and Welfare was taken by surprise and was completely unprepared for its administration. Aid programs often result from pressures applied on Congress by particular interest groups. States will suddenly discover that still another aid program has been created without their consultation. The legislature must either vote a matching appropriation or face criticism for failing to take advantage of Federal aid.

(8) The scope and complexity of Federal aid programs, proceeding as they do through the labyrinthian bureaucracy, is making it increasingly difficult for States and their subdivisions to maintain sensible communication and to obtain essential information concerning available aids. Many jurisdictions fail to participate in Federal programs because they do not have personnel who are familiar with the programs or who can master the bureaucratic intricacies.

(9) Federal programs that deal directly with municipalities sometimes unsettle the State's relationship with their subdivisions. Direct Federal-local arrangements should exist only when the State provides no suitable mechanism for the Federal aid program.

By describing the "squeak" points in intergovernmental relations I do not mean to suggest that there is much evidence on the part of the States of basic dissatisfaction with Federal programs. One of the revealing aspects of the many intergovernmental studies is the lack of criticism on the part of States concerning ongoing Federal programs. We recently conducted a survey in Minnesota to evaluate the effectiveness of Federal programs. Our administrators uniformly approved the programs and voiced apprehension over any prospective diminution in them.*

The speaker was Orville L. Freeman, then (1958) Governor of Minnesota and currently Secretary of Agriculture.

Recurrent reference to governors' conferences suggests one additional source for obtaining in a systematic fashion the collective views of the governors on matters of federal-state relations. We attempted to systematize and summarize the 160 formal policy resolutions passed by the Governors' Conference from 1946 through 1966. Of these resolutions 24 or 15 percent could be identified as relating either directly or indirectly to aspects of grants-in-aid. These resolutions were about evenly balanced between calling for more expansion of grant programs and criticisms of grant implementation requirements, further confirming our earlier characterization of the governors' contrasting perspectives on grants.

We carried the analysis of these resolutions one step further by categorizing the nature of the policy action called for by each of the 160 resolutions, pro and con federal activity. The results of our analysis appear in Table 12.

These results further document the governors' varying perspectives on intergovernmental matters. The governors were about equally disposed to recommend more federal action and more state action. A lesser but significant number of resolutions, twenty-six, were identified as calling for less federal activity. However, more resolutions urged greater inter-state activity than less federal involvement. The governors evidently and perhaps realistically, evince a greater confidence and desire in "horizontal" federalism than in an effort to turn the clock back regarding federal activities.

* SOURCE:
To Establish an Advisory Commission on Intergovernmental Relations, Joint Hearings before the House Intergovernmental Relations Subcommittee and the Senate Committee on Government Operations, 86th Congress, 1st Session, June, 1959, p. 187–89.

TABLE 12
RESOLUTIONS OF THE GOVERNORS' CONFERENCE
BY TYPE OF ACTIVITY RECOMMENDED, 1946–66

Type of activity recommended	Number of resolutions
Less Federal activity	26
More Federal activity	68
More State activity	73
More Local activity	15
More Inter-State Activity	34
	216*

* Adds to more than 160 because of double-counting some resolutions.
SOURCE OF RESOLUTIONS: *State Government,*
1946–66.
SOURCE OF TABULATIONS: author's files.

State Administrators and Grants. The first known survey of state grant executives was conducted by a committee of the National Municipal League in 1928. At that time federal grants were only $100 million and the Committee's questionnaire survey covered only 264 state executives administering grants in six program areas: forestry, agricultural extension, highways, national guard, vocational education, and child-hygiene. Twenty years later, when the Council of State Governments (COSGOV) repeated portions of the survey, grants approximated $2 billion and over five hundred state grant executives in ten major program areas were contacted. More than three hundred responded. Three of the questions in the 1948 survey were identical with those included in the 1928 study. The results for these are shown in Table 13.

So far as stimulation and the positive effects of federal supervision were concerned, there was no significant change in state executives' views between 1928 and 1948. In both surveys over 90 percent concurred that federal grants had stimulated state activity and more than two-thirds felt that federal supervision had improved state standards of service and administration. The changes over twenty years did produce a marked rise in the proportion of state administrators

TABLE 13
RESPONSES OF STATE EXECUTIVES IN FEDERAL GRANT
PROGRAMS TO QUESTIONS ON GRANTS
1928 AND 1948

Question	Percentage of executives replying "yes" (number of cases in parentheses)	
	1928	1948
Have federal grants stimulated state activity with respect to the aided programs?	90.9 (264)	93.8 (325)
Has federal supervision improved state standards of administration and service?	68.6 (264)	70.3 (317)
Has federal aid led to interference in state affairs?	6.1 (264)	35.8 (321)

SOURCE: Council of State Governments, *Federal Grants-in-Aid: Report of the Committee on Federal Grants-in-Aid* (Chicago: 1949), p. 280.

who averred that grants had led to "interference" in state affairs. It is difficult to give a precise interpretation of the kind and extent of federal "interference" perceived by the state administrators. It does seem evident, however, that the second survey tapped an underlying element of discord with the "interference" question that was much more in evidence in 1948 than in 1928. How much this "interference" dimension remains in federal grant relations and in which direction it has moved since 1948 will be disclosed by a repeat survey planned by the author in 1968.

In addition to the three questions replicated from the 1928 study, the COSGOV survey in 1948 posed seven other grant-related questions to the state executives. The results for these questions are provided in Table 14. The dominant theme discernible from the percentages is the majority satisfaction with existing financial arrangements and with grant expansion. This is not surprising given administrative proclivities toward the status quo organizationally and expansion programmati-

TABLE 14
RESPONSE OF STATE EXECUTIVES TO QUESTIONS
ON FEDERAL GRANTS, 1948

Question[1]	Percentage responding "yes"	Total number of respondents
Should federal grants for the program be increased?	77.6	299
Should the system of federal grants be expanded, i.e., new programs added?	51.6	277
Are existing provisions relative to matching arrangements satisfactory?	73.9	268
Are existing provisions relative to the apportionment of funds among the states satisfactory?	68.6	290
Are existing provisions relative to the allocation of funds among the various portions of an aided program satisfactory?	78.0	241
Should federal aid be subject to the same financial control as other state funds?	87.8	312
Does federal aid tend to unbalance overall state programs?	28.5	298

[1] These are not necessarily the verbatim questions asked; some have been changed slightly to facilitate simplified and consistent tabular presentation.

SOURCE: Council of State Governments, *Federal Grants-in-Aid: Report of the Committee on Federal Grants-in-Aid* (Chicago: 1949), pp. 276–80.

cally. In some respects state grant executives harbor attitudes similar to those of their federal counterparts.

There were some partial departures from a pattern of administrative protectionism and expansionism, however. Nearly 90 percent of the state executives acknowledged the desirability of making federal grants subject to the same kinds of budgetary and financial controls as general state revenues and expenditures. The near unanimity with which the idea is endorsed is exceeded only by the lack of progress in achieving reforms. Apparently the source of opposition and difficulty lies not with state grant-in-aid executives. They are disposed toward compliance with financial controls that could conceivably run counter to their program interests.

A different perspective on the part of a minority of these executives also showed through in response to the last question in Table 14. More than one-fourth of the administrators indicated that from their viewpoint federal grants led to an imbalance among state programs. This result of grants, frequently referred to as the "budget distortion" effect, has long been discussed but, as we noted in a fiscal context, has rarely if ever been objectively identified or operationally measured. Here the distortion effect is acknowledged by those executives in a central role to judge its existence. These same executives are also in a position where (a) they would be the least likely to be aware of budget distortion (b) they would be the most likely to benefit from the "unbalancing" in terms of their own program. Under these circumstances it is perhaps surprising to find more than one-fourth of the state grant administrators noting its existence.

From the COSGOV study nearly two decades ago we shift to two recent studies that gathered intergovernmental attitudinal data from state executives. The first, initiated in 1963, focused on the heads of major state departments and agencies in all fifty states. Although major interest was on state executives administering grants, large numbers of other agency heads not connected with grants were contacted. Out of nearly 1400 circularized, 933 responded and of these 310 were responsible for programs involving federal aid.

The second survey focused in depth on state executives in two states, Iowa and Minnesota, during 1965. It replicated several questions used in the 50-state study plus additional ones on different intergovernmental matters. The response rate in this latter survey was slightly over 60 percent, producing about 250 replies in Iowa and 200 from Minnesota. The state departments receiving federal grants ranged from 12–18 depending on state administrative organizational structures. These departments varied from Aeronautics, Education, and Health to Highways, Natural Resources, and Welfare.

Identical questions on the impact of federal grants were asked in both surveys of all three groups of administrators. In all three samples about one-third of the administrators were serving in departments where federal aid constituted 50 percent or more of that agency's budget. This finding underscores heavy reliance of the states' fiscal-administrative structure on federal grants. The attitudinal responses of the three groups are provided in Table 15.

There was a substantial minority, nearly a majority, that responded affirmatively to a question intended to ascertain the stimulative character of federal grants. Like the distortion issue, whether grants are in reality stimulative in their impact remains to be determined by objective fiscal data. Whatever

TABLE 15

AMERICAN STATE GRANT ADMINISTRATORS VIEWS ON FEDERAL
GRANTS-IN-AID, NATIONALLY AND FOR IOWA AND MINNESOTA,
1963 AND 1965

Questions	Nationally (1963)	Iowa (1965)	Minnesota (1965)
	(percentages responding "yes")		
Do federal funds increase the amount of funds raised by the state?	52	47	38
Does federal aid seem uncertain and difficult to estimate?	40	34	51
Is your agency less subject to supervision and control by the governor and legislature because of federal aid?	50	63	48
If federal aid did not have restrictions on how the money is spent would you allocate the funds differently from the way they are presently spent?	54	51	52
N = (approximately)	(300)	(150)	(120)

SOURCES: Deil S. Wright and Richard L. McAnaw, *American State Administrators,* Study Code and Marginal Tabulations for the State Administrative Officials Questionnaire (Department of Political Science and Institute of Public Affairs, The University of Iowa, Iowa City, Iowa, January, 1965), 40 pp. mimeo. Deil S. Wright and Catherine D. Papastathopoulos, *State Executives in Iowa and Minnesota* (Institute of Public Affairs, The University of Iowa, and Department of Political Science, The University of North Carolina, October, 1967), 69 pp. mimeo.

such objective results might reveal, an important proportion of state executives responsible for federal grant programs perceive their fiscal effects as stimulative.

It is noteworthy that the recent proportions agreeing that federal grants are stimulative are considerably less than the 90-plus percentages disclosed by the 1928 and 1948 surveys. This may be accounted for in two ways. First, the questions posed, and therefore the operational definition of stimulation, differed as between the former and latter two surveys. The earlier surveys simply posed the question of whether state activity was stimulated by grants. In other words, is the state doing more because of federal grants? In the two recent surveys the definition of stimulation was more narrowly and precisely defined. To respond affirmatively the executives had to view grants as raising the amount contributed by the states to the aided programs. A second interpretation is that, objectively speaking, federal grants are no longer perceived to be as stimulative as they once were. Given the expansions in scope and the large consistent financial increases in federal grants, these altered perceptions by state executives probably reflect some actual changes in the effects of grants on state programs.

One administrative problem often mentioned at the state level is the uncertainty of estimating available federal funds. From one-third to one-half of the executives from the three groups affirm that the uncertainty does exist. We have no data from other times or places to document any trend.

Several references have been made to the independence and insulation from policy control of administrators at all levels in the grant-in-aid field. The third question in Table 15 was designed to explore this independence as perceived by state grant administrators. Any initial reservations concerning the candor with which grant administrators would respond about their own independence were considerably dispelled. Large numbers freely acknowledged that where federal aid programs were involved they felt less subject to the supervision and control of state policy organs—the governor and legislature. Approximately half of the state grant executives nationally and in Minnesota concurred with this view. In Iowa, where the governor has weaker formal powers than in Minnesota, the proportion agreeing exceeded 60 percent. It would be difficult to imagine a clearer demonstration of the policy and administrative impact of federal grants on the organization and functioning of state governments than the self-admission of autonomy by half or more of state grant administrators.

How do state executives feel about the distorting or imbalancing effects of federal grants? Rather than employ possibly prejudicial terms such as "distortion" and "imbalance" we simply posed the hypothetical situation in which the executive would be free to allocate the funds differently. The question, of course, was: Would he? From the last line of figures in Table 15 it is evident that a slight but consistent majority of all three groups of grant executives would spend the funds differently. In other words, there is a substantial and majority segment of state executives who believe that the present program distribution of funds under federal grants is not the most desirable allocation of fiscal resources.

Persistent through the detailed figures and their variations in Table 15 is a remarkably consistent overall theme. That theme or pattern might, for lack of a better term, be called "modal centrist." The percentages tend to hover around 50. Since these proportions approximate only about half of the respondents, the affirmative half, this centrist pattern actually represents a fairly sharp division of opinion among state executives regarding the effects and relationships engendered by federal grants. In one sense the state grant executive is like the governor. He perceives benefits accruing from grants but finds their constraints, complications, and consequences less than uniformly desirable. This conflict situation prevails with respect to both individual executive roles and the aggregate character of grant administration at the state level.

The systematic empirical data marshalled here force a qualification of the terminal observation that "there are more satisfactions than complaints." For the few areas probed by these surveys of state executives the majority does not uniformly lie on the side of satisfaction. A more accurate characterization would identify the cleavage and ambivalences among state administrators regarding federal grants.

Local Officials and Grants. When we turn our attention below the state level to ascertain participants' perspectives toward grants and the federal system we are confronted with two difficulties. First there is the dilemma of choosing from among numerous different types of local officials (a) which particular group should be surveyed or (b) whether to lump all local officials into a composite but polyglot group. The second problem, closely related to the first, is the extensiveness of the disparate officials in relation to the paucity of attitudinal data available on any one type or the aggregate of all local officials.

One attitude survey that does command attention was conducted by the Senate Subcommittee on Intergovernmental Relations in 1963, *The Federal System as Seen by State and Local Officials.* This study has one major qualifying condition; less than five hundred officials (8 percent) responded to the six thousand questionnaires sent out. Despite that limitation we rely on the survey as the best and only basis for generalizing about local officials' attitudes on grants in particular and the federal system in general.

Four attitudinal positions emerged. The first category was termed "Orthodox States Righters." This group viewed the issues raised by the Committee's inquiry from an ideological position consistent with the classical tenets of "dual federalism." Their view of the federal system laid emphasis on independence and separateness of activities among the levels of government. On the subject of grants-in-aid these respondents contended that there were far too many programs already, that no new ones should be initiated, and that most of the existing grant programs should be terminated.

A second major attitudinal constellation was identified as the "Neo-Traditionalists." Respondents in this category shared some of the states' rights sentiments concerning dual or compartmentalized federalism; they expressed many anti-centralist ideas. What set them apart from the first group was their reality-oriented positions. When confronted with existing relationships and specific issues among governmental units, they bowed to the practical necessity and/or the status quo and were unwilling to reduce the present extent of federal activity. This group accepted the existing (1963) levels of grants, albeit reluctantly, and did acknowledge that the federal government had an appropriate but restricted role in using the grant device and other techniques to alleviate certain common problems.

In the third attitude category fell the "Pragmatic Cooperative Federalists." These respondents avoided any general ideological commitments in their questionnaire responses. They appeared to accept fully the "marble-cake" view of the federal system. The acceptance of practical, work-a-day necessities of intricate federal-state-local relations did not preclude criticisms of existing patterns and relationships. The criticisms and recommendations stemming from this group, however, were within the context of the major programmatic features of cooperative federalism. Inherent in this position was the absence of a general principle on which further extensions of federal power via grants or other devices might be seriously challenged. This position, while prevalent among many public officials, has been best elaborated by the late Professor Morton Grodzins in *The American System: A New View of Government in the United States.*

The fourth attitude subdivision contained the "New Nationalists." These respondents adhered to a consistent pro-federal stand. The federal government was assigned and expected to fulfill a major role in the resolution of public problems. At least skepticism, if not distrust, was the pervading outlook toward state and local governments. None of these respondents elaborated arguments favoring a unitary system but none suggested either a reduction in the role of the federal government or a reduction in the present role of state and local governments. These New Nationalists did oppose or reject, however, most of the measures offered to strengthen the power position of states and local governments. Further extensive use of grants was strongly supported as a highly appropriate technique for asserting the senior role of the national government.

The percentage distributions of local officials by the four attitude positions are presented in Table 16. Somewhat surprisingly, the Neo-Traditionalist holds a plurality position. The polar positions of the continuum, when combined, constitute about one-fourth of the respondents and are about evenly divided between the two extremes. The Pragmatic Cooperative Federalist category contains about a third of the officials. Significantly, however, the two middle groups dominate participants' perspectives toward American federalism.

TABLE 16
ATTITUDINAL POSITIONS OF LOCAL OFFICIALS
CONCERNING THE U. S. FEDERAL SYSTEM

Attitudinal Position	Percentages
Orthodox States Righter	11%
Neo-Traditionalist	43
Pragmatic Cooperative Federalist	33
New Nationalist	13
	100%

SOURCE: *The Federal System As Seen By State and Local Officials,* Subcommittee on Intergovernmental Relations, U. S. Senate, 88th Congress, 1st Session (Committee Print, 1963), pp. 203–5.

A central question arises as to what extent, if any, there is common ground between these two attitudinal groupings. If such a common ground exists, we then need to ask: what are the elements that compose a broad-based agreement on the current character and future development of our federal system? Although an ideological distinction partially separates the two groups, that distinction more clearly identifies the common outlook they share in the realm of realistic and practical approaches to present-day problems. The Senate Committee study, in its concluding section (p. 206–7), summarized the nature of the overlap between the two groups and elaborated the components of a theory drawn on these two attitude dimensions. The principal tenets of this composite theory embody both normative and descriptive features and include the following:

(1) As a practical matter, Federal, State, and local governments are viewed as loosely related parts of one overall system. Each level, however, vigorously maintains its separate institutional identity and freedom of action in policymaking.

(2) The domestic functions of government are not neatly parceled out among the three levels; instead, several governmental activities are assumed jointly by each governmental level with significant and continuing responsibilities being assumed by all.

(3) Decisionmaking in the intergovernmental process is shared fairly equally among various public bodies on the three planes, thus preserving a cardinal principle of traditional federalism.

(4) The administration of programs of joint concern is a mutual undertaking. Such devices as joint boards, joint inspection, the sharing of specialized information and use of another level's technical personnel reveal the benefits of this collaboration among equals; competition rather than collaboration, however, is produced when administrative regulations are unilaterally imposed without full consultation with another level's officials and without recognition of the merit of some administrative practices of other jurisdictions.

(5) The Federal grant-in-aid is and will continue to be an inescapable and important feature of contemporary intergovernmental relations. It provides a necessary means whereby the three levels of government can collaborate to fulfill common purposes. If not encumbered with excessive administrative redtape, it can also serve to strengthen State and local governments, since it utilizes the existing institutional frame-work for administering these activities of common concern.

(6) Representative, responsive, and responsible State governments are vital for the proper operation of Ameri-

can federalism. They have a vital role in collecting a sizable proportion of total revenues, directly administering several important governmental services, providing vital assistance to their local units of government and serving as political laboratories for testing new policies.

(7) When properly empowered, financed, and aided, county and municipal governments singly and in voluntary association with one another can meet many of the challenges that ubiquitous urbanization have created.

(8) Intergovernmental relations should be viewed primarily as a network of functional, financial, and administrative arrangements which seek to advance the commonweal. Parity with respect to the power positions of the various levels is an indispensable ingredient for successful collaboration in this area. Inequality after all, undermines the voluntarism that is so essential for any full-fledged cooperative endeavor.

(9) Every level has a fundamental duty to preserve the interlevel balance, but a primary responsibility for implementing this ideal rests with Congress. Its past enactments constitute the greatest single force shaping the federal system under which we live, and its future actions will exert no less an impact.

These nine propositions are the suggested bases on which a majority of local officials' sentiments concur. There are no doubt points on which particular participants would disagree. On a general basis, however, these statements accurately and summarily characterize the attitudes of local officialdom toward our federal system. Proposals for changing intergovernmental relationships and for improving or altering the status of various governmental levels will have to be generally consistent with this broad attitudinal base.

Summary Observations

Grants-in-aid and the attendant joint and cooperative activities based on them are primary examples, if not the core base, of what has been called the "new federalism." Alternate terms have also been employed, such as "functional federalism" and "cooperative federalism." Whatever the term selected, it has been used to characterize the tendencies toward national-state-local collaboration in the conduct of public functions. Although the beginnings of cooperative federalism ante-dated the New Deal, there is little question that federal action during the Great Depression greatly expanded and firmly institutionalized the new federalism. The two decades since World War II have seen the new federalism elaborated to the point where several dominant trends may be discerned:

(1) grants have grown in number, type, functional focus, and fiscal importance;

(2) equalization through formula grants has become an explicit and approved aim, particularly for many HEW grant programs;

(3) grant authorizations were initiated with specific program objectives in mind and subsequent extensions and additions have produced extremely categorized results;

(4) increased professionalism has produced growing tensions between federal program administrators (professionals) and:

    a. popularly elected officials and administrative generalists;

    b. professionals at other levels in the same program field;

    c. professionals in other functional programs at the same level;

(5) greater professionalism has been accompanied by a trend toward the tightening of federal administrative standards governing state action with varying effects on basic state policies;

(6) wholesale expansion of project grant programs, including many for research and demonstration purposes, has resulted in direct and final federal approval of each grant application;

(7) there has been a trend toward closer federal review of state decisions on specific projects, project priorities, and

state plans to the extent that state actions on grant applications are preliminary, with federal "review" constituting the effective final decision;

(8) there is measurable ambivalence and increasing criticism of the specific operations and cumulative effects of grants-in-aid by state, local, and some federal participants in the grant process.

The first five trends noted above are generally consistent with research and theorizing about new or cooperative federalism. The latter three, while originating from prior tendencies, constitute important departures in the extent and nature of federal involvement. The significance of this development is sufficiently different in degree and kind that it deserves an appellation different from new federalism. To some extent these latter tendencies might be traced to and classified under "creative federalism" except that (a) the administration seeks to use the phrase in a strongly positive context whereas these trends are not uniformly wholesome, and (b) "creative federalism," despite widespread use, remains a formally undefined and ambiguous concept. Two other terms that might satisfy our lexicon are "direct federalism" and the "new, new federalism."

Whatever designation is chosen to characterize these recent developments it is clear that one chief consequence is to vest far greater discretion in the hands of federal administrative officials than has previously been the case. Such discretion presents the opportunity to accomplish desirable results. But it also places a heavy burden of calculation on the same administrators to weigh both programmatic *and* political payoffs from their grant determinations. These calculations and complications are considerably reduced for the administrator under formula grants.

The results of direct federalism, apart from the by-passing of units of general government, appears to be the general withdrawal by the Congress from basic policy determinations in the allocation of federal grants. This is not to say that particular committees or key Congressmen fail to influence grant or project allocations. It is to say, however, that with

direct federalism legislatively mandated grant policies have
become increasingly ambiguous or non-existent guides to administrators in the allocation of project grant funds to diverse applicants for federal assistance.

Furthermore, under direct federalism the "applicants" for
federal grants are of a different character than under the
new federalism. Under new federalism the chief applicants
and recipients of federal grants were the states and, second-
arily, local units of government. Direct federalism and its
attendant project grants has overlaid the former concept with
an expansion of grants directly to individuals, specialized public agencies, quasi-public groups, and even private firms.
The granting of funds to applicants in the last two categories
has prompted a further elaboration of federalism that will not
be explored here, namely, "private federalism" or, the "new,
new, new federalism."

What remains to be mentioned, but likewise not explored,
are the several alternatives to the present state of affairs. In
other words, what is to be done? We propose no specific
prescriptions here nor do we evaluate the pros and cons of
the various alternative approaches. We conclude first, by indicating the two major constraints within which these approaches must be considered and second, a brief list of the
several alternatives.

This discussion occurs in the context of two highly significant qualifying conditions: (1) the Vietnam War and (2)
President Johnson's "creative federalism." The harsh fiscal
and non-fiscal realities of our policies in Southeast Asia cause
a continuous rethinking and revision of domestic policy directions. Vietnam may have temporarily obliterated the prospect of a federal surplus and "fiscal drag." But most of us,
perennial optimists that we are, continue to look toward a
time when more viable fiscal policy choices are before us
than the tension-ridden ones that now confront the nation.

The second major constraint on this discussion is the
rhetoric and practice of "creative federalism." The term finds
extensive use in connection with Great Society programs. In
fact, it was born a twin of the "great society" phrase in the

President's commencement speech at the University of Michigan in May 1964. Evidently the terms were not conceived as identical twins. The Great Society has been elaborated and accorded a status equal to the New Frontier, Fair Deal, and New Deal. But for more than three years the administration has used without full elaboration the creative federalism phrase. At one point, in his State of the Union message in 1966, the President recommended the creation of a commission of "distinguished scholars and men of public affairs" to assist in a definition and development of the concept. The commission was never created, nor has a long-promised message on the subject ever emerged from the White House. At the abstract level the term seems to be a blanket phrase, covering a fundamentally pragmatic and philosophically unguided approach to intergovernmental relations. Filling in the verbal void on creative federalism are the positive actions of the Johnson administration and the Congress from 1964 through 1966.

It seems clear that the realities of creative federalism are pinned on two action orientations: (1) an extensive expansion of existing and new categorical grants, and (2) the wholesale extension of project-type funding authorizations that are more narrowly specified than even the categorical program grants.

The additional constraint, then, on the discussion and observations offered here is a commitment by the executive toward an extension of past patterns in intergovernmental fiscal relations. From the standpoint of this paper that commitment is treated as provisional. It is seen as subject to change (a) by an alteration in outlook and priorities by the present incumbent or (b) by his replacement with a chief executive less disposed toward the extremes of the categorical and project grant approaches. Two political givens, the Congress and the Republican Party, might induce either of these altered conditions. Hints of some thinking tending in the reverse direction have started to appear in recent Presidential messages. Much of the credit on this score should go to the prodding by Congress and by the Advisory Commission on

Intergovernmental Relations. Within the administration the Department of Housing and Urban Development appears to be exerting positive leadership.

The basepoints of this paper on the present status of federal-state fiscal relations can be briefly summarized. First, federal grants-in-aid are an integral part of our federal system; they are here to stay and there is no way to turn the clock back. Second, politically the dominant party in Congress plus the executive have supported major expansions in grant programs. Third, grant expansions have reached a stage where their consequences, both fiscally and administratively, have generated measureable amounts of ambivalence and negative reactions among diverse segments of officials connected either directly or indirectly with grant programs. Fourth, these perspectives and reactions have generated an active interest in various proposals to correct, reduce, alter, or circumvent the undesirable effects of grants. Among the alternatives that should be explored by both political parties as well as by the Congress and the Executive Branch, *with meaningful involvement by state and local officials,* are the following:

(1) Negative income tax,

(2) Guaranteed annual income

(3) Tax credits against federal income taxes

for state and/or local taxes paid,

(4) Improvement in existing grant-in-aid operations by:

    a. clearer statement of Congressional intent and periodic subsequent review of grant programs,

    b. policy consistency on allocation formulas and matching requirements,

    c. consolidation of many specialized grant categories into larger program or bloc grants,

    d. numerous administrative and procedural changes,

    e. major organizational changes and restructuring to create a better basis for planning and coordinating grant programs,

(5) Revenue sharing of the type suggested by several prominent persons and public officials—Walter W. Heller, Former Chairman of the Council of Economic Advisers un-

der Presidents Kennedy and Johnson; Joseph Pechman, Economist at the Brookings Institution; Congressman Henry S. Reuss (D., Wis.); Congressman Charles E. Goodell (R., New York); Senator Jacob Javits (R., New York); Congressman Melvin R. Laird (R., Wis.).

THE CASE FOR REVENUE SHARING
by Melvin R. Laird

MELVIN R. LAIRD, Chairman of the House Republican
Conference, was first elected to Congress from the 7th
District in Wisconsin in 1952 after six years' service in
the Wisconsin State Senate. Congressman Laird is the
ranking Republican on the Labor, Health, Education,
and Welfare Appropriations Subcommittee and second
ranking on the Defense Appropriations Subcommittee.
Chairman of the Republican Party's Platform Committee
in 1964, Laird was the first Congressman in either party
to introduce Revenue Sharing legislation in modern
times.

Mr. Laird was the editor of the *Conservative Papers,*
published by Doubleday in 1964, and is the author of
A House Divided: America's Strategy Gap (1962). He
was the recipient of the 1967 Distinguished Service
Award of the American Political Science Association
and the Lasker Medical Research Award.

In a nation beset with as many problems as America today,
there is obvious need for rethinking basic programmatic approaches to problem-solving. The scope of our problems and
the success so far in meeting them are delineated in later
chapters.[1]

One thing is clear: despite an enormous increase in the
financial commitment of the federal government toward solutions in areas such as poverty, hard-core unemployment,

[1] See especially, Chapter 2, "Crime in America"; Chapter 3,
"Poverty, Welfare and Jobs"; and Chapter 5, "Toward Better
Housing."

housing, education, crime, when the results are measured we seem either to be standing still or to be regressing.

Detroit has become the classic example of a city held up as a model both in terms of the amount of federal aid provided and in terms of the use to which that federal aid was put. Yet Detroit experienced what has been described as the worst riot in our nation's history. New Haven (another "model city"), Newark, Watts, and a host of others experienced similar turbulence in varying degrees during the past three summers.

With the coming of each new summer in America, the dread of similar eruptions grows and becomes more widespread. Clearly something is drastically wrong with the way we are doing things.

The growing national debate on revenue-sharing has had at least one beneficial effect: it has focused attention on methodology and away from goals. This is all to the good, for it means a departure from the irrational debate over which side recognizes or cares more about our enormously complex problems. It means also that the emphasis has been shifted to the more relevant confrontation over how best to attack commonly recognized problems. And, perhaps most fortunate of all, it signals a new awareness of and interest in evaluating existing programs in order to determine whether in fact they are contributing meaningfully to the solution of our many ills.[2]

For too many years, America's leadership has viewed our domestic problems in a piecemeal fashion. From this perspective that same leadership has devised, perhaps without fully realizing it, a generalized approach to problem-solving that has fragmented the attack and made it less effective than it might otherwise have been.

The generalized approach, as we have seen in the preceding paper, is the categorical grant-in-aid. The extent to which it has fragmented the attack is systematically and brilliantly presented by Professor Wright.

[2] See Chapter 11, "Oversight and the Need for Congressional Reform."

DISILLUSIONMENT

The phenomenal increase in categorical grants-in-aid in the past three years has brought with it a corresponding rise in the degree of disillusionment with the categorical technique. Governors, for example, are becoming more outspoken than in the past. A representative illustration of this was given by Godfrey Sperling in his report on the 1966 Governors' Conference:

> For even the "liberal" Governors, who like nothing better than seeing the federal funds moving into their states, are disenchanted over the current programs flowing out of Washington.
>
> Governor after Governor here got up and said he not only didn't understand upcoming federal legislation, but that he didn't understand the legislation already passed and which gave him responsibilities for administrating programs at the local level. (Christian Science Monitor, December 20, 1966.)

Within the Johnson administration itself, there is similar disenchantment on the part of some key officials. Assistant Secretary and Comptroller of the Department of Health, Education and Welfare, James F. Kelly, for example, told the Federal Government Accountants Association on June 15, 1967, that

> . . . the narrow categorical grant approach which has been followed has sharply handicapped governments at all levels in adapting their budgets and programs to current and emerging needs and has sometimes hindered the development of adequate central planning and control in state and local governments.

Daniel P. Moynihan's paper, which appears later in this volume, reflects a similar disenchantment. He went a step further in his illuminating remarks before the National Board Meeting of the Americans for Democratic Action on September 23, 1967:

> . . . liberals must divest themselves of the notion that the nation, especially the cities of the nation, can be run from agencies in Washington.
> . . . the biggest problem of running the nation from Washington is that the real business of Washington in our age is pretty much to run the world.
> As far as I can see, an American national government in this age will always give priority to foreign affairs. A system has to be developed, therefore, under which domestic programs go forward regardless of what international crisis is preoccupying Washington at the moment. This in effect means decentralizing the initiative and the resources for such programs.

It is the argument of this paper that a broad "system" of revenue-sharing, instituted as a replacement for many existing categorical grants and as a deterrent to the creation of a large number of new ones, would present the most rational way for "decentralizing" both the initiative and the resources for domestic programs. More than that, it would create a better framework within which to unleash the diverse forces of our society, governmental and private, for a more coordinated, concerted and effective attack.

SCOPE OF THE PROBLEM

The task that lies before us is staggering. If we focus just on the cities, ignoring all other problems outside the metropolitan centers, the agenda for this generation and the next is difficult to comprehend fully.

Mayor Lindsay of New York reportedly testified that that city alone will need $50 billion over the next ten years. The 1966 Ribicoff Hearings produced an estimate that our cities will require more than a trillion dollars in the next decade.

The National Planning Association estimated the cost for renewing our cities at two trillion plus.

Add to all of this the economic development requirements in the Appalachias of America, sewer and sanitation needs in the smaller communities, environmental pollution control, housing, education, health and jobs outside our central cities, and the scope of our agenda begins to emerge.

Against such a backdrop, President Johnson told the Nation's Governors in March of 1967 that federal grants-in-aid to the states will quadruple in the next five years from the then current $15 billion to some $60 billion. The President's recommendations in the 89th Congress and in the First Session of the 90th Congress make clear that the bulk of that fourfold increase will fit the mold of the narrow, categorical grant. Included in the past three years, for example, were such major categorical programs as the Elementary and Secondary Education Act, the Law Enforcement and Criminal Justice Assistance Act, the Juvenile Delinquency Prevention and Control Act,[3] the so-called Anti-Poverty program, the Economic Development and Assistance Act, Pollution Control programs, and a host of others.

EFFECTIVENESS OF CATEGORICAL GRANTS-IN-AID

The categorical grant has become our nation's chief tool in fashioning the "Great Society." Yet in the face of the Detroits, the Newarks and the New Havens, no one can argue that substantial progress toward such a goal has truly been achieved. On the contrary. Many today would argue, myself included, that the categorical grant has often compounded the very problems it is designed to correct.

A classic example which illustrates the problem under categorical grants has been our recent experience with water pollution control programs. The recently created Department of Housing and Urban Development administers

[3] For a fuller discussion of the Anti-Crime and Juvenile Delinquency Acts, see Chapter 2.

a sewer construction and expansion program that was created under the Housing Act of 1965. It authorized $200 million per year in 50 percent matching grants. In fiscal years 1966 and 1967, the President requested $100 million for the program. For fiscal year 1968, he requested $165 million.

The program was and still is a very popular one. By February of 1967, the Department of Housing and Urban Development had on hand applications totalling more than $5 billion.

Two conclusions can be drawn from this:

1) For every community that gets its sewer construction funds from the federal government, a great many will not. Those that do not in most cases will postpone taking action on their own precisely because the federal program "exists" and because it would be politically suicidal for the Mayor of a city to float a bond issue or try to spend local funds on a problem where federal funds supposedly exist.

2) The federal government itself obviously does not have and will not acquire in the foreseeable future sufficient revenue to make adequate funds available for all or even most of the more than 400 separate categorical grant programs it is currently administering, let alone any new ones it may be disposed to create.

In light of this cold fact, it is a continual source of wonderment to many of us in Congress in both parties why there is such a persistent demand for more categorical grant programs on the part of the administration.

ARGUMENTS FOR FEDERAL CATEGORICAL AIDS

Proponents of categorical assistance to the states and local units of government usually base their argument on one or more of the three following assumptions:

1) the states lack the resources to tackle the problems alone:

2) they lack the innovative ability to fashion effective solutions; and

3) they lack the motivation to do the necessary job.

LACK OF RESOURCES

It is certainly true that the federal government with its progressive tax system has largely preempted the more lucrative tax sources in America. Recent studies have shown that federal revenues (because of progressive tax policies) tend to increase at a faster rate than the nation's economic growth while state and local revenues (because of regressive tax policies) tend to yield revenue increases at rates equal to or less than the growth in Gross National Product (GNP).[4]

In his projections to 1975, Professor Weidenbaum sees continual growth in federal revenues under existing tax rates which could translate into potential federal surpluses. On the other hand, he sees a potential deficit situation continuing to face state and local governments. He concludes:

> The actual responses of state and local governments to their potential deficit positions customarily take a variety of forms. They are almost continually raising tax rates, utilizing new tax sources, raising property assessment ratios, and *deferring desirable programs*. Each of the existing sources of funds will continue to be utilized, but some of them have severe restrictions. Debt increases are often limited by constitutional ceilings. New or increased taxes encounter increasing voter resistance and accentuate problems of interstate competition. (emphasis added).

> Hence, a basic conclusion of this study is that the nation will begin to solve its long-term governmental budget problems if it links its actions on the potential

[4] Murray L. Weidenbaum, *Prospects for Reallocating Public Resources,* American Enterprise Institute for Public Policy Research, 1967.

federal surpluses with the anticipated deficits in state and local budgets.

Dr. Weidenbaum goes on to make an extremely pertinent point about the use of anticipated revenue increases on the federal level:

> The possibility certainly exists that the nation may use up potential increases in national revenues for *relatively low priority,* federal programs, while state and local governments are forced either to defer more worthwhile projects or to increase taxes still further. (emphasis added)
>
> Hence, simply reacting to specific program demand . . . may result in losing an important opportunity for reallocating public resources; a deliberate decision to use federal funds to strengthen state and local governments may succeed in raising the aggregate level of public services in the United States and/or avoiding or reducing the need to expand the overall level of taxation.

The problem of resources at the state and local level has been compounded in recent years by a drain of top-level talent as well. A very preliminary investigation was conducted in the late summer of 1967 with the assistance of the Civil Service Commission's new data processing equipment. Recognizing the severe limitations that existed in our survey, an attempt was made to determine the effect of these vastly proliferating categorical grant programs on the availability of middle and top-level management personnel to administer state and local government requirements in the general areas of health, education, welfare, and budget analysis.

At my request, the CSC ran a computer study which took a selected sample of 7812 individuals who are currently employed in the grades of GS-15 through GS-18 throughout the federal government. These 7812 represent a sample of more than ⅓ of the total number of 19,677 GS-15 through GS-18 federal government employees. These pay grades are, of course, generally considered top-level management positions for the Federal Service, ranging as they do from $18,404 to $27,055.

Of the 7812 cases, some 856, or 10.59 percent have had experience at the state and local governmental level. Unfortunately, from the data available, it was impossible to determine if the 10.59 percent had come directly from state and local government, or if their state and local service was at some earlier stage in their careers.

However, the 10.59 percent figure is by no means the most significant one in this study. At my further request, the CSC broke the figures down by major governmental agencies. The results of this tabulation are shown in Table I.

From Table I, it is clear that the four agencies of the federal government which have the greatest proportion of the high-level employees with prior state and local experience are:

Department of the Interior	34.1%
Bureau of the Budget	31.6
Department of Housing and Urban Development	28.6
Department of Health, Education and Welfare	28.5

Caution is, of course, indicated in drawing conclusions from this study. It is quite clear, however, that the areas where states and localities are most in need of trained, competent, managerial-level personnel are precisely in the areas of budget analysis, and the general administration for such programs as those administered by Interior, HUD and HEW.

It may be unfair to accuse the federal government of the twin sins of usurping tax sources and "pirating away" the talent at the state and local level. We can, however, assert that the following effects flow from the loss of these individuals from state and local payrolls:

1) It removes trained top-level management from the states where they can closely and effectively deal with state and local level problems.
2) It imposes an undue burden on the states and localities in terms of training and related costs for their top-level managerial help.

TABLE I
FEDERAL GS-15 THROUGH GS-18 EMPLOYEES WITH PRIOR STATE AND LOCAL GOVERNMENT EXPERIENCE

Agency	Total full-time GS-15 through GS-18 employees in the agency	Total employees in the sample (includes some part-time consultants)	Employees with state and local government experience	Percent of employees with state and local government experience
Arms Control and Disarmament Agency	26	17	2	11.8
Atomic Energy Commission	2	1	–	–
Department of the Air Force	1184	289	22	7.6
Department of Agriculture	973	600	74	12.3
National Foundation on the Arts and Humanities	7	5	–	–
Department of the Army	2056	1058	99	9.2
Bureau of the Budget	141	57	18	31.6
Department of Commerce	1343	456	45	9.9
White House Conference on Civil Rights	1	1	–	–
Civil Service Commission	126	17	2	11.8
Office of the Secretary of Defense	509	168	10	6.0
Department of Justice	623	323	47	14.6
Department of Labor	388	55	7	12.7
Export-Import Bank	38	28	3	10.7

Agency	Total full-time GS-15 through GS-18 employees in the agency	Total employees in the sample (includes some part-time consultants)	Employees with state and local government experience	Percent of employees with state and local government experience
Federal Coal Mine Safety Board of Review	1	1	—	—
Federal Communications Commission	128	38	5	13.2
Federal Radiation Council	2	2	—	—
National Advisory Commission on Food and Fiber	3	3	—	—
Farm Credit Administration	14	13	1	7.7
Federal Trade Commission	170	109	11	10.1
General Services Administration	334	157	15	9.6
Department of Health, Education and Welfare	1270	274	78	28.5
Department of Housing and Urban Development	288	119	34	28.6
Information Agency	112	82	8	9.8
Interstate Commerce Commission	235	19	1	5.3
Department of Interior	823	41	14	34.1
National Commission on Food Marketing	1	1	—	—
National Science Foundation	38	89	7	7.9

TABLE I (cont'd)

National Capital Housing Authority	2	1	1	—
National Labor Relations Board	221	72	6	8.3
National Aeronautics and Space Administration	2033	333	14	4.2
National Capital Planning Commission	6	3	2	—
Department of the Navy	1599	489	38	7.8
Office of Emergency Planning	96	48	10	20.8
President's Commission on Consumer Interests	4	1	—	—
Post Office Department	206	75	8	10.7
Renegotiation Board	35	21	1	4.8
Railroad Retirement Board	36	40	5	12.5
Small Business Administration	127	44	7	15.9
Securities and Exchange Commission	88	31	1	3.2
Smithsonian Institution	67	18	3	16.7
Department of State	468	312	36	11.5
Tax Court of the United States	5	5	—	—
Transportation Department	265	6	37	13.6
Office of Special Representative for Trade Negotiations	2	—	—	—
Department of Treasury	1217	584	60	10.3
Veterans Administration	1442	375	124	8.6
Water Resources Council	5	2	—	—

3) It makes the state and local level career service less attractive, as fewer individuals are willing to start there, only to have to move on when it becomes clear that the federal level is where they can be the most productive.
4) It perpetuates and aggravates the imbalance which has been built into the present categorical grant-in-aid system.

If a personal note may be permitted, the question has sometimes been raised why, as a former member of the Wisconsin State Senate, I chose to move to the national level to serve as a Member of Congress. Quite frankly, although some may scoff at this, I would still prefer the challenge of the Wisconsin State Legislature if true federalism could be restored. My major reason for departing that institution was the frustration caused by the growing preemption on the part of the national government of major decision-making opportunities with regard to state problems. Both the legislature and the state executive establishment in Wisconsin and elsewhere more and more have become "administrative arms" of the national government. With each passing year, the area left to state legislatures and executives for unfettered decision-making has been greatly narrowed.

In my own case, this was perhaps the overriding reason for leaving state public office in favor of national public office and I do not believe I am unique in this respect.

LACK OF INNOVATIVE ABILITY

It is often charged that governmental personnel at the state and local level lack the creativity to tackle these problems effectively. Our social problems seem to have reached the "crisis state" during the same period when categorical grants have burgeoned and state and local fiscal capacity has approached a crisis. This makes it difficult to determine which set of circumstances played the major role in fostering the twin crises of social and economic problems and the states' reduced capacity to deal with them.

Dr. Moynihan, in his remarks before the ADA, shed considerable light on this question:

> It is indeed a fact that it is so much more pleasant to be able to stroll across Lafayette park to endorse or to veto a public works program than it is to have to go through the misery of persuading fifty state legislatures. But that has to do with the personal comfort of middle-aged liberals, *not with the quality of the government action that results,* and in a time of some trouble, comfort cannot be the sole consideration.

> The . . . theory involved is that the national government and national politics is the primary source of liberal social innovation, especially with respect to problems of urbanization and industrialization. *I do not believe history will support this notion.* The fact of the matter is that it has been from the cities and to a lesser extent the State governments that something like a preponderance of social programs have come in the twentieth century, for the most part, of course, cities and states of the North. There are many reasons for this, of which probably the most important is that until recently these have been the areas where such problems first appeared, and where the wealth and intellect—and political will— existed to experiment with solutions . . . *If this potential has not been much in evidence of late, it is mostly, I believe, because we have allowed State and local government to get into such fiscal straits that they have no resources for innovation left to them.* But the impulse and potential remains, and it is to be found there rather than in Washington. (emphasis added)

LACK OF MOTIVATION

A third assumption on which many proponents of federal categorical assistance rest their case lies in the area of motivation. It is often charged that state and local officials are apathetic or indifferent to the needs of their citizens and must be "primed" by federal "seed money" and "motivated" by federal guidelines to take enlightened action.

It is my own tendency to reject such an assumption out of hand. I have had the privilege of knowing and working with too many state and local officials to be persuaded that as a general indictment such a charge has any merit. But even if partially true, the argument goes to the heart of the question concerning what kind of governmental system we prefer in this country. Under our representative form of government, we place ultimate reliance upon the good sense of the citizens who vote public officials into office. Prior to the "one man, one vote" decision of the Supreme Court, there may have been some validity in the argument that elected state officials as a body were not "responsive" to the demands of a majority of the electorate. That argument's validity has been considerably reduced by the Supreme Court action.

If we sincerely believe in and wish to preserve representative government, it seems to me our efforts should be directed towards strengthening state and local ability to respond to requirements for service rather than attempting to bypass the states and localities through the categorical device.

REVENUE-SHARING

Our states today are hamstrung in three vital ways: first, the federal government has largely usurped and dried up revenue-raising sources. This limits drastically the commitment a state or a locality can make on its own to solve its most pressing problems. Second, narrow categorical federal grants with their matching formulas and "free" funds force states and localities to follow federal priorities with available resources rather than their own determination of what is most urgently required. Third, the burgeoning federal bureaucracy more and more is attracting top talent in specialized fields from the states and localities. This reduces still further the state's ability to solve its own problems.

Revenue-sharing, at least in part, would reverse these processes. A revenue-sharing package designed to substitute for additional categorical aids and to replace many of the existing ones would provide a better framework within which to tackle the domestic problems that beset our nation.

Clearly, it is neither possible nor desirable to attempt a clean substitution of revenue-sharing for the present proliferated grant-in-aid structure. But it is both possible and highly desirable to institute a different type of federal-state-local fiscal arrangement that would minimize present deficiencies in the grant-in-aid technique and maximize a more effective utilization of federal dollars expended.

Like other broadly descriptive terms, revenue-sharing means different things to different people. For the purpose of this paper, the broad concept of revenue-sharing is used to include all of the following:

a) a return to the states of a percentage of federal income taxes collected coupled with an equalization formula and a tax-effort ratio. The equalization formula is designed to assist the poorer states while the tax-effort ratio recognizes those states whose own tax policies reflect relatively greater attempts to meet their own problems.

b) bloc grants which are instituted to consolidate many formula and project grants into larger, less restrictive functional grants.

c) tax credits both for state and local taxes paid in order to free additional tax sources to the states and their political subdivisions and for specific purposes such as educational tax credits and the Human Investment Act.[5]

The legislative "package" which I envision as the most prudent and effective way of instituting a basic change in the

[5] For a fuller discussion of the Human Investment Act by its original House sponsor, Rep. Thomas B. Curtis, see Chapter 3.

fiscal arrangements of our federal system contains two separate sets of actions, one immediate and one longer range.

The principal components of the "package" which should be implemented as soon as possible are contained in legislation introduced by me early last year, H.R. 5450. This bill combines percentage rebates with tax credits for state and local taxes paid.

The longer range "package" entails a series of legislative actions implemented over a limited number of years. Included, for example, would be gradual consolidation of many of the existing categorical grants into a small number of broad functional grants. Also included would be additional use of the tax credit device for specific areas of great national need. One notable example would be tax credits to those who bear the cost of education and might include tax credits for donations to institutions of learning as well. Another would be tax credits to industry to create additional incentives for utilizing devices to control air and water pollution.

Laird Revenue-Sharing Bill

My own legislation, H.R. 5450, which combines percentage rebates with tax credits for state and local taxes paid, could and should be implemented in the immediate future. It would return 5 percent of the income taxes collected by the federal government to the states. Ten percent of the total rebate in any given year would be distributed among the poorest ⅓ of the states in the form of supplementary grants. Ninety percent would be distributed on the basis of a tax-effort ratio which is the ratio between the sum of all taxes collected by the state and its subdivisions and the total personal income for the state.

Because of the demands of Vietnam and the continuing prospects of massive deficits in the Administrative Budget, the argument has often been made that revenue-sharing is nice to talk about but it cannot be implemented until we balance the budget or until Vietnam is behind us. This is a valid argument on the part of those who urge revenue-sharing as a *supplement* to existing grants-in-aid. During this war period, however, H.R. 5450 directs Congress to reduce appropriations under existing categorical grant programs by the amount rebated in a given year. If, for example, the amount to be returned under revenue-sharing in fiscal 1968 were $3 billion and the total categorical grant-in-aid disbursements were estimated at $18 billion, then Congress would be directed to reduce disbursements under the categorical programs a total of $3 billion, or from $18 billion to $15 billion. In other words, there would be no net increase in aggregate domestic expenditures. The primary purpose of the percentage rebate portion of the "package" is to effect a change in the *structure* of federal assistance without creating unnecessary havoc. The additional increments in financial assistance—whether small or massive—that might be required are provided through other devices such as tax credits and bloc grants.

Table II, based on original budget projections for fiscal year 1968, illustrates the distribution of state allocations under the Laird revenue-sharing bill.

TABLE II

STATE ALLOCATION TABLE FOR LAIRD REVENUE-SHARING BILL

	Basic grant	Supplementary grants	Total grant
Alabama (47)	$45,931,540	$24,957,240	$70,888,780
Alaska (2)	3,043,656	–	3,043,656
Arizona (35)	26,562,820	14,042,280	40,605,010
Arkansas (49)	26,286,120	13,183,800	39,469,920
California (8)	319,030,490	–	319,030,490
Colorado (19)	30,713,260	–	30,713,260
Connecticut (1)	35,140,390	–	35,140,390
Delaware (3)	6,087,310	–	6,087,310
District of Columbia[1]	8,854,270	–	8,854,270
Florida (28)	83,285,500	–	83,285,500
Georgia (40)	59,212,940	35,473,620	94,686,550
Hawaii (12)	11,344,540	–	11,344,540
Idaho (34)	11,621,230	6,132,000	17,753,230
Illinois (5)	128,940,340	–	128,940,340
Indiana (14)	68,343,910	–	68,343,910
Iowa (24)	43,994,660	–	43,994,660
Kansas (20)	35,693,780	–	35,693,780

TABLE II (cont'd)

	Basic grant	Supple- mentary grants	Total grant
Kentucky (43)	$41,781,100	$24,528,000	$66,309,100
Louisiana (41)	58,106,160	27,502,020	85,608,180
Maine (37)	14,941,580	8,431,500	23,373,080
Maryland (10)	44,824,750	—	44,824,750
Massachusetts (9)	74,431,220	—	74,431,220
Michigan (11)	119,532,670	—	119,532,670
Minnesota (23)	61,426,510	—	61,426,510
Mississippi (50)	37,539,600	13,735,680	51,275,280
Missouri (22)	53,679,020	—	53,679,020
Montana (29)	11,067,840	—	11,067,840
Nebraska (25)	18,815,330	—	18,815,330
Nevada (4)	6,364,010	—	6,364,010
New Hampshire (26)	8,577,580	—	8,577,580
New Jersey (6)	83,562,190	—	83,562,190
New Mexico (39)	17,155,150	8,646,120	25,801,270
New York (6)	292,744,370	—	292,744,370
North Carolina (44)	66,960,430	37,619,820	104,580,250
North Dakota (36)	10,514,480	5,672,100	16,186,580
Ohio (16)	120,639,460	—	120,639,460
Oklahoma (38)	35,417,090	20,971,440	56,388,530
Oregon (17)	28,222,990	—	28,222,990
Pennsylvania (18)	148,862,450	—	148,862,450
Rhode Island (15)	12,451,320	—	12,451,320
South Carolina (48)	33,480,220	17,660,160	51,140,380
South Dakota (42)	12,174,620	5,457,480	17,632,100
Tennessee (46)	50,912,060	28,912,380	79,824,440
Texas (31)	138,071,300	—	138,071,300
Utah (32)	15,771,670	—	15,771,670
Vermont (32)	6,640,700	—	6,640,700
Virginia (30)	52,018,850	—	52,018,850
Washington (13)	45,654,840	—	45,654,840
West Virginia (45)	24,349,250	13,766,340	38,115,590
Wisconsin (21)	70,834,180	—	70,834,180
Wyoming (27)	5,257,220	—	5,257,220

[1] District of Columbia per capita income ($3,673) is the highest in the Nation.

NOTES. The number in parenthesis indicates the State's per capita income ranking. New Jersey and New York share the same rank of 6; Vermont and Utah share the same rank of 32. In order to have the lowest rank equal to the number of States presented, the numbers 7 and 33 are omitted.

Total revenue-sharing grants under Laird 5 percent formula equal $3,100,000,000.

Formula based on budget projections, fiscal 1968.

The tax credit portion of H.R. 5450 would work in the following way: beginning with a ten percent credit for state and local taxes paid in the first year of operation, it would increase each year by ten percent until a full 40 percent credit is available in the fourth year.

The distinction between a tax credit and a tax deduction is a simple one. The tax deduction permits an individual to lower his net income for computing his federal income tax liability. A tax credit, on the other hand, is applied to the total tax obligation of an individual and is treated in the same manner as if it were a cash payment on the federal income tax which an individual must pay.

The tax credit portion of my bill is primarily designed to return additional tax sources to the states and localities by reducing the federal tax burden on individual taxpayers. Under the provisions of the bill, the decision to utilize the tax credit in place of the deduction is an optional one for the individual taxpayer. The impact on an average family of four of the tax credit portion of H.R. 5450 is illustrated in Table III.

A glance at Table III indicates that at 10 percent, no matter what the income level, every taxpayer would be better off taking the deduction provided under existing law. This was done in order to preclude any drain on the federal treasury in the first year both because of the Vietnam War and in order to provide time for the states to plan their own tax programs after the legislation is enacted.

The Laird revenue-sharing "package" is designed to provide an orderly transition to a more rational and effective fiscal arrangement among the various levels of government. It will (1) stop or greatly slow the creation of large numbers of new categorical programs, (2) provide additional tax sources to state and local governments, and (3) maintain the present flow of federal dollars to the states but in a combination that gradually removes the federal "strings" on many of these programs. Such a "package" implemented immediately would provide a rational framework for the longer-range actions to follow.

TABLE III

COMPARISON OF ESTIMATED TAX BENEFITS BY VARIOUS INCOME LEVEL TAXPAYERS FROM (1) DEDUCTION FOR STATE AND LOCAL TAXES UNDER PRESENT LAW, AND (2) TAX CREDIT IN LIEU OF DEDUCTION, AS PROPOSED IN THE LAIRD REVENUE-SHARING BILL, H.R. 5450 (90TH CONG.)

[COMPUTATIONS BASED ON A FAMILY OF 4]

Income level[1]	Income tax liability[2]	Average deduction for State and local taxes	Tax benefit from deduction of State and local taxes	Estimated tax credit, and net tax benefit[3] therefrom, for State and local taxes							
				10-percent credit		20-percent credit		30-percent credit		40-percent credit	
				Amount of tax credit	Net tax benefit	Amount of tax credit	Net tax benefit	Amount of tax credit	Net tax benefit	Amount of tax credit	Net tax benefit
$3,500	$36	$217	$30.38	$21.70	−$8.68	$43.40	$13.02	$65.10	$34.72	$86.80[4]	$56.42[4]
$5,500	281	319	47.85	31.90	−15.95	63.80	15.95	95.70	47.85	127.60	79.75
$7,500	555	438	74.46	43.80	−30.66	87.60	13.14	131.40	56.94	175.20	100.74
$12,500	1,386	679	129.79	67.90	−61.89	135.80	6.01	203.70	73.91	271.60	141.81
$17,500	2,348	962	222.17	96.20	−125.97	192.40	−29.77	288.60	66.43	384.80	162.63
$35,000	7,228	1,541	564.63	154.10	−410.53	308.20	−256.43	462.30	−102.33	616.40	51.77
$75,000	24,783	3,394	1,798.82	339.40	−1,459.42	678.80	−1,120.02	1,018.20	−780.62	1,357.60	−441.22

[1] All income is assumed to be earned income.

[2] Tax computations made on the following assumptions (and rounded to the nearest dollar): (a) The taxpayers itemized their deductions. The amount of deductions used in the computations were the average deductions for the respective income classes. These were derived from basic data in "Preliminary Report, Statistics of Income—1964, Individual Income Tax Returns." (b) Taxpayers use the tax rate schedule.

[3] The net tax benefit is equal to the tax credit (allowed under H.R. 5450) less the deduction allowed under present law. A minus figure for the net tax benefit indicates that the deduction will provide a larger tax saving than the tax credit will.

[4] Since the credit is limited to the tax liability of the taxpayer, before applying the credit, the net tax benefit, in this example, would be limited to $36. (A tax credit of $66.38 (i.e., $30.38 + $36) would provide this maximum benefit.) It has been suggested that under these conditions, the taxpayer be allowed to file for a rebate. See Chapter 3, "The Case for the Negative Income Tax."

Longer Range Actions

In addition to immediate implementation of legislation like H.R. 5450, the longer-range components of revenue-sharing would include essentially bloc grants and other forms of tax credits.

A priority goal would be consolidation over time of many of the existing categorical programs into broad functional bloc grants. Such functional grants, for example, might fall into the following categories: 1) Agriculture; 2) Natural Resources; 3) Transportation; 4) Housing, Community Development, and Commerce; 5) Health; 6) Education; 7) Public Assistance and Economic Opportunity; 8) Unemployment Compensation; and 9) General Government. Such consolidation has already begun in programs like the Republican-sponsored Comprehensive Health, Planning and Services Act of 1966 which combined some sixteen separately administered formula and project grants into a single bloc grant. Under this approach, the states themselves develop comprehensive plans, establish their own priorities and coordinate their own activities. The bill provides more than $900 million for comprehensive health grants to the various states during the next three years.

An interesting sidelight connected with this program was the much publicized rat control legislation proposed by President Johnson early in 1967. The administration bill would have established a specialized categorical program administered by the Department of Housing and Urban Development aimed specifically at rat eradication. The House refused to consider this program but instead through the amendment process authorized additional funds in the Comprehensive Health Planning Act which could be used by the various states either for rat eradication or for their more pressing health problems.

Significant steps were also taken by the House of Representatives in the first session of the 90th Congress in such fields as Crime, Juvenile Delinquency, Air Pollution Control, the Meat Inspection Act, and the Elementary and Secondary Education Act.

In all of these cases, the administration proposal offered categorical and formula grant programs. The House, to varying degrees, restructured these programs to more closely resemble the bloc grant concept.

An all-out effort was made by the Minority in the First Session, for example, to consolidate the Elementary and Secondary Education Act into a bloc grant. Led by Representative Albert H. Quie of Minnesota, a ranking minority member of the House Education and Labor Committee, Republicans sought to restructure and redirect the program to provide for the following:

1) A two-year authorization, beginning in Fiscal Year 1969, for federal assistance through lump-sum grants on a scale that would have been somewhat greater than the existing authorization.

2) Amendments providing for effective state administration of federal aid for our schools.

3) Consolidation of a number of federal programs so as to lessen the confusion, duplication and paperwork inherent in a profusion of narrow categorical federal aids.

4) Provision for state coordination of preschool and early elementary education programs for deprived children, with administration through the U. S. Office of Education and participation of the state educational agencies, while preserving the advantages of a major role for community action agencies and the active participation of parents.

The bill was designed to maintain a desirable focus upon improving educational opportunities of educationally deprived children, while affording greatly increased flexibility in the use of federal funds at the state and local level to attack educational problems on a broad scale. It would have continued and provided for expansion of participation of non-public school teachers and pupils in the benefits of federal programs.

Though partially successful in attaining these goals, the Elementary and Secondary Education Act as enacted by the

Congress remains primarily a package made up of formula and project grants.

Tax Credits for Education

On the general question of support for Education, Republicans continue to press for early enactment of a general tax credit for those who bear the cost of education.[6] This remains the single, most effective step Congress could take in increasing substantially its support of the educational activities of our nation, both public and private. Such credits would make it more feasible for our educational institutions to bring their charges into better line with actual operating costs. Tax credits for education could quite logically include donations to institutions of learning in order to create further incentives for private support of educational institutions.

CONCLUSION

This decade has witnessed both a tremendous increase in the number of federal categorical grant programs and a marked upsurge in the number and complexity of our nation's domestic problems.

Despite our increased commitment, we seem not to be making significant inroads in our attempts to resolve these problems. With the exception of the bureaucratic administrators of categorical grants and others with a clear vested interest in their continuation, there seems little significant defense of the categorical technique remaining. On the other side of the coin, there is growing support of Revenue-Sharing as a better, more effective device for tackling these problems.

America seems once again to be faced with a choice, a

[6] See especially Laird Bills H.R. 781 and H.R. 782, 90th Congress. Both would provide tax credits for education. H.R. 781 would provide a tax credit up to $325 for Higher Educational costs; H.R. 782 would provide credits for high school costs as well.

very old choice, between centralization and decentralization. We have experimented for the past thirty years on the premise that "national" problems demand "national" solutions, nationally administered.

That theory has now been tested and found woefully inadequate to the needs of a modern America. The only broad alternative offered thus far that seems both feasible and possible of execution is a system of revenue-sharing which would include percentage rebates, tax credits and bloc grants.

The problems of domestic America are the problems of all levels of government and all elements within our society. The narrow categorical technique bypasses many of those elements and often hampers effective action by the complicated requirements that attend them. The will, the resources and the talent exist in America to tackle our diverse problems effectively. But to do so requires a basic change in the present and projected structure of our federal system.

Revenue-sharing would provide that change. It would restore a system that provides for true partnership among the various levels of government, permits maximum unleashing of the diverse forces within our society, and fosters more steady progress toward the goals we all seek for America. The restoration of a climate in America that enhances and encourages creativity and "solution-finding" at the state and local level remains the best hope for a better America in the last third of the twentieth century. History can yet record that the decade of the 1960s was a period in which Americans rededicated themselves to the attainment of new heights and to the achievement of a better life for all Americans through a creative federalism that kept in step with modern times.

With the enactment of Revenue Sharing in the next Congress, I am confident that history *will* so record.

Chapter 2

CRIME IN AMERICA

CRIMINAL JUSTICE IN THE UNITED STATES 1967:
A SURVEY

by G. Robert Blakey

PROFESSOR G. ROBERT BLAKEY teaches Criminal Law
and Criminal Procedure at the Notre Dame Law School.
Prof. Blakey has served as a Consultant to the President's Commission on Law Enforcement and the Administration of Justice and, prior to 1964, was a Special
Prosecutor in the U. S. Department of Justice. A graduate of the University of Notre Dame and the Notre Dame
Law School, Prof. Blakey is a member of the North
Carolina and District of Columbia Bars and has been
admitted to practice before the United States Supreme
Court.

"It is of great importance in a republic not only to
guard the society against the oppression of its rulers, but
to guard one part of the society against the injustice of
the other part." Madison, *The Federalist* No. 51.

IDEOLOGY AND CRIMINAL JUSTICE

What Cardozo said of law may be said of criminal justice.
Each man tends to see it through "his own eyes." Many perspectives could, of course, give us a better view. Yet all too
often insight tends to turn into ideology. Our earliest traditions saw the criminal law simply as a substitute for revenge,
an instrument to promote the peace. Religious thought, particularly following the Reformation, tended to identify law
with morality. Crime became sin and punishment found its

rationale in expiation. The Enlightenment soon followed the Reformation. Criminal proscriptions then became a means of crime prevention through deterrence. Modern man, on the other hand, has turned away from any view bottomed on moral or individual responsibility. Crime is now seen as the product of environment or the aberrations of personality. Its explanation lies not in concepts like original sin or conscious choice, but in poverty, passion, discrimination or disease. Reformation is the goal.

None of these insights—obviously—is wholly wrong or wholly right. If each had emerged merely to supplement, but not to supplant the other, we would indeed have developed a better perspective, for criminal justice is all of these things, yet none of these things. Discussion about our system of criminal justice today, however, is characterized and marred by "hawks" and "doves." Some feel the need for peace, denounce our loss of a sense of personal responsibility, and tend to support the forces of law enforcement. Others see a threat to liberty, chide our insensitivity to social injustice, and tend to seek alternatives to effective law enforcement. Instead of constructive action on all fronts, proposals from each side are viewed as opposing alternatives. Debate too often becomes emotional and polarized. Division, deadlock and delay are the result. Stubborn ideology faces stubborn ideology. But if ideologies are stubborn, so too are facts.

CLASSIFICATION OF CRIME

Traditionally, we have classified crimes in terms of individual actions—murder, rape, robbery and the like. When the task is the assessment of a social problem, this technique is not only inadequate, but misleading. Crime must be analyzed in terms of more than legal definitions. For present purposes, it is, therefore, more meaningful to speak of a typology such as street crime, white collar crime, and organized crime, that is, to put chief emphasis on the people involved and the consequences of their actions on others.

Street Crime

Next to race relations, Americans today generally consider crime the number one domestic problem. Rightly or wrongly, they believe crime is on the rise, and the crime they fear is the crime that affects their personal safety, especially in our streets. While our primarily rural population of yesterday could view crime as characteristic of the remote and immoral city, our primarily urban population of today views crime as more directly threatening.

Rather than walk in their neighborhoods at night, one-third of our people stay behind locked doors. Poor people spend money they cannot afford on a taxi because they are afraid to use public transportation. Moreover, the fear of many is a fear of the stranger, often the stranger of another race. Fear of crime makes one-fourth of our people want to move from the neighborhood in which they live. It is a fear which seems to be ubiquitous and it is a fear which is impoverishing the lives of many Americans. P.T.A. meetings and church services are not held at night. Library facilities and other cultural opportunities are underused. We are becoming indeed an intimidated society.

Today, it is not unusual, moreover, for a victim of crime to go unaided. In 1964, for example, the murder of Kitty Genovese in New York City was witnessed by no less than thirty-eight of her neighbors, yet none even called the police. Everywhere the normal bonds of community seem to be breaking up. People are reluctant "to get involved." Crimes also go unreported to the police, for people feel—perhaps rightly—that they cannot do anything. People are not only afraid, but hopeless.

Public alarm is, indeed, founded in fact. Fully 60 percent of all major crime against the person—rapes, robberies, and assaults—occurs on the street or in other public places. There are honest disputes about the figures, but our best indicators tell us that street crime is increasing. The over-all crime rate is in fact probably increasing about seven times as fast as our population. Arrests among the young are increasing about twice as fast as their numbers. Our crime figures are corroborated, moreover, by other statistics, especially among the young. For example, the illegitimate birth rate in the fifteen-nineteen age group in 1940 was forty per 1000, while today it is 115 per 1000. Property crimes are up about a half. Depending on the offense, unreported crimes are probably two to ten times higher than reported crime. Certainly, there is reason for alarm about street crime.

Yet all public fears are not justified. Apart from robbery, most crimes against the person—murders, rapes, and assaults—are committed by family members, friends, or other persons previously known to their victims. It is true that race is a factor in street crime. The ratio of Negroes among perpetrators is about four times that of whites. However, if other factors relating to socio-economic conditions are correlated, there seems to be no important distinction in the white vs. non-white ratio. Street crime is not, furthermore, significantly interracial. Non-whites are also disproportionally victimized by street crimes—with the exception of larceny. A Negro man in Chicago, for example, runs a victimization risk six times that of his white counterpart; a Negro woman, eight times.

The statistics also tell us something else. While crime is on the rise in suburban areas, it is still largely a problem of the city ghetto. Both the criminal *and* his victim tend to be of a broken home, poor, uneducated, unemployed, and a member of a minority group. Street crime is plainly related to socio-economic factors.

It is not possible, of course, to talk of street crime without talking about the Negro riots that have rocked the ghetto areas of our cities in the last few years. The statistics alone are disturbing. In 1967, for instance, seventy-eight people were killed, 3120 were injured, and $524 million property damage was done—in some forty-two "civil" disturbances.

Again, however, popular impressions are only partially correct. Civil disturbances are not new to our cities. No Negro riot yet has been worse in any respect than the Irish draft riot in New York City in 1863. Over 2000 casualties were suffered. Federal troops had to be pulled out of Union lines to put it down. Indeed, Meade's army was so weakened that he was unable to resume the offensive after Gettysburg. Extremist elements have, of course, exploited bad situations, but the recent riots themselves have been largely spontaneous. Indeed, the riots may, in a sense, be an indication the situation is improving. De Tocqueville once sagely observed that it is when "certain abuses have been remedied . . . that others . . . appear more galling."

Unquestionably, the riots are related to the frustrations of a people whose hopes have been stirred by the indication that progress is possible. The riots seem to be, in short, but an exaggerated outgrowth of many of the same social and economic conditions which play a major role in the other forms of street crime. Our proper course of immediate action lies in effective law enforcement or, if necessary, martial law; but the underlying conditions must be removed if progress is to be ultimately made in the area of street crime—in all its forms.

White Collar Crime

Too little is said today of white collar crime—fraud, embezzlement, tax evasion, price-rigging, double dealing in securities and the like. In 1949, Sutherland published his seminal study, *White Collar Crime,* which was an analysis of the crimes committed by seventy of the largest manufacturing, mining, and mercantile corporations in this country. Over an average "life career" of forty-five years, the seventy corporations had an average of four criminal convictions each. Today, however, no one systematically collects statistics on these crimes. Attention is focused elsewhere. People do not find white collar crimes in the headlines each day so it is not a matter of interest or concern to them.

Some groups also do not speak of it, because it does not fit neatly into their ideology. How can it be "crime" if it is not the product of ignorance, poverty, discrimination, or disease? Others do not speak of it, embarrassed that they might have to attack members of their own socio-economic class. Its impact on our nation, however, is plainly great. Just one conspiracy, for example, involving the collapse of a fraudulent salad oil empire in 1964 had an economic price tag probably twice that of all criminal assaults for the same year. Economically, petty theft merely transfers wealth, usually from the rich to the poor. Yet price fixing and the collusive allocation of markets undermine our free enterprise system, most often transferring wealth from the poor to the rich and unfairly eliminating small businesses. When an individual in the upper middle class evades taxes, less revenue is available for needed social services, and persons whose wealth is more visible must make up the difference. There is a cause for concern here, too, but plainly more knowledge is needed before a more accurate evaluation can be made or specific action can be recommended.

Organized Crime

While people are concerned about street crime and white collar crime is largely ignored, our attitude toward organized crime is strangely ambivalent. A majority of our people probably do not believe that a group like the Mafia even exists. Others feel organized crime only "services" our moral failings. Touched by its corruption, many political leaders also minimize its significance. Yet a growing number of people see it as a threat.

The core of organized crime today consists of twenty-four highly structured groups operating in our largest cities across the Nation. Their internal organization is patterned after the Mafia groups of Sicily. They are, however, more than mere criminal cartels. They are also para-governments within our society. They are active in professional gambling, the importation and distribution of narcotics, and loan sharking, each an offense parasitic, corruptive, and predatory in character, and with its chief impact on the urban poor. The economic price tag of organized crime, moreover, is put at twice that of all other crime combined. Organized crime, in addition, clearly affects street crime. Who can say that juveniles do not try to emulate the "success story" of the top men in organized crime? Street crime is also involved in other ways. For example, estimates place at 50 percent the percentage of theft in our large cities related to the need to acquire funds for narcotics. Significantly, too, the organized crime groups have not confined their activities to traditional criminal endeavors, but have increasingly undertaken to subvert legitimate businesses and unions. The viability of large spheres of economic life is threatened. More importantly, these criminals have everywhere established corrupt alliances with the processes of our democratic society: the police, the prosecutors, the courts, and the legislatures. Freedom from legal accountability is secured, often under a rhetoric of liberty. In many ways, organized crime is thus the most sinister kind of crime in America. In a real sense, it is dedicated not only to subverting American institutions, but our decency and integrity. The cause here for concern is real.

LOCAL LAW ENFORCEMENT

To understand the administration of criminal justice in our society today, we must first appreciate the problems of the administration of justice in a largely stable, homogeneous, pioneer, agricultural community of the first half of the nineteenth century. It is then necessary to understand the problems of the administration of justice in our mobile, heterogeneous, urban industrial community and the resulting difficulties involved in meeting those problems with legal doctrines and social institutions first inherited from England and then adapted to an American society of the last century.

We inherited from England a medieval system of sheriffs, coroners and constables, devised for a rural society and fashioned out of the history of a struggle between the Crown and Parliament for political and religious freedom in the seventeenth century. A professional police force was then unknown. Not until 1844, in fact, was the first unified night and day police force established in this country in New York City. Its primary function was street patrol. Today there are some 400,000 people working for approximately 40,000 separate police agencies that spend more than $2.5 billion a year. Nearly one-half of the personnel of every city department, nevertheless, remain primarily involved in street duty. The rest back up the patrolman in detective work and staff positions. Police work, in short, has changed comparatively little since 1844.

Popular fiction notwithstanding, scientific crime detection is a limited tool. The radio and the automobile have had a greater impact on day-to-day police work than the best a crime laboratory has to offer. Police work today is still largely looking, questioning and listening—under the best conditions and in the best of departments.

The performance of the local police is hardly impressive. Putting aside the question of community relations—often non-existent in the ghetto—the clearance rate by arrest of crimes against the person in 1966, for example, was fortunately high —88 percent for murder, 62 percent for rape, and 72 percent for aggravated assault. Yet it should be recalled here that most often the perpetrator was known to the victim—and it has been in this area that the greatest growth of crime has occurred. Under present law enforcement practices, the 1966 statistics demonstrated, in short, that crime does pay. Only 30 percent of the robberies, 22 percent of the burglaries, 23 percent of the auto thefts and 18 percent of the larcenies were even cleared by arrest. Excluding automobiles, only approximately 10 percent of all stolen property is ever recovered. The year 1966 was, unfortunately, a typical year. Note, too, that these figures are clearance by arrest only. Something will be said of convictions later.

The truth is that the nation's local police officers are poorly paid, undertrained, and overworked. Professionalization is only just beginning. All too often politics, if not corruption, taints their work. The experts agree that few departments are well organized. There is a need for area wide planning and state wide coordination, but local law enforcement is fragmented, complicated and frequently overlapping. America is essentially a nation of obsolete, small police forces. The statistics tell the story. In small cities, for example, the median annual pay for a patrolman is $4600; in large cities, it is $5300. Nevertheless, 90 percent of police budgets go for salaries. Only about 10 percent of the total personnel in metropolitan departments have college level training. Only a few states—notably California, New York, and New Jersey—have attempted to set up statewide standards. Police personnel have remained stable, while population and crime have increased. How much could be done just with more adequate personnel, moreover, has been often demonstrated. An experiment known as Operation 25 was undertaken in 1954 in northeast Harlem in New York City. When manpower was doubled, street crime was halved. Muggings—which nationally account for over 50 percent of all robberies—were virtually eliminated. A similar experiment was recently conducted on Manhattan's West Side. Comparable results were obtained. There is something that can be done. But more than experiments are necessary. The needs of local law enforcement, in short, are massive.

STATE LAW ENFORCEMENT

As the state's chief executive, the governor of most states must see to it that the laws of the state are enforced. The governor, too, is usually the head of the National Guard, which backs up the police agencies in civil disturbances. Traditionally —and today in some forty-seven states—the state attorney general, however, is the state's "chief law enforcement officer." In this capacity, he generally has supervisory power over law enforcement in the state. State concern with law enforcement, moreover, is widespread. No less than twenty-eight states have programs for police training. Another thirty-one have identification and laboratory facilities open to the local police. On the other hand, statewide police forces, now found in a majority of states and in all of the populous states save

California, have been a comparatively new development. Principally because local county sheriffs or constables—institutions with a few notable exceptions now anachronistic—were unwilling or unable to enforce the law, state police agencies were established, first in Pennsylvania in 1905. Today, they are the fastest growing of the police agencies, they employ some 40,000 people and they spend some $315 million each year. From the beginning, they have been characterized by a high degree of professionalization, largely free of corruption, and not dominated by politics. Usually, it is their job to train local officers, maintain statewide laboratories, keep statewide intelligence and other files, and otherwise back up local forces. In many ways, state law enforcement is the hope of the future.

FEDERAL LAW ENFORCEMENT

Unlike the states, the federal government has no common law jurisdiction in the area of criminal justice. Like Topsy, the federal police agencies have "just growed." In 1789, the Revenue Cutter Service was started. Since then, innumerable different agencies have been established. Enforcing 2800 federal statutes, they employ 23,000 full time men and spend $220 million a year. Located in various departments of the federal government, the chief agencies are, among others, the Secret Service, the Bureau of Narcotics, the Internal Revenue Service, and the Federal Bureau of Investigation. Although small in numbers—New York City has more police officers than the whole federal establishment—the impact of the federal agencies on criminal justice (federal, state and local) has been great. The Federal Bureau of Investigation, under the leadership of J. Edgar Hoover since 1924, has been, for example, widely responsible for the increased use of the tools of science in crime detection, higher training standards in police work, and the general move toward professionalism. In 1966 alone, the Bureau participated in 5337 police training schools, which were attended by 163,149 officers (half the number of full time local personnel), while in its national laboratory, open to all law enforcement agencies, the Bureau made 284,304 examinations, and, in its Identification Division, through fingerprint searches, identified 22,614 fugitives.

While the attention of local and state agencies has been primarily directed at street crime, the burden of responding to white collar and organized crime has largely fallen to the federal government. Evaluation of the federal effort, however, is difficult, because there are so few objective measures. What information we do have is not encouraging. In the area of organized crime, for example, the federal government is spending about $20 million a year. Nevertheless, little progress has been made against the hard-core of organized crime. Estimates place the probable membership of La Cosa Nostra at 5000. Since 1961 convictions have been secured only against approximately 2.6 percent. The failure to do more has been attributable—basically—to a failure to secure legally admissible evidence. Organized crime has too often shown a willingness to threaten, bribe, and murder those who would testify against its members. In the first four years, for example, of the present drive—which began in 1961—twenty-five informants were killed, often horribly tortured to death. The need for new evidence gathering techniques, such as electronic surveillance, seems manifest. Until they are authorized, as Robert F. Kennedy put it, we will continue to do little more than "tread water." There are thus things that can be done to improve the performance of law enforcement on the federal level, too.

COURTS

It is not possible to talk about criminal justice without talking about the courts, both state and federal. Popular fiction makes much of the drama of the criminal trial. It is supposed to be, of course, a contest between the forces of good and evil from which the truth emerges—established in a process characterized by a high regard for individual rights. Attention also is focused on the work of our appellate courts, particularly the Supreme Court. There we are told rights are vindicated and justice done. The facts bear little relation to popular fiction.

Well over half of all criminal defendants are poor—and poorly represented at trial. Seldom is a defendant judged by a jury of his peers—his guilt is usually established as a result of bargaining process with the prosecutor in which the merits of the case are not always the chief consideration. Popular fiction notwithstanding, criminal justice today is thus largely administrative not judicial. When cases do go to trial, moreover, the conviction rate for the offense as charged is seldom different from the exoneration rate, a disturbing result from any point of view. And some 20 to 25 percent of these convictions are reversed on appeal. Nowhere is the breakdown of our system of criminal justice more manifest than in the prosecutions growing out of the recent riots. In the Detroit riot 7231 persons for example, were arrested, yet nearly half had to be released without charges for lack of evidence; in Newark, 1300 were arrested, but again less than half could be formally charged. In large measure, this result is the product of factors wholly unrelated to guilt or innocence or the protection of real liberty. Our courts today operate with rules of evidence and criminal procedure that were fashioned in an age dominated by the death penalty and fearful of the suppression of religious or political dissent. Law enforcement was consciously debilitated. Insistence today upon the common law rights of an Englishman of the latter half of the eighteenth century, pressed to the limits of their logic in our formative years by a Puritan and pioneer distrust of all government itself, now produces a complicated, expensive and time-consuming process that has largely broken down. The adjudication of guilt or innocence today, in short, is at best a matter of chance. A system designed for the leisurely pace of a rural society is now operating as a mass production scythe of the poor and a means of avoiding legal responsibility for the rich. Volume alone—now staging 2.5 million cases a year—makes a mockery of justice.

We have experienced in the last decade, moreover, a revolution in criminal procedure, led by the Supreme Court, which has been both good and bad. The elimination of the third degree—now largely an accomplished fact—was a reform crying for implementation. In 1936, for example, in *Brown* v. *Mississippi,* the Supreme Court overturned a conviction because it was based on a confession obtained by physical torture. No other result was possible. But as the Court has moved on and on to more and more attenuated questions of "fairness," the single-minded pursuit by some jurists of individual rights defined by an eighteenth-century ideology, but applied to a twentieth-century society is threatening to alter the nature of the criminal trial from a test of the defendant's innocence or guilt to an inquiry into the propriety of the policemen's conduct—with possible adverse consequences to us all. For example, in 1957, in *Mallory* v. *United States,* a rape conviction was overturned merely to discipline the police because they questioned the defendant at the wrong time, even though his confession was otherwise voluntary. The defendant, after his release, raped another woman. In another case, following the reversal of another rape conviction, this time for the second time, the outraged husband of the ravished woman shot and killed the defendant during the course of the third trial.

While few do not have sympathy with the goals of the Court—accurate fact finding, the recognition of human dignity, the preservation of privacy—it must be questioned whether the judicial process is the proper instrument for the modernization of criminal justice. The tool of reversal, the only one generally available, is much too blunt. Among other things, better training, higher pay, in short, fair minded professionalism will do more for these goals than judicial exhortations. The improvements necessary cannot be implemented by the judiciary. They must come through legislative and executive action. It is in this direction that the hope of the future lies.

CORRECTIONS

If it is necessary to talk about courts, it is necessary, too, to talk about corrections—probation, institutionalization, and parole. Our criminal justice system, in short, should be viewed as an integrated whole—even if it is not in practice. On any given day—nationwide—our correctional institutions are responsible for a staggering 1.3 million offenders. Each year they spend some $1 billion. Here, too, the central role of the states is evident. All states have prison and parole systems. There are forty-five states that operate or underwrite adult court and probation systems. Yet correction does not correct. Life in many institutions is at best barren, at worst unspeakably brutal and degrading. Most institutions are confronted with serious problems of rackets, violence, and homosexuality. Treatment is aimed at the offender, while many of the causes of his crime were in his environment, which is left untouched. Probation or parole is often a joke. Caseloads of the probation or parole officers are out of proportion. Although over half of the adult offenders are "supervised" frequently this supervision is limited to a ten- or fifteen-minute interview once or twice a month with an officer carrying over a hundred other cases. Trained officers are an exception. Parole decisions are often related to little more than institutional capacity—the necessity to release or parole as many as are newly added to the prisons. Personnel resources and adequate facilities are everywhere in short supply.

We speak of rehabilitation, yet 80 percent of those in corrections are involved in custody and maintenance. Twenty-five of our major state institutions are over a hundred years old. Our recidivism statistics, which are inadequate because they depend on catching the offender the second time, indicate a measure of our failure. For example, 75 percent of those who are arrested have been arrested before, and 70 percent of these individuals were first arrested under twenty-five. On the average these individuals are rearrested five times. Their criminal careers span ten years. Their six arrests produce three convictions and two imprisonments. Our repeat offenders tend to repeat for burglary, robbery, narcotics, and fraudulent checks. Frequently, there is a progression toward violence. These data, although incomplete, sadly document the existence of a persistent or hard core offender, who contributes substantially to the over-all crime problem.

CONCLUSION

No short survey can do more than touch on the high points. There are, however, certain conclusions that can be drawn. The remarkable thing about our crime problem is not that it is bad, but that it is not worse. The problems are everywhere massive. For too long now we have dissipated our energies in ideological debates over issues often of symbolic value only —consensual homosexuality, capital punishment, police review boards, coddling of criminals, and the like. The problems of crime, of course, involve more than criminal justice. Long term solutions must be sought to underlying problems. Symptoms, however, must be treated, too. Every part of the criminal justice system is undernourished. There is insufficient manpower, and what there is, is not well paid, trained or organized. Our legal theories were developed in another age to deal with other problems. We have tended, moreover, to forget that the liberty of the King's subjects presupposes the establishment of the King's peace. Virtually every aspect of the present system must be rethought—and the rethinking must include questions touching on administration as well as theory. "The balance of power within our society," Walter Lippmann has observed, "(is turning) dangerously against the peace forces—against the police and the courts." America has too much crime—of all kinds. More than it need have. It is time we did something besides lament it.

SELECTED BIBLIOGRAPHY

The Courts The Public and The Law Explosion, The American Assembly (1965).

The Challenge of Crime in a Free Society: A Report of the President's Commission on Law Enforcement and Administration of Justice (1967) (and supporting Task Force volumes).

Radzinowiz, *Ideology and Crime* (1966).
Roscoe Pound and Criminal Justice, Gluck (ed.) (1965).
Uniform Crime Reports—1966: U. S. Department of Justice,
    Washington, D.C.

A REPORT AND CRITIQUE OF THE CURRENT EFFORTS OF THE FEDERAL GOVERNMENT TO CONTROL AND COMBAT CRIME IN AMERICA

by Richard H. Poff

RICHARD HARDING POFF was born and educated in Virginia, receiving his law degree from the University of Virginia a year after he passed the State Bar. His education interrupted by military service in World War II, Poff received the Distinguished Flying Cross after flying 35 combat missions over Europe.

In 1952 at the age of twenty-nine, he became the first Republican ever to represent the 6th District of Virginia in the Congress and has been re-elected by increasing majorities ever since. Second ranking Republican on the House Judiciary Committee, Poff is Chairman of the House Republican Task Force on Crime and Vice-Chairman of the National Commission on Reform of Federal Criminal Laws. He is a member of the Republican Leadership team of the House, the Joint Senate-House Republican Leadership and the Republican Coordinating Committee.

"There is much crime in America, more than ever is reported, far more than ever is solved, far too much for the health of the Nation."

(Quoted from *"The Challenge of Crime in a Free Society"* A Report by The President's Commission on Law Enforcement and Administration of Justice)

I. Introduction

An appropriate point to begin this report is January 23, 1967, the day the President's Commission on Law Enforcement and Administration of Justice submitted its historic report to the President. The Commission had spent eighteen months and almost $2 million in its intense study of law enforcement and criminal justice in America. Its 10 volume report contained over two hundred specific recommendations for dealing with the problem of crime. Many of these recommendations call for action by the federal government.

Tribute is due the Commission, its staff, its advisers and consultants. Its report and recommendations have made a significant contribution to the cause of law enforcement and it has illuminated many dark corners in our system of criminal justice. The Commission has laid the foundation for a productive dialogue.

The Commission, chaired by former Attorney General Nicholas Katzenbach, was truly a Presidential Commission. It was constituted by Presidential order; its members were appointed by the President; it served under the President, at the pleasure of the President; and it reported its findings to the President.[1] As such, many in Congress anticipated that the President would recommend an equally historic and comprehensive anti-crime program to implement the recommendations of his Commission. He did not. But this is not to say the President ignored all Commission recommendations. To the contrary, on February 6, 1967, the President sent his Mes-

[1] The President's Commission on Law Enforcement and Administration of Justice was created by Executive Order 11236 (July 23, 1965). The members of the Commission were: Nicholas deB. Katzenbach (Chairman), Genevieve Blatt, Charles D. Brutel, Kingman Brewster, Garrett H. Byrne, Thomas J. Cahill, Otis Chandler, Leon Jaworski, Thomas C. Lynch, Ross L. Malone, James B. Parsons, Lewis F. Powell, Jr., William P. Rogers, Robert G. Storey, Julia D. Stuart, Robert F. Wagner, Herbert Wechsler, Whitney M. Young, Jr., and Luther W. Youngdahl.

sage on Crime to the 90th Congress, calling for enactment of a number of proposals based on the Commission's findings and recommendations.[2] These proposals, their strengths and weaknesses, will be examined in the course of this paper.

The President, however, is responsible for far more than proposing legislation. To place the crime fighting efforts of the Johnson administration in context, this paper will first look at the respective roles and activities of the federal and state governments. It will then focus on two fundamental roles of the federal government: assisting state and local law enforcement and enforcing the federal criminal laws. The discussion of assisting state and local law enforcement will be limited to a review of the President's proposed new grant-in-aid legislation. The discussion of the effectiveness of federal law enforcement will be limited to a review of the organization of federal law enforcement and the efforts to combat organized crime. Obviously, there are other vital topics that might be discussed in this report and which the author regrets he is unable to discuss because of limitations placed on the scope of this paper. Nevertheless, the selected topics give the reader a representative report on current federal efforts to control and combat crime in America.

II. The Federal Role

Law enforcement and the administration of criminal justice are fundamentally responsibilities of local and state governments and are based on local and state laws and controlled by local and state officials. Crime, however, knows no boundaries. Crime is a national problem affecting all parts of the country. The national dimensions of crime have necessarily evoked the use of federal power.

In 1789 Congress enacted the first federal criminal law, which imposed a $500 fine on a ship's master for failure to report on imports and vessel tonnage.[3] Since that date, Con-

[2] See House Doc. No. 53, 90th Cong., 1st Sess. (1967).
[3] Section 11, Chapter 5, of Vol. 1, U. S. Statutes (July 31, 1789).

gress has defined and re-defined the criminal jurisdiction of the federal government. In brief, the federal power has been invoked to protect the federal government or any of its agencies, property, personnel, functions or interests from harmful behavior. Federal power is invoked when the offense occurred in federal territory or enclave, when the offense occurred on an American vessel on the high seas, when the offense involved the use of the facilities of interstate commerce, or if the offense infringed upon a federal, statutory, or constitutional right. Today there are more than 2800 criminal statutes to protect these basic interests of the federal government.[4]

To enforce these criminal statutes, the federal government maintains over twenty law enforcement or investigative agencies, ranging from the FBI to the Fish and Wildlife Service and involving no less than eight separate Cabinet departments, the Executive Offices of the President, and four independent agencies. The federal government employs some 23,000 law enforcement officers. There are some 425,000 full-time law enforcement officers in the entire United States. The federal government also operates a system of criminal courts and a correctional establishment which houses about 5 percent of the 400,000 prison population of the United States.

The federal government, primarily through the FBI, has for many years provided information, advice and training to state and local law enforcement agencies. Under The Law Enforcement Assistance Act of 1965 the Department of Justice has been giving state and local agencies financial grants for research, demonstration projects and planning. Similarly,

[4] Republican sponsored legislation in the 89th Congress created the National Commission on Reform of Federal Criminal Laws to review, revise, recodify and reform the existing federal criminal laws and improve the federal system of criminal justice. The existing criminal code is premised on 18th century concepts of criminal justice and has been kept current by patchwork amendments and periodic revisions. The mandate of the Commission is to modernize the criminal code and eliminate the ambiguities, gaps and anomalies which now exist. (*Editor's Note:* This legislation was drafted by Congressman Poff, who has been selected by the Commission to serve as Vice-Chairman.)

under The Juvenile Delinquency and Youth Offense Control Act of 1961, the Department of Health, Education and Welfare has been giving financial assistance to state and local agencies for research and demonstration projects in the field of juvenile delinquency.

III. THE STATE'S ROLE[5]

The National Council on Crime and Delinquency, a nonprofit, voluntary organization founded in 1907 to promote and develop through research practical methods of crime prevention and control and advice on programs for the effective treatment of offenders, states that:

> Responsibility for crime control is shared by state and local governments, with the role of the states expanding steadily. The growth of intercounty and interstate crime, the inability of local governments to provide services, and the complexity of local crime control have demanded greater state and federal involvement. Local agencies cannot meet the problem because effective law enforcement, as well as courts and corrections, cannot be operated by individual communities acting alone.[6]

The problems of crime in America are most acute in large metropolitan areas. The Uniform Crime Reports issued by the FBI show that 83 percent of crime in the United States is committed in the 212 Standard Metropolitan Statistical Areas. Metropolitan areas encompass both a central city and outlying suburbs. Generally, a large portion of the metropolitan area is outside the law enforcement jurisdiction of the city it encompasses. Efficient law enforcement in these areas

---

[5] In preparing this sketch of the role of the state and local governments in crime control, the author is indebted to material gathered by the National Council on Crime and Delinquency and the Council of State Governments.

[6] National Council on Crime and Delinquency, press release of October 6, 1967.

demands coordination, regionalization and sharing of facilities and services by several jurisdictions: city, suburban, and state.

State and local law enforcement and criminal justice agencies do not (and should not) exist in isolation: organizationally or functionally. They are all part of a statewide system. For example, when a crime is committed in a metropolitan area the local police are called, and it is their responsibility to investigate and apprehend the suspect. In turn the local police may ask for laboratory and criminal identification assistance from the state police, or they may seek state assistance in apprehension if they think the suspect may have fled the city. Even when the arrest is made by the city police, if the crime committed violated a state law (and all felonies and most misdemeanors are violations of state law) the suspect will be prosecuted by a state prosecutor in a state court. Upon conviction, he will be committed to a state institution and given rehabilitative training by the state education system. If placed on probation, he will be in a state system. When his term ends, he is released into the state parole system, and the state employment service helps him find a job.

It is currently being argued that the states have no responsibility or experience in law enforcement.[7] If law enforcement is viewed as part of a larger system of criminal justice, the importance of state government becomes clearer. All states run prison and parole systems. All states operate courts and probation systems. All states have systems of prosecution. In forty-seven states the attorney general is the chief law enforcement official, and has broad authority. The governor of

[7] Attorney General Ramsey Clark contends: "Typically, throughout the country, the local police department has secured no assistance from state government—financial or supervisory. State government experience in local police work has been quite limited. More than 75 percent of all state police are highway patrolmen and in many states the highway patrol really all the state police do and that is as much traffic control as any other function." *Hearings before the Subcommittee on Criminal Laws and Procedures of the Committee on the Judiciary,* United States Senate, 90th Cong., 1st Sess. on S. 300 *et al* (1967) at p. 366.

every state has a mandate to maintain law and order within his state.

Even in law enforcement, narrowly confined, the states have basic responsibilities. They determine the division of police responsibilities among jurisdictions and agencies; they decide what will be done by the state police, county sheriffs, and city, township, borough, and village police; they define by law the permissible behavior of police dealing with suspects.

It is not true, as some contend, that the principal law enforcement responsibility of states is limited to traffic control.[8] Twenty-eight states have programs of police training. In Connecticut, the State Municipal Police Academy trains all police. Increasing numbers of states are adopting the Model Police Standards Code, and, as in Oregon, are setting standards for local forces within the state. Governor Spiro T. Agnew of Maryland, concerned about local inability to solve growing problems and support new programs, developed a state assistance program for local police. Thirty-one states operate criminal identification bureaus and laboratory facilities, which provide assistance to local police. The Michigan attorney general and state police are developing a cooperative attack on organized crime. State responsibility in law enforcement has developed steadily and is growing rapidly.

As the state role in law enforcement has expanded, so has interstate cooperation. All states belong to the Interstate Compact for the Supervision of Parolees and Probationers. Nearly all the states have ratified an agreement dealing with detainers lodged against prisoners in other states, making possible speedy trials for multiple offenders. Twelve Western states and all six New England states are members of regional corrections compacts. Four of the New England states have formed a police compact to provide for central collection of police intelligence and mutual aid. New England also has a well-developed cooperative program for advanced training of state police officers. All such compacts have the congres-

---

[8] See Footnote 7.

sional approval required by the Constitution under a blanket
ratification statute.[9]

IV. FEDERAL ASSISTANCE TO STATE AND LOCAL LAW ENFORCEMENT

On January 19, 1967, the Republican Leaders of the House
and Senate—Congressman Gerald R. Ford (R. Mich.) and
Senator Everett M. Dirksen (R. Ill.)—presented to the American people an appraisal of the State of the Union and a call
for action. Congressman Ford observed:

> At all levels of government a massive effort should
> be made to reduce crime by attacking some of its basic
> causes: poverty, slums, inadequate education and dis-
> crimination. However, our laws and actions should never
> be based on the theory that a criminal is solely the prod-
> uct of his environment. Fear of punishment remains an
> important deterrent to crime.
>
> Most Americans will resist any trend toward the es-
> tablishment of a national police force or the unwarranted
> intrusion of federal power into local law enforcement.
> Yet, there is a proper place for federal assistance and
> leadership.
>
> The primary responsibility for law enforcement must
> remain with the states and local authorities. In the last
> analysis, public safety depends upon the courage and
> character of the policeman patrolling his beat. The fed-
> eral government can properly help in making law en-
> forcement a more attractive and professional career.[10]

Within less than a month the report of the President's
Crime Commission, echoing the words of Congressman Ford,
called for the federal government to make "a dramatic new
contribution to the national effort against crime by greatly ex-

[9] 48 Stat. 909; 4 U.S.C. 111 (1964).
[10] *Congressional Record,* Vol. 113, January 23, 1967 (daily ed.)
at p. H460.

panding its support of the agencies of justice in the states
and in the cities." The Commission's report noted that in the
field of law enforcement, delinquency prevention and the
administration of criminal justice, the federal contribution is
still very small. To implement this Commission recommendation, the President submitted two legislative proposals to the
Congress: The Safe Streets and Crime Control Act of 1967
and the Juvenile Delinquency Prevention and Control Act of
1967.

(A) *Safe Streets and Crime Control Act of 1967*.[11] The
proposed Safe Streets and Crime Control Act—subsequently
given the more descriptive title of Law Enforcement and
Criminal Justice Assistance Act of 1967 by the House Judiciary Committee—authorizes a grant-in-aid program for state
and local institutions and agencies of law enforcement and
criminal justice. Federal grants would be available for planning, action programs and research to improve and strengthen
all phases of crime prevention and control, including police,
prosecution, courts, probation, corrections, and parole. Attorney General Ramsey Clark told the Congress the program
would reach an annual federal expenditure of $1 billion and,
as one distinguished witness testifying before the Congress
noted, the impact of such expenditures "will determine the
whole evolution of law enforcement."

Combined expenditures of local, state and federal government for law enforcement and the administration of criminal
justice today are slightly more than $4 billion annually: $2.8
billion for police; $1.03 billion for corrections; and $350 million for courts and prosecution. Approximately 7 percent of
this total expenditure is federal. Federal expenditures for juvenile delinquency constitute an even smaller percentage.

[11] Introduced in the House of Representatives by Chairman of
the Judiciary Committee Emanuel Celler (H.R. 5037) and introduced in the Senate by Chairman of the Subcommittee on Criminal Laws and Procedures John McClellan (S. 917). At the time
of writing this paper the Senate has completed hearings but taken
no formal action on the proposal. This discussion is limited to actions taken by the House of Representatives.

The President's proposal was cast in the form of a typical "Great Society" grant program, bypassing the governors of the states and containing no priorities, no formula to assure equitable allocation throughout the nation of the federal funds, and vesting absolute discretionary authority for administering the program in a non-elected official in Washington.

Republicans commended the goals of the proposal, but challenged the means the President had selected to reach those goals. Evidence from experiences under similar "Great Society" grant programs in the areas of education, housing, employment, transportation and welfare supported the Republicans' conclusion that applicants, sorely in need of funds, would quickly become skilled in the art of grantsmanship and tailor their applications to what they believed the Department of Justice would approve. Stated another way, Republicans felt that the President's scheme for distributing the much needed money contained unwise and unnecessary federal encroachments upon state and local law enforcement.

The fact that large grants could and would be made directly to cities and towns wholly bypassing the states raised the possibility of a direct dependency link between the localities and the federal government, undermining in the process the position of the states. Constitutionally, it is the states which possess independent political power, not the localities which are mere creatures of the state. Practically, bypassing the state could result in fragmentation and duplication by localities in planning programs and implementing projects and would defeat statewide coordination.

The absence of priorities in the President's proposal raised the question of whether it sought to undertake too much, too soon, with too little. The President asked Congress for $50 million for the first year and $300 million for the second, with no indication of how the money would be spent during the formative phases of the program. Unfortunately, there is not enough money in the Federal Treasury to do immediately all that needs to be done eventually in the field of crime control. Enthusiasm for the whole cause should be tempered with an emphasis upon its most important parts first. Among all the desirable goals, a catalogue of priorities should be established.

Certainly a high priority is education and training of law enforcement officials and personnel. Any police chief will tell you that what he needs is better trained men. Everyone agrees. Another high priority is the urgent need for more scientific and technological research into causes and control of crime. The President's Crime Commission called research "the greatest need" of law enforcement and recommended that a National Institute patterned after the National Institutes of Health be established.[12]

Efforts of Republican members of the House Judiciary Committee to amend the "Great Society" formula for distributing federal money or establish priorities were in vain. The Democrats held the votes and the administration was determined to hold the line. Republicans caucused and agreed that these issues should be presented to and resolved by the House of Representatives in floor debate. Every Member would be given an opportunity to vote on each issue:

Does the President's proposed grant scheme encroach upon the independence of state and local law enforcement by vesting undue discretionary authority in the Attorney General and the Department of Justice?

Should federal assistance money be granted directly to the states for statewide crime control planning and programs to improve state and local law enforcement and criminal justice?

Should this legislation contain a distribution formula

[12] Congressman Gerald Ford (R. Mich.) in his Appraisal of the State of the Union Message on January 19, 1967 stated: "A National Law Enforcement Institute, similar to the successful National Institute of Health, should be established for research and training and for the dissemination of the latest techniques in police science." Congressman William Cramer (R. Fla.) introduced such legislation (H.R. 6052) on February 23, 1967, and the Cramer bill formed the basis for the Republican amendment to incorporate such an Institute in the President's proposal.

to assure equitable allocation of the federal funds to the state and local governments?

Should the federal government establish a National Crime Research Institute comparable to the National Institutes of Health?

Each of these questions was answered on August 8, 1967, with a resounding YES when both Republican and Democratic Members of the House from all parts of the country overwhelmingly voted to adopt the Republican Amendments offered by Congressmen Bill Cahill (R. N.J.) and Bob McClory (R. Ill.).[13]

(B) *The Juvenile Delinquency Prevention and Control Act of 1967.*[14] Cast from the same die and paralleling the proposed Safe Streets and Crime Control Act, the President also recommended that Congress pass his Juvenile Delinquency Prevention and Control Act of 1967. This bill was designed to complement the Safe Streets bill by giving federal financial assistance to encourage the development and improvement of state and community rehabilitative and prevention services for delinquent youths and those in danger of becoming delinquent. This assistance would be available to courts, correctional systems and community agencies concerned with the prevention, treatment and control of juvenile delinquency.

Information compiled by the President's Crime Commission shows that the single, most disturbing aspect of the nation's crime problem is the growing involvement of young people in crime. The cost to the nation of such crime has been estimated at $4 billion annually. Several indices docu-

[13] For a full discussion of these amendments and the votes thereon see *Congressional Record,* Vol. 113, August 2, 3 and 8, 1967, (daily ed.) at pp. H9788–H9810, H9888–H9915, and H10060–H10108.

[14] Introduced in the House of Representatives by Congressman Pucinski (H.R. 7642) and introduced in the Senate by Senator Dodd (S. 1248). At the time of writing this paper the Senate has completed hearings but taken no formal action on the proposal. This discussion is limited to the action of the House of Representatives.

ment the startling increase in juvenile delinquency that our nation is experiencing. A graphic example of this increase is found in the fact that in 1960 approximately 440,000 children aged ten to seventeen were referred to courts for their offenses; in 1965, court referrals of this age group (excluding traffic violations) increased to 601,001. This represents a 36 percent increase in court referrals, while the population increase of this age group was only 16 percent during this period.

Indeed, the need for assisting state and local governments in dealing with the problem of juvenile and youth offenders is immediate. Money properly spent today will be money saved tomorrow. The loss of young people to a life of crime today will be a loss to the nation tomorrow in terms of community leadership, manpower resources and economic losses to society arising from the growing costs of law enforcement, crowding court dockets and necessary corrective efforts.

The goals of this legislation were beyond question, but the machinery the administration was urging to reach these new goals raised the same fundamental issues which had confronted the Congress with the Safe Streets and Crime Control Act.

On September 26, 1967, when the House Committee on Education and Labor presented this legislation to the House of Representatives, Congressman Tom Railsback (R. Ill.) offered a comprehensive Republican amendment similar to the amendment Republicans had offered and incorporated in the Law Enforcement and Criminal Justice Assistance Act. Adoption of the Railsback amendment would mean that the states would be directly involved in administering the programs, that there would be an equitable distribution of the available funds throughout the nation, and absolute discretionary authority to administer the program would not be given to a non-elected Washington official (in this case the Secretary of Health, Education and Welfare).[15]

Again, Democrats from all parts of the country joined

[15] For a full discussion of the Republican amendment and the vote thereon see *Congressional Record*, Vol. 113, September 26, 1967 (daily ed.) at pp. H12445–H12489.

Republicans in overwhelmingly adopting this approach for granting federal money to assist state and local governments in dealing with the vital problem of juvenile crime.

V. THE EFFECTIVENESS OF FEDERAL LAW ENFORCEMENT

(A) *Organization.* It is the duty of the Congress to define and that of the President to enforce federal criminal law. It is the responsibility of both the Congress and the President to maintain effective law enforcement within the confines of the national government's criminal jurisdiction. Effective law enforcement at all levels of government demands efficient organization and delegation of responsibilities. On March 15, 1967, twenty-three Republican Congressmen called for a full scale investigation of the adequacy of the federal government's organization to fight crime. Based on their own preliminary study of the organization of the federal government's crime control effort they found that "today that organization is less than optimum."[16]

This Republican study indicates there is little system, little method, little coordination and little order in the federal government's approach to crime. Today it is a crazy-quilt of departments, bureaus and agencies with competing responsibilities, duplicative staffing, poor communications and self-defeating jealousies and suspicions. This confusion, duplication, competition and jurisdictional jealousy occurring in the Executive Branch among its twenty different law enforcement and investigative agencies, four independent agencies and eight Cabinet Departments with investigative and enforcement authority can be easily illustrated.

Federal control over the use of *narcotics* is the responsibility of: The Department of Justice and within the Justice Department the FBI and the Immigration and Naturalization Service; the Department of Health, Education and Welfare and within

---

[16] The complete Report will be found in the *Congressional Record*, Vol. 113, March 21, 1967 (daily ed.) at pp. H3110–H3114.

HEW the Public Health Service and the Food and Drug Administration; the Department of Treasury and within the Treasury Department the Bureau of Narcotics, Customs Agency Service, Interpol, and the Internal Revenue Service; and the Department of Post Office. Some of these departments, bureaus, and agencies have law enforcement authority, some have investigative authority only, some have both while others have neither.

Federal control over *organized crime* is the responsibility of The Department of Justice and within The Department of Justice the Criminal Division and particularly its Organized Crime and Racketeering Section, the FBI and the Immigration and Naturalization Service; the Department of Treasury and within the Treasury Department the Secret Service, the Bureau of Narcotics, and the Internal Revenue Service including its Alcohol and Tobacco Tax Division; the Department of Post Office; the Securities and Exchange Commission; and the Department of Labor, particularly its Labor Management and Welfare Pension Reports Office. Again, some of these departments, bureaus, agencies and divisions have law enforcement authority, others have investigative authority, some have both and others have neither.

Problems of juvenile delinquency prevention and control are handled by six Executive Departments and seventeen different bureaus, agencies and divisions.

Corrections and rehabilitation of criminal and juvenile offenders is the responsibility of four Executive Departments and twelve bureaus and agencies within the Executive Branch.

Research and development projects in law enforcement and crime prevention are undertaken by some fifteen different departments, bureaus, agencies and divisions.

The federal law enforcement establishment has become so complex and overlapping that no one knows how much duplication really exists. No one knows how frequently two or more agencies are working on the same problem or case. No one knows how extensive inter-agency competition and suspicion really is. No one knows when one agency may, in effect, be counteracting another.

The answers to these questions—and other related questions —regarding the effectiveness of the organization of the Executive Branch to deal with crime prevention and control are extremely difficult for anyone other than the President to obtain. If the Congress were to probe, it could be embarrassing to the President; thus it is very unlikely that a Democratically controlled Congress would undertake such an investigation. Even if it would, however, it might be confronted either with the cloak of "Executive Privilege" and denied all information or provided with such scant and irrelevant bits and pieces of information, meaningful correlation would be impossible. The President's Crime Commission, for its own reasons, did not focus on the problems of the federal government's organization to fight crime.

Structural reorganization is a job for the President. The Congress has, by the Reorganization Act of 1949, empowered the President to undertake reorganization of the Executive Branch of government. All available information indicates that such a reorganization is long overdue. The new legislation to assist state and local governments in fighting crime will increase the responsibilities of the federal government and in turn further compound this problem of organization. If new federal efforts are to achieve optimum results, there should be horizontal coordination at the federal level and vertical coordination with the state and local governments. It is hoped that the President will undertake this necessary reorganization.

(B) *Federal Efforts against Organized Crime.*

The magnitude of organized crime in America is staggering. *** If the rule of law is to survive (in America), organized crime—an entrenched enemy within—must be eliminated.[17]

> *Robert F. Kennedy*
> Attorney General of the United States
> September, 1963

[17] Notre Dame Law School Symposium on Interstate Organized Crime, *Notre Dame Lawyer,* Vol. 23, No. 6 (1963) at p. 637.

Organized crime means money. So much money is involved that it is virtually impossible to calculate. ***
Organized crime means power. Its vast capital and far flung organization inescapably means the corrosion of legitimate social institutions. . . . And organized crime means terror. It is difficult for someone who does not regularly see reports of nationwide criminal activity to comprehend fully the toll of violence and death.[18]

> *Nicholas deB. Katzenbach*
> Attorney General of the United States
> July, 1965

I know how deeply all of you share my concern over the scope and power of organized crime in America. It constitutes nothing less than a guerrilla war against society.[19]

> *Lyndon B. Johnson*
> President of the United States
> May, 1966

Organized crime is a 'tiny part' of the entire crime picture . . .[20]

> *Ramsey Clark*
> Attorney General of the United States
> May, 1967

The President's Crime Commission reported that "Organized crime affects the lives of millions of Americans, but because it desperately preserves its invisibility, many, perhaps most, Americans are not aware of how they are affected, or even that they are affected at all." It is very disconcerting that the present Attorney General of the United States seems

[18] *Hearings before the Subcommittee on Administrative Practice and Procedure of the Committee on the Judiciary,* United States Senate, 89th Cong., 1st Sess. on Invasions of Privacy (1965) at p. 1157.
[19] Remarks of the President reproduced in *Hearings before the Committee on Government Operations,* 90th Cong., 1st Sess. on The Federal Effort Against Organized Crime (1967) at p. 12.
[20] *The New York Times,* May 19, 1967, p. 23, col. 1.

to be attempting to perpetuate this profound public misconception, when he is (or should be) aware of the magnitude and dimensions of organized crime in America. It is equally, if not more disconcerting, that the present Attorney General is directing the federal efforts against organized crime as if it were truly as he has said, only but a "tiny part" of the total crime picture.

Despite Congressional investigations, periodic national magazine articles, daily newspaper stories, television news reports, and much talk, the average citizen has only a vague idea of what organized crime is and what it does. The public's conception of organized crime seems to be more like an old movie depicting the Prohibition Era of gangland warfare, bigshot hoodlums dressed in blue serge suits with silk shirts and white ties, with only an occasional prosecution for some tax violation, because the hoodlum's "mouthpiece" has been able to "fix" a state case of murder, extortion, or bribery. Although this conception is not totally inaccurate, it is sadly incomplete and badly dated.

The present Attorney General has made no effort to dispel this public misconception of organized crime. It goes almost without saying that no national effort against organized crime can be successful without strong public support. The present Attorney General is performing a great disservice to the nation in his efforts to anesthetize the public to the problems of organized crime.

Today, organized crime is a multi-*billion* dollar service industry—supplying illegal services such as gambling, loan sharking, numbers, narcotics, prostitution and other forms of vice to countless numbers of customers. It operates within structures as complex as any large international corporation and employs and involves thousands of criminals. Its actions are not impulsive; rather they result from carefully contrived and intricately executed conspiracies, sometimes spanning a period of several years and aimed at gaining control over entire fields of activity as a means of amassing huge profits.

Because the average American labors under a misconception about the nature and impact of organized crime, a notion constantly fed and fostered by the disinterest and inaction of the Department of Justice, he is unaware that he is a principal victim of organized crime. For example:

The average American is affected by organized crime if he is a businessman. Organized crime affects businessmen in a variety of ways. When the syndicate commits arson, it raises the insurance rates businessmen pay. Fraudulent bankruptcies, pre-planned and cleverly executed, cost businessmen millions of dollars a year in bad debt losses.

But in a larger sense, organized crime is a threat to the entire American free enterprise system. Trafficking in vice and greed and all the ignoble human frailties, syndicated crime has a gigantic earning power. This earning power has filled a reservoir of wealth unmatched by any legitimate financial institution in the nation. Organized crime has tapped this reservoir and invested its funds in wholly legitimate business activity.[21]

With resources practically unlimited, the crime syndicate has the power through massive purchases and sales on the stock market to manipulate capital values and influence price structures. By careful, methodical, clandestine infiltration of several segments of an industry, organized crime can create monopolies and, by coercive methods, restrain commerce among the states and with foreign nations.

The average American is affected by organized crime if he is a wage-earner. By intimidation or infiltration of honest labor unions, hoodlums contrive to control the labor supply, frustrate the rank and file, extort money as the purchase price of labor peace, and gain access to mammoth union pension funds.

The average American is affected by organized crime if he

[21] Republicans have introduced legislation to activate the criminal clauses of the antitrust laws to deal with the unfair competition and unconscionable trade practices which arise from the investment of illegally obtained funds in legitimate business. See H.R. 11266, H.R. 11268, S. 2048 and S. 2049 (90th Cong., 1st Sess.) and a statement of explanation in the *Congressional Record,* Vol. 113, June 29, 1967, by Senator Roman Hruska (R. Neb.) at pp. S9144–S9147.

is a consumer. Although the housewife may not know it, the price of a loaf of bread may go up 1¢ as a direct result of an organized crime conspiracy. The housewife who purchased inferior detergent at the local A&P store did not know it had been pushed unwanted upon the food chain. When A&P resisted, five stores were bombed and two store managers were killed.

The consumer most brutally affected by organized crime is the sick man who depends upon drugs and is subject to the counterfeit and spurious drug products palmed off by organized criminals.

The average American is affected by organized crime if he is a taxpayer. The revenue loss from organized crime is staggering. A classic example is the revenue loss in untaxed liquor which the honest taxpayer must make up. A more recent example is the untaxed cigarette. Governor Rockefeller has said that his state loses $50 million a year to cigarette bootleggers.

Two years ago the Internal Revenue Commissioner testified that his office had recommended over a four-year period assessments against organized crime operations totalling $219 million. How much more was not discovered or assessed can only be imagined. If organized criminals paid income tax on the profit involved in the syndicate's gross take (estimated at up to $50 billion a year), there would be little need for the 10 percent surtax the President requested.

The average American is affected by organized crime if he is a victim of poverty. For fiscal year 1968, the President asked Congress for a little over $2 billion to fund the War on Poverty. Organized crime's profits from illegal gambling are about $7 billion a year, possibly half of which comes from the numbers racket. Much of the money involved in the numbers racket is extracted not from the affluent, but from poor who look upon it as a chance to escape poverty. The urban poverty program cannot work when the mob is skimming off 50 percent more money in gambling profits than the taxpayers are contributing.

The average American is affected by organized crime if he

is a victim of street crime. Unknown to many, much local crime is the direct result of organized criminal conspiracies. Arson practiced by organized crime frequently destroys adjacent real property owned by innocent landlords. Car theft rings are skillfully organized and operate interstate. Burglary and jewel thefts reportedly are completely organized in many cities. The occasional local crook frequently must obtain prior permission from the mob before he can make a "score." The mob acts as a "fence" and always gets its cut.

Even in cases where local crime is not organized, there is a direct relationship between organized crime and street crime. Indeed, in a very real sense, organized crime is the seed-bed of street crime. The classic illustration is narcotics traffic. A high percentage of the crime committed against persons and their property is the result of the compulsive passion of the addict to acquire the money necessary to feed his loathesome habit. One district attorney has estimated the figure as high as 50 percent.

In still another way, organized crime has a measurable impact upon street crime. The syndicate thrives and survives only where it succeeds in corrupting local law enforcement. The corrupt policeman who takes a bribe and closes his eyes to the numbers racket and dope traffic is all too likely to be blind to other forms of crime as well.

In short, any person who operates a business, earns a wage, keeps house, pays taxes, lives in poverty, or falls victim to street crime, is also directly or indirectly a victim of organized crime. A victory against organized crime is a victory for the average American citizen.

What is the record of the Johnson administration's war against organized crime? On August 29, 1967, a group of twenty-three Republican Congressmen cited that record.[22] These Republicans reported that the President had promised in the 89th Congress legislation to "strengthen and expand" the fight against organized crime, but no such legislation ever appeared. The only proposals recommended by the Johnson

22 The complete Report will be found in the *Congressional Record*, Vol. 113, August 29, 1967 at pp. H11431–H11435.

administration to fight organized crime are measures which
have been under active consideration by the Congress for
several sessions and pre-date the Johnson administration.[23]

A most alarming fact reported by these Republicans is the
substantial decrease in vital activities by the Organized Crime
and Racketeering Section of the Department of Justice, which
is the principal federal organ involved in combating organized
crime. It was reported that the number of man days of
Section personnel in the field has decreased by over 48 percent since 1964; the number of man days before grand juries
has decreased by over 72 percent since 1963; and the number
of man days in court has decreased by over 56 percent since
1964.

The Johnson administration has quoted ever-climbing numbers of indictments and convictions relating to organized
crime[24] and has reported a recent increase in the personnel
in the Organized Crime and Racketeering Section.[25] On their
face, these facts appear to substantiate a claim of increased
and effective effort to fight organized crime. Closer analysis,
however, belies any such claims.

The truth is that the indictment and conviction record
claimed for the Organized Crime Section represents a great
number of inconsequential cases against minor hoodlums—not
the leaders—of organized crime. Also, these statistics are
"padded" by cases relating to many areas over which the
Section has "supervisory jurisdiction," but which have little or
no relation to organized crime. These cases include such matters as violations of Indian Territory liquor laws, interstate
liquor traffic laws, and criminal prosecutions under the Taft-

---

[23] See House Doc. No. 53, 90th Cong., 1st Sess. (1967). The
President recommended enactment of a witness immunity bill
(S. 677) and a bill preventing the obstruction of criminal investigations (S. 676). This legislation had originally been formulated
during the Eisenhower administration and also recommended during the Kennedy administration. See H.R. 3021 (87th Cong., 1st
Sess.) and H.R. 6909 (87th Cong., 1st Sess.).

[24] *Hearings before the Committee on Government Operations,*
House of Representatives, 90th Cong., 1st Sess. on the Federal
Effort Against Organized Crime (1967) at pp. 5–31.

[25] *Ibid.* at pp. 51–52.

Hartley (Labor) Act. The Section's supervisory jurisdiction was explained by Assistant Attorney General Vinson (the head of the Criminal Division of the Department of Justice) as "involving areas *often related to organized criminal activity* . . . In this way, the Organized Crime and Racketeering Section is able to insure uniform standards *even though many of the cases do not involve organized criminal groups.*"[26] (emphasis added.)

Although there have been increases in personnel in the Organized Crime and Racketeering Section, these increases followed the severe drop in personnel which occurred when the Johnson administration came to power. This addition of manpower was necessary, and the administration must be commended for making the necessary increase. But the question is not how many men there are, but what they are doing. The fact that there has been an increase in manpower makes the downward trend of the Section's activities (cited above) even more alarming.

The President's Crime Commission found that the means used by law enforcement to fight organized crime are primitive when compared to organized crime's methods of operation. They declared that "law enforcement must use methods at least as efficient as organized crime's."

The problems of law enforcement in combating organized crime are basically problems of proof. The leaders of organized crime insulate themselves, operate in secrecy, and minimize their own direct involvement in overt criminal acts. "From a legal standpoint," the Commission reported, "organized crime continues to grow because of the defects in the evidence-gathering process. Under present procedures, too few witnesses have been produced to prove the link between criminal group members and the illicit activities that they sponsor." The Commission recommended a detailed program "to destroy the power of organized crime." It urged that the Congress adopt six new statutes to facilitate the war against organized crime. The Commission endorsed a general witness

[26] *Hearings before a Subcommittee (State, Justice and Commerce) of the Committee on Appropriations,* House of Representatives, 89th Cong., 2nd Sess. re the Department of Justice, at p. 77.

immunity statute, the elimination of special standards of proof
in perjury cases, the extension of the prosecution's right to
appeal from pretrial rulings suppressing evidence or confessions, the establishment of federal residential facilities to
protect witnesses, empowering courts to impose extended sen-
tences on organized crime leaders, and the creation of a
permanent Joint Congressional Committee on Organized
Crime.

To date, the President has largely ignored these Commission
recommendations, and is, in fact, actively opposing legislation introduced by Republicans to implement many of them.[27]
This opposition has centered principally on legislation introduced by Congressman William M. McCulloch (R. Ohio)[28]
and co-sponsored by forty-seven other Republicans, which
would authorize restricted use (under prior court authorization and continuing court supervision) of electronic surveillance equipment by law enforcement officers to gather vital
evidence necessary to prosecute the leaders of organized
crime.

District Attorney Frank Hogan of New York, one of the
nation's most experienced and successful organized crime
fighters, told the President's Crime Commission that electronic
surveillance is:

[27] The Republican Organized Crime Package includes: witness
immunity—H.R. 6053 (Cramer), H.R. 7095 (McClory) and H.R.
13485 (McDade, Andrews, Bell, Cahill, Dellenback, Esch,
Findley, Frelinghuysen, Harvey, Horton, Mathias (Md.), Morse,
Mosher, Reid (N.Y.), Robison, Schneebeli, Schweiker, Schwengel,
Shriver, Stafford, Stanton and Whalen); elimination of special
standards of proof in perjury cases—H.R. 13485 (same sponsors
as H.R. 13484); appeals from pretrial rulings suppressing evidence or confessions—H.R. 8654 (Railsback), H.R. 9680 (Mize)
and H.R. 10813 (Collier); Federal residential facilities for protection of witnesses—H.R. 13487 (same sponsors as H.R. 13484);
Criminal Procedure Revision Act—H.R. 11267 (Poff, Rhodes,
Laird, Bob Wilson, Arends, Conable, King (N.Y.), MacGregor,
Price (Tex.), Moore, Hutchinson, McClory, Taft, Smith (N.Y.),
Wylie, Cramer, Smith (Calif.), Devine, Meskill and Roth); and
establishing a Joint Congressional Committee on Organized Crime
—H.R. 6054 (Cramer) and H.R. 13488 (same sponsors as H.R.
13484).

[28] H.R. 13275 (90th Cong., 1st Sess.).

"The single most valuable weapon in law enforcement's fight against organized crime. . . . It has permitted us to undertake major investigations of organized crime. Without it, and I confine myself to top figures in the underworld, my own office could not have convicted Charles 'Lucky' Luciano, Jimmy Hines, Louis 'Lepke' Buchalter, Jacob 'Gurrah' Shapiro, Joseph 'Socks' Lanza, George Scalise, Frank Erickson, John 'Dio' Dioguardi, and Frank Carbo. . . ."

The Commission agreed.

The list of knowledgeable law enforcement officers who have also testified to the need for and benefits of electronic surveillance equipment in combating organized crime is endless. A representative sampling of the list would include: former Attorney General William P. Rogers; former Attorney General Robert F. Kennedy; former Attorney General Nicholas Katzenbach; Assistant to the Director of the FBI, Cartha D. DeLoach; Director of the Intelligence Division of the Internal Revenue Service, William A. Kolar; the former Department of Justice prosecutor who put Jimmy Hoffa in jail and successfully prosecuted Bobby Baker, William O. Bittman—not to mention hundreds of other federal, state, and local law enforcement officers.

Despite what appears to be an undisputable fact that the one really valuable tool of law enforcement against organized crime is electronic surveillance, the Johnson administration insists that it is of no real value at all. Contrary to his predecessors, Attorney General Ramsey Clark contends that electronic surveillance is neither "effective nor highly productive."[29] Mr. Clark has said that "all my experience indicates that it is not necessary for the public safety. It is not a desirable police investigative technique and it should only be used in the national security field where there is a direct threat to the welfare of the country."[30]

[29] *The New York Times*, May 19, 1967, p. 23, col. 1.

[30] *Hearings before Subcommittee No. 5 of the Committee on the Judiciary,* House of Representatives, 90th Cong., 1st Sess. on H.R. 5037 *et al* (1967) at p. 319.

Authorizing the use of electronic surveillance by law enforcement officers involves two fundamental issues. One is the right of privacy of the individual. The other is the right of society to be safe from crime. Any legislation which ignores either is faulty. Any legislation which fails to strike a proper balance between the two is itself unbalanced and dangerous.

The legislation sponsored by Republicans is based first, on a bill prepared for and endorsed by the President's Crime Commission Task Force on Organized Crime and secondly, on the constitutional blue print drawn by the Supreme Court in the recent electronic surveillance case of *Berger* v. *New York* (June 12, 1967).[31] The Republican bill completely outlaws all forms of wiretapping and bugging practiced by private citizens, but authorizes *limited* electronic surveillance in *specific* criminal investigations by *law enforcement officials* acting under *court order*. In the absence of a court order or when limitations of the court order are violated, the legislation imposes not only substantial criminal penalties against the officer, but civil sanctions as well. Those Republican sponsors of this legislation earnestly and honestly believe that this bill strikes a true balance between individual privacy and society's safety.

The President has proposed legislation which bans all use of electronic surveillance equipment, except in cases involving "national security."[32] No court order or other procedural safeguard is provided for determining whose conversation the President might seek to overhear in a "national security" case. Furthermore, the President's proposal does not classify organized crime as a matter of "national security." The windfall beneficiary of the President's ban on electronic surveillance would be organized crime. For that reason, it fails to strike a true balance.

The concept and thrust of the Republican measure has enjoyed the most respectable support from every echelon of government. It has the support of the Judicial Conference of the United States (headed by Chief Justice Earl Warren), the Association of Federal Investigators, the National Association of Attorneys General, the National Association of District

---

[31] 388 U.S. 41 (1967).
[32] H.R. 5386 (90th Cong., 1st Sess.).

Attorneys, the International Association of Chiefs of Police, the National Council on Crime and Delinquency and the American Bar Association.

It is a matter of amazement that the present Attorney General of the United States stands almost alone in opposition to this legislation. Moreover, he stands rigid, inflexible and unyielding. No statistic, no fact, no circumstance, no crisis seems sufficient to move him. This posture is impossible to justify until he proves that every soldier in the war against organized crime is out of step but the General.

VI. Conclusion

During the opening days of the 90th Congress, the Republican Leadership of the House of Representatives held an informal meeting with experts in the fields of law enforcement, prosecution and corrections to discuss what action the Congress—and the Republicans—could take to control crime in America.

Emerging from that meeting was a conviction that Republicans had a responsibility of focusing public attention upon the problems of crime and the proposed solutions, offering legislative proposals to implement recommendations of the President's Crime Commission, and developing amendments and new proposals to improve upon crime legislation offered by the Johnson administration. To assist Republican members of Congress in carrying out this program, the Committee on Research and Planning of the House Republican Conference established a Task Force on Crime. The Task Force conducts research, prepares statements to dramatize the problem and serves as a catalyst in developing legislative solutions to the problem of crime in America.[33]

Republicans have been criticized for "making an issue of

[33] The Members of the Republican Task Force on Crime are Richard H. Poff (Chairman), Robert Taft, Jr. (Vice Chairman), Barber B. Conable, Jr., William C. Cramer, Samuel L. Devine, John N. Erlenborn, Carleton J. King, Clark MacGregor, Robert B. Mathias, Robert Price, Thomas F. Railsback, Henry P. Smith III, Chalmers P. Wylie and Louis C. Wyman.

crime." Republicans do not apologize. Former Attorney General Katzenbach recently observed that "it was not so long ago that the perennial basic concern and problem of law enforcement was how to get adequate public attention and concern."[34] Republicans believe that a concerned and aroused citizenry is a prerequisite to sustained and meaningful action by all levels of government. Accordingly, they have played a major role in helping to educate the public about the national problems of crime. However, it is well recognized that real and lasting solutions will come only from bipartisan efforts.

In this paper concern has frequently been expressed over the failure of the President to implement the recommendations of his Crime Commission. It is not expected that the President will agree with all the recommendations. The Commission members themselves did not always agree, nor would the Congress agree on all the recommendations. However, most—if not all—Commission recommendations represent answers to some of the underlying problems. No one disputes that problems exist, or that solutions must be found. Disagreement arises over proposed methods of solution. Republicans believe that if the President disagrees with the solutions recommended by his Commission, he has a duty to recommend alternative solutions. He cannot simply ignore the problem.

Over thirty-six years ago the National Commission on Law Observance and Enforcement (the Wickersham Commission) submitted a report equally as comprehensive and historic as the Report of the President's Crime Commission. For the most part its recommendations were ignored. Republicans will not let history repeat itself.

Plagued with a plethora of foreign and domestic problems, the President has seriously neglected the crisis of crime in America. Crime waits for no man. The nation can afford no further delay. The war against crime must be escalated. The time for action is now.

[34] First National Conference on Crime Control, Proceedings, March 28–29, 1967, Address by Nicholas deB. Katzenbach at p. 20.

Chapter 3

POVERTY, WELFARE, AND JOBS

WHERE LIBERALS WENT WRONG
by Daniel P. Moynihan

DANIEL P. MOYNIHAN is Director of the Joint Center for Urban Studies of the Massachusetts Institute of Technology and Harvard University. He is also Professor of Education and Urban Politics at Harvard, a Member of the Institute of Politics, and of the faculty of the John Fitzgerald Kennedy School of Government. A life long Democrat, he served on the staff of Governor Averell Harriman of New York, and was an Assistant Secretary of Labor under Presidents Kennedy and Johnson. He is the co-author with Nathan Glazer of *Beyond the Melting Pot,* and winner of the 1963 Anisfield-Wolf Award in Race Relations.

THE PAST IS PROLOGUE

Nothing that we could say could add to the impressiveness of the lesson furnished by the events of the past year as to the needs and dangerous conditions of the neglected classes in our city. Those terrible days in July—the sudden appearance, as from the bosom of the earth, of a most infuriated and degraded mob; the helplessness of property owners and the better classes; the boom of cannon and rattle of musketry in our streets; the sky lurid with conflagrations; the inconceivable barbarity and ferocity of the crowd . . . the immense destruction of property were the first dreadful revelations to many of our people of the existence among us of a great, ignorant, irresponsible class, who were growing up without any permanent interest in the welfare of the community, of

the success of the government . . . of the gradual formation of this class and the dangers to be feared from it,
the agents of this society have incessantly warned the
public for the past 11 years.—(Draft riots in New York,
c. 1863)

This description of New York in 1863 could be of Newark
or Detroit, or of a dozen other American cities in which
violence has raged in the streets this summer. But it describes
the aftermath of the great Civil War draft riots in which the
Irish masses of the city exploded in blind fury at what they
perceived to be the injustices of the society in which they
found themselves.

The nation was then in the midst of the great crisis of
slavery. We are now in the midst of another moment of
maximum danger that has evolved from our failure fully to
resolve that first crisis, and our unwillingness to see that this
second one was developing in an urban setting for which the
attitudes, and to some degree the machinery, of American
government are desperately ill-suited.

The streets of the Negro slums contain the wreckage of a
generation of good intentions on the part of American liberals, and good people generally, who have foreseen this outcome or at least insisted on the urgency of the problems that
we must suppose have led to it. Many of our proudest achievements are a ruin as well.

CONSIDERATION FOR LIBERALS

Liberals, to be sure, are not the only people in America
who have been hurt and damaged by the violence of this
summer. But they, and the poor themselves, are the only
ones who deserve much consideration. The racists and reac-
tionaries and so-called conservatives in Congress, the shrewd
careerists in the administration who have learned so well how
to get along with them while keeping up appearances, and
the great indifferent American mass who wanted it that way:
for them there need be no sympathy.

When one reads the Democratic chairman of the House Appropriations Committee, describing Mayor Cavanagh of Detroit as "this arrogant man" for daring to suggest that the federal government was not facing up to the needs of our cities, it becomes clear that the leaders of Congress have not only learned nothing from their failure, but that neither do they propose to forgive anyone who warned them against it. They had all but destroyed the legislative program of John F. Kennedy when he was murdered, and only thereafter relented somewhat.

Now that American cities are being assaulted one after another across the land, they appear to have decided against any further display of weakness. These are familiar men in history. They are the ones who lose wars, waste opportunities, squander time and destroy civilizations.

They will commonly do so, while invoking the Chairman's principles of "discipline, self respect . . . law and order." Yet it is not ordained that they should prevail, and in the great crises of the American past they have not. Whether they shall do so now is the issue before the nation.

The outcome is likely to be determined now by persons of good will—who actively desire to see American society continue to succeed, who accept the fact that it has in ways failed, and realize that only great and costly effort can reverse the course of events.

SOURCES OF FAILURE

We liberals must inquire into the sources of our own failure, for surely we have not succeeded in bringing the nation along with us. It is not only useless and tasteless to get into a name-calling contest with our presumed opponents; it is also a sure way to avoid facing the possibility that we have some explaining to do about the sources of the present crisis.

We ourselves have lost battles and opportunities, and with time growing short we would do well to ask "why?"

First, in our concern to protect the good name of the poor,

especially perhaps the Negro poor, we have entangled ourselves in positions that have led us into preventing effective
action to help them.

Second, in our eagerness to see some progress made we
have been all too willing to accept the pathetically under-
financed programs which have normally emerged from Congress, and then to oversell them both to ourselves and to those
they are designed to aid.

Third, in our desire to maintain public confidence in such
programs, we have tended to avoid evidence of poor results,
and in particular we have paid too little heed to the limited
capacities of government to bring about social change.

These failings have been accompanied, moreover, by a
formidable capacity for explaining them away.

In the aftermath of the Newark riots one could already
detect our self-defense system at work. Newark, we were
beginning to say, was after all a backward city, doubtless run
by the Mafia. Unemployment was high. The mayor was fighting with the poverty program. The police were brutal and
corrupt. Newark, we were almost saying, deserved a riot. But
Detroit . . . what have we to say after Detroit?

Detroit had everything the Great Society could wish for a
municipality; a splendid mayor and a fine governor. A high-
paying and, thanks to the fiscal policies of the national government, a booming industry, civilized by and associated
with the hands-down leading liberal trade union of the world.

Moreover, it was a city whose Negro residents had every
reason to be proud of the position they held in the economy
and government of the area. Two able and promising Negro
Congressmen are from Detroit. Relations between the Negro
community and City Hall could hardly have been better.
Detroit Negroes held powerful positions throughout the city
administration, and to cap matters, the city was equipped
with the very model of a summer task force, with a solid
program and a twenty-four-hour watch to avert violence.

Urban Under Class

How then could Detroit riot? The answer lies in the question, "Who rioted?" The rioting was begun and probably largely continued by young persons whom sociologists would describe as an urban under class. They happened in this case to be Negro and American, yet their counterparts are to be found in the slums and in the literature of nations throughout the Western world.

Marx despaired of getting any help for his revolution from persons whose main impulses seemed to be so destructive, both to themselves and the society around them.

Most agree that the life of this stratum of society is profoundly different from that of most working people, and certainly most middle-class people. As one middle-aged Negro declared on television, at the height of the Detroit disturbances, "You don't see a family man out here." He may or may not have been right about that moment, but his understanding was sound: violent and criminal behavior set this group apart from the rest of society.

Where did this under class come from? How did it form? There does not seem to be any satisfactory answer, save that something like it has always been present in most cities in America, and that there are reasonably good signs by which to detect it. The Children's Aid Society of New York had foreseen the formation of such a class among the Catholic immigrants of the city, and indeed was formed to help the wretched young people—orphans and foundlings—involved. Their first annual report, dated 1854, said:

> It should be remembered that there are no dangers to the value of property or to the permanency of our institutions so great as those from the existence of such a class of vagabond, ignorant, and ungoverned children. This dangerous class has not begun to show itself as it will in 8 or 10 years when these boys and girls are ma-

tured. Those who were too negligent or too selfish to
notice them as children will be fully aware of them as
men. They will poison society. They will perhaps be
embittered at the wealth and luxuries they never share.
Then let society beware, when the outcast vicious, reck-
less multitude of New York boys, swarming now in every
foul alley and low street come to know their power and
use it.

A decade or so ago we began to detect the formation of
a Negro version of this class growing up in our northern
cities. Just as certain, we did little or nothing about it.

THE DEPRESSION UNENDED

The basic conditions that would appear necessary for the
formation of such a class have clearly existed in our cities
for a generation now. First, and uppermost, is unemployment. The Depression has never ended for the slum Negro.

To unemployment, add low wages, add miserable housing, add vicious and pervasive forms of racial discrimination,
compound it all with an essentially destructive welfare system and a social scientist would have every ground on which
to predict violence in this violent country. Moreover, there
were many specific warnings.

1. The increase in welfare dependency. Something like six
out of every ten Negro youths reaching eighteen have at
some time been supported by the Federal Aid to Dependent
Children program.

2. The increase in certain types of crime. For the crimes
of burglary, larceny, and auto theft, the Negro crime rate
increased 33 percent between 1960 and 1965. White rates
also increased but not as much.

3. The missing men in the census count. At least three
years ago we began to realize that the number of Negro males
enumerated in the 1960 census was far fewer than it should
have been. We now know that altogether we missed 10 percent

of the Negro population, with a much higher loss rate in young adult males. Something like one male in six, in effect, had simply dropped out of organized society.

4. Educational failure. For five years or more, we have known that Negro children were doing very badly even in schools that would have to be described as quite good. For some time we have known that the net results, the failure rates on Selective Service examinations, were horrendous: until recently, something like 56 percent of Negro youth called up for the draft have been failing the mental test—a sixth-grade examination.

5. The steady deterioration of family structure in low-income neighborhoods. Probably not more than a third of the children of low-income Negro families who now reach eighteen have lived all their life with both their parents.

This last point is often misunderstood. Probably the best available evidence we have of the increase or decrease in the size of lower-class populations lies in the statistics about family life. Breakdown in family relations among poor persons is a pretty good clue that an under class is forming. Many persons—the more liberal a person is the more likely he will be to react this way—interpret the statement to mean that the plight of the poor is being blamed on the state of their families. In other words, that the poor are to blame for their troubles. But just the opposite is the truth; the state of the families is the best evidence of what is happening to the poor.

AVAILABLE EVIDENCE

It happens that this evidence was available not only for the nation but specifically for Detroit. In 1966 the Detroit Urban League published a special study of "The Detroit Low-Income Negro Family," which summarized these developments in an urban area whose Negro population had grown in that half century from a few thousand to two-thirds of a million. The captions over the bar charts in the Urban League

report portray the life of the Negro poor in a typical northern city:

> Nearly one-third of Detroit area non-whites under 18
> live in broken homes (1960) . . . Almost one Detroit
> area non-white family out of five is headed by a woman
> (1960) . . . About 20 per cent of Detroit area non-
> white females who were ever married, are divorced or
> live apart from their husbands (1950–1960) . . . One
> out of seven persons in Detroit area non-white house-
> holds are not members of the husband-wife-child family
> (1960) . . .

In Detroit, the report continued, the non-white illegitimacy
ratio rose from 138.0 per thousand live births in 1950 to
156.7 in 1957, to 228.4 in 1964. (In line with national trends,
the white illegitimacy ratio during this period rose from 15.0
to 34.5, but for every two white illegitimate children born in
the city there were three non-white.)
In a 1965 study of low-income households in Detroit,
Greenleigh Associates reported "24.9 percent of the Negro
households reported out-of-wedlock children and only 4.0 percent of the white households did so. . . . A common pattern
found was for older children to be legitimate and younger
children to be illegitimate."
It would be outrageous and unforgivable at this moment
to pretend to understand more than we do, but we do know
that these were signs of trouble coming. The Negro community was splitting: on the one hand, there was a large and
growing group for whom progress was real and unmistakable.
On the other hand, there was another group for whom things
were not working.
Relatively they grew worse off, not just when compared
with white society but also when compared with other Negroes.
Negro leaders have naturally and properly wished to draw
attention to their great achievements and even greater potential. Trapped in their own decencies, liberals have agreed;
and so in a hundred ways, great and small, the problem of
the burgeoning urban lower class was concealed.

If there was delinquency in the slums, we told ourselves that well-to-do kids in the suburbs were just as unruly but were never brought to law—which is not true, but which leaves everyone feeling better. If there were fatherless children in the slums, we told ourselves that white middle-class fathers were never at home either—which is true, but has nothing to do with the matter. It also, somehow, leaves those children in the slums needing help and not getting it.

A CRUCIAL OPPORTUNITY

When the new frontier began formulating its programs, these were designed for an essentially different class of person; the competent, reasonably well-motivated individual who happened to be out of work or out of skills, and who would surely take advantage of opportunities offered him. Our one crucial opportunity came with the major amendments to the welfare system in 1962, but we did nothing then except to confirm the conventional wisdom that, for example, portrayed the typical mother requiring aid for dependent children as a West Virginia miner's widow. The system was enlarged somewhat but not changed.

Last summer, with something like one New York City child in five living on welfare, Dr. Mitchell Ginsberg of the Lindsay administration declared the system "bankrupt. It was just as bankrupt five years ago, but somehow we could not, would not, see it then."

There has been a massive loss of confidence on the part of Negroes as to white sincerity. Two years ago, during the rioting in Watts, comedian Dick Gregory tried to help calm things. He was shot for his troubles, and told the young man who had done it, "All right, you shot me. Now go home." Two months ago at a Black Power rally in Washington, Gregory was shouting over and over again: "Watts was legal!"

Our programs might have had far greater impact if only they had been of sufficient size. The amounts of money going to cities and to the poor increased, but in nothing like the amounts or for the purposes demanded by the situation.

Anyone who was involved with the establishment of the War on Poverty knows that it was put together by fiscal mirrors; scarcely a driblet of new money was involved. Even an element of fraud entered the picture: the Bureau of the Budget began calculating interstate highway funds as part of the financial aid going to cities.

Such money is of considerable aid to General Motors and the United Automobile Workers, and to the Association of General Contractors, but as for the poor, the best that can be said for it is that it destroys a lot of bad housing.

Here again it was fear of, and after a point too sophisticated a knowledge of, the fiscal conservatism, and also social complacency in the Congress that held us back, that even somehow kept us from telling ourselves the truth.

Huge-sounding bills were passed, but mini-appropriations followed, and after a point both ends of Pennsylvania Avenue were co-operating in this process. Instead of taking what we could get, but insisting that it was not enough, liberals both within and without the administration gave in to an orgy of tub thumping.

It does not automatically follow that we raised hopes out of all proportion to our capacity to deliver on our promises, but if we did, and we *must* have, we have only ourselves to blame.

Ourselves and the federal bureaucracy. Somehow liberals have been unable to acquire from life what conservatives seem to be endowed with at birth, namely, a healthy skepticism of the powers of government agencies to do good.

The American national government is a superb instrument for redistributing power and wealth in our society. One person in ten in the United States, for example, now gets a Social Security check every month. But as an instrument for providing services, especially to urban lower-class Negroes, it is a highly unreliable device.

THREE RECOMMENDATIONS

The more programs, the less impact. The 1966 White House conference "to fulfill these rights" produced a hundred pages of recommendations, which meant that the conference was a failure and a disaster. If it had produced three recommendations, it might have been a success. I shall propose three.

First. The United States government must become the employer of last resort, so that anyone looking for work and not finding it is automatically given a job. Put to work. If this is done stupidly it will turn out to be a WPA, but with just a little administrative energy it can be worked out that such jobs are distributed throughout the labor market, so that in fact they are not visible as such. The government must see to it that everyone looking for work finds work, and correspondingly that those without work have no excuse for their situation.

Second. We have got to get more money directly into the hands of the poor. The best way to do this, or at least the best known way, is through a family (or children's) allowance. The United States is the only industrial democracy in the world that does not have such a system of automatic payments for families who are raising minor children. We are also the only industrial democracy whose streets are filled with rioters each year. The connection may not be direct, or may not exist at all, but then it may.

Such a payment would have the advantage that everyone would get it, not just a special segment artificially defined as below a certain income line or across a certain racial line.

It has worked well all over the world, including Canada, and for $9 billion a year, it would be a sound investment in the future as well as in the present.

Third. We must rebuild, or at least clear, the burnt-out neighborhoods. The federal government has a dozen ways to do this, and it must. Otherwise the ruins remain a symbol of the injustices that led to them. Accompanying such a clearance and rebuilding program, we simply must enact a form of federal reinsurance of small business in such areas. Otherwise they will become deserts.

The problem, of course, is that it is unlikely we shall do any of these things, or any other things. Never has the national instinct and the national interest appeared more divergent. The mood of the administration in Washington is one of paralysis. There is no political will for the Executive branch to move in any direction, and nothing but fear as to what direction Congress will take if it should seize the initiative.

SOURCES OF PARALYSIS

This paralysis derives from several sources. The first, understandably, is disappointment, and not a little bitterness at what has happened. This is a mood tinged as well with exhaustion. Many men in Washington have been at their desks for eight years. The first few years were exhilarating, but of late an entirely understandable exhaustion seems to have set in.

The second source of paralysis is the conviction within the administration that the public mood is one of fierce dislike for Negroes and adamant determination that there be "no reward for rioting."

But the third is the decisive one: There is no money. The war has used up all the available income and taken us beyond that to a massive deficit. Washington does not dare spend another nickel, and indeed appeared to be in the process of quietly cutting back many domestic programs when the rioting resumed in June.

The result has been a curious process of backward reasoning. First: "We can't do anything." Second: "We won't do anything." Third: "We shouldn't do anything."

And, above all, not giving ammunition to the Republican enemy by suggesting perhaps there were some deficiencies in our approach to date. Beyond that, we are to pray and to await the report of the presidential commission, which will solemnly reassure us that the FBI has found no evidence of Communist conspiracy and that the problem of rioting lies in despair and hopelessness in the ghetto.

We might get away with it. Just possibly. Or we might march directly into a political crisis that will spoil the rest of the twentieth century for the American people. Such a disaster would be the election, next year or five years from now, of a determined right-wing President.

The task of American liberals would seem to be clear. We cannot do anything without the President, and the President seems determined to do nothing. Worse, he is denying it. Talk about that rat bill is meaningless. The rat bill was nothing.

The administration is not unwilling to do what is needed. The matter is more complicated. It seems to feel that the Congress is not going to do anything, and that therefore it will be useless and worse to ask and be refused. Not only will the obstructionist majority say "no," but from elsewhere there will come a chorus of charges that the war in Vietnam is the reason the President will not move.

This is true, but also irrelevant. The President dares not and will not scrap the war in order to save the cities. Somehow he must be enabled to scrap other things, and raise new funds, in order to proceed with both. It is a time to ponder his oft-repeated statement, in those sweet days so soon past, that he is the only President we have.

The experience of the Vietnam protest will hardly encourage the thought that he responds to pressure, much less to name-calling (and much less to expressions such as this). The only serious option open to us seems to be that of trying to persuade the public at large that we can do something about the causes of Negro violence which will help not only the rioters but everyone. It is time for this fabulously rich nation to declare a dividend. A family allowance would be a good beginning, guaranteed full employment a logical accompaniment. But perhaps there are better, more feasible, programs that will work in the slums and yet assert the unity of the nation. Let us look for them.

The one thing going for us is the apparent fact that how-ever disturbed the nation might be by events, it is nonetheless trying to understand them. If there is much white hatred abroad, it has been hesitant so far to show itself in public. The fact is that we are not the racist nation we used to be.

We are facing a problem we do not fully understand and certainly do not know how to solve. But to face such situations with calm and competence is what marks us as the people we are. It is what John F. Kennedy would have expected of us. It is what we have a right to expect of Lyndon B. Johnson. And a responsibility to demand of ourselves.

THE UNTRUTH OF THE OBVIOUS
by *Yale Brozen*

YALE BROZEN is Professor of Business Economics in the
Graduate School of Business of the University of Chicago. He is also Director of the Research Management
Program of the Graduate School of Business. Prof.
Brozen studied at MIT and received his doctorate in
economics from the University of Chicago. He has
taught at the University of Minnesota, Illinois Institute of
Technology, and Northwestern University, where he held
a joint appointment in the Technological Institute and
in the Department of Economics. Prof. Brozen has
served as a consultant to business firms, and to governmental and private research agencies. He is a member
of the Committee on Economic Policy of the U. S. Chamber of Commerce, the Education Advisory Committee
of the National Association of Manufacturers, the National Thrift Committee, and the Advisory Board of
the Center for Modern Economics.

This is the age of science. It is an age when men search for
laws to explain and help them understand the world they
live in. After many years of painstaking research, Professor
C. Northcote Parkinson discovered the law, "Expenses rise
to meet income." If he were to extend his research to include
the current federal administration, he would probably amend
his law to read: "Expenditures always exceed income, no
matter how great income is."

Lee Loevinger, a lawyer and a member of the Federal
Communications Commission, has also discovered a useful
law for explaining many things. His law might be called "The

Law of Irresistible Use." It says, "If a boy has a hammer, it proves something needs pounding. The political science analogy is that if there is a government agency, this proves something needs regulating."

Let me suggest a "law" of my own—perhaps not universally valid but nonetheless a helpful guide to straight thinking in the field of public policy today. It is the following: *Economic policy propositions that are obviously "true" tend, in fact, to be false. As a consequence, policies based on such propositions tend to be self-defeating.* The reason for this is that, in economics, obvious effects too often are superficial effects—only part, and usually the first part, of a complex chain of events set in motion by a given policy action. These obvious effects are so easily observable that they obscure less obvious, indirect and more fundamental effects that tend to work in the opposite direction.

What are some obviously "true" policy propositions that are false? An excellent example, and a tragic one because of its far-reaching consequences, is the widely believed proposition that higher minimum wage rates help low-wage workers.

In 1966, the Fair Labor Standards Act was amended to raise the federal minimum wage from $1.25 an hour to $1.40 by February 1967 and $1.60 by February 1968. And the coverage of the act was extended to millions more workers. Supporters of this action argued that the $1.25 rate provided only $2476 a year for a full-time worker (after deducting social security taxes), and that this was below $3130 a year, the official line an income must cross if the recipient were not to be poor (assuming a family of four). Obviously, then, if the minimum were raised, there would be fewer people living in poverty.

A minimum wage rate of $1.60 an hour provides an annual income of $3180 (after social security taxes). Since no one can be paid less, obviously all poverty resulting from "substandard" wage rates has been eliminated—not taking into account, of course, occupations not covered by the Fair Labor Standards Act, or recently covered occupations where the rate had not yet reached $1.60.

Despite all the obviousness of this argument, it is demonstrable that increases in the statutory minimum have, as a matter of record, hurt the poor and increased unemployment for unskilled workers.

When the minimum wage is raised, some people's wages go up. First, there will be those who remain employed at the higher rate. In addition, others who had already been receiving more than the minimum—workers enjoying some advantage of skill, training or location—will find their wage rates and their firms better insulated against competition from low-wage workers and low-wage areas of the country.

But the far more important effect will be lower incomes for a great many other people and more unemployment in general. Why? Because unskilled labor markets in the U.S.—and these are the markets most directly affected by minimum wage legislation—are competitive. This means that a number of employers are bidding for such labor and, consequently, prevailing wages are generally in line with, and not below, worker productivity. Thus when wage rates are forced up artificially, by law, the number of jobs will decrease. Employers who find it uneconomical to pay the higher rate will substitute machinery or skilled workers for unskilled workers, discontinue product lines requiring large inputs of unskilled labor, or close their plants. So, what higher minimum wage rates really do is price some unskilled workers out of their jobs—except in a few isolated situations where labor markets are not competitive (only three counties in the U.S., according to one study).[1]

There is ample evidence this is the case. A *New York Times* story (February 13, 1967, datelined Greenville, Miss.) reported that spot checks by civil rights workers indicated 100,000 cotton choppers were losing their jobs because "large" farms, covered by the Fair Labor Standards Act for the first time beginning 1967, were required to pay a minimum rate of $1.00 an hour. A *U. S. News and World Report* story

[1] Bunting, Robert, *Employer Concentration in Local Labor Markets* (University of North Carolina Press, Chapel Hill, N.C., 1962).

(August 17, 1964) described the closing of a handicraft shop in Paintsville, Kentucky—which destroyed the jobs of its 200 part-time employees—when the new local wage-and-hour office pressed for strict compliance with the $1.25 minimum wage. A *Wall Street Journal* sampling of retailers (August 31, 1961) found that package wrappers and substandard employees were being dismissed and work weeks were being shortened because the Fair Labor Standards Act was being extended to retail stores effective September 3, 1961.

The Southern Pine Industry Committee testified in Senate hearings that the $1.00 an hour minimum imposed in 1956 was a major reason for the closing of numerous saw mills in the South.[2] A study of selected low-wage industries demonstrated that employment adjusted for output and trend fell in saw mills, men's cotton garment plants and other industries when the minimum was raised to $0.75 in 1950.[3] Another study found a 13 percent drop in seamless hosiery mills whose *average* wage was below the minimum when the $0.25 an hour minimum was imposed in 1938 and subsequently raised to $0.325 in 1939. This employment drop did not include any decrease resulting from mills going out of business.[4]

Of course, the firing of cotton choppers in 1967, novelty shop employees in 1964, package wrappers in 1961, saw mill workers in 1956, cotton apparel plant employees in 1950 and seamless hosiery workers in 1938 does not necessarily mean that unemployment rose as a consequence. Supporters of minimum age legislation argue that it will expand purchasing power and protect high-wage employers against competition from low-wage employers. Therefore, they conclude, workers losing their jobs because of the rise in the minimum will be able to replace them with better jobs.

[2] Labor and Public Welfare Committee, Hearings on *Amendments to the Fair Labor Standards Act,* 87th Cong., 1st Sess., pp. 691–93.

[3] Peterson, John, "Employment Effect of Minimum Wages, 1938–50," *Journal of Political Economy,* LXV (October, 1957).

[4] Hinrichs, A. F., "Effects of the 25-cent Minimum Wage on Employment in the Seamless Hosiery Industry," *Journal of the American Statistical Association* (March, 1940).

The weight of theory and fact is to the contrary. Wage rates rise because of rising skill levels, increases in the quantity and quality of tools needed to help workers become more productive, and the freedom of workers to leave low productivity, low-wage jobs to take better jobs created by enterprises applying improved technology in advantageous locations. The number of better jobs increases because enterprise patiently mobilizes the capital accumulated by savers and risks investment in research programs which, when successful, improve technology and productivity. Laws cannot hurry the process (except in a few instances, e.g., motivating investment in research by providing patent protection), although tax legislation and governmental competition for capital in the securities markets can and do slow it down.

Minimum wage legislation that prematurely forces wage rates up for less skilled workers, or for people living in towns and rural areas remote from major markets, destroys low-wage jobs before higher wage jobs become available. Such impatience causes unemployment for some, and forces others into lower paid jobs in the increasingly smaller number of occupations not covered by the Fair Labor Standards Act. These effects can be seen by looking at what happens to groups most directly affected by minimum wage laws.

For instance, the evidence is clear that every increase in the statutory minimum wage in the post-war period has been accompanied by a rise in teenage unemployment (see Table 1). Following these increases, teenage unemployment then begins to decline as the normal process of rising output per man-hour provides more of the more productive jobs needed to absorb teenagers entering the labor force. But for some teenagers the recovery in job levels comes too late. Moreover, despite this recovery, the secular trend in teenage unemployment measured relative to general unemployment has been persistently upward. Increases in the minimum have been following too closely on the heels of previous increases with the result that one increase is not fully digested before another is enacted. As a consequence, the ratio of teenage to general unemployment has not only been higher after each

TABLE 1

UNEMPLOYMENT RATES FOR TEENAGERS (AGES 16–19)
(SEASONALLY ADJUSTED)

Month	Minimum wage		Teenage unemployment rate	
Dec. 1949	$0.40		15.4%	(13.7)
Jan. 1950	0.75		15.2	(17.7)
Feb. 1956	0.75		11.4	(12.6)
March 1956	1.00		11.5	(11.4)
August 1961	1.00		17.1	(13.8)
Sept. 1961	1.15	(1.00)	18.0	(15.8)
August 1963	1.15	(1.00)	16.2	(12.6)
Sept. 1963	1.25	(1.15)	17.4	(15.2)
August 1965		(1.15)	13.9	(10.6)
Sept. 1965		(1.25)	14.8	(12.8)
Jan. 1967	1.25		11.0	(11.7)
Feb. 1967	1.40	(1.00)	13.2	(13.2)

NOTE 1: Minimum wage figures in parentheses are for jobs not covered prior to the minimum wage increases of September 1961 or February 1967. Unemployment rate figures in parentheses are raw data not adjusted for seasonal influences.

NOTE 2: The fall in the seasonally adjusted unemployment rate from 15.4% in December 1949 to 15.2% in January 1950 occurred despite a fall in the number of teenagers employed. Teenage employment fell by 37,000. Officially defined unemployment was lower, nevertheless, because 52,000 teenagers gave up looking for jobs and were no longer classified as unemployed. (On a non-seasonally adjusted basis, teenage employment fell by 306,000 and unemployment rose by 121,000.)

The downward seasonal adjustment for January 1950 appears to be unduly large, particularly in view of the fact that an adjustment of the same proportion as that used in the mid-1950s would have produced a seasonally adjusted unemployment rate of 16.6%.

SOURCE: Bureau of Labor Statistics, *Employment and Earnings and Monthly Report on the Labor Force*, March, 1967.

minimum wage increase than it was before but has mounted by more than 50 percent since the enactment of the $0.75 minimum in 1949 (see Table 2).

TABLE 2

COMPARISON OF TEENAGE AND GENERAL UNEMPLOYMENT RATES
(AVERAGES OF MONTHLY SEASONALLY ADJUSTED DATA)

Twelve months	Minimum wage[1]	Teenage unemployment rate (Ages 16–19)	General unemployment rate	Ratio— teenage/ general
Jan. 49–Dec. 49	$0.40	13.5%	6.1%	2.2
Jan. 50–Dec. 50	0.75	12.2	5.2	2.3
Mar. 55–Feb. 56	0.75	11.0	4.2	2.6
Mar. 56–Feb. 57	1.00	11.0	4.1	2.7
Sept. 60–Aug. 61	1.00	16.4	6.6	2.5
Sept. 61–Aug. 62	1.15 (1.00)	15.4	5.8	2.7
Sept. 62–Aug. 63	1.15 (1.00)	16.4	5.6	2.9
Sept. 63–Aug. 64	1.25 (1.15)	18.3	5.4	3.4
Sept. 64–Aug. 65	(1.15)	15.6	4.8	3.3
Sept. 65–Aug. 66	(1.25)	13.2	3.8	3.5

[1] Minimum wage figures in parentheses are for jobs not covered prior to September 1961.

SOURCE: Bureau of Labor Statistics, *Employment and Earnings and Monthly Report on the Labor Force*, Vol. 13, No. 9.

A comparison of unemployment rates for two other groups, white teenagers and non-white teenagers, is even more striking (see Table 3). In 1954, the unemployment rate for non-white teenagers was 1.36 times the rate for white teenagers. It moved up to 2.27 times the white teenager rate in 1966 and 2.5 times for the first seven months of 1967. When the minimum wage went to $1.40 in February 1967, white teenage unemployment rose from 9.6 percent in January to 11.5 percent in February, a significant increase. But the rate for Negroes jumped even more—from 20.9 percent to 26.2 percent, and then on up to 34 percent in May.

In other words, for many teenagers and particularly for Negro teenagers, the minimum wage has destroyed the beginning jobs where they would normally acquire the skills and

TABLE 3
COMPARISON OF WHITE AND NON-WHITE TEENAGE
UNEMPLOYMENT RATES
(AGES 16–19)

Year	General unemployment rate	Teenage unemployment rates Non-white	White	Ratio— non-white/ white
1954	5.5	16.5	12.1	1.36
1955	4.4	15.8	10.3	1.53
1956	4.1	18.2	10.2	1.78
1957	4.3	19.1	10.6	1.80
1958	6.8	27.4	14.4	1.90
1959	5.5	26.1	13.1	1.99
1960	5.5	24.4	13.4	1.82
1961	6.7	27.6	15.3	1.80
1962	5.5	25.1	13.3	1.89
1963	5.7	30.4	15.5	1.96
1964	5.2	27.2	14.8	1.84
1965	4.5	26.2	13.4	1.96
1966	3.8	25.4	11.2	2.27
1967 (Jan.–July)	3.8	25.9	10.4	2.5

SOURCE: Bureau of Labor Statistics, *Employment and Earnings and Monthly Report on the Labor Force*, August, 1967; *Manpower Report of the President*, March, 1967.

discipline to make themselves more productive. Many end up frustrated or face a more difficult task equipping themselves for higher skilled jobs as adults. Some are doomed to a life on welfare.

Analysis of the wage experience of workers who retain their jobs in low-wage industries despite the increased minimum suggests that the limited benefits of such increases are a poor trade for the costs. These workers receive unusually large wage increases at the time the higher minimum goes into effect (leaving out of account the drop to zero in the earnings of workers who become unemployed). However, their wage increases in the following years are then unusually low relative to increases in other industries (see Table 4). The net result of the minimum wage for workers who do not lose their jobs appears to be merely a change in the timing of wage increases they would have received anyway. They enjoy

TABLE 4

WAGE RATE CHANGES FOR SELECTED INDUSTRIES[a]
1949–52

Industry	Rate/hour 1949	Percentage change 1949–50	Percentage change 1950–52	Total change
Seamless Hosiery	$0.853	10.2%	10.7%	20.9
Cigars	0.884	9.6	10.4	20.0
Men's & Boys' Furnishings	0.920	7.6	9.1	16.7
Men's & Boys' Shirts & Nightwear	.927	6.6	9.3	17.9
Men's & Boys' Separate Trousers	.963	6.7	9.0	15.7
Women's & Children's Underwear	0.980	6.4	9.3	15.7
Women's & Children's Undergarments	0.999	6.4	12.0	18.4
Average		7.6	10.0	17.6
Average—All Manufacturing	1.378	4.5	14.6	19.1

1955–60

Industry	Rate/hour 1955[b]	Percentage change 1955–56[c]	Percentage change 1956–60[d]	Total change
Seamless Hosiery	$1.13	10.6%	12.8%	23.4
Cigars	1.19	8.4	11.6	20.0
Men's & Boys' Furnishings	1.13	11.5	5.8	17.3
Men's & Boys' Shirts & Nightwear	1.15	10.0	4.4	14.4
Men's & Boys' Separate Trousers	1.15	9.6	7.4	17.0
Women's & Children's Underwear	1.20	10.0	5.7	15.7
Women's & Children's Undergarments	1.25	8.0	7.4	15.4
Average		9.7	7.9	17.6
Average—All Manufacturing	1.87	5.4	14.7	20.1

[a] Industries were selected whose average hourly rates were within 25¢ of the new minima.

[b] Mar. 1955–Feb. 1956 average of monthly hourly rates.

[c] Change in average monthly rates from Mar. 1955–Feb. 1956 to Mar. 1956–Feb. 1957.

[d] Change in average monthly rates from Mar. 1956–Feb. 1957 to the twelve months of 1960.

SOURCE: Bureau of Labor Statistics, *Employment and Earnings Statistics of the United States, 1909–60.* Bulletin No. 1312, U. S. Government Printing Office, Washington, D.C., 1961.

no long-run increase in purchasing power. But there is a decline in the purchasing power of the workers who lose jobs, or are prevented from finding jobs in the first place, or are forced into lower wage jobs in uncovered occupations.

If the minimum wage only changed the timing of wage rate increases, there would be little to concern us. However, in the interval between the time the minimum is raised and the time productivity catches up, tens of thousands of people are jobless, thousands of businesses fail that are never revived, and teenagers (particularly Negro teenagers) are barred from obtaining the low-wage jobs that have traditionally been their stepping stones to opportunity and advancement. This is a very large price to pay for impatience.

There are other adverse effects of minimum wage legislation, some of which are more indirect. It prolongs segregation in plants where segregation would have gradually disappeared. Why? Because it reduces the number of jobs, and employers have found they could fill the reduced number of jobs in any given plant with the available white workers. Moreover, it hastens the migration of Negroes to the big cities of the North and West—by eliminating both actual and potential jobs in the rural South where most of the Negroes are. Some migration would occur anyway as a normal response to the development of better opportunities in the cities. However, in the absence of rapid increases in the minimum wage, more industry would move into the South and fewer Negroes would have to move out. Forced migration has only led to a greater problem of assimilation, higher welfare loads and a breakdown of order in overcrowded slums.

Minimum wage laws also hasten automation, as noted in passing above. This so-called automation effect really amounts to a redistribution of income from the unskilled who produce a product directly to the skilled who produce it indirectly by making automated machinery. Since machinery industries are mostly concentrated in the North, this in turn has had the effect of benefitting one section of the country at the expense of another.

Another effect of minimum wage legislation has been to

depress wage rates in occupations not covered by the legislation, such as domestic service and—until recently—farm work. Workers losing their jobs in covered occupations have swollen the supply of people looking for work in non-covered occupations.[5] And ironically, yet another effect has been to reduce employer training for the unskilled, just at the time when the government has been mounting large programs to provide the training itself.

Finally, the minimum wage, like all artificially high wage rates, causes a misallocation of capital and lowers the average level of productivity in the economy compared to what it would have been otherwise. Higher minimum wages force the modernization of some plants and the non-modernization of others, because capital is drained into plants that must buy machines to replace the labor that is not worth employing at the minimum wage rate. The result is less capital for the rest of the economy, which means that productivity and wage rates will rise more slowly elsewhere.

Summing up, the minimum wage does very little good and much harm. The reason this is not more widely understood is that its limited good effects—higher wages for a few—are easy to see. But the bad effects—unemployment, generally lower wage levels, restricted opportunity, plus the social costs that accompany these effects—are indirect and more difficult to see.

OTHER UNTRUE TRUTHS

There are a large number of other instances where the government has intervened in the economy with seemingly obvious methods for reaching a desired goal. In many of them, however, sooner or later the results turn out to be the opposite of those expected by the well-intentioned supporters of the program or policy. Let me summarize some instances, but in less detail.

[5] Brozen, Yale, "Minimum Wage Rates and Household Workers," *Journal of Law and Economics,* V (October 1952).

Direct public assistance was initiated as an obvious way to help needy persons until they could become self-supporting. Today this program is credited with prolonging the poverty of its recipients, in some cases for generations. Since the program requires that the recipient lose a dollar of welfare payments for each dollar earned, it constitutes a positive disincentive to getting a job. In effect, any part-time or short duration job amounts to working for nothing, and the net gain from a full-time job is significantly reduced. The same 100 percent deduction applies to payments to parents under Aid to Families with Dependent Children (until recently, to the children also) and to adults participating in work training and employment programs under the Economic Opportunity Act (Title V). A partial deduction from payments applies to other public assistance programs, and to social security and pension programs for disabled veterans as well. In addition, the *level* of welfare and retirement income benefits also influences incentives to seek employment and training. Recent studies have found that higher payment levels correlate with the extent to which people fall into poverty categories or are unemployed.[6] Income supplements are needed. However, in thinking about how to provide them, it is important to recognize that the disincentives built into current welfare programs defeat one major objective of those programs by increasing the odds against welfare recipients becoming self-supporting.[7]

Public policy has encouraged the development of trade union power as a protection for the working man. Without questioning the need for strong union organization, it must be noted, however, that one effect of this policy has been to restrict opportunities—to help some American workers at the expense of others. Recently, for example, discrimination

[6] See Brehm, C. T. and Saving, T. R., "The Demand for General Assistance Payments," *American Economic Review* (December 1964); and Gallaway, Lowell E., "The Aged and the Extent of Poverty in the United States," paper to Southern Economic Association, November 1965.

[7] Peterson, John, "Incentives for Employment," (unpublished paper dated October 16, 1967).

against Negroes in union membership and union apprentice-ship programs has received wide publicity. It is still less widely understood, however, that this is a logical, though not commendable, use of the power some unions have attained —because people can be expected to try to promote their self-interest, sometimes even if it means foreclosing opportunity for others.

Union wage-fixing arrangements can also restrict opportunity. The Chicago elevators' union, for example, succeeded in imposing a wage of $2.50 an hour for elevator operators in downtown buildings, driving the cost of two-shift manual operation to over $10,000 a year. Since operating costs of automated elevators (including taxes, insurance, interest and depreciation) amount to only $8000 a year, it began to pay owners to convert to automated elevators. The result has been more jobs for skilled workers who make automated elevators at the expense of jobs for teenagers and the unskilled who ran the elevators.

Excessive or artificial wage rate increases, as noted in the review of the minimum wage, cause not only unemployment. They also mean lower wages for workers in other sectors of the economy and, in general, a slower rate of growth in productivity and *average* wage income than otherwise would have occurred. I would estimate that 10 percent of the U.S. labor force receives wage rates about 15 percent higher than it would in the absence of wage laws and concentrated union power, while the remaining 90 percent receives wage rates about 5 percent lower. The *net* result is greater inequality in the division of income and about 3 percent less total wage income for all U.S. workers as a group—or about $10 billion less—than they would otherwise earn.[8]

Federal urban renewal and public housing had the dual objectives of reviving the central city and providing better housing for the poor being "cleaned" from slums. Billions of dollars and years later, some downtown areas are cleaner—some

[8] For the data on which this estimate is based, see H. G. Lewis, *Unionism and Relative Wages in the United States* (University of Chicago Press, Chicago, 1963), pp. 8–9, 286–95.

just emptier. But several unexpected results have become apparent. Landowners received inflated prices, and tangled procedure kept properties off local tax rolls for unreasonably long periods. More significant in human terms, renewal projects tore down a great deal of existing low income housing, replacing it in most cases with more expensive apartments and non-residential buildings. Public housing, for many reasons, never did its job of building the needed replacement housing for the poor. With the reduced supply of low rent units that resulted, poor families typically had to pay higher rents. For example, one Chicago Housing Authority study showed that the median rental paid by 161 families relocated in 1957 increased 51 percent, from $51/month to $77/month. Unquestionably, three major effects of our efforts to improve urban conditions have been to hurt the poor and destroy the livelihoods of thousands of small businessmen, while merely transferring slums from one part of a city to another.[9]

A similar perverse effect operates in the area of regulation to protect consumers. For example, transportation regulation —such as that carried on by the ICC in the case of railroads, trucks, barge lines and oil pipelines, by the CAB in the case of airlines, by the Federal Maritime Commission in the case of ocean carriers, and by the Federal Power Commission in the case of gas pipelines—was designed to protect consumers from high and/or discriminatory rates. Instead, rates tend to be higher[10] and in some cases more discriminatory than they would have been in the absence of governmental regulation.[11]

To cite a few cases: In the early 1950s the railroads, finding their rates for transporting cigarettes unnecessarily high, sought ICC permission to reduce them in order to compete

[9] Johnson, Thomas F., Morris, James, and Butts, Joseph G., *Renewing America's Cities* (Washington, D.C.: Institute for Social Science Research, 1962); and Anderson, Martin, *The Federal Bulldozer* (New York: McGraw-Hill Book Co., 1967), rev. ed.

[10] MacAvoy, Paul W., *The Economic Effects of Regulation: The Trunk-Line Railroad Cartels and the Interstate Commerce Commission Before 1900* (Cambridge, Mass.: The M.I.T. Press, 1965).

[11] Lochlin, D. Philip, *Economics of Transportation* (Homewood, Ill.: Richard D. Irwin, Inc., 1960), p. 139.

with lower truck rates. The ICC settled the competitive problem not by agreeing to the railroads' request for lower rates but by *raising* the truck rates on cigarettes.[12] The CAB withdrew certification from North American Airlines and drove it out of business after that company had pioneered air coach transportation.[13] The Federal Maritime Commission requires subsidized ship lines to join ocean conferences that cartelize rates at higher levels than those set by operators not members of the conference.[14] It also follows policies that result in the inefficient design and operation of American ships.[15] Because of FPC regulation, field prices of natural gas sold to interstate pipeline companies are about 7 percent higher than they would otherwise be.[16] The fact is that most of these regulatory agencies have ended up setting price floors to protect industry, not price ceilings to protect consumers—and regulated industry has tended to become more inefficient as a result.

Several studies of gas and utility regulation have reached similar conclusions. In general, prices for gas and electricity are higher in states where regulatory commissions restrict the rate of return on investment to less than 6½ percent than in those which do not. The reason is that utilities permitted to earn more than 6½ percent are in a better position to attract the capital needed to install cost-saving equipment. This, in turn, makes possible lower rates for the consumer.[17]

[12] Nelson, James C., *Railroad Transportation and Public Policy* (Washington, D.C.: The Brookings Institution, 1959).

[13] Peltzman, "CAB: Freedom from Competition," *New Individualist Review* (Spring 1963), pp. 16–23.

[14] Colberg, M. R., Forbush, D. R., and Whitaker, G. R., *Business Economics* (Irwin, Homewood, Ill., 1964), pp. 130–31.

[15] Ferguson, A. R., Lerner, E. M., McGee, J. S., Oi, W. O., Rapping, L. A., and Saboeka, S. P., *The Economic Value of the United States Merchant Marine* (Northwestern University Press, Evanston, Ill., 1961).

[16] Gerwig, R. W., "Natural Gas Production: A Study of the Costs of Regulation," *Journal of Law and Economics,* Vol. V (1962), pp. 69–92.

[17] See Stigler, G. J., "The Government of the Economy," in Stigler, G. J. and Samuelson, P. A., *A Dialogue on the Proper*

Usury laws are supposed to protect borrowers from extortionate interest rates. And to some extent, they may accomplish this objective. However, another effect should be considered. They apparently bar poor credit risks from obtaining legal loans, because legal lenders will not lend where risks are so high that the legally allowed return is not compensatory. Thus they open the way for the illegal credit racket. Clearly, borrowers from illegal lenders pay much higher interest rates than they would if there were no usury laws.

The farm program is supposed to help farmers by stabilizing farm prices at "equitable" levels. Years ago, it seemed obvious that this could be done by a judicious combination of price supports and production controls. However, farmers simply cultivated more intensively, increasing output well beyond demand and setting off a chain reaction of weaker *real* prices, enormous surpluses, and higher costs for the support and storage program. To compound the problem, soil bank programs for restricting output to more manageable levels have been offset by government-sponsored research programs to increase farm productivity and multi-million dollar reclamation programs putting more land under cultivation. The main effects have been to decelerate the necessary movement of farmers to better opportunities off the farm, to raise the price of necessities and to place a greater tax burden on all. It is finally becoming clear that the farm program has helped very few farmers, and mostly the large ones, at great expense to everybody else.[18]

We are concerned about poverty and have attempted to meet the problem with various devices—e.g., poverty programs, provision of job training facilities, larger relief programs, more federal grants for general and special purpose education, to name a few. These are obvious ways. What is

---

Economic Role of the State (University of Chicago Graduate School of Business, Selected papers no. 7, 1963); and Stigler, G. J. and Friedland, C., "What Can the Regulations Regulate? The Case for Electricity," *The Journal of Law and Economics,* V (October, 1962), pp. 1–16.

[18] Houthakker, Hendrik S., *Economic Policy for the Farm Sector* (Washington, D.C.: American Enterprise Institute for Public Policy Research, 1967).

unobvious is that it is the government itself that causes much of the hardship and poverty that concerns us, partly by its many interventions in the free market and partly by the taxes required to support these programs.

The difficulty is that too often policy makers perceive the obvious, direct effects of a proposed policy and not the less obvious, indirect effects that tend to work in the opposite direction. To achieve a desired goal, they try to reverse or ignore free market forces, rather than ride with them and use them to their advantage. They forget that intervention in the operation of a free economy will, more often than not, simply establish power centers that one interest group can take over and use to exploit another. And almost invariably, they succumb to the iron law of organizational immortality, the law which ensures support for a policy or agency long after its task has been completed or its ineffectiveness—even outright destructiveness—established.

Fortunately, there is growing understanding of this difficulty. Both economists and social workers are beginning to pay attention to the disincentive effects of welfare programs. The public is increasingly aware that overly permissive labor policies have made it easier for some unions to win wage increases in excess of productivity and to restrict entrance into apprenticeship programs and higher paying jobs—a restriction used primarily against Negroes. The outcry against urban renewal and public housing is loudest from the traditional supporters of these programs. Studies by economists are demonstrating the costs of transportation and utility regulation and suggesting better approaches to the problem of natural monopolies. Everybody—including the farmers—seems to agree that traditional farm programs have done far more damage than good. And, getting back to where we began, economists overwhelmingly agree that minimum wage laws are a major cause of the poverty and structural unemployment that a host of other government programs are designed to cure.

There is, in short, a growing conviction that it is time to stop asking government to do what it cannot do well—and start maximizing opportunities by relying more heavily on the creative strengths within the free society.

POVERTY IN AMERICA

by Charles E. Goodell and Albert H. Quie

REPRESENTATIVE CHARLES E. GOODELL first came to Congress in 1959 at the age of thirty-three. Since that time he has served on the House Committee on Education and Labor and is considered an expert on the subject of poverty legislation.

In 1962 he co-authored the Manpower Development and Training Act, which has become the nucleus of training programs for the unemployed throughout the United States. As a member of the House Administration Committee, Mr. Goodell won wide bipartisan support in the 90th Congress for the proposed Goodell Election Reform Bill, the first effective attempt to re-write the laws dealing with reporting and disclosure of campaign financing. The Congressman is a member of the House leadership and has actively served in a number of Republican Committee functions at the National level.

CONGRESSMAN ALBERT H. QUIE (R., Minnesota) is now serving his eleventh year in the U. S. House of Representatives. Before his election to Congress, he served as a Minnesota State Senator. An authority on education, Congressman Quie is the second ranking Republican member of the House Education and Labor Committee and has played a major role in shaping educational legislation passed by Congress in recent years. He is also a member of the House Republican Policy Committee. Mr. Quie was the co-author with Charles E. Goodell of the Republican alternative to the administration's War on Poverty program, known as the Opportunity Crusade.

Poverty is an intractable and self-perpetuating complex of conditions. Its root causes are seen only "through a glass darkly." Elimination of poverty in the America of the 1970s demands bold innovation now.

Developing a comprehensive program to alleviate and eliminate poverty is no simple matter. Vast amounts of data must be studied and collated. No single agency of government today collects and analyzes the necessary data for a rational poverty program. No single agency evaluates the impact and the inter-relationship of hundreds of separate federal programs, spending between $25 and $40 billion annually on poverty problems.

In 1964, when the poverty war was launched, Republicans urged a National Commission on the causes and cures of poverty. The suggestion was rejected. Today the wilderness of the poverty sector remains largely unexplored. Four years and 5½ billion dollars after President Johnson declared his War on Poverty, Americans still have no clear insight into the causes and cures of poverty.

It is our belief that the present poverty war cannot be abandoned. It can be dramatically improved. Major changes and new directions were incorporated in an entire substitute for the poverty war known as the Republican Opportunity Crusade. They entail administrative revamping, government incentives for massive involvement of private enterprise, increased involvement of the poor themselves in their own programs, emphasis on the traditional American concept of Community Action, and true partnership among federal, state, local and private agencies.

To provide a continuing evaluation and a basis for future improvements, we suggest a new Council of Economic Opportunity Advisers in the Office of the President. This council should be patterned after the present three-man Council of Economic Advisers, with comparable stature and independence. It would have full responsibility for poverty research, analysis of pertinent data, and evaluation of the myriad exist-

ing programs. It would be mandated to chart the course of a
true crusade to insure full economic opportunities for all
Americans.

THE CHALLENGE OF POVERTY

Before we can help the poor, we must know who they are.
Devising a reliable and workable definition of "poverty" has
proven to be no easy task.

One of the earliest definitions of poverty was offered by
the President's council of Economic Advisers. In its 1964
Annual Report, the Council defined poverty in terms of a
minimum annual cash income. A family unit of two or more
persons with a total annual cash income of $3000 or less or
an "unrelated" individual receiving a total annual money income of $1500 or less was categorized as "poor."

The serious shortcomings of this definition evoked widespread criticism. By ignoring differences in family sizes, in the
ages and special needs of individual family members, in the
geographic location of family residence, in the disparities between the cash needs of the urban and rural poor, and in the
important fact that minimum decency of living standards are
not constant but are subject to fluctuation over time, this income benchmark was destined, at the outset, to be woefully
inadequate.

Raising a family's annual cash income to an arbitrary level
does not necessarily move it out of poverty. In many instances,
the causes of poverty and its perpetuation can be attributed
to a lack of basic education, a lack of marketable job skills,
a lack of steady employment with ample opportunities for
advancement—and a lack of personal motivation and incentive.

Our goal should not be limited to bringing the poor to a
minimum income level—a level that will do little more than
sustain human life. Our goal must be one of providing every
person with an equal opportunity to develop his potential capabilities to the fullest so that he may be able to provide for

himself and his dependents those goods and services that are necessary to maintain a decent and comfortable standard of living, and more!

A second definition of poverty was developed by the Social Security Administration on the basis of consumer-expenditure patterns that showed that a low-income family member's food needs could be satisfied with an expenditure of no less than seventy cents per day. This data also suggested that the total cash expenditures for food of a poor family should account for not more than one-third of its total living costs. Family size, the age and sex of the head of the household, and the lower cash income needs of the rural family (now estimated to be 30 percent lower than those of a nonfarm family) were taken into consideration by the SSA poverty index.

While the SSA index does represent an effort to be more specific, our tools for measuring poverty are still crude and inadequate—our methodology unsophisticated. It is imperative that we develop improved techniques for identifying and measuring the poor.

The SSA index, though not an ideal measuring device, does recognize the existence and relationship among a number of variables that relate to individual and family needs. Because it affords a greater degree of accuracy and flexibility, it has virtually phased out the earlier "$3000–$1500" income benchmark definition. The SSA poverty index now serves as the basis for the administration of the present War on Poverty programs.

The following table shows the initial SSA annual cash income thresholds, in terms of 1963 money income.

Adjustments made for 1966 food prices would raise the current SSA poverty threshold for a nonfarm family of one to $1635; a farm family of one to $1145; a nonfarm family of four to $3335; a farm family of four to $2345 and nonfarm and farm families of seven to $5430 and $3790 respectively.

While the SSA index is currently relied upon, it should be noted that other definitions of poverty have been advanced. Depending on the criteria that one chooses to apply, the in-

WEIGHTED AVERAGE OF POVERTY INCOME CRITERIA FOR FAMILIES
OF DIFFERENT COMPOSITION, BY HOUSEHOLD SIZE, SEX OF HEAD,
AND FARM OR NONFARM RESIDENCE, 1964

| Number of family members | Nonfarm | | | Farm | | |
	Total	Male head	Female head	Total	Male head	Female head
	Weighted average of incomes at economy level					
1 (under age 65)	$1,580	$1,650	$1,525	$960	$990	$920
1 (aged 65 or over)	1,470	1,480	1,465	885	890	880
2 (under age 65)	2,050	2,065	1,975	1,240	1,240	1,180
2 (aged 65 or over)	1,850	1,855	1,845	1,110	1,110	1,120
3	2,440	2,455	2,350	1,410	1,410	1,395
4	3,130	3,130	3,115	1,925	1,925	1,865
5	3,685	3,685	3,660	2,210	2,210	2,220
6	4,135	4,135	4,110	2,500	2,495	2,530
7 or more	5,090	5,100	5,000	3,055	3,065	2,985

SOURCE: Social Security Administration

WEIGHTED AVERAGE OF POVERTY AND LOW-INCOME CRITERIA[1] FOR
FAMILIES OF DIFFERENT COMPOSITION BY HOUSEHOLD SIZE,
SEX OF HEAD, AND FARM OR NONFARM RESIDENCE,
MARCH 1967

| Number of family members | *Weighted average of incomes at poverty level* | | | | | |
| | Nonfarm | | | Farm | | |
	Total	Male head	Female head	Total	Male head	Female head
1 member	$1,635	$1,710	$1,595	$1,145	$1,180	$1,110
Head under age 65	1,685	1,760	1,625	1,195	1,230	1,140
Head aged 65 or over	1,565	1,580	1,560	1,095	1,105	1,090
2 members	2,115	2,130	2,055	1,475	1,480	1,400
Head under age 65	2,185	2,200	2,105	1,535	1,540	1,465
Head aged 65 or over	1,970	1,975	1,955	1,380	1,380	1,370
3 members	2,600	2,610	2,515	1,815	1,820	1,725
4 members	3,335	3,335	3,320	2,345	2,345	2,320
5 members	3,930	3,930	3,895	2,755	2,755	2,775
6 members	4,410	4,410	4,395	3,090	3,090	3,075
7 or more members	5,430	5,440	5,310	3,790	3,795	3,760

[1] Required income in 1966 according to Social Security Administration
poverty or low-income index for a family of a given size and composition.
Family income criteria weighted together in accordance with percentage
distribution of total units by number of related children and sex of head,
as of Current Population Survey, March 1967.
SOURCE: Social Security Administration

cidence of poverty in the United States assumes somewhat different proportions. Persons included on the poverty roster according to one definition may well be excluded under the terms of another.

AMERICAN POVERTY IN PERSPECTIVE

It is important that we see American poverty in clear perspective as compared to world poverty. The United States has a serious problem. It in no way implies complacency or underestimates that problem to emphasize the fact that we have done better than most other nations. Comparative figures are elusive but it is clear that per capita personal income in the United States is more than double that of the next highest nation in the world. Great Britain and West Germany vie for second place. Per capita personal income of non-white American citizens is approximately at the same level as per capita personal income in West Germany and Great Britain. As we recognize the fact that the United States is doing reasonably well in comparison to performance of other nations, we must face the crucial danger of a widening gap between the poor and the affluent in America.

Between 1950 and 1960 the percentage of poor families in the United States dropped from 28.9 percent to 19.5 percent. From 1960 to 1966 the percentage of poor families dropped from 19.5 percent to 14.3 percent. (Economic Report of the President—February 1968.) Significantly, the rate of reduction was greater in the 1950s than in the past six years. In perspective, these figures raise some doubt about the efficacy of the highly advertised federal programs of recent years.

A CLOSER LOOK AT THIRTY MILLION

Working within the general SSA poverty guidelines, in 1966 an estimated 29,657,000—or 1 out of 7 of our total noninstitutionalized population—were among the poor. Of these 29.6

million, 4,821,000 were "unrelated" individuals while 24,836,-
000 were members of family units.

Among those identified as poor are approximately 5.4 million persons age sixty-five or older. Senior citizens who, with
few exceptions, must rely exclusively on income-maintenance
are inadequately served by present programs. The SSA reports that poverty stricken aged families received 60 percent
of their income from social security benefits. In 1965, almost
35 percent of aged social security beneficiaries were living in
poverty.

An estimated 12.5 million children under age eighteen com-
prise a second major grouping among the poor. Nearly
4,386,000 are preschoolers under age six. The young, like the
elderly, must look to others for support.

Younger children—especially those age six or under—present a special problem. Not only are they unable to provide
for their personal needs, but they also require steady supervision and care by an adult. Parental responsibility often
precludes contribution to the overall family income by an
adult, who might be capable of joining the labor force.

Women (regardless of their age, unemployment status, or
family responsibilities) are more poverty-prone than are men.
The incidence of poverty is especially high among older
women who live alone and younger women who are heads of
households that include small children. In 1966, 35 percent,
or 1.8 million, of households headed by women are classified
as poor. Here again, existing programs are inadequate.

Educational achievement bears a direct relationship to employment opportunities, projected lifetime earnings and ability
to provide adequately for a family's basic needs.

Poor children tend to drop out of school sooner. Possessing
minimal job skills, the non-graduate encounters major difficulty in securing permanent employment. Reduced earning
capacity lowers his standard of living. High school dropouts
tend to marry and assume family responsibilities at an earlier
age than do their counterparts who remain in school. Limited
educational credentials and restricted employment opportuni-

ties circumscribe the upward economic mobility commensurable with growing family responsibilities.

While a husband-wife wage earner team might command a joint income sufficient to meet its needs, the presence of smaller children virtually excludes a wife from working. And with a larger number of children, the incidence of poverty is greater.

PERCENT OF FAMILIES WITH MALE HEAD AND
INCOME BELOW THEIR POVERTY LINE

Total family members	None	1	2	3	4	5	6 or more
			Number of children under 18				
2, head 65 or older	23	1					
2, head under 65	7	23					
3	5	6	1				
4	5	5	6	1			
5	4	4	9	8	1		
6 or more	1	5	8	10	13	22	34

[1] Percentages not shown for base less than 100,000
SOURCE: Social Security Administration

Moreover, the level of professional or vocational achievement and attendant earning limitations has a direct relationship on the incidence of lifelong poverty.

While there is a tendency to associate abject poverty with the urban ghetto, our rural dwellers continue to be poorer than our urban population. In 1964, more than one-third of all individuals living on farms had cash incomes that fell below the poverty threshold. The farm income criterion is 30 percent lower than non-farm to allow for on-farm production.

The incidence of rural poverty has declined twice as fast as non-farm in recent years. Migration of farm families to the cities has increased. It is obvious that rural poverty has joined the urban migration.

On a nationwide basis, poverty continues to zero in on our nonwhite population. In 1966, 33⅓ percent of all nonwhite families were poor as contrasted with approximately 10 percent of all white families.

INCIDENCE OF POVERTY AND LOW-INCOME STATUS, 1966: NUMBER AND PERCENT OF HOUSEHOLDS BELOW SSA POVERTY LEVEL AND ABOVE THAT LEVEL BUT BELOW LOW-INCOME LEVEL, BY NUMBER OF CHILDREN UNDER AGE 18 AND SEX AND COLOR OF HEAD

[NUMBERS IN THOUSANDS]

Type of household	All households					With male head					With female head				
		Poor		Near poor			Poor		Near poor			Poor		Near poor	
	Total	Number	Percent	Number	Percent	Total	Number	Percent	Number	Percent	Total	Number	Percent	Number	Percent
All households															
Total	61,291	10,906	17.7	4,334	7.1	48,314	5,552	11.5	3,341	6.9	12,977	5,354	41.3	993	7.7
Unrelated individuals	12,367	4,821	39.0	781	6.3	4,564	1,277	28.0	281	6.2	7,803	3,544	45.4	500	6.4
Under age 65	7,489	2,124	28.4	312	4.2	3,279	712	21.7	146	4.5	4,210	1,412	33.5	166	3.9
Aged 65 and over	4,878	2,697	55.3	469	9.6	1,285	565	44.0	135	10.5	3,593	2,132	59.3	334	9.3
Families	48,924	6,085	12.4	3,553	7.3	43,750	4,275	9.8	3,060	7.0	5,174	1,810	35.0	493	9.5
With no children	20,332	2,204	10.8	1,436	7.1	18,118	1,874	10.3	1,247	6.9	2,214	330	14.9	189	8.5
With children	28,593	3,877	13.6	2,118	7.4	25,634	2,399	9.4	1,814	7.1	2,959	1,478	49.9	304	10.3
1 child	9,081	843	9.3	433	4.8	8,034	491	6.1	331	4.1	1,047	352	33.6	102	9.7
2 children	8,491	869	10.2	454	5.3	7,665	503	6.6	359	4.7	826	366	44.3	95	11.5
3 children	5,416	694	12.8	458	8.5	4,949	406	8.2	411	8.3	467	288	61.7	47	10.1
4 children	2,923	543	18.6	361	12.4	2,629	342	13.0	323	12.3	294	201	68.4	38	12.9
5 children	1,396	387	27.7	206	14.8	1,262	281	22.3	195	15.5	134	106	79.1	11	8.2
6 or more	1,286	541	42.1	206	16.0	1,095	376	34.3	195	17.8	191	165	86.4	11	5.7
White households															
Total	54,801	8,402	15.3	3,644	6.6	43,826	4,272	9.7	2,808	6.4	10,975	4,130	37.6	836	7.6
Unrelated individuals	10,786	4,026	37.3	677	6.3	3,820	1,007	26.4	224	5.9	6,966	3,019	43.3	453	6.5

Under age 65	6,296	1,626	25.8	241	3.8	2,688	540	20.1	110	4.1	3,608	1,086	30.1	131	3.6
Aged 65 and over	4,490	2,400	53.5	436	9.7	1,132	467	41.3	114	10.1	3,358	1,933	57.6	322	9.6
Families	44,026	4,373	9.9	2,967	6.7	40,006	3,265	8.2	2,584	6.5	4,013	1,111	27.7	383	9.5
With no children	18,759	1,863	9.9	1,268	6.8	16,823	1,607	9.6	1,111	6.6	1,936	256	13.2	157	8.1
With children	25,257	2,509	9.9	1,701	6.7	23,182	1,656	7.1	1,476	6.4	2,075	853	41.1	225	10.8
1 child	8,164	616	7.5	340	4.2	7,337	372	5.1	258	3.5	827	244	29.5	82	9.9
2 children	7,721	599	7.8	373	4.8	7,114	373	5.2	303	4.3	607	226	37.2	70	11.5
3 children	4,865	461	9.5	394	8.1	4,533	278	6.1	358	7.9	332	183	55.1	36	10.8
4 children	2,498	336	13.5	280	11.2	2,321	235	10.1	252	10.9	177	101	57.1	28	15.8
5 children	1,125	217	19.3	165	14.7	1,063	175	16.5	159	15.0	62	42	67.7	6	9.7
6 or more	884	280	31.7	149	16.9	814	223	27.4	146	17.9	70	57	81.4	3	4.3
Nonwhite households															
Total	6,488	2,506	38.6	690	10.6	4,487	1,281	28.5	533	11.9	2,001	1,225	61.2	157	7.8
Unrelated individuals	1,584	796	50.3	105	6.6	744	270	36.3	58	7.8	840	526	62.6	47	5.6
Under age 65	1,196	499	41.7	72	6.0	592	172	29.1	37	6.3	604	327	54.1	35	5.8
Aged 65 and over	388	297	76.5	33	8.5	152	98	64.5	21	13.8	236	199	84.3	12	5.1
Families	4,898	1,712	34.9	585	11.9	3,743	1,011	27.0	475	12.7	1,161	699	60.2	110	9.5
With no children	1,568	341	21.7	166	10.6	1,293	267	20.6	134	10.4	275	74	26.9	32	11.6
With children	3,333	1,371	41.1	421	12.6	2,449	746	30.5	341	13.9	884	625	70.7	80	9.0
1 child	916	228	24.8	94	10.3	696	119	17.1	73	10.5	220	109	49.5	21	9.5
2 children	770	270	35.1	82	10.6	551	130	23.6	57	10.3	219	140	63.9	25	11.4
3 children	550	231	42.0	64	11.6	416	128	30.8	53	12.7	134	103	76.9	11	8.2
4 children	424	209	49.3	82	19.3	308	108	35.1	72	23.4	116	101	87.1	10	8.6
5 children	271	170	62.7	43	15.9	198	107	54.0	38	19.2	73	63	86.3	5	6.8
6 or more	402	263	65.4	56	13.9	280	154	55.0	48	17.1	122	109	89.3	8	6.6

SOURCE: Derived by the Social Security Administration from special tabulations by the Bureau of the Census from the Current Population Survey for March 1967.

As might be expected, racial discrimination intensifies the virulence of poverty among minority groups. Age-old patterns of social and economic injustice continue to take their heavy toll among Americans principally of African, Asian, Latin and indigenous Indian origin. A realistic appraisal of poverty in America demands consideration of this factor. Until dominant contemporary attitudes of heart and mind are changed, it is unlikely that we will eliminate poverty amidst plenty.

These conditions are amenable to legislative solution only in the framework of changed attitudes.

THE REPUBLICAN OPPORTUNITY CRUSADE AS AN ALTERNATIVE TO THE ANTI-POVERTY PROGRAM

by Charles E. Goodell and Albert H. Quie

THE BASIC APPROACH

The key to success of any national poverty program lies in finding the proper role of the federal government in the sophisticated society of the late twentieth century. Government programs must incorporate certain basic tenets:

1) The poor themselves must be energized through participation in planning, policy formation and program implementation;
2) The total community with all its constituent resources must be mobilized;
3) The efforts of all levels of government must be supplementary to this independent action.

The Economic Opportunity Act proposed in 1964 by President Johnson touched around the edges of these concepts but failed to incorporate them clearly and provide for their effective implementation.

THE BACKGROUND

Three years before the so-called Poverty War, Republican Members of the House Education and Labor Committee began to develop new programs to help the underprivileged. That year Republicans suggested highest priority attention to the deprivations of the very young children of the poor. The

objective was to equip children of the poor to compete successfully with their more affluent peers as they moved into the
regular school system.

Significantly pre-school programs in the Poverty War were
not even specifically mentioned in the law. Head Start was
funded as an afterthought of community action.

Similarly, in 1961 Republicans developed new approaches
to job training and employment opportunity with emphasis on
programs designed to assist hardcore unemployables. In 1962,
this program was substituted for President Kennedy's proposals and was enacted into law as the Manpower Development
and Training Act. In 1963, Republicans worked with forward-
looking Democrats in Congress to revamp old vocational education laws. The result was the landmark Vocational Education Act of 1963.

From 1961 to 1964 Congressman Goodell waged a continuing fight to authorize an experimental residential skill center in the District of Columbia. This was finally approved in
1963 as a precursor of the Job Corps, but no money was ever
provided. How much better it would have been had we tried
out a few of these ideas and learned how to administer them,
before we plunged into mass production of job corps camps
in 1964.

With the declaration of the Poverty War in 1964, Republicans were constantly frustrated by partisan manipulation of
the legislative process to prevent improvements in the White
House proposals. Democrats went so far as to lock out the
Republicans from several House Committee meetings in which
the poverty law was being drafted. Accordingly, House Republicans began to put together our own suggestions which
culminated in the so-called Opportunity Crusade proposal. We
were determined to conform the Poverty War as closely as
possible to the realistic needs of the poor in contemporary
America.

THE ROLE OF THE FEDERAL GOVERNMENT

In any domestic program such as the War on Poverty, the federal government should never be more than a partner— with no more dominant role than a co-equal with state and local government. It should establish national policy and co-ordinate the efforts of the fifty states. Project-by-project approval of grants from local groups should be only of a short-term nature and, as soon as possible, be supplanted by one wherein each state will develop its policy to meet the overall needs of the communities within its boundaries. This same community planning will permit utilization of federal funds in a versatile way which will enable them to meet their particular and peculiar needs within the broad policies laid down at the state and federal levels.

The federal government is now encouraging local communities to move faster by providing assistance through grants directly from the federal to the local levels. Often, in order to receive funds for projects that will benefit the community, additional proposals for projects that are not needed must be incorporated to obtain OEO approval for any money. This grantsmanship will, in the long run, thwart the efforts of individuals at the community level.

In the future, only necessary and innovative programs in which the federal government might wish to experiment and demonstrate should be funded on a project-by-project basis.

The federal government should offer leadership, encouragement, incentives, and seed money. It cannot dominate. It cannot direct or impose programs from above. It cannot buy success. It must lead and persuade for it is the unique catalyst which can breathe life into the great coalition which is the American community.

The national anti-poverty program must match the pressing needs of the poor with the services of government and available resources from the independent sector. Except in programs of an institutional nature, such as education, purely governmental activities should be confined to new frontiers where no existing forces can be mobilized.

STATE AND LOCAL GOVERNMENTS

Of major importance in the poverty effort is involvement of the states. The vast majority of social welfare programs are organized and administered at the state level. Without enlightened state participation, the proper balance of comprehensive social planning within the framework of differing regional needs is beyond attainment. The poverty of the great urban centers and the wealth of the suburban complex which surrounds them must be interrelated in a way that only state powers can accomplish. The resources of the great state universities frequently are least available where they are needed most. The moral leadership of the governors and other officers of state governments is of major importance to focus the attention of the affluent on the communities outside their normal vision.

Local governments play a vital role in combating poverty. They provide indispensable municipal services in the immediate community in which the poor reside. Complex regulations in urban centers often virtually preclude traditional self-help activity. They can be eased only by local authorities. For example, some cities charge a fee for a permit to place a ladder on a sidewalk to paint a house. Clean up campaigns accumulate trash. City ordinances designed for regular trash collection create major difficulties in disposing of any abnormally large accumulation. Even such routine daily problems as this must be handled through some form of coordination between the efforts of the people and the municipal structure.

Independent, uncoordinated activity among these various sectors has marked anti-poverty efforts for years. The War on Poverty to date has done little to weld these forces together. In many instances, the operations of OEO have been more disruptive than coordinative. This major deficiency contravenes one of the primary roles of meaningful community action. At the federal level, particularly, the function of the community action program is to coordinate, encourage and lead. Such has not been the case under the present act. Meaningful coordination of new and old programs can be the difference between solution and failure.

MOBILIZATION OF THE TOTAL COMMUNITY

Mobilization of support of the total community is imperative if programs to eliminate poverty are to be meaningful. The poor, the affluent and governments each play a vital role.

It is the people themselves, and the independent sector, which must provide most of the expertise and resources required to eliminate poverty. Non-governmental sectors provide more than 80 percent of the job opportunities in America today. The vast majority of highly skilled professionals capable of providing counseling, legal, medical and testing services are privately employed. Volunteers with special expertise must be drawn from the ranks of those who can contribute their own time.

Government action is obviously necessary to stimulate, guide and supplement private efforts. Republicans have made a variety of proposals along these lines outside the specific confines of the poverty war itself. For example, the bulk of housing needs for our nation's poor cannot be met by public housing alone. The Percy-Widnall housing proposal would provide realistic inducement for private industry to make massive investments in the urban ghettos. The Republican Human Investment Act, sponsored by Rep. Thomas B. Curtis (R., Missouri) and over one hundred other Members of Congress, would give a tax credit to employers who invest in human beings through private training programs.[1] Tax incentives and subsidies have been offered as a means to bring industry into the ghettos and rural areas. Rural redevelopment, as an alternative to the poverty programs' encouragement of migra-

---

[1] See paper following.

tion to the cities, is imperative. Federal revenue sharing has been proposed to provide states and local governments the means to solve many of their own problems without the administrative waste and stifling bureaucracy of federally centralized programs. These specific Republican approaches are covered elsewhere in this volume and are certainly an important part of the necessary total assault on poverty in America.

COMMUNITY ACTION

Community action programs must involve the total community. Unfortunately, misunderstanding and misdirection of community action has created widespread negative reaction to the concept. Community action has served man throughout his experience with social organization. It is a technique widely employed today throughout the world from the most primitive to the most advanced societies.

It is a curious phenomenon that community action is not understood in America today. The Englishmen who invaded the wilderness of the New World at Jamestown and Plymouth Rock survived through this technique. These small colonies were set down with minimal supplies and no government. They lived only because each contributed in the spirit of one for all and all for one. Their homes, their forts, even the stockades which protected them against the ravages of animals and unfriendly Indians, were the product of community action. Utilizing these techniques, they shared their labor in the quest for food.

Community action typifies social, political and economic organization of every frontier from Virginia to Alaska. From it stems the now quaint customs of "quilting bees" and "barn raisings."

The sophisticated public education system, of which America is so justly proud today, found its beginnings in community action. Common defense of the early settlements was improvised through community action techniques. Organization of the colonies for the looming revolution was a complex manifestation of the technique.

The curious combination of geographic and political factors which came to bear in the North America of the seventeenth and eighteenth centuries left no other alternative. Community action in practice paralleled the political theories of Voltaire and Locke. It was, however, community action which created the matrix from which emerged the Declaration of Independence. The Constitution forged two centuries of community action experience into a unique system of government.

Emerging power of the United States in the nineteenth century was a phenomenon which confounded political sophisticates of the European ruling class. In consequence, many, including Alexis de Tocqueville, traveled in the New World in an effort to understand the essence of this "revolution."

After lengthy travels throughout the nation, in 1835 he described the source of America's strength in these words:

"Americans of all ages, all conditions, and all dispositions, constantly form associations. They have not only commercial and manufacturing companies, in which all take part but associations of a thousand other kinds—religious, moral, serious, futile, general or restricted, enormous or diminutive. The Americans make associations to give entertainments, to found seminaries, to build inns, to construct churches, to diffuse books, to send missionaries to the antipodes; they found in this manner hospitals, prisons, and schools. If it be proposed to inculcate some truth, or to foster some feeling by the encouragement of a great example they form a society. Wherever at the head of some new undertaking you see the government in France or a man of rank in England, in the United States you will be sure to find an association." (Democracy in America)

As the twentieth century dawned, the tradition continued to mature. Successive waves of European immigrants, banding together, used community action as the vehicle for their assimilation into the mainstream of American life. This proud tradition is perpetuated and manifested in the multiplicity of ad hoc organizations of private citizens which flourish today.

Americans need only the catalyst of believable and enlightened leadership, with sensitive government support, to initiate massive self-help activities. An infinite variety of self-help measures, from clean up and recreational campaigns to remedial and household education, can proliferate in the slums.

Neighborhood organizations, functioning through neighborhood centers located within walking distance of the needy, bring the services of old line agencies into the areas where they are most desperately needed. When these centers are used as a base by competent, well-trained community action workers, greater impetus is given to directing the strength of the poor themselves into constructive, mutually beneficial programs.

An excellent case can be made that the major ingredient of urban alienation in today's society is the isolation of people from the power centers of the community. How can a ghetto dweller influence policies of a school board, of a sanitation department or a housing agency in a major metropolitan area today? Two-way communication between the ghetto dwellers and decision-makers is critically lacking. The slum poor feel no momentum of which they are a part.

Involvement of parents in Head Start has been a striking success. The principle must be extended to involvement of parents in policymaking functions of neighborhood schools. From there the principle extends to virtually every agency affecting the vital daily problems of the urban ghetto dweller. Neighborhood organizations provide an ideal structure for accomplishing this.

Even under the community action programs, constructive efforts toward true involvement of the total community in pursuit of sound solutions has been given too little attention. Here too, the federal government has attempted to structure its War on Poverty from the top down. As a result, only a limited number of the programs, such as Head Start and Legal Services, are in fact programs supported by the rank and file. From the beginning, the Office of Economic Opportunity read things into the community action title that were never intended by Congress. Social reform by force and by abrasive relations between community action agencies on the one hand and existing agencies on the other were confused with constructive community effort.

Office of Economic Opportunity personnel organized and directed confrontation and demonstrations against public officials leading to major tensions and community disruption. Too frequently these displays of hostility have coincided with racial unrest which polarized the Negro and white communities.

Lack of coordination and cooperation between community action agencies on the one hand and school officials, welfare agencies, housing authorities and representatives of private enterprise on the other, alienated community leaders.

Irresponsible handling of large sums of money and lack of fiscal accountability continue to plague community action programs.

Community action has bypassed significant numbers of the poor. There is little evidence that large numbers of the poverty stricken are being assisted in tangible or visible ways. Under the Opportunity Crusade, clear guidelines structuring the proper role for each of the necessary elements of the community are provided. Detailed provisions to encourage meaningful community action should, hopefully, prevent future mismanagement and misuse of the community action technique.

A bold new concept in keeping with these ideas is introduced in the Opportunity Crusade. Job Opportunity Boards, structured to resolve the problem of hardcore unemployables, are created. The membership of these boards is divided between the poor and representatives of industry and labor who can provide meaningful jobs and job training. These boards are directed to make maximum utilization of volunteers and voluntary contribution of services, particularly the kind of simple supportive help so desperately needed by an individual on a downward spiral of job experience.

This new approach to employment opportunity is the refinement of several similar programs which have developed simultaneously in the private sector or as part of local community action programs. A major contribution to this concept has been made by the Committee for Employment Opportunity, which is a joint venture conducted by the Indianapolis Chamber of Commerce in the Center for Independent Action. This program has been highly successful in identifying, counseling and placing hardcore unemployables in meaningful permanent jobs through the community effort. Now in its second year, the program has a demonstrated cost of less than $45 per poor person placed.

COORDINATION

A major function of any community action program is coordination. This term implies many things and the function takes a number of forms in a national anti-poverty program. The concept is well understood elsewhere in the world where community action has proven highly successful. Unfortunately, it is neither understood nor has it been implemented under the OEO. Even its most obvious meaning has been ignored through preoccupation with the operational role which OEO has elected to serve. The agency has failed effectively to mobilize and simplify the availability of services provided by existing governmental agencies at all levels.

Coordination is a "word of art" in nations such as Venezuela, which has utilized community action techniques with a high degree of success. Coordination implies recognition of the supportive role of a national government in implementing the community action concept. In this century, advanced societies have increasingly provided social services, which prior to the twentieth century were provided, if at all, through independent action. The resulting social complexity has provided a galaxy of services and independent bureaucracies. Both program and services often overlap. Administrative demands have created relatively complicated processing procedures to determine eligibility of individual applicants.

Thus the forgotten man is faced with an almost insurmountable obstacle when he approaches his government to share in the services to which he is rightfully entitled. In America it is rare to find fewer than two independently administered programs providing essentially the same service. Each jealously seeks to preserve its funds and to expand its constituency. Incredibly time-consuming delays thus confront the individual who may well have spent his last penny to arrive at the agency's doorstep. The mystique of this bureaucratic complexity frustrates the typical victim of poverty, who often has only the most rudimentary level of literacy. As the sophistication of programs and the sum of available funds increases, the complexity compounds.

The individual faced with such enormous bureaucracy is virtually helpless. Accordingly, one of the major functions to be served by a federal anti-poverty agency is coordination. Coordination is the process by which this maze should be simplified and its services made readily available to those who need them most. It is the very opposite of proliferation, a fact that is seldom understood by poverty program administrators. Coordination is of primary importance at every level of the poverty war. The federal agency should serve as a catalyst. It manifestly must be a source of funding in poor areas.

INVOLVEMENT OF THE POOR

Psychological and pragmatic reasons place the highest priority on maximum feasible involvement of the poor. History amply demonstrates the validity of this approach. Upward movement towards a poverty free society in the United States has been characterized by involvement of people in their own destinies. With the exception of income maintenance for those incapable of self-support, government's most effective role remains the structuring of conditions in which individuals can realistically help themselves or organize to help each other.

The sociological impairment which flows from simply stig-
matizing the poor with hand-outs would seem to be evident
on its face, yet precious little attention has been directed to
this impediment. The respected urbanologist, Daniel P.
Moynihan points out elsewhere in this volume:

> "Last summer, with something like one New York City
> child in five living on welfare, Dr. Mitchell Ginsberg of
> the Lindsay administration declared the system 'bank-
> rupt. It was just as bankrupt five years ago but somehow
> we could not, would not see it then.' "[2]

Social and economic decay has thus set-in in the very areas
where it could do the most damage. Tucked away in their
misery, isolation and despair, the poor have been largely out
of sight.

The net result of these and many other factors is the loss
of sociological momentum among the poor themselves. The
loss of life and property in both the long hot summers and
the winters of discontent of recent years is in large measure
the price of national indifference to the failures of the past
thirty years. These failures have been compounded by the
loud exhortations of leaders who promise an "instant tomorrow" they cannot deliver and who conceive of solutions only
in terms of unavailable massive infusions of federal dollars
in the pattern of past failures.

Thus urban poverty today demands, even more than might
be expected, the sociological impetus which flows from maximum involvement of the poor. The major contribution of the
War on Poverty to date is the creation of a clearly identified
program which the poor regard as their own. In spite of its
many tragic administrative asininities, the regeneration of hope
in the hearts and minds of some of the poor themselves is the
first meaningful sign of progress in the Poverty War.

The psychological impact of involvement of the poor was
a gratuitous and often unpleasant surprise to the overlords
of the War on Poverty. The Economic Opportunity Act of

2 See p. 137.

1964, as presented to the Congress, incorporated the concept only by implication in community action programs. True involvement of the poor was not the intent of many of the original planners.

Adam Yarmolinsky, a member of the President's original poverty task force, explained it in these words:

"What we meant then though, or at least what I understood, was that the activities which were then being carried on for poor people should be carried out by poor people for other poor people . . . It was not a matter of giving poor people who lived in the area a place on the boards of community action organizations . . ."

As the implications of involvement of the poor rapidly unfolded, the overlords of the War on Poverty beat a hasty retreat. Agitation to limit this "disquieting" development mounted.

By 1966 a Democratic coalition of Southern governors and big city machines had formed. It sought increasing control of local community action boards. Republicans met this threat to involvement of the poor with the Quie Amendment which earmarked at least one-third of the seats on local community action boards for representatives of the poor, chosen by residents of impoverished areas.

Undaunted, the established coalition continued its fight to curtail independent involvement of the poor. Fueled by local political reaction, their drive culminated in regressive curtailment of community action in the 1967 poverty law.

In addition to its sociological value, involvement is a pragmatic must. Secretary of Housing and Urban Development, Robert C. Weaver, has characterized the urban renewal programs as failures, citing as the principal reason the failure to involve the poor themselves. Consistent with this attitude, in implementing the Model Cities Program, the Secretary announced on December 1, 1967, a policy of direct consultation with the poor in establishing the priorities of that program at the local level. The poor themselves, who are immersed in poverty conditions twenty-four hours of every day, are

best equipped to determine the things that rankle the most and
will bestir participation of the poor in their solution. They
possess the great advantage of being on the scene and readily
accessible to those whom they can help.

The approach of the poverty warriors to involvement of
the poor has too often bordered on the cavalier or the doc-
trinaire. The poor have been told what is best for them. Significant understanding of the subculture of poverty seems to
be lacking. There is a distinct difference between joint cooperative action and condescension.

The Republican Opportunity Crusade builds into programs
an expanded involvement of the poor at all feasible levels,
in letter as well as spirit. It assures representation of the poor
on independent local community action boards. Selection of
the representatives of the poor is regularized under appropriate democratic procedures. Representation of the poor on
State Community Action Commissions is required, thus permitting the voice of poverty to be heard in establishing comprehensive state-wide social action programs and providing
state partnership in the crusade. Special boards which are
created to meet specific needs, such as job opportunities,
legal services and education, require representatives of the
poor.

JOB CORPS

The hard core of unemployable youth requires innovative
institutional programs. The Job Corps, which has received a
major portion of funds allocated to job training, was designed
to fill this void. It is by far the most expensive type of program. The cost per enrollee year is conceded by OEO to be
$6950. More accurate estimates which include all the costs
of administration in conformity with accepted accounting
principles place the cost at $8100 per enrollee year.

Three years after the War on Poverty was launched, the
only substantial evaluation Job Corps officials could provide
Congress was a survey done by a well-known pollster under

contract with OEO. A sampling of Job Corps graduates and terminees was contacted in the poll to determine what had happened to youngsters after their Job Corps experience. This is appalling evidence in itself of the lack of sustained follow-through in the Job Corps program.

In its initial stages the Job Corps program was mass produced. Effective screening and referral of enrollees was virtually non-existent. Discipline in camps was loose and permissive. Administrative costs were excessively high and many instances of waste and poor judgment were uncovered. Tighter and more realistic administration has corrected many of these deficiencies, but basic faults remain.

Perhaps the most serious error in the whole Job Corps program was rejection of the idea that Job Corps Centers should serve community and regional needs. Ninety-one percent of Job Corps enrollees returned to their home areas. A distant Job Corps Center could be of little assistance to these enrollees in securing a job. Only 6 percent of Job Corps graduates had any help from the Job Corps in getting a job. Most of them were simply referred to the local employment office and there they were largely ignored. Job Corps officials then shifted responsibility for placement to small regional offices totally incapable of doing the job. Subsequently, the Job Corps has improvised with a variety of private volunteer groups to help Job Corps trainees find employment.

The Job Corps program arrogantly ignored the experience of those who had been working with residential training for years. The training facility must assume responsibility for testing, counseling, training and placement. This can be done most effectively if the training facility itself is community oriented. Great flexibility would be possible in providing single centers that would serve the needs of multiple communities in a region. Wherever possible such facilities should be integrated with non-residential area vocational schools and technical institutes. Facilities for hard core, Job Corps type youngsters would be provided at full federal expense without requirement of state or local matching. By combining facilities with on-going programs, however, the cost per enrollee could be reduced, the diversity of available training expanded and the stigma of sending enrollees to a "center for rejects" avoided. The latter problem in the Job Corps is likely to be of increasing significance as the program matures.

The failures and shortcomings of the Job Corps program are many. They are not limited to excessive costs and poor administrative planning. Job Corps officials proclaimed in hearings before Congress that 57 percent of "graduates" obtained jobs immediately. This sounds impressive until one examines the figures more closely and finds that 53 percent of them had jobs at the time they entered the Job Corps. In addition, the figures apply only to those enrollees who finished their training. One-third of the enrollees dropped out in the first three months and another third in the second three months. According to Job Corps' own survey, youngsters remaining in the Job Corps less than six months receive very little if any significant benefit. As of the summer of 1967 that included two-thirds of the enrollees.

Other evaluations cast considerable doubt on the coordination of training with available jobs. Only 23 percent of total Job Corps enrollees indicated that they were using the training they received.

It is tragic that the basically sound concept of residential training for youngsters who cannot respond in their present environments has been given a black eye by the early mistakes of the Job Corps. The concept must not be abandoned. The program must be redirected on a more realistic basis. Enrollees must be carefully screened to see to it that only the hard core who cannot respond elsewhere are admitted. Extravagant administrative costs must be cut. The Job Corps Centers must be community oriented. They must be integrated with vocational and technical institute programs. States and private enterprise must be given a far greater role in organizing and running the programs. Most important of all, enrollees must be carried through all the way to placement in meaningful jobs at the end of the road.

Neighborhood Youth Corps

Another poverty war program to help young people is known as the Neighborhood Youth Corps. The "in-school" Neighborhood Youth Corps program was designed to give part-time jobs to youngsters who might drop out of school for economic reasons. This program, administered largely by school officials, has worked reasonably well, but should be expanded to provide part-time jobs in private employment as well as public and non-profit employment. The Opportunity Crusade concentrates on this aspect by providing for full-time counselors in the schools for that purpose.

The "out-of-school" Neighborhood Youth Corps program was conceived as a means to provide both job-training and income maintenance for the youthful poor. In the first two years, only 10 percent of the participants received any training at all. In the third year, by the most generous definition of training, only 32 percent of the participants received any training. Unfortunately, the job opportunities in the Neighborhood Youth Corps are limited to public and private non-profit employers. Too often the jobs provided have been contrived and dead-end. Providing such temporary jobs may take young people off the streets and help prevent riots, but it ends up compounding their frustrations. They want jobs with a future, along with the kind of training that will help them move up the economic ladder.

Industry Youth Corps

The Opportunity Crusade would add a new dimension to the Neighborhood Youth Corps. It would emphasize on-the-job training for young people in private profit-making enterprises. Administered locally by Community Action Boards, the Industry Youth Corps would permit reimbursement to employers for all costs of training and a portion of the wages paid to young people who are not fully productive. Employers would pay three-fourths of the wages—the federal government one-quarter. Under the Neighborhood Youth Corps, the federal government pays 100 percent of the wages and other expenses. The Industry Youth Corps would thus employ at least three times as many youths per federal dollar spent as the Neighborhood Youth Corps, while assuring more effective job training and permanent productive employment.

PHASE OVER

New programs, once nurtured beyond the experimental stage, must be transferred to existing agencies for permanent administration. Continuing review and transfer serve sound organization of government while enhancing the innovative role of the anti-poverty agency. Resultant savings in administrative costs and personnel resources increase the number of poor who can benefit directly. Also, new methods of operation which are more successful in alleviating poverty will then infect older agencies and enable their entire program to function more effectively.

Accordingly, the Crusade transfers a number of established programs to old line agencies.

For example, the Job Corps program is transferred to the Vocational Education division of the Department of Health, Education, and Welfare (HEW). The program is restructured to provide quality training at lower costs. Residential Skill Centers located in areas of need are established. The development of job and career opportunities in the immediate community is encouraged. There is a requirement that continuous liaison with employers in the area served by the center be maintained. The director is required to establish a placement program for graduates.

In the same manner, Head Start, Early Years, Upward Bound and similar remedial education programs are placed under the jurisdiction of the Secretary of HEW as the 1967 amendment to the Economic Opportunity Act of 1964 did with Follow-Through and previous amendments did with Basic Adult Education and Work Study at the college level. This move consolidates these activities under a single department, thus providing a comprehensive overview of needs that must be met and simultaneously avoiding duplication of effort and unnecessary administrative costs.

The Crusade also seeks to encourage an awareness of community action in the existing bureaucracies. For example, the transfer of the remedial education programs to HEW is designed to encourage that Department to utilize community action techniques in meeting the problems of poverty. Republicans believe that the established agencies of the federal government are sincerely dedicated to aiding the poor. The repeated assertions by Democrats that departments such as HEW or Labor will destroy programs designed to help the poor border on slander.

Wherever feasible, the federal tax dollar is used to focus the energies of all Americans on the solution of the problem of poverty. To this end, private industry and commerce are involved to the maximum feasible degree in job-oriented programs. A special emphasis is placed on such programs in accordance with the priorities voiced by the poor themselves.

Within this legislative framework, men and women in the Executive departments can develop more fully the innovative role which the national government must play. The Office of Economic Opportunity is invited to be a dynamic organization, which evolves new ideas, proves them and develops a program of demonstrable value. The War on Poverty must generate innovation. It must offer the organizational flexibility which encourages constant evolution to meet changing problems and conditions. This is the role the Opportunity Crusade seeks to mold for the federal government.

Thus the Opportunity Crusade gives meaningful redirection to the federal anti-poverty program. It encourages every segment of American society to participate in a meaningful way in solving a major social crisis of the late twentieth century. It offers positive hope to those trapped in the misery of poverty. This program holds out to the American people the hope of structuring a united nonpartisan campaign to realize the American Dream in today's world. We believe it offers the American people a realistic opportunity to reduce poverty. As the late President Kennedy so aptly stated:

> "In the end the people must choose and the people must help themselves . . . let each devote his energies to the betterment of all so that your children and our children . . . can find an ever richer and a freer life."

THE CASE FOR THE REPUBLICAN HUMAN INVESTMENT ACT

by Thomas B. Curtis

REPRESENTATIVE THOMAS B. CURTIS (R., Missouri) was first elected to Congress in 1950. He is a member of the House Committee on Ways and Means, the Senate-House Joint Economic Committee, and the Senate-House Joint Committee on Internal Revenue Taxation. Since 1964, he has served as a Congressional Delegate for Trade negotiations.

Congressman Curtis, who is a member of the Republican Task Force on Job Opportunities and Welfare, was active in the development and enactment of the Manpower Development and Retraining Act. As spokesman for Congress in the economic sphere, he was a leader in writing laws extending Social Security to cover disability and in producing the major tax reform legislation of recent years. He was a participating author of the Tax Code of 1954, the 1962 and 1964 Revenue Acts and is an advocate of Congressional reform, having helped write and enact the recent reforms in legislative procedure as well as those still pending. As ranking member of the bipartisan Joint Senate-House Committee on the Organization of Congress, he proposed to establish a permanent Ethics Committee to oversee the standards and ethical codes of the Members of Congress.

Congressman Curtis, an authority on government procedure and economics, is the author of *87 Million Jobs: A Dynamic Solution to End Unemployment.*

Years ago unemployment seemed to be a simple matter for most Americans to discuss. Calvin Coolidge, for example, said that when there was a scarcity of jobs, unemployment results. To make a job, someone had to make an investment—to meet a probable demand for goods or services. The grocery clerk saved his money to open a store of his own. The mechanic saved his money to open a small shop of his own. The rich shifted money to new enterprises that promised better markets. And the nation grew as savings built new plants and businesses.

The depression of the thirties drastically altered this simple economic model. Emphasis should be taken off capital, academic observers argued, and placed instead upon consumption, aggregate demand, or the creation of more consumer spending. In such a system planning could be more orderly, they argued, because government by controlling money flow, could also control consumption. The advocated step was simply that of making government the prime factor of job creation rather than continuing enterprise and investment as the prime factors.

This in a nutshell is the theory of the "new economics" upon which our current employment policies are based. Underlying the economic thinking of the new economists for the past generation has been the notion that all that needs to be done to prime prosperity's pump and to create jobs is to increase the consumption of goods and services. Yet the economic statistics available reveal that there are currently over three million unemployed in the United States; that there are certainly many times this number who are underemployed (those who are working at a lower skill level than their capabilities or desires warrant); that at the same time there are reports in most every newspaper and periodical of jobs literally going begging; and on top of all that government spending certainly has never ever been so high.

There is again a crisis in economic thinking. The new economists are prone to look upon jobs as a simple pliable mass locked up in a squeezeable plastic dispenser, with government-dictated spending policies constituting the pressure which squeezes out just enough jobs to go around. The fundamental flaw is that the public spending approach regards the employment problem basically as one that melts away as soon as government controls produce the right volume of spending. Today it is necessary to face up to the need for more pinpointed action in the area of job escalation, not the crudely broad methods of the spenders. Our primary task today is that of upgrading individuals to match the unfilled jobs generated by our dynamic economy.

In addition to offering an ineffective approach to solving our current unemployment problems, the advocates of increased government spending may in fact make life even more miserable for the unemployed—and everyone else for that matter. Positive harm may result because the current unemployment in the economy is "frictional" and "structural" in nature and not due to lack of aggregate demand but to lack of specific types of training and retraining. Any beneficial effect of heavy government expenditures will be blocked and reversed by this lack of skills bottleneck and inflation, not more jobs, will ensue. This has been the experience of the past few years, and far from helping the very poor on the bottom of the skills ladder, it crushes them brutally.

Institutionalized government training programs, while better in theory than the aggregate spending approach, in practice are inefficient and do not often zero in on the specific types of training needed. Private industry perforce knows better than government what jobs are available, how best to train individuals for these jobs, and will be more efficient in handling the over-all operation of training and retraining. For this reason as much training as possible should be transferred from the public to the private sector of our economy. Those who fear a retrenchment of the over-all amount of manpower training programs if this comes about are ignoring the figures to the contrary. The Department of Labor estimates that the government spends $1.5 billion annually while some economists, as reported by Sylvia Porter of the *Washington Star* of May 24, 1967, estimate that private industry spends between $14 and $18 billion annually. And we could—and should—receive even more from American industry.

One of the most compelling arguments for increased training in the private sector over that by government is that the training in the private sector will undoubtedly be job related. This means economy in the training programs and an inestimable amount of psychological benefit for the trainee. In this context it is ironic to note that some of the strongest promoters of government institutionalized training programs have done the most to prevent proper correlation of training with available jobs. An essential part of intelligent government institutional training programs should be the collection of Job Vacancy Statistics indicating what jobs are available and what skills are in demand. Coupled with the collection of comprehensive job vacancy statistics is the need for constantly updating the Dictionary of Occupational Titles which is the nomenclature which helps to make these statistics feasible and usable.

The Subcommittee on Economic Statistics of the Joint Economic Committee concluded that the statistics would be most useful in raising the efficiency of the nation's manpower programs and urged that the Department of Labor spend the $2.5 million needed for this purpose.

Despite the unanimous recommendation of the Joint Economic Committee subcommittee, no request for funds was made by the Johnson administration and no appropriations were forthcoming from the Subcommittee of the House Appropriations Committee. Significantly, the only voice opposing the development of job vacancy statistics is that of big labor. Mr. Nathaniel Goldfinger, director of research for the AFL-CIO, was the lone dissenter appearing before the subcommittee of the Joint Economic Committee in 1966 and he argued against the compilation of the data solely from the standpoint of its possible misuse. However, also obvious to most economists was labor's vested interest in keeping control of jobs within the established guidelines of unions in being. Some of the theorists in the Research Digest of AFL-CIO also are seeking to protect the assumption of the "new economists" that unemployment is entirely "cyclical" and a result of "inadequate aggregate demand" which would then call for "heavy Federal expenditure programs" to correct.

If unemployment is largely frictional and "structural" then its underlying cause is essentially a lack of training in skills in demand. Inside the House Appropriations Subcommittee, as well as in the Department of Labor pressure was brought to bear by AFL-CIO to defeat the appropriation for the collection of job vacancy data. Now the administration has silently dropped the request.

In order to develop proper manpower policy, two things must be borne in mind about our dynamic economy. First, the economy grows and often veers sharply from the past by creating new jobs, not simply more jobs of the same kind. It has been creating skilled job needs which usually are not entirely filled—while at the same time it has been eliminating jobs at the lower end of the ladder of skills. Unfortunately, public emphasis has been placed almost entirely on the jobs that have been eliminated. The perfectly understandable cries of despair when an old factory closes down have been drowning out the busy sounds of work where a modern one has opened.

A second major concept that must be borne in mind is that there is in the economy a "ladder of skills" which is continually moving upward carrying the lowest level along with it. Job training programs must be alert to its movement to insure that the maximum number of workers can be aboard. There is really no problem of job reduction due to automation in the large sense. Automation creates more—and better—jobs than it destroys. Those who persistently resist these facts ignore the new jobs that a new age has created, and concentrate angrily, wistfully and confusedly, on the jobs at the lower end of the hiring scale that are being eliminated.

This is not to say that those with little training or none at all should not receive attention. They definitely should. Yet those unskilled individuals who need help most would be as poorly served by an attempt to leapfrog them immediately to high rungs on the skill ladder as to conclude they are economically useless. Such efforts are doomed to an excruciatingly large percentage of disappointments. Instead the entire job spectrum should be viewed as a whole in order to best aid the man on the bottom rung—or not yet on the ladder at all. When one individual's job becomes vacant by his taking on (through training) a better job, an individual below him on the ladder upgrades himself so that he can move into the spot. The same process of upgrading tends to occur across the whole of an industrial and service landscape. This, in general, is the nature of the process by which adjustments are made involving literally millions of jobs each year. This is true job escalation.

THE HUMAN INVESTMENT ACT

How do we stimulate this job escalation? The recent Republican effort began with Operation Employment in 1961–62, a full scale study under the aegis of the Republican Policy Committee which asked many leading authorities on employment and unemployment from all parts of the nation to prepare papers on the aspects of their expertise. A ground work of theory and data was laid for fully comprehending the problem of structural unemployment and the role of manpower development and training in an advanced industrial economy. This research and scholarship gave the impetus to and was incorporated in the Manpower Development and Training Act of 1962. Unfortunately, partly because of the lack of certain tools needed to administer the MDTA, it has not been as successful as it should be (an up to date Dictionary of Skills is one of the tools which is lacking). Furthermore, other fundamental approaches were also needed.

The Human Investment Act contains a more fundamental approach to manpower training and retraining. As such it has broad support from Republicans and many others. Republican members totaling 109 in the House and Senate sponsored the bill in the 89th Congress, including all twelve members of the joint House-Senate Republican leadership. In the 90th Congress this number swelled to over 130 House members and 29 Senators.

The Human Investment Act is premised upon the fact that

the most effective job trainer in the nation is the private sector of the free enterprise economy. Business and labor, working together, have consistently been able to conceive and develop sound training programs superior in quality to—without the inefficiency inherent in—government-operated programs. Business has recognized that a rapidly advancing technology requires continuous programs of training and retraining. It conducts formal as well as informal training during business hours or after work in plants, offices, and classrooms. Instruction is provided by skilled supervisors or outside experts and teachers. No one else is as capable of teaching the skills business needs and of teaching those skills well.

Furthermore, businesses will actually assist in paying part—and sometimes all—of the tuition costs of night school or vocational school. This is all directed along the line of upgrading the skills of our people.

The Human Investment Act seeks to encourage training by providing a tax credit of ten percent for various allowable training expenses. Among these expenses are wages and salaries of enrollees in on-the-job training programs under the Manpower Development and Training Act, or under cooperative education programs. Tax credits are also allowed on tuition or course fees paid to a college, business, trade, or vocational school. These can include expenses for home study courses. In addition, and most consistent with the philosophy of this bill, the taxpayer-employer can obtain a tax benefit for the expenses of an employee training program shaped particularly to his specific needs. The bill includes expenses for the taxpayer's own training program; or, if his business is too small for this to be feasible, the bill allows a credit against the expenses of a training program contracted by him but run by another taxpayer. Another tax credit specifically includes trade associations, apprenticeship committees, joint labor management groups, and similar organizations.

The virtue of this approach over institutionalized programs lies in its flexibility to the employer and encouragement to the trainee. A businessman knows what skills he needs and how best to train a man for these skills. The employee in turn knows that the skill he is learning is in demand, and that almost certainly a job awaits him at the completion of his training. Because of the advances in technology, businessmen should be given the freedom to shape their own programs. Also, because lack of assurance of a job puts a trainee in a discouraging psychological limbo, everything possible should be done to make the training mesh with the job.

Frankly, there should be nothing startlingly new about this concept of encouraging upgrading of skills across the board. Industry has been doing it all along. What is new is the vital need for governments to recognize and emphasize it. The Human Investment Act will remove outmoded tax impediments standing in the way of private capital investment in training and retraining. Many workers will be afforded the opportunity to upgrade their skills to a level where their productivity is well above their former job. When an old job becomes vacant, an individual lower on the skill ladder upgrades himself so that he can move into the spot. Again, this is job escalation.

GOOD TAX THEORY

The Human Investment Act, in allowing a 10 percent credit against the expenses by an employer for certain training and retraining, is good tax theory from a number of points of view. First, one of the very important purposes of the Human Investment Act is to remove from the tax code the imbalance which favors machinery over human beings. The 1962 Investment Tax Credit on Machinery—which was abortively suspended and then almost immediately restored by the Johnson administration in early 1967—provides for a 7 percent tax credit against the cost of investment in certain equipment and machinery. If we are going to have a tax credit for capital investment in machines, surely we must do the same for human beings who in this respect are in competition with machines. Capital investment in training human beings should not be made unequal in favor of capital investment in machines. This is particularly inappropriate in an economy where training and retraining are already lagging behind the accelerated pace of automation.

The Human Investment Act 10 percent credit for training expenses is in contrast to the 7 percent allowed for machinery in the 1962 Investment Credit Act. The reason for this apparent disparity stems from the fact that an employer who invests in an employee's training has no title over the employee, unlike the title he has over the new machine, and may lose his investment to another firm. This risk requires some differential. The question is whether the 3 percent additional is sufficient differential and not whether there needs to be a differential.

The second reason why the Human Investment Act is good tax theory is because it is in accord with what I term the "neutralist" and classical tax theory. This theory holds that we should not tax money spent for a beneficial social purpose which if not so spent the government would have to spend. A prime historical example in our Federal income tax code are the tax deductions for charitable contributions to hospitals, schools and community chest agencies etc. Many Republicans and I have proposed other tax exemptions or credits where the federal government has determined a social need to be important by adopting direct governmental expenditure programs. These proposals range from a tax credit for expenses of higher education to credits for expenses borne by industry for the installation of air and water pollution equipment.

According to classical tax theory these suggested provisions should not be looked upon as tax *benefits* to the particular taxpayers involved, but are more realistically viewed as the government's efforts to remove tax *impediments* to expenditures for important social activities. For this reason opponents of the Human Investment Act who charge that it represents a tax subsidy of the business community are off base even if they fail to view it as the counterpart of what has already been given to business in the 7 percent tax credit for investment in machinery. If we do not remove, at least in part, the tax impediment to employee training and retraining, government funds will have to be spent for programs that do a much less efficient job with much less beneficial results.

The third reason why this proposal is sound tax theory is that it sets forth what Republicans have been arguing for a long time—that expenses for training, retraining, and education are, and should be looked upon as capital expenditures. As such they should be taxed as capital expenditures. Education and training investments in our citizens is a capital investment for which over the lifetime of the individual great returns will be paid.

The Human Investment Act is focused upon the employers' expenses for job training and retraining. This is sound and suggests immediately the counterpart of removing the burden of taxation on money spent for training and education borne by the taxpayer-trainee himself. The correlation between the amount of education and training a person gets and the amount of income he will then receive has been clearly established. Money invested in education can be paid off as a relatively small percentage of the increased earnings the person obtains from the education. Society as well as the individual benefits from this process.

Attention should be paid to the concept of spreading income anticipated in the future to cover the costs experienced during the period when an individual is learning his trade or profession. An individual's needs and wants do not conform to those forty-five years of his life (age twenty to sixty-five) when he is gainfully employed. Our tax laws should recognize this and be updated to facilitate income averaging and particularly capital expenditures for education and training by allowing the costs thereof to be treated as capital expenditures.

Our society, based as it is on the theory that men should be permitted to rise to the limits of their abilities and initiatives, is not well served by an economic and tax system that permits only those who have assisting parents or inheritance to gain the necessary funds to get the education they can absorb. Nor is it well served by the alternative system of having a political bureaucracy set up a system of endowments and scholarships and select through whatever procedures they might develop who shall be more fully trained and educated and who shall not. Allowing a person to capitalize his educational and training expenditures with the assistance of consumer credit mechanisms and then to deduct the cost as return of capital from his future earnings, may be a way out of this dilemma.

An important beginning toward the goal of capitalization of educational expenses in the specific area of vocational training is the Human Investment Act. The Human Investment Act calls for a partnership of business and labor, working together, to identify the great variety of jobs becoming available in our dynamic economy and to develop intelligent manpower training programs to meet these increasing demands for skills. It calls for a re-examination of the most beneficial and efficient role for the federal government. And most of all, it calls for faith in ourselves—management, the working man, blue collar or white collar, and the labor union —to persevere in our efforts for job escalation which can be accomplished without decisions emanating from bureaucratic authority in Washington but from actions originating in the broad base of the pyramid of America's economic and political strength—in the heart and soul of a strong and free people.

THE CASE FOR THE NEGATIVE INCOME TAX

by *Milton Friedman*

MILTON FRIEDMAN is Paul S. Russell Distinguished Service Professor of Economics at the University of Chicago. He is also a member of the research staff of the National Bureau of Economic Research. Professor Friedman received his B.A. from Rutgers University, his M.A. from the University of Chicago, and his Ph.D. from Columbia University. A frequent contributor to professional economic and statistical journals, Professor Friedman is also the author or co-author of many books, the most recent of which are *Essays in Positive Economics* (1953), *A Theory of the Consumption Function* (1957), *A Program for Monetary Stability* (1960), *Price Theory* (1962), *Capitalism and Freedom* (1962) and *A Monetary History of the United States, 1867–1960* (1963). Professor Friedman has been a member of the Board of Editors of the American Economic Review and was elected President of the American Economic Association for 1967.

A minimum annual income is now guaranteed by government to all U.S. residents. In some states, Illinois and New York, for example, the guarantee is explicit: the law provides that individuals or families are entitled to receive payments from the state to make up the deficiency between other sources of income and the amount required to support some specified standard of life. In other states, and I believe in most of them, the law does not explicitly guarantee a minimum income. But the complex of welfare and assistance programs financed by the federal, state, and local governments do provide such a guarantee in fact.

The existence of such a governmentally guaranteed minimum is a justifiable source of both pride and dismay.

It is a source of pride because the existence of the guarantee and even more the level of the guarantee testify to the success of our economic and political system in providing higher levels of living to all and especially to the relatively disadvantaged among us.

The level of support guaranteed to persons dependent on governmental assistance is low by the standards of affluent America. But it is high by any absolute standard. It provides a level of living higher than that attained today by the great majority of the world's population, a level that most of them regard as simply unattainable. It provides a level of living higher than that attained by most U.S. residents a few generations earlier. Today's poverty standard is yesterday's standard of comfort if not opulence.

A competitive enterprise system has proved the greatest engine mankind has yet discovered for producing economic development and progress and for eliminating low incomes. But a low income is not the same as poverty. Poverty is a relative concept. Economic progress and development have not and will not eliminate poverty. And this is something to be proud of, not something to be deplored. It is a sign of our affluence that we regard as poverty what in other circumstances we would regard as abundance. It is a fine thing that a society in which the condition of the ordinary citizen is improving and reaching levels hitherto deemed unattainable should set itself higher standards for the relatively less advantaged, even though the less advantaged have a higher absolute income than their counterparts at an earlier date.

PRESENT PROGRAMS

The existence of a governmentally guaranteed minimum is a source of dismay, as well as pride, because the present welfare programs that provide the guarantee are such a mess. They are costly, inefficient, destructive of the pride, self-reliance, and incentive of the people helped, and interfere seriously with the effective operation of the economic system.

Direct Relief and Aid to Dependent Children

The most obvious components of the present *de facto* guaranteed minimum income are direct relief and aid to dependent children.

These programs have at least one merit: the people who are assisted for the most part have lower incomes than the people who pay the taxes to finance the programs. This may seem like a trivial or obvious merit. But it is not. Of the great host of so-called welfare programs in the U.S., these are the only programs which unambiguously benefit people with lower incomes than they burden. For some other programs, like social security, the redistributive effect is uncertain, for still others, like urban renewal and agricultural price supports, the programs quite clearly benefit people with higher incomes than those who pay the cost.

Offsetting this great merit, the present direct relief and aid to dependent children programs have major flaws. For one thing, they have the worst possible effects on incentives. If a person on relief earns a dollar, and obeys the law, his or her relief payment is reduced by a dollar. Since working generally involves costs—if only for better or different clothes—the effect is to penalize industry or honesty or both. These programs therefore tend to produce poor people, and a permanent class of poor people living on welfare, rather than to help the unavoidably indigent.

No less important are the effects of these programs on the personal freedom and dignity of both the persons being helped and the bureaucracy administering the programs. To qualify for assistance, a man or woman must submit to a detailed and personal examination of his or her circumstances, resources, relatives, and so on. Once on assistance, a government official tells the recipient how much he or she may spend for food, rent, and clothing. He or she must get permission from an official to rent a different apartment, to buy second-hand furniture, to make a deposit with the gas company. Mothers receiving aid for dependent children may have their male visitors checked on by government investigators at any time of the day or night. We are providing material help to the people on welfare—but we are also depriving them of personal liberty, freedom, and dignity.

The taxpayer who pays the bill to support people on relief has the moral and legal right to see to it that the money is spent for designated purposes. But it seems to me neither prudent nor noble for him to exercise this right. The major effect is simply to weaken the self-reliance of the recipients, diminish their humanity, and make them wise in the stratagems for evading the spirit of the restrictions imposed on them. And the effect on the administrators is no more salutary. Instead of bringing aid and counsel to the poor, the welfare workers become detectives and policemen; enemies to be outwitted. That is a major reason why it is so hard for large cities to staff their welfare agencies and why they experience such high turnover.

It would be far better to give the indigent money and let them spend it according to their values. True, they may spend much of it in ways we disapprove of—but they do now, and not all the red-tape in Washington will keep them from finding ways of doing so. If we spent the same amount on the poor in total, they would have more to spend—because of savings in administrative costs—and they would get more satisfaction per dollar spent—because they would waste less in circumventing the bureaucracy and would use the money for what they value most. In addition, at least some would grow in the course of making their own decisions and would develop habits of independence and self-reliance. And surely, if social workers are hired on government funds they should devote their energies to helping the indigent, not spying on them.

Other Welfare Programs

The direct relief and aid to dependent children programs are only the tip of the welfare iceberg. There is a maze of detailed governmental programs that have been justified on welfare grounds—though typically their product is illfare: public housing, urban renewal, old age and unemployment insurance, job training, the host of assorted programs under the mislabeled "war on poverty," farm price supports, and so on at incredible length.

Estimates of how much we are now spending on welfare programs vary widely depending on what specific programs are included. A modest estimate, which excludes entirely veterans' benefits and educational expenditures, is that federal, state and local governments are spending more than $50 billion a year. Of this total, only about $7 to $8 billion goes for direct relief and aid to dependent children. Much of the rest of the money is simply wasted—as in the agricultural programs. And most of it goes to people who cannot by any stretch of the imagination be classified as poor.

The welfare iceberg includes also measures that do not require direct government expenditures, except for enforcement. The most obvious is minimum wage rate legislation. Other items are the Walsh-Healy and Davis-Bacon Acts—which require government contractors to pay "standard" wages to their employees on both government and non-government work and thereby introduce governmentally set minimum wages for many categories of employees—and the whole range of legislation conferring special immunities on trade unions.

Though such legislation is always enacted in the name of helping the disadvantaged, its *effect* is to increase the number of indigent people. The minimum wage rate, for example, prices many unskilled workers out of the market and is the major explanation, in my judgment, for the tragically high unemployment rate among teenagers, especially Negro teenagers. These measures involve a confusion between *wage-rate* and *family income*. Persons who are capable of earning only low wage-rates are for the most part youngsters or extra family members whose earnings supplement those of the main breadwinner. But even where the worker is the main breadwinner, it is surely better that he be free to earn what little he can than that he be unemployed, and better that if government funds are to be used to aid him, they be used to supplement his earnings, not to replace them.

THE NEGATIVE INCOME TAX

There is a far better way to guarantee a minimum annual income to all than our present grab-bag of programs. That way is to use the mechanism by which we collect the bulk of our taxes, namely, the personal income tax. At one time, citizens were required to contribute to the support of the commonwealth by payments in kind—forced collections of food or timber or forced labor on public projects. That is still the rule in many backward areas and is widely practiced in all totalitarian countries. Both freedom and efficiency were fostered by substituting taxes in money for taxes in kind.

In our welfare programs, we are back in the earlier era, dispensing largess in kind, or trying to, and examining the detailed physical circumstances of the recipient. Here, too, the route to progress is to substitute payments in money for payments in kind and the single numerical means test of income for the ambiguous means tests we now use.

I have termed this device for helping the poor a *negative income tax* in order to stress its identity in concept and operation with the present income tax. The essential idea is to extend the income tax by supplementing the income of the poor by a *fraction* of their unused income tax exemptions and deductions.

Under present law, a family of four is entitled to exemptions and deductions of not less than $3000 (precisely this sum if the family uses the standard deduction). If such a family has a total income of $3000 it pays no tax. If it has a total pre-tax income of $4000 (and uses the standard deduction), it has a *positive* taxable income of $1000. At the current tax rate for that bracket of 14 percent, it pays $140 a year in taxes, leaving it with $3860 in income after taxes (see table). If such a family had a total pre-tax income of $2000, it would have unused exemptions and deductions of $1000, or in other words, it would have a *negative* taxable income of $1000 [$2000–$3000]. Under present law, it gets no benefit from those unused exemptions and deductions. Under a negative income tax, it would be entitled to receive a payment, the amount depending on the tax rate.

If the tax rate were the same as for the first bracket of positive income, or 14 percent, it would be entitled to receive $140, leaving it with a post-tax income of $2140. If the tax rate were 50 percent, the highest rate that seems to me at all feasible, and the one I have used for illustrative purposes, it would be entitled to receive $500, leaving it with a post-tax income of $2500.

If the family had a zero pre-tax income, it would have a negative taxable income of $3000. With a 50 percent rate, it would be entitled to receive $1500 leaving it with a post-tax income of $1500.

EXAMPLE OF INCOME TAX INCORPORATING 50 PERCENT
RATE ON NEGATIVE TAXABLE INCOME
(Family of four; existing exemptions and standard deduction;
existing rates on positive income)

Total income before tax	Exemptions and deductions	Taxable income	Tax rate	Tax	Income after tax
0	$3,000	$-3,000	50%	$-1,500	$1,500
1,000	3,000	-2,000	50%	-1,000	2,000
2,000	3,000	-1,000	50%	- 500	2,500
3,000	3,000	0			3,000
4,000	3,000	+1,000	14%	+ 140	3,860

For each size of family, this plan defines *two* incomes: the *break-even* income, at which the family pays no tax and receives no payment—in the example, $3000—and the *minimum guaranteed* income—in the example, $1500.[1] For different

---

[1] Note that under present laws, negative taxable income could be more than $3000, since a taxpayer who uses actual rather than standard deductions could have exemptions plus deductions of more than $3000. This is a point that deserves much more

sizes of families, these incomes are different, both the break-even income and the minimum guaranteed income being higher, the larger the size of the family.[2]

As a practical matter, payments under the negative income tax could not wait for an accurate determination of the amount due, since that would mean postponing payments until after the end of the year. Here again, the situation is precisely the same as under our present personal income tax and the same devices would be used. Wage-earners now have taxes deducted at source throughout the year. Recipients of other incomes now file advance estimates of anticipated income and make advance payments of estimated taxes. Both groups reconcile payments with amounts due after the end of the year. Similarly, under a negative income tax, wage earners who are entitled to payments because they receive wages less than the break-even amount would receive their extra payments along with their wages. Others would file estimates of anticipated income and anticipated amounts to which they

---

attention than it has received. On the one hand, it offers the possibility of introducing a desirable flexibility into the program. For example, it would offer a far better way than medicare or socialized medicine to finance by tax funds abnormal medical costs: simply permit such costs to continue, as now, to be a deduction in computing income. On the other hand, this point gives still more importance to undesirable deductions and exclusions under the present income tax. Such deductions and exclusions mean that a family with high income from tax-exempt sources or with large deductions could not only avoid tax as it now does but could also qualify for subsidies.

[2] With a 50 percent rate on negative taxable income, and present law with respect to exemptions and standard deductions, these are as follows:

Family size	Guaranteed minimum income	Break-even income
1	$ 450	$ 900
2	800	1,600
3	1,150	2,300
4	1,500	3,000
5	1,850	3,700
6	2,200	4,400

are entitled, and would receive their payments at regular intervals—weekly, or biweekly, or monthly—throughout the year. Again, there would be a reconciliation at the end of the year.

To facilitate advance estimates, and revisions of estimates, use could be made of local post offices or perhaps social security offices to supplement internal revenue offices. However, the whole program would be administered by the Internal Revenue Service as part and parcel of its administration of the regular personal income tax.

In effect, the addition of the negative income tax would require everyone to file an income tax return. This universal filing requirement would have the incidental advantage that it would improve the administration of the positive income tax, making it easier to check evasion of the tax.[3]

There are many other details that would have to be worked out in an operating negative income tax—definition of the family unit, treatment of items like charitable receipts and welfare payments in computing negative taxable income, and so on. All these are problems that now arise under the positive tax. The general rule should be to follow precisely the same rules in computing negative as in computing positive taxable incomes. There appear to be no special problems peculiar to the negative income tax.[4]

ADVANTAGES OF THE NEGATIVE INCOME TAX

The negative income tax would guarantee a minimum income while at the same time avoiding most of the defects of present welfare programs.

1. *It concentrates public funds on the poor.* By comparison

[3] It is interesting to note that in the 1930s, when Pierre S. Dupont was tax commissioner of the State of Delaware and was subsidizing the office out of his own pocket, he introduced universal filing solely for the purpose of reducing evasion of the state income tax.

[4] Many of these problems are discussed in detail in Christopher Green, *Negative Taxes and the Poverty Problem,* The Brookings Institution, 1967.

with the host of present programs, the negative income tax has the great virtue that it would concentrate public funds on supplementing the incomes of the poor—not distribute funds broadside in the hope that some will trickle down to the poor. It would help people because they are poor, not because they are old or disabled or unemployed or farmers or tenants of public housing. No doubt, these characteristics are often associated with poverty, but the association is very far from perfect.

2. *It treats indigent as responsible individuals, not incompetent wards of the state.* By giving help in the form of money by the objective impersonal criterion of income, the negative income tax would give the indigent responsibility for their own welfare, and thereby promote the development of habits of independence and self-reliance.

3. *It gives indigent an incentive to help themselves.* Present direct assistance programs in effect embody a 100 percent tax rate on additional income of people receiving assistance: for every dollar earned, their assistance payments are reduced by one dollar. There has come to be wide recognition of the serious disincentive effects of this arrangement and numerous suggestions have been made to avoid this effect. For example, New York City is experimenting with a program whereby welfare recipients will be permitted to keep a flat amount of outside earnings plus a fraction of earnings above that flat amount without reducing their welfare benefits. All such proposals linked to present direct assistance programs have a fatal defect: two individuals holding the same job at the same salary may have different total incomes because one was on welfare before getting the job, while the other was employed throughout. The first will be getting welfare payments to add to his income; the second will not. This is highly inequitable and is likely to be productive of much justifiable objection on the part of low income people who have managed to support themselves.

The negative income tax with a fractional rate is the only way so far proposed that treats all equally while at the same time maintaining an incentive for the indigent to help themselves by small and gradual steps. At the 50 percent rate used for illustration, recipients of aid would keep 50 cents out of every additional dollar earned. This is less of an incentive, of course, than if they could keep the whole dollar, but far more of an incentive than exists at present when they can keep nothing. For incentive purposes, it would be desirable to have as low a rate as possible, but this objective has to be balanced against the need to provide a tolerable level of income maintenance. Under present income tax exemptions, any rate very much lower than 50 percent would cut negative income tax payments to so low a level that they would not provide a major alternative to present assistance programs.[5]

4. *It would cost less than present programs yet help indigent more.* Because the negative income tax is directed specifically at poverty, it would both help the indigent more and yet cost far less than our present collection of programs. As noted we are now spending over $50 billion a year on all welfare programs of which some $7 to $8 billion is going for public assistance (direct relief, aid to dependent children, old age assistance, aid to the blind, and to the permanently and totally disabled). The gross cost of the 50 percent plan outlined above would be somewhat greater than the amount we are now spending on direct assistance programs but only about a fifth of the total amount that we are now spending on all welfare programs.[6] Clearly, the elimination of public assistance plus only a modest reduction in other programs would be enough to finance that particular negative income tax with no net cost. Yet that plan would make most of the needy better off than they are under present programs.

Moreover, these figures greatly overestimate the net cost. They make no allowance for the effect of the greater incen-

[5] I would prefer much higher exemptions and a lower rate, but that would require major reform of the positive income tax. Though desirable in its own right, that is a separate issue.

[6] Christopher Green estimated for 1964 that the cost of the 50 percent plan would be $7 to $9 billion (if public assistance payments are excluded from the income base used in calculating taxable income), compared with public assistance payments in that year of $5.1 billion. *Op. cit.*

tive to earn income on either the number of the needy or the amount of income subject to positive tax. And they make no allowance for the increased receipts under the positive income tax from the reduction of evasion as a result of universal filing of tax returns.

5. *It eliminates bureaucracy and political slush fund.* The negative income tax would enable us to eliminate almost entirely the cumbrous and expensive welfare bureaucracy that is required for present programs. The worthy people who now staff that bureaucracy could devote their talents to more useful activity. The possibility of using the bureaucracy for political patronage would be eliminated. A related advantage is that the negative income tax cannot be used as a political slush fund, as so many current programs—notably in the war on poverty—can be and have been used.

OBJECTIONS TO THE NEGATIVE INCOME TAX

A number of objections have been raised to the negative income tax—by both the left and the right. Most of these seem to me to arise either from misunderstanding or utopianism.

1. *The negative income tax removes a means test.* One frequent objection is that, by making the receipt of payments a matter of right, the negative income tax eliminates any means test and introduces a new principle in the relation between citizens and the government.

This is simply a misunderstanding. The negative income tax retains a means test, but the test is the single straightforward numerical test of income not the present complex. It uses the same means test for deciding who shall receive assistance as we now use to decide who shall pay the expenses of government.

Similarly, the negative income tax introduces no new principle. As noted at the outset, we now have in fact though not always in law, a governmentally guaranteed minimum.

2. *The negative income tax destroys incentive.* Some proponents of a guaranteed annual income have proposed in

effect a negative income tax at a rate of 100 percent. They
have proposed that the government fill the gap between some
specified income level and the actual income of each family,
thereby making the break-even income and the minimum guaranteed income identical. Such plans would indeed destroy incentive. They retain the worst feature of the present direct
assistance program but would be far more costly because they
eliminate the features of present programs that discourage
applicants for welfare. I regard such plans as thoroughly irresponsible, undesirable, and impractical.

Though superficially similar to a negative income tax,
such a plan is in fact radically different—just as a positive income tax levied at a 100 percent rate differs radically from
one levied at a fractional rate.

A negative income tax at a fractional rate, as already
stressed, gives greater incentives to earn income than our
present programs, which mostly have an implicit 100 percent
rate. Compared with a hypothetical world in which there are
no government welfare programs at all, the negative income
tax, even at a fractional rate, would indeed weaken incentive.
But, whether desirable or not, that is not our world and there
is not the remotest chance that it will be in the foreseeable
future. Those, like myself, who would like to see the role of
government reduced, only harm our own cause by evaluating
a program by such an unreal standard.

3. *The negative income tax cannot be adjusted to the specific
needs of each indigent family.* This is of course entirely true.
The question is whether it is an objection. A federal negative
income tax is being proposed as a general nationwide program to set a floor under the incomes of the disadvantaged.
But conditions differ widely from state to state and even within
states. Prices vary, so that it requires different sums of money
to purchase the same level of living. Average income varies,
so does the level of living that is regarded as a poverty level,
and so also the economic capacity of the communities to assist the less fortunate. These variations are reflected now in
the wide differences among states in the levels of assistance
given under present programs—differences that seem to me
much too wide. The negative income tax with a 50 percent

rate would establish a nationwide minimum standard well above the level now achieved in many, probably most states. It would be well below the level now achieved in some of the wealthier states.

However, it is designed to provide a nationwide program. There is nothing to prevent states from supplementing the benefits paid under the negative income tax out of state funds, and there is every reason to encourage them to do so. The best way for them to do so, I believe, would be to enact a supplementary state negative income tax, just as they now have supplementary state positive income taxes. They could have different exemptions and different rates but they could, as many now do under the positive income tax, coordinate state enforcement with federal enforcement.

Undoubtedly, there would also be special problems within each city or state. Being general and impersonal, the negative income tax cannot be adapted to cases of special hardship, and no doubt such cases would exist. However, by providing a basic minimum, it would reduce such cases to a manageable number, which could be taken care of by supplementary state programs or, preferably, by private charity. One of the great costs of the proliferation of governmental welfare programs is the elimination of a basic role for private charity, with its flexibility, diversity, and adaptability. An indirect advantage of the negative income tax is that it would provide an important place for private charity to serve precisely that function which private agencies can serve best—handling the special case.

4. *The negative income tax would be divisive.* The objection has sometimes been made that, by dividing the community into those who receive checks from the government and those who send checks, the negative income tax would fragment the community. Clearly, this objection has no force at all if the negative income tax is compared with present programs. They are far worse in this respect. However, the objection is raised mostly by proponents of family allowances.[7] They

---

[7] It was brought to my attention by Daniel P. Moynihan in oral comments at a recent conference on problems of social welfare.

argue that giving a straight cash subsidy to parents of all children in proportion to the number of children would unify the community by comparison with a negative income tax. Yet, they say, the economic effect would be similar, since, if the family allowance is included in taxable income, much of it would be recovered from higher income families in the form of additional taxes.

A negative income tax is partly a family allowance, since large families have higher exemptions under the income tax than small families and so would receive larger benefits for any given family income. However, it gives a family allowance only to families defined as needy, not to all families.

In principle, there always exists a universal subsidy (sometimes called a "social dividend") plus a tax system that would produce identically the same results as a negative income tax. For example, consider the illustrative 50 percent negative income tax plan. The equivalent universal subsidy (or family allowance plan) would be a subsidy to each family equal to the break-even income under that plan, inclusion of the subsidy in taxable income, elimination of the present minimum exemptions and deductions under the income tax, and a tax rate of 50 percent on an initial bracket equal to the break-even income. Each and every family would be in the same position as under the negative income tax plan when the extra tax is deducted from the subsidy.[8]

The problem in practice is that this system involves mailing out checks to 200 million people in order to help 20 or 40 million, and then having the 160 or 180 million others mail back checks. This is highly inefficient. Equally important, it is complex and confusing politically. It is not clear what is being done. Both administratively and politically, it seems to me far better to net out the payments and extra taxes.

The apparent budgetary cost of even small children's al-

----

[8] To illustrate, a family of four with no other income would receive $3000 as a social dividend, giving it a taxable income of $3000 subject to a tax rate of 50 percent. Its tax would be $1500, leaving it with an after tax income of $1500, just as under the illustrative negative income tax.

lowances is extremely high because checks are being sent to ten families in order really to help one or two. The reverse flow through higher taxes is disguised and uncertain. Hence, any children's or family allowance is likely to be so small as not to permit the elimination of any substantial part of the present welfare programs. The end result would be to add another rag to the bag while retaining the present highly divisive welfare programs. Universal family allowances therefore seem to me undesirable.

5. *The negative income tax would be another rag in the bag.* I have urged the negative income tax as a substitute for existing programs. But, it is said, in practice the negative income tax would simply be piled on other programs and not be a substitute for them, so that the argument I have just made against family allowances applies equally to the negative income tax.

This objection clearly cannot be dismissed out of hand and is, indeed, in my opinion, the most weighty of those I have listed. There is a tendency in government for old programs never to die, or even to fade away, but simply to be continued, whatever their success in meeting the problem for which they were enacted. If they are failures, the only effect is that still more programs are enacted.

One not very satisfactory answer to this objection is that it is a counsel of despair. If those of us who regard governmental programs in any area as bad do not fight for better programs as a substitute, but simply engage in delaying actions, then the objection is certain to be valid. That course of action makes it a self-fulfilling prophecy.

In the present instance, as it happens, I believe there is a more satisfactory answer to the objection than this general answer. While the negative income tax is unlikely to be adopted as a substitute for *all* welfare programs—as I should prefer—it does seem to me highly likely to be accepted as a substitute for the direct public assistance programs. There are two reasons why this seems to me so. The first is that the defects of those programs—particularly direct relief and aid to dependent children—are so great, so glaring, and so widely recognized, that there is a desire in every part of the political spectrum to find a substitute for them. The second is that the usual bastion of an existing program—the pressure group formed by the bureaucracy administering it and by the people who can use it for patronage—is less potent in this instance than usual. It is less potent because the mass of jobs are so unattractive that it is hard to fill them. The turnover is high and there are few patronage plums.

Despite these favorable conditions, the negative income tax may not be introduced as a complete substitute for the direct public assistance programs. But even then, it is likely to be used as a partial substitute and it is almost certain to be a substitute for other additions to the program. The political reality may be that the programs will be expanded in one way or another. If so, far better that it be in this way.

Finally, we must look to the future. Whatever may be the original intent, I believe that a negative income tax will be so much more effective than current programs that, in the course of time, it would increasingly replace them, in the process diminishing the problem toward which all of the programs are directed.

6. *The negative income tax will foster political irresponsibility.* If we adopt an open and above board program for supplementing the incomes of people below some specified level, will there not be continued political pressure for higher and higher break-even incomes, for higher and higher rates on negative income? Will the demagogues not have a field day appealing to the have-nots to legislate taxes on the haves for transfer to them?

Clearly these dangers exist. But, like the incentive question, they must be evaluated in terms of the world as it is, not in terms of a dream world in which there are no governmental welfare measures. The relevant political question is whether the negative income tax is more susceptible to these dangers than alternative programs of the kind we now have or are likely to get.

When I first proposed in print the negative income tax, I wrote that it might well be more susceptible to these dangers than other programs.[9] As I have thought further about the subject, and have participated in the public discussion of the proposal, I have been led to change this opinion. I now believe that there are strong reasons to believe that the negative income tax is less susceptible than other proposals to the political dangers.

Because the negative income tax is intimately linked with the general income tax structure, there is no way to raise the break-even incomes without raising the exemption for tax purposes, which clearly requires a higher rate on incomes above the exemption. The cost of the payments is in one lump sum that can be calculated and that will be painfully obvious to every taxpayer. It will be obvious that every rise in the rate applied to negative taxable income raises the cost. Finally, the negative income tax does not, as do other welfare programs, generate a large bureaucracy that has an interest in expanding the program and it cannot be used as a political slush fund.

CONCLUSION

The problem we face in the welfare area is to halt the proliferation of the bad programs we now have and ultimately to dismantle them. But while these programs are on the whole bad, more or less incidentally they do help some people who are disadvantaged. Can we in good conscience mount a political attack on them unless we can provide an alternative way to achieve the small amount of help they do provide the disadvantaged? Can we be effective, unless we have a satisfactory answer to the inevitable charge that we are heartless and want to let the poor starve? And would we not be guilty of the charge, if we had no alternative? Most of these programs should never have been enacted. But they have been enacted and they now must be dismantled gradually, both to

[9] See Milton Friedman, *Capitalism and Freedom* (University of Chicago Press, 1962), p. 192.

promote social stability and because the government has a responsibility to meet commitments it has entered into.

The negative income tax offers a way to replace the existing programs gradually. As a proposal, it offers a platform from which an effective political attack can be launched on existing undesirable programs. Once in operation, it would assure assistance to the needy now getting help under present programs, and so make it feasible to repeal them or permit them to wither away as current commitments are met. Once in operation, too, it would remove the specious excuse now offered for every suggested expansion of the federal authority —that it is "needed" to help one or another disadvantaged group.

These are the negative advantages, as it were, of the negative income tax. The positive case for it is no less strong. "It is directed specifically at the problem of poverty. It gives help in the form most useful to the individual, namely, cash. It is general and could be substituted for the host of special measures now in effect. It makes explicit the cost borne by society. It operates outside the market. Like any other measure to alleviate poverty, it reduces the incentives of those helped to help themselves, but it does not eliminate the incentive entirely, as a system of supplementing incomes up to some fixed minimum would,"[10] and it reduces incentives less than other measures that are now in operation or that have been suggested. Finally, it treats all members of the community alike, with a single impersonal means test for all, the same for those who in a particular year pay taxes and for those who in that year receive benefits.

[10] Quoted from *Capitalism and Freedom, op. cit.,* p. 192.

APPENDIX TO CHAPTER 3

LETTER FROM MELVIN LAIRD TO THE PRESIDENT OF
THE UNITED STATES ON THE HUMAN INVESTMENT ACT

August 31, 1967

The Honorable Lyndon B. Johnson
President of the United States
The White House
Washington, D. C.

My dear Mr. President:

I write this letter reluctantly and with some foreboding lest
it be interpreted as partisan in nature. Nothing could be further from my intentions, but events of recent weeks here in
our nation compel me to transmit my thoughts to you.

We are all sick at heart over the turmoil and disruption that
has marked many of the cities in our nation during these past
three summers. This turmoil has given rise to charges and
countercharges from all levels of government and from all
sides of the political spectrum concerning the continuing
breakdown in our society. Debate has raged around the question of whose lack of foresight and action has been primarily
to blame.

All of us, I think, can agree that it is time to shift the
emphasis from debate to action, that it is time to stop seeking
scapegoats and start implementing solutions.

The Urban Coalition which met here in Washington last
week had this to say in its "Statement of Principles, Goals, and
Commitments:"

Confronted by these catastrophic events (the riots of

the past three summers), we, as representatives of business, labor, religion, civil rights, and local government, have joined in this Convocation *to create a sense of national urgency* on the need for positive action for all of the people of our cities. (emphasis added)

Mr. President, I applaud the efforts of the Urban Coalition, as I am sure you do, for attempting to create the "sense of national urgency" that is so vitally needed.

Unfortunately, they—like all other segments of our society save perhaps the Presidency itself—operate at a distinct handicap when it comes to translating this "sense of national urgency" into meaningful and effective action.

Mr. President, we have already had three summers of growing turbulence in our cities—each one worse than the one before. Yet, we continue to delay immediate action on the apparent premise that the nation is incapable of action without specific statutory authority from the Congress.

The Urban Coalition itself, demonstrated its recognition—if only a partial one—that the nation can act without necessarily awaiting Congressional Action. Its call for the creation of one million jobs for the presently unemployed with emphasis on private sector activity is worthy of serious consideration.

Frankly, Mr. President, I am more disturbed than I care to admit over the repeated allegations that somehow the nation has been frustrated by Congressional inaction on urban programs.

Your own letter to Senator Mansfield listed 23 programs that have been pending before Congress since January. If Congress gave you tomorrow every cent you requested in those programs, the total amount available for, as you phrase it, "an all-out commitment to . . . our cities" would only be $6.7 billion to be disbursed in varying amounts over many thousands of communities throughout these United States.

Over the past weekend, the nation's press quoted Secretary of Housing and Urban Development Robert Weaver as having taken a "show me" attitude with regard to the recommendations of the Urban Coalition. According to the Baltimore Sun, he said, "I want to know how they're going to get the million jobs."

Your Press Secretary, Mr. Christian, is reported to have said that you are postponing the adoption of any major new recommendations that might emanate from your task forces on urban problems until they can be "unveiled" in next January's State of the Union message. This I cannot bring myself to believe, Mr. President, for I know how deeply you and all Americans desire to get on with the job of building a good society here in America now.

In Syracuse, New York, last August, you yourself warned, "this is no time to delay . . ." in references to the grave problems that face our cities. In your letter to Senator Mansfield on August 16, you said:

> The task before us is immense. But we have charted a beginning—and we have done so with the help of the best and most experienced minds in the nation. I believe the enactment and funding of these programs (the 23 pending before Congress) is the first step in making this commitment a reality for the people of America.

Mr. President, I commend you for the sentiments you expressed in that letter and in the many public statements you have made concerning the grave problems that face our cities. But I would respectfully differ with your conclusion that "the enactment and funding of these programs is *the first step* in making this commitment a reality for the people of America."

We do not have to wait for the enactment of another program or the appropriation of another dollar by Congress in order to get on with the job of reducing the problems we face throughout urban America.

Rather, through enlightened leadership on the part of the President, we could begin immediately toward accomplishing the goal set forth by the Urban Coalition of "putting at least one million of the presently unemployed into productive work at the earliest possible moment."

Specifically, Mr. President, I recommend that you as the

Chief Executive of our great nation call together an emergency conference of all 50 governors, the mayors of at least the major cities if not all of our cities, as well as national leaders in the fields of business, labor, and religion for a very specific purpose.

The primary purpose of such an emergency conference convened by you would be to lend the prestige and persuasive powers of your office to the end that private industry throughout our nation and especially in the larger metropolitan areas would begin immediately to implement a program which, in the words of the Urban Coalition's statement of principle, would "seek out the unemployed and underemployed and enlist them in basic and positive private training and employment programs" for existing jobs in individual enterprises and industries.

Such a conference, convened by you as our Chief Executive would, I am convinced, mobilize this nation and provide the added impetus so necessary to compel the governors and mayors throughout our nation to call their own conferences of key business and civic leaders in their respective states and communities in order to put such a program into effect in the immediate future.

As you know, Mr. President, we in the Minority have urged enactment by the Congress of the Human Investment Act for the past three years. The Human Investment Act would provide a 10% tax credit to industry for the training costs incurred under such a program. However, it is my own view that we need not await legislation by Congress in order to persuade private enterprise throughout our nation to begin implementation of such a program now.

Certainly, I would hope, that we in the Congress and you, as Chief Executive, would pledge early efforts to enact a program similar to the Human Investment Act which would provide tax credits for training costs. However, it is not necessary, in my view, to await such action by Congress before urging private industry to undertake or step up such programs now.

Mr. President, I cannot tell you how deeply I feel the need

for some such action on the part of the Chief Executive of our nation. We all hunger for the kind of decisive leadership only the office of the President can provide and I urge you as President of all the people to undertake such a step now.

With best wishes and kindest personal regards, I am

Sincerely yours,

Melvin R. Laird
Member of Congress

Chapter 4
CIVIL RIGHTS

MAN WAS BORN TO BE FREE:
TOWARD FULFILLMENT OF THE DREAM
by William M. McCulloch

WILLIAM M. MCCULLOCH has represented the 4th District of Ohio in the House of Representatives since 1947. A graduate of the College of Law of The Ohio State University, Mr. McCulloch was a member of the Ohio House of Representatives for six terms, and served as the Republican leader from 1936–39, and as Speaker for three terms.

He is the ranking Republican member of the House Committee on the Judiciary, a member of the Joint Committee on Atomic Energy, and a member of the Joint Committee on Immigration and Nationality Policy. He is currently a member of the Antitrust Subcommittee of the Committee on the Judiciary. Congressman McCulloch is also a member of the President's National Advisory Commission on Civil Disorders. Mr. McCulloch belongs to the American Political Science Association and was a recipient of the Congressional Distinguished Service Award.

The Declaration adopted by the Representatives of the United States of America, in General Congress Assembled, on July 4, 1776, and ever after called the Declaration of Independence, contains this brave and hopeful manifesto:

"We hold these Truths to be self-evident, that all Men

EDITOR'S NOTE: Unlike other papers in this volume, this one focuses on the historical record from the standpoint of the Republican Party's contribution. This was dictated by the current misunderstanding on the part of many concerning Republican policy and attitudes in the field of civil rights. The author is the House member who has had more to do with writing the legislative record in this field than any other man in this century.

are created equal, that they are endowed by their Creator with certain unalienable Rights, that among these are Life, Liberty, and the Pursuit of Happiness—That to secure these Rights, Governments are instituted among Men, deriving their just Powers from the Consent of the Governed. . . ."

Eleven years later the Congress, acting under the Articles of Confederation, adopted the Ordinance of 1787 for the government of the Northwest Territory which had been ceded to the United States by the several states which made up the Confederation.

The drafting and passage of the Ordinance was one of the most effective and far-reaching achievements under the Articles of Confederation. Its chief draftsmen were Rufus Putman and Manasseh Cutler whose efforts and political and economic philosophy had a deep and lasting beneficial influence on the emerging nation, that was soon to become the giant of the Western world, and now the leader of and for free people everywhere.

Article VI of the Ordinance of 1787 foreshadowed the Thirteenth Amendment, as the Supreme Court was to note in 1911 in *Bailey* v. *Alabama*. For Article VI declared that "There shall be neither slavery nor involuntary servitude in the said territory, otherwise than in the punishment of crimes, whereof the party shall have been duly convicted. . . ."

In 1788, The United States in Congress Assembled reported that the Constitution transmitted to the legislatures of the several states had been properly ratified by the required number and that such duly authenticated ratification had been received.

Thereafter, on the 4th day of March, 1789, George Washington, who had been unanimously elected the first President of The United States, took his oath of office. A new nation was born.

Notwithstanding the Declaration of Independence and the Ordinance of 1787, the new nation was so engrossed in becoming strong enough to stay free that the brave and hopeful words of those great documents remained merely words of unfulfilled promise.

Nevertheless at this early date, farsighted men like Franklin and Hamilton were instrumental in founding societies for the abolition of slavery. Thus by the time of Washington's inaugural, abolition societies were operating in seven of the ten states.

REPUBLICANS AND CIVIL RIGHTS: EARLY YEARS

Such societies did not let a nation forget the disparity between its noble preachings and deplorable practices. Thus as passions rose and the pro-slavery forces won a legislative victory with the passage of the Kansas-Nebraska Act of 1854, many people felt it was time to form a new anti-slavery party. A convention was held at Jackson, Michigan, where on July 6, 1854, it was resolved to oppose the extension of slavery and "be known as 'Republicans' until the contest be terminated." Thus, with the avowed purpose of fulfilling the promise of the Declaration of Independence for all the people, the Republican Party was formed.

The first platform of the new party proclaimed that it was "both the right and the duty of Congress to prohibit in the territories those twin relics of barbarism, polygamy and slavery."

Four years later, in 1860, the Republican Party elected their first Presidential candidate, Abraham Lincoln. The slavery issue shortly thereafter drew the nation into civil war.

In April 1862, a Republican Congress passed the District of Columbia Emancipation Act. The bill was sponsored by Henry Wilson, then a Republican Senator from Massachusetts and later Vice-President under Ulysses S. Grant. It was managed by Senator Lot Morrill, a Republican from Maine. The Act abolished slavery in the District of Columbia.

On January 1, 1863, the first Republican president issued the Emancipation Proclamation which abolished slavery in the rebellious states. On February 10, 1864, Lyman Trumbull, a Republican Senator from Illinois, presented a Constitutional

Amendment, based on Article VI of the Ordinance of 1787, which was designed to abolish slavery in all the states. The proposal passed the Senate easily but failed in the House of Representatives.

Lincoln interceded. In his last annual message to Congress in December, 1864, he exhorted the House of Representatives to reconsider its action. It did. The states quickly ratified the proposal which, on December 18, 1865, became the Thirteenth Amendment.

Soon after the ratification of the Thirteenth Amendment on December 18, 1865, Southern states passed a series of laws known as the Black Codes which, in effect, seriously restricted, if they did not completely prevent, the Negro from using and enjoying his civil rights.

To neutralize the Black Codes, certain Republicans in Congress sponsored legislation which stands as a landmark in American history—the Civil Rights Act of 1866. The Act is one of the most comprehensive civil-rights bills ever enacted. It was passed by a Republican Congress that followed Republican leadership. Some of its provisions are still in force today. It provided in part:

> "That all persons born in the United States and not subject to any foreign power, excluding Indians not taxed, are hereby declared to be citizens of the United States, and such citizens, of every race and color, without regard to any previous condition of slavery or involuntary servitude, except as a punishment for crime whereof the party shall have been duly convicted, shall have the same right, in every State and Territory in the United States, to make and enforce contracts, to sue, be parties, and give evidence, to inherit, purchase, lease, sell, hold, and convey real and personal property, and to full and equal benefit of all laws and proceedings for the security of person and property as is enjoyed by white citizens, and shall be subject to like punishment, pains, and penalties, and to none other, any law, statute, ordinance, regulation, or custom to the contrary notwithstanding."

The Act, although noble in purpose, was susceptible to constitutional attack. The Thirteenth Amendment alone provided no support for protecting the Negroes more than the whites against not only state discrimination but also private discrimination as well.

Thus a Republican Congress, again under Republican leadership, passed and proposed a new amendment to the Constitution which history would later prove to be the most important Constitutional amendment, the most frequently employed, and the most far-reaching basis for civil-rights legislation. In fact, today, its reach is still being debated and extended, *e.g. United States* v. *Guest.*

There were several Republican sponsors of the various sections of the proposed amendment. But the sponsor of Section 1, which is the heart of the amendment, was John A. Bingham, a Republican from Ohio.

Thus on June 13, 1866, two months after the enactment of the landmark Civil Rights Act, Congress transmitted the Fourteenth Amendment to the states. Ratification was completed on July 9, 1868.

However, the Negro remained a long way from legal equality. The Republican Party was distressed by Negro disenfranchisement. Consequently, three Republicans—William P. Fessenden of Maine, James G. Blaine of Maine, and John Howard of Michigan—sponsored the Fifteenth Amendment which provided that "the right of citizens of the United States to vote shall not be denied or abridged by the United States or by any State on account of race, color or previous condition of servitude." It was proposed by Congress on February 26, 1869. Ratification was completed on March 30, 1870.

In view of the growing invisible empire of the Ku Klux Klan in the South, the Fifteenth Amendment needed enforcement. Thus John Bingham of Ohio sponsored the Second Enforcement Act which provided federal machinery to supervise elections in the states and which made criminal the discriminatory interference with federal or Constitutional rights. The bill was passed by a Republican Congress on May 31, 1870.

But the continuing success of the Ku Klux Klan made further legislation imperative. Again under Republican leadership a wide-sweeping civil rights bill was enacted by Congress. The Act of April 20, 1871, known as the Ku Klux Klan or Anti-Lynching Act, forbade conspirators to go in disguise upon a public highway to deprive a person of his federal or Constitutional rights. It also forbade individual action under color of law which deprived a person of such rights. Criminal sanctions were provided.

These provisions, sponsored by Representative Samuel Shellabarger, another Republican from Ohio, are still the basis for the prosecution of present-day civil-rights violations.

But the most far-reaching civil rights legislation was yet to come. In 1870, Senator Charles Sumner, a Republican from Massachusetts, introduced a public accommodations bill providing for Negro equality in railroads, steamboats, public conveyances, hotels, theatres, houses of public entertainment, common schools, all institutions of learning authorized by law, churches, cemeteries, and juries in federal and state courts.

The sweep of the bill made many hesitate. But five years later Sumner's diligent efforts bore fruit. On March 1, 1875, a Republican Congress passed the broadest civil rights bill ever. Since it was predicated on the Fourteenth Amendment, not on the Commerce Clause, it was intended to apply to all forms of private discrimination against Negroes seeking to enjoy public accommodations.

However, the 1875 Act marked the high-water mark of the Republican program. In 1876, the Republicans lost the House of Representatives to the Democrats. In 1877, the Democrats tried to repeal certain key civil rights provisions, but the Republican President Hayes vetoed the effort.

Thus on the twenty-fifth anniversary of the Republican Party, it could boast not only that it had fulfilled the purpose of its creation which it declared under the oaks at Jackson, Michigan, but also that it had legislated for the Negroes a comprehensive program of civil rights covering every possible aspect of equality.

However, the sudden revolution in the Negro status which the Republican Party had championed had made the country weary. The diligence necessary for effective enforcement of the civil rights laws was lacking. And moreover, in 1883, the Supreme Court held that the 1875 public accommodations bill could not be supported by the Fourteenth Amendment which merely prohibited discrimination by the states.

Reaction continued. In 1894 a strongly Democratic Congress repealed no less than thirty-nine provisions of the Republican Reconstruction program. Federal protection of Negro voting rights was completely abolished. But this time there was no Republican President in office to veto the measure. The door to the polling booth was now closed to Negroes in the South. It was to remain locked until a Republican President, well over a half century later, gave the Negro a key.

The legislatures of the northern states quickly filed the legislative gaps made by restrictive Supreme Court decisions and the Democratic program of repealing Reconstruction legislation. But at the same time, the southern states, no longer restricted by federal law, continued to repress the Negro.

REPUBLICANS AND CIVIL RIGHTS: MODERN ERA

Resurgence of the civil rights movement had to await a proper time. A global war, a depression, and then another global war forestalled all hopes.

"A time for a change" was the campaign slogan of the Republican Party in 1952. Although some efforts to rejuvenate the Negro cause had been made since 1875, they were all abortive.

One such notable attempt was made by George Bender, an Ohio Republican, who introduced a bill in 1947 to abolish the poll tax as a qualification for voting. On the House floor, Mr. Bender proclaimed:

"Every instinct for justice and political decency cries out

against the existence of" poll tax provisions which "disfranchise 10,000,000 of our citizens—Negro and white alike."

An Illinois Republican, Everett McKinley Dirksen, added his eloquence to the cause, calling the elimination of the poll tax "the unfinished business of this generation." He continued:

"Liberty is always unfinished business. Equality is always unfinished business. So, quite aside from some of the remarks, intemperate and otherwise, that have been made here, one of the great responsibilities and one of the great objectives of the Republican Party since its birth has been equality and freedom. So, this is the unfinished business."

The bill passed the House easily, but the Senate failed to consider the matter. The time was not yet ready.

However, with the election of President Dwight Eisenhower in 1952, the time was near.

On August 13, 1953, President Eisenhower issued Executive Order 10479 to establish a new Government Contract Committee to promote compliance with anti-discrimination clauses in Government contracts.

In 1954, the Supreme Court handed down its historic decision in *Brown* v. *Board of Education* holding unconstitutional a state law providing "separate but equal" schools for Negroes. That decision reawakened the sleeping civil-rights conscience of the nation.

In 1955, President Eisenhower, by Executive Order 10590, established the President's Committee on Government Employment Policy to combat discrimination in federal employment.

In 1956, President Eisenhower, in his State of the Union Message, asked Congress to create a Commission on Civil Rights to investigate charges that "in some localities . . . Negro citizens are being deprived of their right to vote."

On April 9, 1956, the Republican administration submitted to Congress a civil rights program calling for 1) creation of a Civil Rights Commission, 2) creation of a Civil Rights Division in the Justice Department, 3) authority for the federal government to use civil procedures to protect civil rights, and 4) broader statutes to protect voting rights.

The bill passed the House with Republicans voting 168 to 24 in overwhelming favor of it while Democrats voted for it by the slim margin of 111 to 102. However, because of parliamentary maneuvering, the bill never reached the Senate floor.

In 1957, the Congress, under the leadership of the Eisenhower administration, finally passed a civil-rights bill, the first since 1875. The 1957 administration bill covered the four points on which President Eisenhower had requested action the year before. But victory did not come easily because Democratic opposition was substantial. The opposition centered on that section of the bill allowing the Attorney General to file civil suits to enjoin discrimination. That section was torn from the bill by Democratic opposition in the Senate despite Republican efforts to save it.

The Democrats further weakened the bill by forcing through a provision that required trial by jury when a person was charged with violating a court order forbidding discrimination in a voting case. The jury-trial feature was designed to make convictions of civil rights offenders more difficult.

The Republican vote on final passage was as impressive as was the Republican record during debate:

HOUSE	YES	NO
Republican	90%	10%
Democratic	52%	48%
SENATE		
Republican	100%	0%
Democratic	62%	38%

The next significant move came again from President Eisenhower on February 5, 1959. He requested enactment of the following seven-point program.

1) An anti-mob bill, making interference with a federal court school desegregation order a federal crime.

2) An anti-bombing bill, making it a federal crime to cross state lines to avoid prosecution for bombing a church or school.

3) A bill to give the Justice Department the right to inspect voting records and requiring the preservation of those records.

4) Extension of the life of the Civil Rights Commission.

5) A bill to give statutory authority to the President's Committee on Government Contracts.

6) A bill authorizing limited technical and financial aid to areas faced with school desegregation problems.

7) Provision of emergency schooling for children of armed forces personnel in the event public schools were closed by integration disputes.

The Eisenhower administration packaged the first four proposals and the last one together with a key to unlock the door of the polling booth for the Negro. This key was called the Referee Plan. Basically it placed responsibility for safeguarding voting rights in the courts.

Under the Referee Plan, when voting rights were being infringed, the Justice Department would file suit in a federal court seeking to enjoin those who were seeking to deprive the Negro of his right to vote because of his race or color. The Attorney General would also ask the court to determine whether there was a pattern or practice of such discrimination.

If the court made such a determination, the Negroes in the area could request that they be registered through the court. The request would be heard either by a judge or by a court-appointed referee. They would determine whether the Negroes were qualified to vote under state law. If they were, the court would issue voting certificates to the Negroes and would notify the state officials. Any official who refused to comply with the court order was subject to contempt proceedings.

The debate was long and sharp. The Republican stand was

clear; the vote on final passage again indicated which party was the more dedicated to civil rights:

HOUSE	YES	NO
Republican	90%	10%
Democratic	66%	34%
SENATE		
Republican	100%	0%
Democratic	70%	30%

On May 6, 1960, President Eisenhower signed the Civil Rights Act into law.

On August 9, 1960, a bill sponsored by Senator Dirksen of Illinois which incorporated administration proposals 1) to provide federal technical and financial assistance to school districts seeking to desegregate and 2) to accord statutory status for a Commission on Equal Job Opportunity was stricken by the Leadership of the Democratic Party.

The record of the Eisenhower administration closed as the most effective since that of a former West Point general who served as a Republican President, Ulysses S. Grant. Not only had Dwight Eisenhower led the fight for the Civil Rights Acts of 1957 and 1960, but he saw to it that the civil-rights laws were enforced. At long last, a President had given the noble words of our history real meaning.

In fact, for the first time in history, a President had shown his sincerity in espousing civil rights by opening all White House social events to Negroes.

The Eisenhower administration was the first to take steps to eliminate segregation in federally financed housing. Moreover, the Eisenhower administration completed integration in the Armed Forces and in Veterans hospitals. It was also instrumental in eliminating segregation in the nation's capital, in bus and interstate travel, in schools on military posts, and in the ranks of civilian employees at naval bases.

Indeed, the record was clear.

For in the prior three decades there had been forty-nine

significant roll call votes in the House and Senate. The Republicans had voted 81 percent in favor of civil rights legislation whereas the Democrats had voted 58 percent against such legislation.

In 1960, a Democrat was elected to the Presidency. Apparently to preserve party unity, the new administration delayed all requests for civil rights legislation for over two years.

In the meantime, in 1962, both the House and Senate with strong Republican support, in spite of Southern Democratic opposition, adopted a constitutional amendment to abolish the poll tax as a qualification for voting. The poll tax had been long employed in some Southern states as a means of preventing the Negro from voting. The ratification of the amendment in 1964 eliminated that practice in federal elections.

On January 31, 1963, over a score of Republicans introduced civil-rights legislation to make the Civil Rights Commission permanent and to authorize it to investigate vote frauds; to establish a Commission for Equality of Opportunity in Employment with authority to enforce nondiscrimination by federal contractors, by labor unions with members employed on federal contract work, and by employment agencies receiving any federal financial assistance; to authorize the Attorney General to enforce school desegregation by civil actions; to provide federal financial assistance to facilitate school desegregation; and to provide a legal presumption for the courts that any one who has completed the sixth grade is sufficiently literate and intelligent to vote.

The administration could no longer ignore the discrepancies between its platform and its program. A month later, it requested civil rights legislation somewhat more narrow in scope. Notably, it recognized the right to vote, but not the right to have that vote counted. It also ignored the very significant problem of discrimination in labor unions and ignored the need for machinery to eliminate discrimination in employment generally.

On March 28, 1963, several Republican Senators intro-

duced strong civil rights legislation—the Republican response
to the relatively weak administration proposal. The bills sought
to establish procedures for public school desegregation, and
technical and financial assistance to facilitate desegregation;
to prohibit racial discrimination in employment by employers
in interstate commerce having fifty or more employees; to
establish a Commission on Equal Employment Opportunity to
encourage and enforce equal employment opportunity in
federal employment, on federal contracts, and on work financed with federal assistance; to ban literacy tests as a requirement for voter registration for persons having a sixth-
grade education, to outlaw arbitrary standards, practices and
procedures for voter registration, to authorize temporary voter
referees under specific circumstances when a voting case is
pending in court, and to require federal courts to give precedence to voting rights cases; to prohibit racial discrimination
in hotels or motels the business of which affects interstate commerce; to amend the Hospital Survey and Construction Act
by outlawing racial discrimination in hospital facilities con-
structed under state plans.

The administration could not ignore this pressure. In June,
it submitted a broader civil-rights bill, including a public-
accommodations provision but excluding an equal-employ-
ment provision.

Immediately, a dispute arose as to the scope of the public-
accommodations section. Was it to embrace all institutions?
The Republicans took the more comprehensive position,
arguing that Congress had the power to do so. Three years
later in *United States* v. *Guest,* the Supreme Court was to
agree with the Republican stand.

In the summer of 1963, the House Judiciary Subcommittee
No. 5 reported out a bill so broad that it lost administration support. Thereafter, Charles Halleck of Indiana, Minority
Leader in the House, together with me as the ranking Republican member of the House Judiciary Committee, and
other Republicans, met with the administration to hammer
out a bill that could muster wide support.

Republicans insisted on eliminating the temporary voting registrar formula in favor of special three-judge federal courts; making the Civil Rights Commission permanent; adding authority for the Commission to investigate frauds; adding a section requiring fair employment practices with enforcement through the courts; and a modified form of the section which the Democrats had torn from the 1957 Act, a section that would permit the Justice Department to intervene in civil-rights lawsuits.

The administration agreed to the Republican terms. The Attorney General, Robert Kennedy, commented that without Halleck's and McCulloch's "support and effort, the possibility of civil-rights legislation in Congress would have been remote." He conceded that the Republican bill was a "better bill than the administration's in dealing with the problems facing the nation."

The new bill went beyond the administration's earlier requests by authorizing Justice Department suits to desegregate public facilities. It permitted the Department to enter any civil-rights suit pending in federal court by requiring, rather than exhorting, government agencies to seek compliance with a nondiscrimination policy in federal programs. It established an Equal Employment Opportunities Commission, covering most companies and labor unions. It required the Census Bureau to collect certain voting statistics by race. And it made reviewable a federal court action remanding a civil rights case to a state court.

On November 20, 1963, the new bill was formally reported by the House Judiciary Committee. On January 30, 1964, the House Rules Committee, with unanimous Republican support mustered through the leadership of Clarence J. Brown, Sr., of Ohio, cleared the bill for debate in the House.

The debate in the House took place from January 31 to February 10.

Clarence J. Brown, Sr., appealed to the members to "conduct this debate on so high a plane that we can at least say to our children and grandchildren, we participated in one of the great debates of modern American history and we did it as statesmen and not as quarreling individuals."

In my own remarks, I said that "not force or fear . . . but the belief in the inherent equality of man induces me to support this legislation . . . No one would suggest that the Negro receives equality of treatment and opportunity in many fields of activity today . . . Hundreds of thousands of citizens are denied the basic right to vote. Thousands of school districts remain segregated. Decent hotel and eating accommodations frequently lie hundreds of miles apart for the Negro traveler . . . These and many more such conditions point the way toward the need for additional legislation . . . This bill is comprehensive in scope, yet moderate in application. It is hedged about with effective administrative and legal safeguards."

The Republicans stood in the forefront of the fight for the bill. Tireless yeoman service was rendered by Charles McC. Mathias of Maryland, Clark MacGregor of Minnesota, and John V. Lindsay of New York. They provided much-needed aid to the Republican leadership of Halleck and myself.

No significant attempt to amend the Republican bill was successful. However, at one moment in the debate, a Democrat from Arkansas, offered an amendment to cut back the provision ending discrimination in federally financed programs.

When the House Democratic Whip supported the proposed amendment, John V. Lindsay, a long-time Republican champion of civil rights, rose to the occasion and denounced the Harris amendment as "the biggest mousetrap that had been offered since the debate on this bill began."

Lindsay expressed his disbelief and dismay while I declared that if the amendment carried, "I regret to say that my individual support of the legislation will come to an end."

But that turned the tide, and the amendment failed on a teller vote.

On February 10, 1964, the House passed the bill by a vote of 290 to 130 and it was sent to the Senate.

There, the Republican Minority Leader, Senator Dirksen,

wrote amendments into the bill which left the House bill little changed in force and effect, but which materially assisted the passage of the legislation in the Senate. The amendments proved acceptable to the administration and to the House.

"No army is stronger than an idea whose time has come," said Victor Hugo the night he died. Echoing that theme, Senator Dirksen declared, "Civil-rights—here is an idea whose time has come." The Senator continued, "Let editors rave at will, but the time has come, and it can't be stopped."

The time had come. On June 10, for the first time in history, the Senate voted to close debate on a civil-rights bill. While only a small majority of Democrats voted for cloture, over 80 percent of the Republicans voted for that action. Nine days later, the Senate passed the bill by a vote of 73 to 27. The Republicans, notably Senator Dirksen and Senator Thomas Kuchel of California, had done their job well.

Because the Senate amendments were minor, House leadership agreed to them. On July 2, 1964, the bill became law.

The Republican record on final passage of the 1964 Act was again outstanding:

HOUSE	YES	NO
Republican	79%	21%
Democratic	63%	37%
SENATE		
Republican	94%	6%
Democratic	73%	27%

Thereafter, in 1965, Senate Majority Leader Mansfield, Senate Minority Leader Dirksen, and Senate Minority Whip Kuchel discussed with the Justice Department the feasibility of a voting-rights bill. A bill was drafted, and on March 17, 1965, it was introduced.

The bill called for a voter registration process supervised by federal voting examiners in states or electoral subdivisions which fail to meet stated standards for allowing qualified applicants to vote. States or voting districts falling short of the bill's standards would be those in which literacy tests or similar devices were used as a qualification for voting on November 1, 1964, and where the Director of the Census determined that less than 50 percent of the persons of voting age residing in the area were registered to vote on that date or actually did vote in the 1964 Presidential election.

The bill was well received in the Senate, whose leaders had drafted it. But in the House, both John Lindsay and I proposed alternative bills which indicated strong Republican support for protecting the Negro's right to vote.

Democratic support was lacking for Republican substitutes. But Republican support for the administration bill which passed was strong. The Republican record on final passage of the 1965 Act was again the better:

HOUSE	YES	NO
Republican	82%	18%
Democratic	78%	22%
SENATE		
Republican	94%	6%
Democratic	73%	27%

The 1965 Act was the last significant civil-rights bill enacted by the Congress. It completes the story to date of civil-rights legislation in the United States.

The Republican Party was formed to combat slavery. It won that battle and started a new campaign, one needing daring and courage—the fight for Negro equality. By the Acts of 1866, 1870, 1871, 1875, 1957, 1960, 1964 and 1965, the Republican Party proved its continuing dedication to the cause of civil rights.

Without exception, the Republicans took the high road in moving toward fulfillment of the dream.

What is that dream? To many, it is the life we take for granted. The right to go to school, to buy a house, to get a job—that is the Negro dream. It is a dream that mirrors the promise of the Declaration of Independence—to enjoy those unalienable rights: life, liberty, and the pursuit of happiness.

The old battles have been won. The Republican Party,

however, is not content with the past. For all the dreams have not come true. There is work to be done. History shows that the Republican Party will be the party, which, in large part, will see that these dreams come true.

HUMAN RELATIONS: THE CHALLENGE
OF TODAY AND TOMORROW

by Clark MacGregor

CLARK MACGREGOR has been a member of the United
States House of Representatives since 1961, representing the Third District of Minnesota. He served as an en-
listed man and U. S. Army officer with the office of
Strategic Services in Southeast Asia during World War
II; graduated with honors from Dartmouth College,
1946, and graduated from the University of Minnesota
Law School, 1948. He is a member of the House Committee on the Judiciary and serves on the subcommittee
which initiates legislation in the field of human rights and
responsibilities. He is also on the special school desegregation guidelines and immigration and nationality subcommittees. In 1967 he served on the select committee to
make recommendations regarding the seating of Adam
Clayton Powell. Much of his work in the Congress has
dealt with the civil rights bills of 1963–64, 1965 and
1966.

The Congress has passed four landmark civil rights laws in
less than ten years, but the mood of America is not civil and
the clamor for "rights" grows daily. Under the prodding and
guidance of Republican Congressmen and Senators, each person now has a federally guaranteed equality of opportunity
to vote, to get an education and a job, to be served, enter-
tained or accommodated in public places; yet riots and violent
civil disorders increasingly mar the image of urban America.

Have we not done enough? Are we failing with solutions
because we haven't analyzed the problem? Is the federal government the best agency, or even the right agency, to look

to for answers? What must be done by individuals, by private groups, by local government?

The struggle for equality fades while the demand for human dignity and justice rises. Important national legislative steps remain to be taken, but the Congress recedes as the primary arena of the civil rights battle.

In 1966 an open housing statute emerged from a bruising debate in the House, but died quietly in the Senate. The House provision was a compromise, drafted and steered to approval by Republican initiative. A Republican effort to persuade the House to adopt a broader and stronger guarantee of equal rights to buy or rent housing of one's choice was beaten down. And in 1967, a new presidential proposal for a 3-stage open housing law lay stillborn in a Democratic Congress.

Apparently a majority of the people of America are not ready for federal action to ban discrimination in the quest for better housing. Perhaps this is an idea whose time has not yet come. But many states and municipalities *have* acted, usually under the leadership of Republican officials, and more must do so. It is a deep affront to human dignity to learn that although your bank balance is ample, your credit rating good, the character and personal behavior of every member of your family above reproach, you may not buy a better home in a better neighborhood because your skin is black.

More and broader open housing ordinances and statutes are needed, but this will touch only part of the housing problem. Many of the poor, white and black, lack the financial means to move. Still others in slum areas do not wish to move, but to improve living conditions where they are. Republicans in Congress are seeking to deal with this aspect of human relations through their almost unanimous sponsorship of the National Home Ownership Foundation Act. We welcome the support of Democrats.

In 1967 this plan for home ownership was originally sponsored by Senator Charles H. Percy, Republican of Illinois, and Congressman William B. Widnall, Republican of New Jersey. The purpose of this program is to upgrade the quality of the nation's housing, to make home ownership available to lower-income families who have or can develop the capacity to accept this responsibility, and to provide needed technical assistance to local community organizations.

The central element of the plan is the establishment of a private, non-profit National Home Ownership Foundation which would raise funds through the sale of federally guaranteed bonds to private lenders. The Foundation would have two major functions:

    1. It would *provide mortgage funds* to non-profit, community organizations equipped to undertake a program of rehabilitation or construction of single or multiple family housing units, to be sold in turn to individual lower-income families. In this way private mortgage financing, private organizations, and local initiative would be mobilized to make home ownership a reality to many for whom the means are unavailable today. Federal funds would be used only to provide a partial interest subsidy to the homeowner, which would be repaid if later his income increases. For each million dollars of continuing federal interest subsidy, private home purchases of approximately $33 million could be supported.

    2. It would provide, when necessary, *technical assistance* to the community organizations to enable them to undertake and manage a sound home ownership program. In addition, it would offer to help these organizations participate in or develop programs such as basic education, job training, credit counseling and other support skills for the prospective home buyer. In helping to supply these tools of successful home ownership, at the same time, the Foundation could provide the service of aiding local organizations and individuals to find their way through the present maze of government agencies and aid programs.

Another feature of the plan would provide for the establishment of a system of mortgage payment insurance, through private companies if possible, to protect home buyers from foreclosures due to temporary interruption of income for causes beyond their control. Also, should the owner decide to sell his property, any capital gain would be his profit, after repaying the Foundation for the interest support he has received. This should encourage home improvements and proper maintenance.

This new plan of action is a most imaginative and constructive approach to improving the quality of our housing and the lives of lower-income families.

Under this plan the enormous resources, imagination, and strength of private organizations would be brought to bear against the problems of housing, particularly in urban areas. The operations of the Foundation and community organizations would encourage involvement of business, labor, the professions, universities, churches, civic groups, and other non-profit organizations, whose talents and energies for assisting in the solution of public problems have not been adequately tapped.

Government activity would be limited to risk-bearing through a federal guarantee of the National Home Ownership Foundation's bonds, and limited financial assistance for the interest subsidy. The emphasis of government would be on these supporting functions and away from direct operations and control.

Also, the residents of our blighted city areas would be encouraged to involve themselves actively in self-help programs leading to better housing, improved skills, and economic advancement. Too often, present programs have failed to generate a sense of self-reliance and self-help which will permit a man to advance through his own efforts.

The Republican National Home Ownership Foundation Act is testimony to our belief that individual dignity, self-help and the involvement of private organizations are indispensable principles in shaping solutions to the complex problems facing urban America.[1]

[1] See Chapter 5 for a fuller discussion of this act.

The Human Investment Act

A good job is as essential to human dignity as a decent place to live. The Civil Rights Act of 1964 moved against racial discrimination in employment, but the law is limited in scope and suffers from lagging enforcement by a Democratic administration.

In addition, the slum and ghetto dweller is particularly hard hit by structural unemployment. Rapid technological change results in a high rate of displacement of labor, especially in lower-paid jobs. White collar occupations and service-rendering industries are rising in importance, and blue-collar jobs are declining. While America experiences an increase of employment opportunities for the well-trained, workers being displaced do not have the necessary skills and work experience to qualify for these opportunities. Negroes and others in minority groups are hardest hit. As unemployment persists in the ghetto, resentment smolders and appeals to violence find an audience.

In June 1964 a task force report of the Department of Labor stated:

> To spur capital investment, the Congress has enacted a Federal Income Tax policy which reduces an employer's tax liability for any year in which he has made expenditures for certain specified capital items. . . .
>
> The same type of incentive could be applied to the development of skills through apprenticeship and training. The amount of such tax credit is not the most important consideration, but the 7% allowed for capital expenditures would serve as a tentative goal.

The Republicans in Congress responded with the Human Investment Act of 1965.[2]

[2] See Chapter 3 for a fuller discussion of this act.

THE ROLE OF INDUSTRY

The most effective job trainer in the nation has always been the free competitive economy. Through the years business and labor, working together, have demonstrated their ability to conceive, organize, and carry out job training programs superior both in quality and in efficiency to government-operated programs.

The proper role of the federal government in 1968 should be to encourage labor organizations and business enterprises to intensify and expand their time-tested programs of job training.

In 1962, Congress adjusted our revenue laws to provide a tax credit toward the cost of plant equipment and machinery in order to spur new investment in these job-creating items. It is now agreed among business analysts that this new provision has made a significant contribution to the increased investment in equipment and machinery.

Republicans believe Congress—and the administration—should now act to encourage a similar investment in human beings—in the American labor force, whose skills are worth far more to the strength of the nation's economy than machinery can ever be. Certainly we should give the highest priority to an investment in human resources, with primary emphasis on the jobless and the underemployed in the deteriorating core city areas of America.

Republicans have suggested the tax credit approach to this problem because it can most easily be designed to reduce to a minimum the burdens of red tape, bureaucracy and governmental intrusion into the affairs of business and labor. The Human Investment Act would promptly become law were it not for the opposition of the present majority party in Congress.

The Human Investment Act and the National Home Ownership Foundation Act could operate together to transform the slums. As Michigan's Governor George Romney has so ably put it:

> ". . . the ghettos are full of the underemployed and unemployed who could quickly and easily be trained in many building skills. They would be eager to learn and earn if they were given the opportunity to work on housing rehabilitation projects.
>
> "No artificial restrictions should be permitted to stand in the way of meeting housing needs so urgent and employment needs so vast.
>
> "Surely, here is an opportunity for private enterprise, with union cooperation and government encouragement as needed, to create a whole new industry in the heart of the ghettos—producing improved housing at a cost the people can afford, reversing neighborhood deterioration, upgrading the skills of the work force, providing meaningful and accessible jobs at reasonable wages where there are none today, and stimulating increased economic progress throughout the central cities."

Republicans would use government to motivate and to encourage innovative action by individuals, labor unions, and business entities. Even enlightened liberals in the Democratic Party are coming around to the view that the nation, especially the cities of the nation, cannot be run from agencies in Washington.

But what of the problem of urban violence? Will better housing and job opportunities, even on a sharply accelerated scale, still the voices of those who cry, "Burn, Baby, burn!"?

America's most critical threat to urban law and order comes from the Negro nihilists, and they are relatively few in number. Our task should be to separate those few who seek to tear down and destroy from the great majority of Negroes and others in minority groups who earnestly desire to help build a better life for themselves within our system of equal justice under law.

No force of program or persuasion can reach the most militant of Black Power advocates who now claim to represent the masses in our cities. Indeed we have no option but to enforce existing criminal law as to these few, while acting to deprive the lawless of the source of their present and potential strength.

Most importantly, Republicans propose to move publicly and privately, as individuals and in groups, to reach out to those in America's slums who feel estranged from our largely white affluence. The greatest gap today is that of communication and understanding. We haven't been listening enough to one another. We haven't made the effort to know each other.

Businesses, labor unions, church groups, civic organizations, trade associations, and local political party units have permitted an understandable process of compartmentalization to shut their members off from those who are not "our kind." But the walls must be broken down. And indeed this progressive step is underway in many communities. As the party founded to enhance the dignity of each individual, the Republican Party in 1968 is dedicated to the success of this Operation Outreach. As former Vice President Richard Nixon stated in New York December 8, 1967, ". . . after this decade of opening doors, we need a decade of preparing people to walk through these doors."

Chapter 5

TOWARD BETTER HOUSING

——◄◆►——

HOUSING, A SOCIAL PARADOX: FACING A TWIN CHALLENGE

by John M. Dickerman

JOHN M. DICKERMAN has been a consultant since 1964 to building material manufacturing, financing and construction firms and to prominent Associations in related fields throughout the United States. He was Executive Vice President for twelve years of the National Association of Home Builders and prior to 1952, was Director of Governmental Affairs for the N.A.H.B. for five years. Mr. Dickerman received the B.A. degree and the LLB degree from the University of Illinois, and has been admitted to practice before the U. S. Supreme Court, the Supreme Courts of Illinois and Ohio, and the District Court of the District of Columbia.

THE HOUSING PROBLEM

On the occasion of urging establishment of the Housing and Urban Development Department in 1965, the President charted the government's concept of tomorrow's urban America and the federal role in urban problem solving and he emphasized the interrelationship of the total urban problem and housing.

He predicted that within a half century our population would double, that by the year 2000 more than 80 percent of our population increase will occur in the urban areas and that within the next fifteen years an additional 30 million people will be added to the cities—a number equivalent to the combined populations of New York, Chicago, Los Angeles, Philadelphia, Detroit, and Baltimore.

To house and service these people, he estimated, we will have to build during the next 40 years as much in our cities as was built since colonial days. Four decades to rebuild the entire urban United States would be another way to express the concept. By 1975 we will need to build at the rate of 2 million new homes per year instead of the 1.2 million to 1.5 million in the early sixties.

In the meantime, he said, "We have over nine million homes, most of them in cities, which are run down or deteriorating; over four million do not have running water or even plumbing."

The concentration of the old, the poor and the discriminated against in the central city slums, amidst physical decay creates crime, school drop outs, delinquency and social disorganization.

"The problems of the city are problems of housing and education," he concluded.

The Task. According to the 1960 Census we had a national inventory of 58,000,000 housing units—urban and rural. Net removals by demolition, natural causes and abandonment are variously estimated from 500,000 to nearly 600,000 per year with projections of 700,000 or more by the 1970s. With production of new houses in the last normal year (1965) at 1½ million units, it can readily be seen that net addition to inventory is less than 2 percent.

During 1966 and 1967 we experienced a "money crunch" which severely limited our ability to maintain even the modest 1½ million unit home building rate of 1965. In fact, we dropped to 1.2 million units in 1966. The availability of mortgage money to support a two million unit rate within our present inadequate home mortgage and credit system should be a matter of grave concern, to which problem inadequate attention is now being paid.

The President pledged to begin the rehabilitation of or the replacement with new homes of nine million deteriorated units. It would seem actions should be taken as well to halt the effects of blight eroding millions of existing older decent homes each passing year to prevent their becoming the slums of tomorrow. These two steps would require additional economic and financial commitments beyond those required for new housing units needed to shelter the population expansion alluded to above.

In summary, according to these projections by the President, America is faced with a Gargantuan residential construction and re-construction task stemming from:

a. A 100 percent population expansion in the next fifty years,

b. Nine million housing units presently in need of repair or replacement plus those units entering this category each year, and

c. The need for streets, sewer, water, and supportive educational, health, recreational, and social service facilities.

The Costs. New house expenditures at the 1½ million unit level including land, material and labor has been approximately $24 billion per year; present remodeling, repair and maintenance expenditures on existing houses are approximately $13 billion per year. Supportive facilities construction costs are currently estimated at about $15 billion annually. These figures provide some tentative dimensions for estimating the order of resources in today's dollars required to achieve the objectives outlined above. Not included in these figures are soft-ware non-construction related expenditures for education, training and social services. No distinction is here made between private and public funds.

As one measurement of the cost of eliminating 4½ million units of substandard urban housing, Senator Abraham Ribicoff, following six weeks of hearings by his Senate Subcommittee on Executive Reorganization, calculated that $50 billion over a ten-year period would be needed.

In spite of the substantial sums contemplated, and in spite of the admitted organizational obstacles to achieving these goals, there is little disagreement over the need to attack the problem. The people to be served are either here or will be shortly. Their needs and desires must be met somehow, some way.

Remaining to be resolved are the methodologies—the systems—the techniques—for reaching the objectives. Precisely here, of course, is where men of good will and intention find themselves at odds.

Before we examine the alternatives, consideration should be given to other—and somewhat unique—aspects of housing.

Unlike the two other essentials of life, housing from primitive times has had a special emotional dimension during mankind's life cycle. The home has enjoyed a special social and legal status for hundreds of years. Values attached to the home, its meaning to family and individual, frequently are not capable of true expression in economic terms.

For these and related reasons housing holds an unusually significant position in a nation's political economy.

Housing Standards. By world standards the typical American lives well. Due in large part to the marvelous productive capacity of our people and of our land, functioning within a framework of private enterprise and governed by a representative democracy, the great majority of our 200 million people are relatively well-housed.

As we move toward even higher living standards under the impetus of a burgeoning technology, criteria for measurement of housing adequacy are revised upward in terms of size and amenity. Inside plumbing and electric lights were once the mark of housing affluence; today absence of this equipment classifies a housing unit as substandard. Norms for protection from heat, cold, moisture and other factors have risen. Environmental elements in the neighborhood—proximity to schools, shopping, transportation—as well as better design and liveability of the housing structure itself are increasingly considered as essential to adequate housing. The lesson of history forecasts a continued rise in and broadening of the scope of housing standards.

An emerging social consciousness in our body politic has brought the realization that, in spite of rising national affluence and the relative housing comforts of a majority of our citizens, a very substantial number of Americans live in deplorable conditions by today's criteria. These are estimated to number more than 20 million persons. Of course, slum conditions, overcrowding, unhealthful environments are not new; these types of conditions have been with us a long time—and exist in other areas of the world often in a more marked degree.

There is a growing national conviction that, to the extent possible such conditions should be eradicated in this country.

The Governmental Role. Commitment of local, state and federal government funds to improving housing in the United States has an extended history. Congress voted money as early as 1892 to investigate city slums. During both World Wars and particularly during the Depression of the 1930s, the federal government launched housing programs to shelter war workers and to stimulate the lagging economy. Special housing benefits for returning World War II veterans were provided in the GI Bill; 6.6 million loans had been guaranteed for new or used homes for veterans of all types to the end of 1966.

Housing for families of low-income incapable of paying economic rents became a prime target of federal action in 1937; slum clearance as a major objective came into focus in 1949 with the passage of extensive subsidy programs by Congress. Virtually every succeeding Congress has enacted additional laws and appropriated additional moneys. These funds were directly or indirectly to stimulate or to subsidize housing for low and middle income families, to clear slums and to provide sewer, water, parks and other environmental facilities and services.

Government Financial Commitments to Urban Problem Solving. The federal government's total cumulative financial investment of tax money in such endeavors through the years has been in the billions; its contingent commitment (through insurance and guarantees) also has been in the billions.

Assessment of the impact of federal funds on housing and related urban benefit programs presents some unique difficulties because of the large number of agencies with urban-related activities ranging from grants, to loans, to insurance. Some subsidy type programs pledge federal payments for up to forty years, but are reported year-by-year as current budget items. True committed expenditures often are thus substantially larger than annual figures suggest.

Secretary Weaver of the Department of Housing and Urban Development testifying before the Senate Subcommittee on Executive Reorganization in 1966 endeavored to shed some light on this subject when he said, "Between fiscal years 1961 and 1964, federal financial commitments making a direct impact on urban problems increased from $15.5 billion to $20 billion, an increase of 10 percent a year. Between 1964 and 1966 they rose by over $8 billion to over $28 billion in 1966, an increase of 20 percent a year and double the rate of increase of the 1961–64 period."

Excluding loan insurance and guarantees, the total federal obligation for 1966 was estimated at $16,847,000,000. HUD's proportion of this was about $4 billion.

So active has housing legislation become in Congress that specially staffed subcommittees have been established in both Senate and House to deal with it. In 1965, the cabinet rank department was established to administer the now extensive federal housing-urban aid program complex in Washington and in branch offices throughout the nation. The local communities' administrative counterparts in the subsidized public housing and slum clearance programs now number more than 2000 local housing and urban renewal authorities. These authorities as of 1967 were government agency landlords managing 635,879 units housing 2½ million people.

Thus, governmental effort has been considerable; its penetration into housing and urban affairs has been growing. But its effectiveness in dealing with the problem, especially among low-income families and in the eradication of slums, has been and continues to be controversial. Criticisms run the gamut from "too little, too late" to "too much, in the wrong way."

Model Cities. A recent major program emerging on this controversial scene was the 1966 Demonstration Cities (Model Cities) legislation. In brief, it is an experimental endeavor to marshal and to coordinate all the applicable governmental programs in limited area projects in selected cities. The model cities approach would provide additional incentive planning subsidies to encourage cities to engage in detailed planning seeking to demonstrate the effectiveness of a total federal program involvement in training people as well as rebuilding physical structures and environments. Supplemental subsidies to defray up to 80 percent of the local costs of approved programs is also available. As with the predecessors of this plan, it encountered strong opposition and was finally funded on a reduced scale. Definitive results are some years away.

The Critical Problem Area. The housing "complex" can be conveniently more than accurately subdivided into a number of categories: that is, families in upper, middle, and lower income levels; rural, suburban and central city locations; economically viable, not economically viable families; and welfare or institutional occupants. There are, of course, gradations and shadings between categories.

The most critical aspect of the complex is the low income family of the non-viable economic category living in a central city substandard dwelling.

This socio-economic demand–supply aspect may be outlined as follows:

1. Housing is needed where people want to live and people generally want to live where employment can be found. Our population is mobile—housing is not.

2. While the upgrading process by which the affluent move into new units and the lower income families move into the vacated units provides decent housing to a greater degree than many will admit, it does not fully answer the need in either the location or price levels required.

3. Likewise at the bottom of the housing inventory deteriorated structures are not effectively removed by a selective or orderly process. Thus, unsound structures remain available to be occupied at prices and in conditions often unfit for human habitation by today's standards. This situation is further compounded by the influx into central city areas of the low income, disadvantaged.

4. The financial ability of cities to cope with housing needs and other problems in the central city is reduced by the flight from the city of taxpaying middle classes and a similar departure by many businesses and some industry.

5. Limitations on choice of housing on the part of any of our citizens, and especially of the lower income segment, serve to perpetuate patterns of inferior housing. This applies especially to negroes although in some areas Mexican-Americans and Puerto Ricans are severely affected by discrimination. Possibly even larger numbers of low income whites suffer not from ethnic discrimination but from economic inability to compete for scarce, decent low cost shelter.

6. The sheer force of numbers of families in a limited market who are often unable to pay full economic rents tends to put a premium on the supply of decent low cost shelter and keeps prices higher; there is little competitive incentive for landlords to maintain their properties; likewise property improvement usually brings higher local tax bills.

Thus the key housing problem for lower income families emerges from a combination of (a) maladjustment in time and place availability of the existing inventory, (b) inadequate inventory maintenance requirements and incentives, (c) impaction of urban central city areas by non-viable economic groups with inadequate training and skills for today's technologically oriented urban employment market, (d) distortion of market forces in the deteriorated real estate due to an excess of limited choice marginal renters and buyers competing for relatively scarce accommodation supply (decent housing in areas traditionally available to certain occupants) (e) inadequate and diminishing local governmental ability to cope with this socio-economic dilemma due to eroding local tax bases, and (f) population growth and mobility in general.

Validity of Government Programs. The extent to which the multiplicity of federal government programs have contributed to a quantative or qualitative solution to these key related problems—the low-income family and slum eradication—is difficult to assess. There exists no objective cost-benefit evaluation of government housing and urban programs. Any evaluation effort would suffer the handicaps of lack of definitive standards by which to measure results, by lack of sufficient comparative statistical bench marks, and by the ideological controversy which has so long swirled around the subject.

Without the programs the situation undoubtedly would be worse; in spite of them, conditions show little incontrovertible evidence of over-all improvement.

A continuation of the programmatic approach so far favored (i.e. the use of federal subsidies partially or wholly to fund solutions and to provide incentives to local communities to use their inherent police powers for good city housekeeping and planning) means to some observers a perpetuation of undesirable multi-layered bureaucratic red-tape, centralized planning, politically directed discretion as to eligibility, conformity to national rather than local patterns of design and performance, among other problems.

Others, while granting the criticisms of delays and red-tape may have substance, would argue that the problem is so complex and that the time elements required by the constitutional, operating, and construction factors fully justify the time delays. Beyond this they would point out that the problem's dimensions are so substantial that the programmatic approach must be given additional time to demonstrate its effectiveness.

Divergent Viewpoints. The fact that slums continue to exist and to fester in spite of almost two decades of federal involvement and the billions spent can be viewed in several ways:

a. As a measure of the extent of the disease calling for massive doses of the similar Federal subsidy medicine or

b. As a demonstration of the inadequacy of this technique and the need to turn to new prescriptions. In the view of some advocates these could include:

   1) Revenue sharing to provide states or local commu-

nities greater financial resources to solve their own urban-housing problems in their own way (assuming they would in fact do so), or

2) Massive tax benefits or other incentives to the major producer of the GNP—private enterprise— to invest its funds and energies in urban-housing problem solving, thus linking the profit motive to social benefit. (Assuming such incentives would, in fact, be sufficient to reach the very substantial private resources necessary and to channel them into the areas of greatest need.), or

3) A combination of current and new approaches designed to harness private enterprise more effectively with Federal government subsidy to achieve social benefit purposes. (Assuming such an effective partnership can be devised.)

Governmental Programs Proliferate. Over the last thirty years increasing federal concern with housing matters has spawned a profusion of government programs—some of longstanding and others of recent vintage. A number, such as the Federal Housing Administration (FHA) and the Federal National Mortgage Association (FNMA), are generally hailed as successful; others such as public housing and urban renewal continue to incur criticism and to provoke debate. Some of the more recent, such as rent supplements and model cities, are so new that advocates at best can only express optimistic hope and opponents view with skepticism. Time will produce facts on which judgments of the newer programs can be made.

This paper cannot undertake a minute examination of *all* the specialized programs such as housing for the elderly and handicapped, college housing, open space and beautification, urban planning assistance, public works planning and so on. Instead, here is a brief look at several of the better known, larger programmatic approaches designed to strike at the most difficult housing problem sector, the low income family in need of decent shelter within its means:

Public Housing

Public housing was first advanced in the early 1930s as a slum clearance and low income family program. Its intended role as an effective slum clearance device has been superseded by the later urban renewal program.

Local and national controversy—sometimes bitter and protracted—has marked public housing's federal subsidization of family rents. Site selection difficulties, the over-income tenant eviction problem, drab barracks-like appearance, failure to house the very lowest income and "problem" families, allegations of political preferences in occupancy, excessive unit costs, reports of property destruction by tenants, crime and disorder in the projects have been among the issues debated in the press and in Congress. In recent years this debate has somewhat subsided.

As of mid-1966, some 848,000 units had reached reservation or later development stages. Projects owned and operated by local housing authorities are located in 2600 communities; since 1937 approximately 9 million persons have lived in public housing. The median incomes of public housing families were reported by HUD as $2580 per year in 1965. Federal subsidies amounted to $250 million (in 1967) to honor forty-year commitments to defray interest and principal on local housing authorities bonds. Thus the ultimate cost to the taxpayer can be calculated at forty times the current budget item for annual subsidy. Once the commitment is made the Congressional appropriation process is automatically necessary to meet this full faith and credit pledge of the government.

Supporters of the program realized several years ago that public housing had accumulated operating handicaps. Particularly was this true in obtaining sites in central city areas and at costs inconsistent with low rental rates, even though subsidized. New amendments to exist-

ing law and administrative actions now permit for public
housing usage:

   a. Acquiring existing private properties,
   b. Leasing existing private properties or portions
      thereof,
   c. Contracting with private developers to buy property
      they have or acquire and rehabilitate or build for
      this purpose,
   d. Private management of projects owned by public
      housing authorities,
   e. Sale of units to public housing tenants who can
      qualify and if the unit lends itself to separate sale,
      and
   f. A mixed private-public ownership of a project.

The recent tendency to employ private enterprise in
production and even management of public housing may
be expected to grow apace. Substantially larger numbers of leased and/or rehabilitated properties as compared to housing authority sponsored new units can be
also anticipated—with corresponding requests to Congress
for increased funding authority.

Urban Renewal

Approved after a four-year Congressional debate, Title
I of the Housing Act of 1949 authorized Federal loans
and grants to local public agencies for slum land acquisi-
tion and clearance. The Federal grants were to be two-
thirds of the net cost of (or loss on) slum cleared land
after resale for approved reuse i.e. a "write down" subsidy. In certain cases the subsidy may be three-fourths
of net cost.

Subsequent amendments to the 1949 Act broadened
its scope from the project to the neighborhood; encompassed conservation of existing properties; required each
community as a condition of eligibility to have a "workable program" for general community improvement; authorized grants to local and state planning agencies (Sec-

tion 701); allowed exceptions (35 percent of grant money since 1965) from the initial predominantly residential requirement; provided demonstration grants for experiments in new techniques for prevention of slums and blight; established a "general neighborhood renewal plan" where the activities were to be carried out in several projects over a long period of time; allowed up to 25 percent of the cost of publicly owned cultural, exhibition or civic structures of benefit to the entire city to be counted toward the local share of urban renewal costs; required relocation of displaced families and businesses with payment of certain expenses; and other refinements and special aids.

Criticisms of the program in its various versions have centered around: (1) delays in carrying out the activities. HUD reports the *median* project execution period from date of HUD approval for loans and grants has been 62 months, but this does not include delays prior to HUD approval; (2) displacement of slum residents causing them to occupy and to create new slums. HUD documents its denial with relocation data indicating that, according to one Census study, 94 percent of displaced families moved to standard housing; (3) rehousing the affluent on the slum-cleared properties instead of the low income; (4) excessive portions of urban renewal projects being devoted to commercial and other non-residential uses thus assisting commerce and industry instead of low income families and altering the original purpose of the program; and (5) selecting large areas for urban renewal well in advance of any action, plus delays, with a resultant discouragement of owners in such areas in repairing and maintaining their properties in the meantime—this has further contributed to existing substandard housing conditions; also (6) demolition of far more living units than are replaced—for all projects as of the end of 1965, 333,-872 units had been demolished and 104,316 built or under construction, but in this case not all land had been committed—where all land cleared had been committed, 102,000 units were demolished and 72,000 replaced.

Estimated budget expenditures for urban renewal activity grants for 1966 were $850 million. By mid-1966 grant reservations had been made to 842 communities on 1994 projects for a total of $5.2 billion. Forty-two thousand acres of land had been approved by year-end 1965 with 31,000 acres acquired and 8800 cleared. Construction was underway on 3100 acres.

With the model cities program placing major reliance on urban renewal the operational delays and other criticisms of this program take on added significance to those concerned about the slow pace of present government efforts to make meaningful inroads on the urban blight problem. The demolition of 333,872 units as compared to Senator Ribicoff's estimate of 4½ million substandard urban housing units and the President's estimate of 9 million substandard units in the Nation suggests the pace must be considerably quickened if any appreciable impact is to be made within reasonable time targets.

In recent years government housing officials have begun—belatedly it is felt by some—to realize the enormity of the task. The diverse programmatic tools forged over the last three decades by piece-meal legislative enactment tended to compartmentalize solution efforts. It has been argued that greater coordination and direction of these related governmental efforts toward a common goal is sorely needed; the establishment of HUD was in part predicated on this concept.

Other significant trends have been noticeable—among which are (1) the realization that *new* construction dependent on subsidized urban renewal results in high unit costs when the real total costs are calculated,—such expense, the difficulties of public funding and the dislocation of families displaced, turned official attention to seek ways to utilize vast quantities of existing housing inventory, structurally sound but in need of rehabilitation; (2) the recognition that private enterprise, a self-generating mechanism with substantial potential resource input, has not been adequately integrated into the search for urban problem solutions. The latter trend has only recently found public expression. If this approach is to be effectively utilized by harnessing the profit motive, much remains to be done in realigning traditional attitudes on the part both of government officials and of private enterprise as well as in reshaping programs and administrative procedures.

Rehabilitation

So large a task as renewing 4½ million deteriorated urban residential units, not to mention the non-urban substandard units of like number, cannot as a practical matter be accomplished with clearance as a principal method. Aside from prohibitive cost and time in pursuing the clearance route is the fact that a great many of these units are basically sound structures representing an enormous investment which would thus be lost.

For these and like reasons rehabilitation has emerged as a basic goal; realization of effective methods to achieve this on a reasonably uniform economic pattern still eludes advocates in spite of a number of significant, and in some instances dramatic, individual project demonstrations.

Several related factors create real problems in utilizing rehabilitation on a large scale:

1. Rehabilitation to be economically sound from a value viewpoint should generally occur on a neighborhood basis. This is difficult to organize with diversity of ownership.

2. Financing in this field is poorly organized, scarce except at high yields and usually for short term. The typical high proportion of on site labor by small firms and individuals precludes financing by contractors; materials needed come from diverse sources and therefore the potential of financing via the manufacturer —distributor—retailer route is generally lacking. The re-

modeling and rehabilitation field has long been beset by problems caused by the so-called "suede-shoe" type operator who takes advantage of unsophisticated owners sometimes in price, or in quality of material and often in financing terms.

3. The uncertainty of estimating due to the prospect of unknown structural or other problems in older buildings being remodeled has often caused bids to rise, and to produce uneconomic results, i.e. greater investment than can be recovered in rents or sale price. Likewise some buildings cannot be economically rehabilitated.

4. A well-organized rehabilitation industry does not exist in many communities for these reasons. As now structured, scattered worksites, difficulties of supervision, quality control and economies of production, cause larger construction firms to shun this type of work in favor of new construction.

In recent years the governmental programs have been modified to encompass rehabilitation. Among these are FHA with its wide ranging specialized insured financing devices, public housing (as noted above), and special direct government loans and grants in connection with urban renewal activities. Except for the long-standing FHA short-term, property improvement insured loans, which are limited amount, high discount devices suited to small jobs, and a new below market interest rate program, there has not been substantial use so far made of the government rehabilitation programs—undoubtedly for the several reasons cited.

The estimated $13 billion total annual expenditures in remodeling, maintenance and repair now occur largely outside of government induced programs. Thus, if government programs can be reshaped or new incentives devised to accelerate rehabilitation, this sector could be substantially increased. The needs and the market opportunities are present; but effective financing and operational mechanisms are required to tap those needs and opportunities.

This brief review of some of the major government housing efforts in terms of achievements to date may provide insight into their effectiveness—and into possible remaining "gaps" in the programs employed to date.

Whether the prevailing governmental approach is a proper one or sufficient in its present and probable realizable dimensions to solve the complex of problems must be determined by an evaluation of the size and nature of those problems. Whether drastically new methods, or a different blending of resources or a different combination of existing devices or an admixture of new and old should be embarked upon is, in a sense, an obligation of interested citizens concerned by recent trends and events in our urban centers and the role therein played by housing.

Unfortunately, housing is too often singled out in considerations of urban problems as an end in itself. Achievement of a given level of housing adequacy without regard to education, training, income levels of families, social conditions, health, transportation, city planning, recreation and other facets of urban living is, we have learned, unlikely to provide lasting and significant results.

Perhaps in part because housing is usually conceptually associated with bricks and mortar and we know *how* to produce it—given enough money, material and manpower, it becomes an easily identified prime target of urban problem solving. We know less about how to change or to improve attitudes, ambitions and habits of the low income or disadvantaged people who are to live in those housing units, who must learn how to live with each other, and who hopefully can become economically self-sufficient enough to pay their own way rather than to become or to remain wards or partial wards of the public taxpayer. In short, we must learn more about how to create a climate of opportunity for such persons to become economic and socially viable citizens in a modern America.

The substantial space here given to a discussion of the low-income family in substandard housing is an indication of the relative importance attributed to this sector of the housing problem complex. It is a front-ranking and critical problem. But it is not the only one.

Other Housing Needs. The President predicted the need to rebuild urban America in the process of accommodating an anticipated 100 percent increase in population in the next fifty years. The manpower, material and particularly financial resources needed for this will be tremendous. Even if the President's figures somewhat overstate the order of magnitude and even with the present decline in birth rate, the demographic indicators point to a population growth in the next thirty-five years of at least 100 million and perhaps more.

On a shorter range scale of a decade this has been estimated by private industry sources[1] to involve a required annual input of 2 to 2.5 million new housing units during the 1970–80 period. On the assumption that 80 percent of such units will be built on land not now used for housing, approximately 8 million acres of land will need to be developed with streets, sewers, water and equipped with transportation, schools and other community facilities. Net new funds required are estimated at $40 billion which present sources show little likelihood of supplying within presently structured limitations.

Sewer and water, while only one factor, illustrate the importance of and interdependence of each element to sound urban growth.

Rising costs of suburban housing, which are dramatized in the popular mind because a house represents a typical family's largest single expenditure (even though many other products and services may have increased proportionally more), tend to price large numbers of lower income families out of the market. Between 1951 and 1965, according to FHA, construction costs rose 68 percent but land costs rose 205 percent. In both cases increase in size contributed to this rise, but in the case of land higher prices were a major factor. A shortage of land is often cited as a reason; translated this often means a shortage of land equipped with sewer, water and other fa-

---

[1] National Association of Home Builders.

cilities and ready to be built on. Improved land utilization practices, zoning and over-all planning can contribute to more economical sites for houses and apartments but a basic ingredient remains—sewer and water.

HUD and three other agencies have federal aid sewer and water programs for local communities. The other three are Economic Development Administration, Federal Water Pollution Control Administration, and the Farmers Home Administration. Experience suggests need for improved coordination between these in making limited funds effective and to avoid unduly disrupting the private financing patterns on which so much of such construction must depend. HUD's grant program in one year showed $99 million committed for 173 projects.

Similar problem areas are present in transportation and highways, schools, recreation and parks.

Trained manpower to put construction volume in place is in increasingly scarce supply; therein lie challenges to equip the low income residents of central cities, now too often unemployed, with the skills to fill this need in the coming years. Since each living unit built is estimated to furnish one man year of employment on the site and one off site, an appreciable increase in housing volume—either in new construction or in rehabilitation—would require additional sources of trained manpower. This becomes both a problem and an opportunity.

Material supplies are not presently considered bottlenecks to achieving the goals set forth assuming adequate lead time is provided to construct needed manufacturing and processing facilities.

Technological research to unlock sudden breakthroughs in cost reduction of housing has periodically been touted; drastic reductions of this type are unlikely to occur in this field given the slow change in consumer acceptance of new products, techniques and designs. Even so, progress has and will continue to be made.

Applied research and improved technical methods have largely accounted for slowing down the rate of housing cost increases in spite of wage scale escalation in the last decade or two. Further progress may be anticipated in product and product application research on which millions of private corporate dollars are now invested annually.

Governmental efforts in this area would best be directed to those areas not duplicated in the private sector. If government does intrude on the private area, a drying up of private research efforts could result. Consideration might be addressed instead to appropriate incentives to private enterprise to invest more heavily in housing oriented research.

Housing Finance. By all odds, aside from the more fully discussed slum—low income family—decent housing problem area, the next most significant difficulty facing the housing industry and government is how to assure a continuing adequate supply of long-term, relatively low-interest rate mortgage money.

The need to manage national fiscal and monetary policies so as not to create periodic feast and famine requiring costly readjustments in housing production for which consumers pay one way or another should now be clear. The latest example of the "money crunch" of 1966 and its causes should be kept vividly in mind.

The use of housing as a countercyclical device on the theory of the "postponability" of housing should no longer be countenanced as an alternative policy in view of the now apparent expanding population's housing needs, and particularly that of the low income family compounding the explosive central city slum areas problem.

Governmental attention at the highest levels should be addressed to structuring the private financing and mortgage credit mechanisms so as to permit the availability of adequate funds. Government loans for limited specialized purposes should at the most serve only temporary, catalytic purposes; the main burden of housing finance should continue to be carried by private lending entities permitted competitively to tap needed long-term investment sources.

CONCLUSIONS

Two central facts emerge from this review—the United States faces (a) a population growth potential of substantial proportions and (b) an urban slum and low-income family socio-economic problem of growing importance to society.

Whether or not the President's population growth prediction of a 100 percent increase in fifty years is overstated or whether some lesser figure is more accurate, the evident order of magnitude is sufficient to justify long range planning to meet the need.

Whether or not there is agreement on root causes of recent civil unrest in the so-called ghetto areas stemming from urban poverty impaction, racial discrimination in employment opportunity, or difficulty in achieving economic opportunity, caused by lack of skills or whatever, the evidence suggests major attention should be directed to this area.

Housing in the latter context should not be regarded as an end but rather as an important part of a total complex of solutions interdependent on each other, including jobs, training, education and necessary health and environmental facilities.

The long-operative governmental programs in the housing field traditionally were divisible into two general types—those, such as FHA, designed for middle income suburbia and those, such as public housing and urban renewal, designed for assisting low income families occupying urban substandard housing. Since the establishment of HUD these distinctions are less sharp and there is an increased effort to use the suburban tools in the central city. This in turn creates some problems of emphasis and accommodation within the agencies.

Relatively less planning is apparently currently underway within government preparing for the population growth needs of the next several decades as compared to the attention directed to the urban area—low income family—slum impaction problem. While this is understandable, it is suggested that *both* should receive *re-doubled* attention.

Governmental answers for urban slums have been forced to undergo a re-thinking and re-orientation in recent years. Hence, the multi-million dollar frankly described "experiments" and model cities type demonstration projects now to be launched in the festering slums. There is need to find answers which seemingly have defied discovery in spite of programs in progress since 1937 and 1949.

No cost-benefit evaluation of these long time programs has been made to discover their quantative or qualitative impact on the urban blight syndrome. Aside from statistics as to number of projects, of acres, of units, of families housed it is difficult to ascertain the degree to which the existent programs have caught up, or not caught up, with the rate of urban decay. There are indications that without the programs the situation would be worse, but there is little hard data showing relative progress against slum growth.

The evident significance for the nation of both the population explosion and of the ghetto problem suggests the need for shaking off the shackles of the programmatic approach. This is the traditional technique in which a "program" is started, becomes a part of the agency stable, is nurtured by the personnel, and usually directs its energies toward a specific and limited objective, vying for funds and visibility within the bureaucratic compound. Top-level government priorities should be established as soon as possible, less important "programs" put on standby or discontinued, with funds and personnel directed toward the selected objectives. Admittedly, this flies in the face of Parkinsonian principles so typically exemplified in government.

Faced with these twin housing-related problems government planners obviously need help. They are groping for substantive procedures to cope with the problems' magnitude and complexity. Unfortunately, not all of them quite realize the limitations of the government as an instrument for effective action beyond the planning (i.e. programing) stage. Some officials do.

The recent hesitant recognition that private enterprise—yes, the much-maligned profit motive—should be harnessed to join hands in effecting public benefits is a significant shift in governmental thinking brought on by hard experience over at least two decades of struggling with construction and reconstruction in urban renewal and public housing. Such a marriage to be effective will require attitude changes on the part of many government officials as well as businessmen—and some program changes. Considering the magnitude of the twin housing-related problems such a marriage is not only desirable but essential; without it the task cannot be done—with it, there is the hope that it can be done.

A REPUBLICAN PROGRAM FOR HOUSING

by *William B. Widnall*

REPRESENTATIVE WILLIAM B. WIDNALL (R., N.J.) is currently serving his tenth term in the U. S. House of Representatives. He is the ranking Republican on the House Banking and Currency Committee and the Domestic Finance and Special Housing Subcommittees. In fifteen years on the Housing Subcommittee, he has authored such programs as the Federal Home Loan Bank Board, leased public housing in private accommodations, a $450 million urban renewal rehabilitation loan fund, the workable program requirement under urban renewal, FHA guaranteed mortgage housing for veterans, and has co-sponsored many related bills, including the Mass Transportation Acts of 1964 and 1966.

A national housing policy must aim at providing an adequate supply of decent and desirable housing for the American people. To reach this goal will require the fullest involvement of the private sector with its initiative, expertise, and capital. Local, state and federal government—in that order—can best serve by providing *stimulus* and *reinforcement,* rather than execution and control.

Too often, in evolving public policy on housing, well-meaning individuals concentrate on specialized programs to aid specific groups at the unnecessary expense of the housing industry as a whole. A strong, growing housing industry, meeting unsubsidized needs of the majority of the American people, contributes a vital element to national economic growth.

This means jobs and tax revenue. It means markets for new products and new techniques. It means the encouragement of savings and investment.

Directly or indirectly, these are contributions to the improvement in the living standards of the less fortunate. New products and new techniques not only lower housing costs, they also produce jobs that create credit stability and purchasing power among lower income families. Savings and investment that increase the available supply of mortgage credit also advance the general rise in living standards. Either through new construction or rehabilitation, this produces an enlarged housing supply particularly for lower income groups.

Attention to this important factor in the past has not been encouraging. Government has been remiss in two ways: not only has it failed to do as much as possible in improving the general housing outlook; government actions have also actually compounded the difficulties facing the industry.

The present rate of housing starts falls roughly between 1.3 and 1.4 million units annually. Anticipated demand for the future indicates a need for some 2.25 to 2.5 million units per year, an increase roughly of a million units.

To reach this goal, a series of steps is needed that includes both changes in existing programs and the inauguration of new ones. In addition, the financial climate must be sound.

REVIEW OF PRESENT PROGRAMS NEEDED

All housing programs now operating must face up to the facts of life and survive on the question of whether they are or are not producing for the body politic. Our financial condition demands it. We must establish priorities, forget about saving face, and remember only the good that certain programs are producing and in what quantities.

I do not mean that we must have the economic realities solely in mind. They are most important, but there is social justice as well to be served. The latter, however, cannot be served by paper shuffling, visions of things to come, and tattered hopes pridefully supported. We must expand our successes, discard our failures, and learn that productive ideas are more important than increased appropriations.

To be more specific, the experience of the concentrated code enforcement program shows that more homes have been targeted for rehabilitation under this operation in one and a half years than have been done under Title I rehabilitation since 1954. This is a sample of what HUD can best learn from its far flung operations and profit greatly thereby. The profit will flow not only to the Department, but also, and more importantly, to the people seeking rehabilitation tools.

HUD could start by reviewing thoroughly its workable program, particularly with respect to progress in code adoption and enforcement and every possible assistance should be provided to localities by HUD to permit them to comply. This is particularly pertinent since statutory provisions on code enforcement must be met.

PROPERTY TAX REVISION

It does no good to encourage a family to rehabilitate and improve its home or place of business if the reward is an immediate and much heavier tax burden. Particularly is this true while the slum landlord reaps benefits from failure to live up to code provisions and the basic needs of his tenants. We should tax him and not the man who improves his property.

What we need is some partnership system between federal and local governments and the property owner that will reward him for neighborhood betterment, penalize him for failing to correct conditions that cause his property to be labeled substandard. I do not think a permanent tax abatement is the answer, but I can conceive of one lasting three years that would help immeasurably. The local government could still collect its previous taxes and look forward to increased revenues after three years.

A NATIONAL HOME OWNERSHIP FOUNDATION

Our goal must and should be to move from a strong basic private housing effort to more specific proposals to meet the needs of our less-fortunate citizens. The provision of sufficient housing, and an adequate choice in housing (as between renter and owner-occupied, for example), utilizing the private sector to the fullest extent and securing some meaningful involvement for those to be benefited, remains the goal.

Whether existing federal institutions and agencies can achieve this goal is questionable.

As hearings before both House and Senate Subcommittees on Housing in the past several years have disclosed, there is a widespread feeling that neither the Department of Housing and Urban Development nor its constituent agencies, are meeting the challenge posed by the Housing Act of 1949—a decent, safe and sanitary home for every American family. In so failing, HUD has ignored Congressional intent, concentrated almost solely on renter-oriented (and *administratively controllable*) housing, and has frozen special assistance funds under FNMA that literally begged to be used.

The Federal Housing Administration has been even more sharply criticized for failing to be helpful in its regulations, administration and attitude. FHA admittedly has been confused by being assigned numerous programs directed toward social goals while its fundamental and original task of encouraging private industry to meet general housing demand has been altered. Thus it has both risk-taking and non-risk-taking functions. The same person may handle suburban housing in the morning and rehabilitation housing in a deteriorating neighborhood in the afternoon. As a result, both functions suffer.

One answer is to separate the two functions into two different agencies within HUD. Another and not incompatible approach would be to create a Congressionally chartered, independent foundation or non-profit corporation to assist in meeting the housing needs of allegedly higher risk families. The administration has pursued neither logical course. Such a Congressionally chartered independent foundation is embodied in the Republican proposal for a National Home Ownership Foundation.

Besides the independent nature of the Foundation, the pro-

posal stresses another overlooked housing idea, home ownership for lower income Americans, and minority groups. According to the 1960 Census, while 64.3 percent of all white
Americans knew the benefits of home ownership, only 38.4
percent of non-whites shared this experience. In ghetto areas,
the figure ranges all the way down to an estimated 1½ percent
in Harlem, with Standard Metropolitan Statistical Area core
cities averaging 31.4 percent. Similarly, on an income basis, in
the decade of the 1950s, the share of all new standard housing was only 5 percent for families with $3–$5000 income
averages. FHA, which in 1950 issued 42.8 percent of its
mortgages on existing homes to families with incomes under
$4000, and 56 percent of its new home insurances to the
same income group, had abandoned these families almost entirely by 1966. Within that year, its activity is estimated at
1.3 percent for existing homes and 1 percent for new construction.

Yet what better way to provide the incentive for family
stability, for respect for property, for neighborhood and
community involvement, and for improvement of credit history and employment patterns, than the time-honored American tradition of home ownership? Not all low income citizens
can take advantage of the program. Many if not most, will
need credit counseling, advice in family budgeting, home-
making, job training, home maintenance and the like. The
program will not meet all the needs for low income housing
assistance, but it is a housing alternative that is so obviously
missing in many areas of the country. If we expect an individual to take the responsibilities of a citizen in a democratic
society, then he must have a stake in it. And ownership of
private property is as meaningful a stake as has ever been
conceived.

Pilot projects sponsored by private non-profit groups in
localities around the country have proven the feasibility of
the idea. Through its operation, poor credit risks have become
good credit risks. Neighborhoods have organized around home
ownership projects to provide the people benefited with a
feeling of responsibility, involvement and meaningful participa-

tion. The National Home Ownership Foundation approach
seeks to build on this experience. That existing federal housing agencies have fought the idea, and ignored home ownership, until recent months, speaks volumes about their attitude
toward government control on the one hand, and the interests
of the ordinary citizen, on the other.

The use of an independent entity like the Foundation, non-
competitive with existing private mortgage financing institutions, yet capable of drawing in additional investment to the
mortgage market to meet a critical need, is another important
objective. Pension funds, for example, have assets of nearly
$175 billion, but only $20 billion invested in mortgages of
any kind. The traditional reluctance of pension trustees for
such investments based on unfamiliarity with the field and
servicing costs could be dispelled by providing a new investment medium, the federally guaranteed bonds of the Home
Ownership Foundation.

Where interest subsidies have been used to lower costs of
renting or purchasing housing units, the traditional method
has been to provide FHA guarantees for below-market-
interest rate mortgages. This is backed up by an immediate
mortgage purchase from the private lending institution by the
Federal National Mortgage Association using funds borrowed
from the Treasury. This is a large current budget item. It
involves a subsidy reflecting the difference between the cost
of borrowing by the Treasury and the below-market return of
the mortgages. To re-involve private funds, FNMA sells
participations in a pool of similar mortgages and loans held
by the government. This requires a second subsidy to meet
the difference between the interest paid on the participation
certificate and the lower interest being received on the mortgages and loans in the pool. It means a double debt for the
federal government.

Interest Subsidization

Whether it be the National Home Ownership Foundation
or the FHA, it makes sense to adopt the position taken by

Republicans on the interest subsidy. This position holds that the interest subsidy should be made directly by the Treasury to the holders of market-rate mortgages. Only one subsidy would be involved; and much less administrative cost. It could be easily reviewed at any time by Congress. It would involve only the use of private mortgage capital; FNMA more adequately could perform its role as a secondary mortgage market; and the budget would be rescued from an increasingly and unacceptable strain. If for example, we take a $10,000 house, a 3 percent interest subsidy, and a thirty-year mortgage, then a $60 million budget item could produce 200,000 new housing units under the Republican approach, while under the FNMA procedure, only 6000 would be built.

Originally conceived for the home ownership program, the direct interest subsidy idea could be considered for other below-market interest rate programs, including direct loan programs by the government in the college housing, elderly housing and urban renewal rehabilitation fields. Sufficient private capital would, of course, have to be available to meet the demand for this type of loan. Nevertheless, a spokesman for the home building industry has described it as an idea that is a breakthrough in the thinking on budget financing for housing programs.

Coops and Condominiums

In core cities, home ownership efforts must emphasize the cooperative and condominium approach. The condominium is closer to the usual fee simple purchase of property associated with single-family dwellings, but it involves an intricate legal mechanism. Unfamiliarity and uncertainty as to how the common law applies has discouraged its use. Much of this confusion and difficulty could be avoided by carefully drawn state laws, similar to those of Illinois or Puerto Rico. The cooperative has a long and relatively successful history and deserves additional encouragement also.

PUBLIC HOUSING

If public housing is to serve a useful purpose other than a high-rise storehouse for problem families or families without hope, it must change its image and its approach. To whatever extent possible, publicly assisted rental housing should provide incentives for the families assisted to improve themselves and become part of a wider community.

One concept that needs to be expanded upon is the sale of units to tenants, a Republican legislative initiative enacted into law in 1966. The condominium or cooperative is adaptable to the program. Those public housing families reaching income limitations for occupancy would be able to convert from renting units to owning them.

Public housing should also be built in relation to community services in the surrounding neighborhood—stores, library facilities, recreational space and the like. Building a self-contained public housing "village" with its own stores and library may have an appeal to the planners, but it has little appeal to the residents of the projects who feel it is only another attempt to isolate them in vertical ghettos.

Rent Certificates

Expansion of the Republican proposal of rent certificates, or leased public housing should be undertaken. The rent certificate program, by using privately owned rental units volunteered by their owners, at public housing rentals and for one to five year terms, eliminates many construction and management costs, architectural and legal fees and similar expenses. The federal costs are less, and the terms more flexible and workable than in rent supplements. Property rehabilitation is encouraged, and more importantly, by using existing dwellings; local communities are able to make a sizable dent in the long waiting lists typical of public housing. By limiting the number of public housing tenants per building, concentration of problems encountered in public housing can be avoided. The private landlord benefits from greater tenant stability, and the community loses nothing from its tax rolls.

Increased use could be encouraged by eliminating unnecessary restrictions on the use of the rent certificate program where vacancy rates are very low for a locality. These restrictions show a lack of comprehension of the fact that vacancy rates are not an appropriate criterion for judging whether or not the program can work in a community. Many public housing eligibles live in rented quarters paying rents beyond their capacity to pay to landlords who may well be eager to participate in the leased public housing program. Present use of the leased approach through rehabilitation by private owners has restored thousands of substandard units to standard condition. Further use can only make better a greatly improved housing condition. Builders are now offering to build, and are building, under the rent certificate program.

Low Interest Rehabilitation Loans

The creation of additional standard housing for use by those of low and moderate income is now being done under the 3 percent rehabilitation loan program as part of urban renewal. This was a Republican proposal enacted in 1964. Coupled with stricter code enforcement this program of property improvement could stand judicious expansion. We do need to find a means of keeping those of low income from ruinous expenditures, but this can be done.

As of now, the loan program is limited to areas with urban renewal projects particularly those of intensive code enforcement. The program area could well be expanded to include all those operations involving the bringing up of buildings to local code standards. To make this work, the eligibility criteria for loan funds should be revised back to the 1964 criterion that an individual must show the impossibility of obtaining and affording home improvement loans from commercial lending institutions. As it now stands, anyone who cannot obtain *comparable* terms can qualify, and that means just about anyone, regardless of income. The latter change was made by Congress because of FHA's unrealistic and unsympathetic application of the original language. When a man has strained his resources to buy a substandard home for $1500, it does him irreparable harm to have a mandatory bill for $3000 plus forced on him on top of his original investment.

Obviously some structures will be so unsound and so expensive to renovate, that rehabilitation will not be realistic. New housing will also be necessary to meet growing demands. Nevertheless, in any one year, existing housing will represent approximately 97 percent of the housing units available. Rehabilitation, together with increased home ownership for people of lower income adds mightily to the preservation of neighborhoods and a family's willingness to join in community involvement and individual responsibility.

Equally important, rehabilitation offers not only many new job openings for present workers of the building trades, plus new employment opportunities for the residents of ghetto neighborhoods or rural areas. Utilization of the "sweat equity" principle, for example, could not only reduce purchase costs to the lower income buyer, but would, with proper training, provide him with marketable labor skills. This principle of self-help has been proven effective in many private pilot projects. Local building trades unions have shown considerable foresight in assisting the process, with realistic wage demands and apprenticeship programs. A re-evaluation of existing doubts and opposition, particularly at the national level, on the part of the building trades, would be of benefit to union members and ghetto residents alike.

Rural and Small Community Housing

Rural and smaller community housing needs are as important as those of the central city. By federal government criteria, 36 percent of the population lived in farm or nonfarm rural areas in 1967. In 1960, the Census found 45.7 percent of the deteriorated and dilapidated housing in rural areas under 2500 population. The twelve largest central cities had only 8 percent of these substandard dwellings. And lest we forget, 56 percent of the population still resides in communities of less than 50,000, while population density is increasing, most rapidly in cities between 50 and 100 thousand in population.

Such similar communities and rural areas can take advantage of home ownership programs. They will be better able to make use of their sweat equity. They also provide unique laboratories for experimenting with new housing techniques and materials, since they are often unburdened by archaic building codes and labor costs are lower. County housing authorities, with the permission of local communities, can also utilize the leased public housing approach where communities themselves would not be able to afford the administrative machinery.

FINANCIAL CONSIDERATIONS

In the fall of 1966, because of tight money, housing starts in October dropped to a twenty-year low at a rate of under 900,000 units a year on a seasonally adjusted basis. In the fall of 1967, money was not much "looser," but housing demonstrated a strong recovery with 1967 October starts at 1,496,000 units on a seasonally adjusted basis.

Why the difference?

In the fall of 1966 banks and savings and loans were loaned to the hilt and experienced a loss of funds to the short term securities market where yields reached a forty-year high. Housing credit accordingly suffered.

The high long-term bond rates have not pulled funds away from our savings institutions which are our principal source of home mortgage credit. The real test, however, lies ahead.

Our huge deficit will force the Federal Treasury into heavy short-term financing in the months to come. This will put upward pressure on short-term interest rates. The 8 percent British bank rate, set after devaluation of the pound, will draw short-term funds from our market and add to upward pressure on short-term rates. And if the Treasury persists in selling Federal National Mortgage Association participations (its highest cost form of financing) this will cause added upward pressure on rates. Recently a billion dollars of participations were offered setting a new high for our current "credit crunch" with rates of 6⅜ and 6½ percent on what in effect is government credit.

It is important to bear in mind the difference between 1967's credit picture and that of 1966. In 1966, mortgage money simply was not available. In 1967, mortgage money was available at a price. In my opinion, mortgage credit on conventional mortgages will continue to be available with interest rates of 6½ to 7 percent in 1968. But the FHA and VA programs with 6 percent or less statutory interest ceilings are in for trouble. Lenders will not make these types of loans with the deep discounts that would have to be charged to make their interest returns competitive in a high interest market.

Setting the FHA and VA mortgage rates at competitive levels should minimize discounts. Congress should so legislate.

At present the Federal National Mortgage Association is providing substantial assistance to the mortgage market. It should continue to do so. Last year the Congress authorized an increase in Treasury subscription to FNMA preferred stock in the amount of $110 million and increased the borrowing ratio from ten to fifteen times capital. As a result of these changes alone FNMA now has unused authorization which would enable it to raise more than $2.6 billion of funds to further assist the home mortgage market. It should act on this.

Conclusion

The myth of federal dominance as a matter of necessity in housing programs is slowly being broken by non-profit groups, private industry efforts in the rehabilitation field, and imaginative local and state programs. Federal efforts must be directed increasingly to the encouragements of this trend. The use of a combination of rent certificates and the turnkey method, for example, would do much towards solving the problem of adequate management and expertise. Under this approach, commercial builders could handle the actual construction efforts, making all savings possible without the suffocating red tape of bureaucracy. Similarly, federal, state, and local tax laws could and should be utilized to encourage rehabilitation and construction for lower income families. States could provide technical assistance funds or "seed" money for non-profit and neighborhood corporations. Anything is imaginatively possible in practical hands.

Any attempt to indicate new approaches to housing and community development must recognize the limitations of knowledge in the field. At the planning and project level, little has been done to make use of the insights that could be provided by sociologists, anthropologists, urban economists, mental health specialists and like experts. At the academic level, the nation's colleges and universities have done little to bring inter-disciplinary knowledge into programs in urban affairs, public administration or urban planning, where these even exist. Research is spasmodic, and the results of separate private, state or local efforts are not widely disseminated, functions that an alert federal government could well perform. In general, neither today's policy makers, nor those of the next generation, are likely to consider housing more than a problem of plumbing. Even citizen participation tends to be made up of those largely unrepresentative of the neighborhood or community affected.

Until we close this knowledge gap, until evaluative statistics are made available for Congress and the American people to judge existing programs by, and until the people themselves find a role in the process, housing programs will remain mere stopgap measures incapable of meeting today's problems or the challenge of tomorrow.

Chapter 6

THE FUTURE OF AGRICULTURE

AGRICULTURE IN MIDPASSAGE*

by Don Paarlberg

DON PAARLBERG is Hillenbrand Professor of Agricultural
Economics at Purdue University. He received his B.S.
degree from Purdue University and his M.A. and Ph.D.
degrees from Cornell University. Prior to his appointment
at Purdue in 1961, Professor Paarlberg served eight
years in Washington during the Eisenhower administration in a variety of capacities—as Food for Peace Co-
ordinator, Special Assistant to the President, assistant to
Secretary of Agriculture Benson, and Assistant Secretary of Agriculture. An authority on agricultural subjects,
Dr. Paarlberg is the author of *American Farm Policy,*
published in 1964 and *Great Myths of Economics,* published in 1968.

If someone had been asked, fifty years ago, to nominate the
vocational group in the United States least likely to request
or accept production controls and government-supported markets, he probably would have named our farm people.

THE AGRICULTURAL CREED

Farm people have had, until fairly recent times, a strong
feeling of self-reliance and independence. To some degree this
attitude still persists. This feeling is found in an agricultural
creed which has been the basis of our national agricultural

* Adapted from Don Paarlberg, *American Farm Policy,* Wiley
and Sons, 1964.

policies until well into the twentieth century. The creed may be expressed as follows:

(1) Farmers are good citizens, and a high percentage of our population should be on farms.
(2) Farming is not only a business but a way of life.
(3) Farming should be a family enterprise.
(4) The land should be owned by the man who tills it.
(5) It is good to make two blades of grass grow where only one grew before.
(6) Anyone who wants to farm should be free to do so.
(7) A farmer should be his own boss.

This creed, which has been called "agricultural fundamentalism" and "agrarianism," was based largely on the teachings of a group of French thinkers called physiocrats. The creed has its roots also in Jeffersonian democracy and in the classical economics of Adam Smith. The philosophy is essentially that which has been described as "the work ethic," or "the Puritan ethic," a belief in diligence and individual responsibility. But physiocratic thought is the most discernible single component of the creed, the articles of which are briefly discussed in the following section.

The Agrarian Society. The physiocrats taught that the physical production of goods, not the merchandising of them, was the basic source of wealth and therefore the most meritorious occupation. And of all goods produced, said the physiocrats, none was so vital, so needed, or so inexhaustible as the annual increase which came from tilling the soil. Therefore the farmer stood high above all others as a man of merit.

Not only did the farmer rank high as a producer of useful goods; he was also a stalwart citizen. He was hardworking, reverent, and less inclined to civil uprisings than his city cousin. He was physically strong, self-reliant, and possessed of manual skills. He made a good soldier. That country would be most wealthy and most stable which had a large share of its population on the land.

All these considerations endow agriculture with a large stock of public good will, the dimensions of which have been estimated with considerable skill by those who propose farm programs. This is the reason we would develop a parity program for farmers but not for barbers or hardware merchants.

A Way of Life. The second article, that farming is not only a business but a way of life, comes from an awareness of and an appreciation for the nonmonetary rewards of farming. These are real to those brought up to appreciate them: independence, family solidarity, visibility of accomplishment, vocational prestige, good neighbors, close contact with nature, and outdoor work. A farmer will add these psychic rewards (measured in accordance with his own sense of values) to anticipated financial returns in comparing farm with nonfarm alternatives. One must conclude that the psychic rewards are substantial if there is to be a satisfactory explanation for the willingness of so many rural people to offer their labor for such low financial returns.

There are in fact not only psychic rewards in agriculture but psychic liabilities as well: long hours, hard work, limited educational opportunities, and relatively few conveniences. But the creed has long emphasized the rewards more than the liabilities, and believers have come out with the view that farming not only *is* a way of life, but that it is a *good* way. They have in mind the continuation of those features of rural living which distinguished it from urban life.

Family Farms. The third item in the agricultural creed is the belief in farming as a family undertaking. This is in preference to corporate enterprise or the plantation system. The family is to work as a unit, with the children serving apprenticeship, confident that they too will in time be farmers. Belief in the family farm is an American reaction against the landed aristocracies and the peasantry of Europe, from which our forefathers fled.

No other single thread of policy runs through our ag-

ricultural history with such consistency—or with such success—as the policy that favors the family farm.

Owner Operation. Not only does the agricultural creed
prescribe the family pattern of farm organization; it pre-
scribes that title to the land should be vested in the family
that tills the soil. The family farm concept in America,
facilitated by our abundant land resources, made it possible to provide the prestige of land ownership to the
many, thereby avoiding the social and economic disadvantages of a landed aristocracy. It permitted the development of an efficient form of agricultural production
which has been able, except for a few specialized products, to hold its own against the large-scale corporate
form of operation.

Two Blades of Grass. A fifth article in the agricultural
creed is this belief, long felt but first articulated by
Jonathan Swift, author of *Gulliver's Travels:* "Whoever
could make two ears of corn or two blades of grass to
grow upon a spot of ground where only one grew before," wrote Swift, "would deserve better of mankind
and do more essential service to this country than the
whole race of politicians put together."

The public puts food in a special category, ranked
above virtually all other goods in basic merit, to be produced in abundance and not to be wasted.

Not only does public opinion require us to avoid
wasting food; it requires that we continue to produce at a
high level. The Land Grant College System, with its
Experiment Stations and its program of rural education,
was founded on the idea that it is good to make two
blades of grass grow where only one grew before. The
same is true of the Reclamation Service. To get the
public land into the hands of people who would make
it produce, to drain the swamp, to irrigate the desert
and to clear the land, these have long been the basic
drives in agriculture, unquestioned until recent years,
and still fiercely defended whenever challenged!

Unrestricted Enterprise. The sixth of the articles in our

agricultural creed is the belief that anyone who wants to farm should be free to do so. Government will recognize the union shop and restrict by franchise the number of firms which can provide this or that public service. But the government has never been willing to restrict entry into agriculture. Part of agriculture's heritage is the belief that the doors should be open, that anyone should have the opportunity to engage in farm production if he considers this his preferred alternative. Indeed, it is believed that the government should help people get started in farming as we have long been doing despite an oversupply of manpower in agriculture.

Independence. The agricultural creed holds that a farmer should be his own boss. Ideally, he should not take orders from an industrialist, a financier, a labor union, an employer, or from the government. The farmer is independent. In this he is pridefully different from the wage-earner. The idea is that the farm operator should be self-reliant. He should be a man of action, not a man of passive acceptance. He should have initiative and enterprise. And it has been part of the creed that these attributes would be rewarded in wealth and position. This spirit subdued the wilderness, settled the plains, and made American agriculture the admiration of the world.

These articles of the agricultural creed were partly inherited from overseas and were partly our own creation. They were consistent, mutually reinforcing, and for many years remarkably well adapted to American conditions. So dominant was the agricultural creed that for 150 years no major piece of farm legislation was enacted contrary to it.

The image and the idea for agriculture, which prevailed until well into the twentieth century and which to some degree still exists, in summary was this:

Family farms in great numbers, owned by the men who operated them, producing a large and growing volume of crops and livestock products.

Farm operators who were sturdy and self-reliant, making their own decisions, turning their farms over to their sons upon retirement, enjoying the satisfaction that comes from an honorable occupation, experiencing a rising level of living, and feeling the prestige that results from land ownership.

It was a mighty vision, never wholly true, but true enough to justify it as an ideal. With this pattern American agriculture went from a wilderness to the most efficient farm plant in the world in a period of a few hundred years. Levels of living rose, the hazards of farm production were diminished, the disadvantages of rural life were reduced, and the social status of the American farmer achieved a high level almost unique in the world. The system of individual enterprise in agriculture proved a tremendous success.

This was the set of ideas with which America entered the twentieth century. By then some strains were showing, and some questions were being asked. The frontier was closing. The free land was almost gone. The industrial economy was advancing. Agrarianism was on the defensive, but the inertia of these dominant agricultural ideas was enormous. It would take a terrific shock to change them.

But this shock was coming. It was a two-stage blow. The system which had withstood war, natural disaster, and economic adversity would be subjected to the hammer blows of a terrible depression and a technological revolution.

There came, then, the clash of an established ideology with a new and harsh set of economic facts. This would change the form and character of agriculture in a few short years. The first of these two hammer blows was the Great Depression of the 1930s.

FARMERS AND THE GREAT DEPRESSION

From 1929 to 1932, prices received by farmers fell 56 percent. Gross farm income in the United States fell 54 percent. Net income fell from $6.3 billion to $1.9 billion.

Anyone who went through the Great Depression without asking questions about individual enterprise lacked economic awareness.

Burned deep and lasting in the memory of every person of farm background, now aged fifty or more and therefore old enough to have been economically sensitive during the 1930s, is that long and terrible experience. When a farmer sits down to do his serious economic worrying, a reoccurrence or an approximation of the Great Depression is what he worries about.

Of course, farmers were not the only ones to suffer from the Great Depression. They took their loss in terms of price. Industry tended to hold prices up but reduced volume. Labor maintained and even increased wages but took its misfortune in the form of unemployment. The service trades suffered both in volume and in returns per unit. All experienced a decline in net income.

What was the impact of the Great Depression on the agricultural creed? It was disastrous—and lasting. The creed was based on the idea that enterprise and hard work would pay out. This idea was shaken. Previously a farm foreclosure was almost clear evidence of mismanagement. But with the Great Depression it was often the good, productive farms which were in greatest distress. And the farmers who worked hard, often for no return, looked with bewilderment and sometimes with anger on the nonworkers with their relief checks. Economic justice seemed to have vanished.

The creed was founded on the belief that the market was an intelligent institution. But here were markets seemingly gone wild with fear, markets that appeared to make no sense.

The creed had extolled the merits of high production, but what were the merits of high production when the market would barely move the then current supplies?

The creed had every farmer being his own boss. But the decisions that individual farmers were making did not seem sensible. Why did farmers persist in producing so much of things which no one seemed to want? The market appeared to be yielding unreasonable answers. Individual decision-making seemed to result in nothing but chaos.

The free economy, so long extolled by the agricultural creed, was without convincing answers to these problems and without remedies. Time was running out and tempers were getting short. In Iowa, farmers threatened to hang a judge who was carrying out his responsibilities in the foreclosure of mortgages. The Farmers Holiday Movement, headed by Milo Reno, undertook to block the movement of farm products to market. Hot-headed farmers were overturning milk trucks and banding together to prevent foreclosure sales.

Into the breach rushed an ill-assorted group: reliefers, reformers, opportunists, and subversives.

Out of a turmoil of diagnosis and prescription there came, finally, a consensus sufficient to permit action. It was the overproduction theory that became accepted in farm policy circles.

The overproduction theory had the merit of simplicity, though it failed to explain the low prices of farm commodities that had not increased in production. And it failed to explain low prices in the nonfarm sector of the American economy. Indeed, it failed to explain the price behavior of the farm and nonfarm sectors in other countries, all of which showed price fluctuations similar to our own.

Whatever the merits of the diagnosis and the prescription, the objective was quickly determined: raise the prices received by farmers to a fair level. What was fair? The prices received in the last "normal" period, a period of neither war nor depression, the "golden age of agriculture," 1910 to 1914. The restoration of price relationships as they existed in 1910 to 1914 thus became the objective. This relationship, by a stroke of political genius, was given the name of "parity," a word that literally radiated justice, fairness, rectitude, and objectivity.

How were we to work toward parity? By reducing production. With production reduced, it was reasoned that prices would rise. Therefore, in an emergency situation and admittedly without much basic analysis, government moved in to restrict farm production and increase prices of individual farm products. This was the long road from which it would be difficult to turn back.

Though production of a few crops was curtailed, the over-all index of agricultural production continued to rise. Its course appears not to have been appreciably altered by the programs. This is wholly understandable, since farmers were allowed to plant anything other than wheat, corn, and cotton on land diverted out of these controlled crops.

Surpluses began at once to accumulate. The fact that they did not become a greater burden is attributable to two droughts (1934 and 1936) and a war (1939).

Finally, the Great Depression came to an end, not conquered by the farm program or the labor program or the industrial program but by the insatiable demands that arose from World War II.

It was a terrible decade. Economic growth had been deferred, long-respected American ideas had been altered, objectives had been questioned, our institutional framework had been shaken, and the relation of the individual to society had been basically changed. The enterprise system had been subjected to ten years of persistent and unrefuted attack.

In agriculture, only one thing was certain: the old order was changed and things would never again be the same.

FARMERS AND THE SCIENTIFIC REVOLUTION

The technological revolution proved to be the dominant agricultural force during the postwar period. Perhaps the most vivid quantification of the agricultural revolution is the fact that twenty-five years ago one farm worker fed 12 people. The most recent figure is 36. Output per farm worker has increased at a rate of over 5 percent per year during the past decade, about twice the nonfarm rate. The farm population has been cut in half during the last twenty years.

There have been more agricultural changes during the lives of people now living than there were in all the previous years since Bible times. If it had been possible, magically, to transport someone from Old Testament times to an American farm as of a hundred years ago, our visitor would have recognized virtually every tool then in use: the rake, the hoe, the plow, the flail. Transported to an American farm today, he would think he was on another planet.

The agricultural revolution has developed a new and portentous idea. Instead of simply accepting what the economists call "the factors of production" (land, labor, capital, and management) as they happen to be combined and at the disposal of one man, the family farm operator, the new concept is to split up the factors of production and reassemble them in optimum form. The economic efficiency latent in this organizational change is, in certain cases, very great indeed. Managerial ability can be recruited, trained, and given responsibility not just for a small unit but for a large one. Capital can be brought in from the outside, not in conventionally sized chunks but in aggregations suited to the capability of the new managerial concept. Farms can be consolidated or operated as associated units, making maximum use of new mechanical equipment and new managerial techniques. Farm labor can be hired and given specific well-defined tasks to perform, as is factory labor. The possible result, if this concept is carried out fully, could resemble the family farm little more than a textile plant resembles the hand loom.

The managerial revolution can take a form called "vertical integration." By this technique the production and market, for example, of broilers, is made into a continuous operation, under single direction. Hatchery, feed supply, financing, the actual raising of broilers, and the marketing of them are related to one another under unified management. The result is standardized quality, controlled movement to market, and reduced over-all cost per bird. The farmer who feeds and cares for the broilers, formerly a farmer in the tradition of family farming, making his own decisions and risking his own capital, becomes essentially a hired laborer or a piece-worker.

The managerial revolution is clearly in its early stages. No one can tell what it will become or where it will go.

The agricultural revolution added a new dimension to the farm policy debate. Could farmers voluntarily make the adjustments required by this revolution? Or should government move in to cushion the impact when change proceeded at a rate more rapid than could readily be assimilated? Should these changes be slowed down, speeded up, or simply accommodated?

So the focus of the farm problem was changed. The original question had been how to overcome a depression. The new problem was to find a way of dealing with an agricultural revolution. Uniquely enough, the legislation originally enacted to deal with the Great Depression was expected to serve the new cause as well.

Characteristically, the problems of the rural people with really low incomes received scant attention in postwar consideration of farm policy. It was the problems of those farm people already on the upper rungs of the economic ladder that were considered. As had been the case in earlier farm policy debates, the rationale was based on the problems of the low-income operator, but the proposals considered were such as to channel the dollars to the operators of the large farms.

Those who believed in economic freedom were quite willing that the agricultural revolution should proceed, feeling strong conviction that if left free to do so, farmers would adapt themselves wisely to it. Those who held the decision-making ability of farm people in low esteem insisted that government should control the pace and cushion the consequences of the agricultural revolution. The pro-control group won most of the battles of this war, just as they had won most of the battles touched off by the Great Depression a decade or so earlier.

WHITHER BOUND?

The agricultural creed received a severe buffeting from the Great Depression and is taking a bad drubbing from the agricultural revolution. We may pause now to assess the present status of this creed, article by article.

(1) *Farmers are good citizens and a high percentage of our population should be on farms.*

The country agrees that farmers are good people. But the agricultural revolution has completely invalidated the objective of a large rural population.

When the agricultural creed was first formulated, our population was 90 percent agricultural. Now it is 94 percent nonagricultural. Advancing productivity per person in agriculture has made it possible to provide food and fiber with a relatively small share of our human and material resources, leaving a relatively large share to provide homes, education, travel, and other social services. This is the necessary condition for a rising level of living.

There is much unjustified grief about those who are "forced out of agriculture." In the first place, it would be more nearly correct to say that they are "attracted to off-farm employment." They go voluntarily, and so at least in their own opinion they better their lot by the change. Studies have shown this to be true. They not only better their own lot, but by reducing the competition for limited farming opportunities they improve the lot of those who remain on farms. If there had been no reduction in the farm population during the past twenty years and therefore the farm population were twice as high as it presently is, it follows that per capita incomes of farm people would be only half their present level.

(2) *Farming is not only a business but a way of life.*

To the degree that this article of the creed considers agriculture a meritorious vocation, agreement continues. But if it is used to justify a cultural barrier between farm and city life, or to rationalize an economic differential adverse to agriculture, farm people are opposed.

The farmer of today wants to see in the "city limits" sign not a social or a cultural or an economic barrier, but simply a line which differentiates one system of local government from another. He wants to preserve what is good about farm life without farmers being made a class apart. He wears his occupational badge with less assertiveness than he once did. He thinks of himself more as a member of society in general and less as the defender of a unique—and archaic—cultural form.

(3) *Farming should be a family enterprise.*

Farming is and for the foreseeable future will continue to be predominantly a family enterprise. About 96 percent of the farm units are organized on a family basis, essentially the same percentage as for many years past. About 70 percent of our farm production is from family farms. The family farm has shown remarkable resilience. It has survived depression, war, and natural disaster. There is reason to believe it can also survive a technological revolution. But to survive it must be able to change with the times. It must be able to grow in terms of acreage cultivated, capital invested, and income earned. To try to hold the family farm in the mold of the past would be to condemn it to obsolescence and indeed to something resembling peasantry.

(4) *The land should be owned by the man who tills it.*

What has been the impact of the technological revolution on this article of the agricultural creed?

The over-all figures look good. Today, nearly 80 percent of the farm operators own the land they operate, or are part-owners. A generation ago the figure was only 57 percent. This rise is a consequence of high earnings in agriculture during the war and early postwar years, which permitted many renters to purchase land.

But there are problems. The percentage of ownership is highest among those on small low-income farms, and lowest for those on farms large enough to provide the operator with a satisfactory level of living. There are, of course, enormous financial obstacles to acquiring ownership of a unit large enough to provide a suitable income. A Corn Belt farm large enough to provide an income considered appropriate by modern standards involves an investment well in excess of $100,000. Increasingly, the large farms, capable of yielding satisfactory incomes, are held within families, with the title changing hands by inheritance or marriage. This may be "family farming with the land owned by the one who tills it," but it means a hereditary land-owning class, not wholly in keeping with the agricultural creed.

(5) *It is good to make two blades of grass grow where only one grew before.*

On this article of the creed the country is bewildered.

Truly we are inconsistent with respect to production policy. In research and educational activities we pursue the policy of agricultural abundance; in acreage reduction programs we go the direction of scarcity. With reclamation projects we endeavor to make the desert bloom; with the emergency feed program we leave the good land idle. With government payments for lime, drainage, and fertilizer we try to make two blades of grass grow where only one grew before; by disking down wheat and cotton to "get into compliance" we destroy the blade already growing.

(6) *Anyone who wants to farm should be free to do so.*

There is little evidence that this article of the creed has been basically weakened by the technological revolution. We are less enthusiastic than we once were about helping people to become farmers, but there is no evidence of any strong move to prevent people from farming, or to set up a board to grant farming licenses.

If one were to count the number of replacement opportunities during the next decade on farms with sales of $100,000 or more per year and then count the number of farm boys who will reach 20 years of age during this period, he would find that only about 8 percent of them will have an opportunity to become successful farm operators.

Obviously not all farm boys can farm. The birth rate on farms is high and the number of farms is diminishing,

putting great pressure on the few new farming opportunities becoming available. The real question is: "How shall
the available farming opportunities be rationed?" There
are basically two ways. One is to leave everyone free to
farm if he wishes, as the creed says, and ration farming
opportunities by the free choice method, with each person sizing up his qualifications, his preferences, and his
probable returns in farming as compared with nonfarm-
ing alternatives. The other way is to ration farming opportunities by some sort of licensing provision, by setting
up some minimum standard, or by some rating scale.

(7) *A farmer should be his own boss.*

It would take an able student of the social sciences to
assess accurately the changes wrought in this article of
the agricultural creed during the past half-century. The
present state or for that matter the earlier state of ad-
herence to this precept is not subject to close calibration.

It is clear, however, that commitment is today less ar-
dent than it formerly was. Every recent major influence
has been to weaken it.

Not just in agriculture but throughout the economy the
ethic of "life adjustment," "acceptance," and "security"
has been, to a degree, substituted for the ethic of individual responsibility. This change is variously attributed
to Karl Marx, to Sigmund Freud, to John Dewey, to
Franklin Roosevelt, and to many others. The true responsibility for this tidal drift is difficult to determine. No
strong spokesman of the older ethic has recently been
able to gain and hold the ear of the American public.

Agriculture entered the Great Depression with a still
high degree of faith in individual responsibility, and put
that faith to the test. The consensus was that individual
responsibility had been weighed in the balance and found
wanting, at least for certain products. Farmers are now
in the midst of a technological revolution and are not all
convinced that the needed adjustments can be made satisfactorily through individual responsibility.

So there is the old agricultural creed. Some articles of the faith are seriously damaged. Others remain almost intact. None has been strengthened.

We continue to pay homage to the old creed in campaign speeches and in official statements, after the manner of a Buddhist spinning his prayer-wheel. But much of the force and conviction has gone out of the exercise.

The old agrarian creed, which once gave us an agreed goal, has been much weakened. No new unifying core of belief has arisen. Small wonder, then, that agricultural policy is in a confused state. Policy is most readily developed when there is agreement on goals and consensus on strategy. It is most effectively implemented when there is an effective power structure to carry it out. On all these counts, agriculture is now in a state of uncertainty, brought about by the agricultural revolution.

It is often said that we are agreed on goals but in disagreement on means. The problem is much deeper than that. We are not only disagreed on whether to take the bus or drive the car; we are disagreed on whether to go to New York or San Francisco, and we aren't sure who will buy the gas for either trip.

Unrest on the farm front is evidence of the psychological trauma through which farm people are going. Things familiar and trusted are being swept away and no new body of belief has arisen to give direction to our endeavors. The farm policymaker of today has a most difficult task. He must write laws for farm people who suffer from goal confusion. He must chart the course for a vessel that has left a port to which it cannot return and is searching for a shore as yet unknown.

FARM PRICES ...
AND FOOD FOR A HUNGRY WORLD
by Odin Langen

REPRESENTATIVE ODIN LANGEN (R., Minnesota) has
been a member of the U. S. House of Representatives
since 1958. A lifetime farmer, he was associated for fifteen years with the national farm program in Kittson
County, Minnesota, where he was chairman of the Production and Marketing Administration. Before his election
to Congress, he served in the Minnesota House of Representatives. As a member of Congress, Representative
Langen serves on the Appropriations Committee, is the
second ranking minority member on the Appropriations
Subcommittee on Agriculture, and is the ranking minority
member on the Legislative Subcommittee. He is serving
his second term as Chairman of the House Republican
Task Force on Agriculture.

Republican concern for the well-being of agriculture both
in the United States and throughout the world is well-founded.
Republican leaders have continuously recognized that a
healthy and economically secure American agriculture serves
to benefit people in all areas of the world. Their constructive
contributions and achievements are proof of this recognition.

It is now a little over one hundred years since the United
States Department of Agriculture was established. On May
15, 1862, President Lincoln, the nation's first Republican
President, signed into law a bill that created this new Department. Agriculture was then regarded as the single most
important economic activity in the nation. It must still be so
regarded today.

In 1889, the new Department was given representation in the innermost councils of government by the action of Congress which elevated the Department to Cabinet status.

Abraham Lincoln, and the Republican Party of his day, forcefully demonstrated their recognition of the importance of the production capacity of food and fiber to the future vitality of this nation and its people. With this beginning, the efforts of succeeding Republican Presidents and Congresses have left a heritage of advances in agriculture that today serve this nation and the world with distinction and fortune.

The growth and development in the American production capacity of quality foods in quantity find no equal anywhere in world history. I shall name but a few of many significant acts of government which helped bring this about.

Republican administrations were responsible for such revolutionary legislative accomplishments as the Homestead Act (1862), the Morrill Land Grant College Act (1862), National Forests Act (1891), National Reclamation Act (1902), Bureau of Plant Industry Act (1902), Pure Food and Drug Act (1906), Meat Inspection Act (1907), Dairy Products Exports Act (1908), Packers and Stockyards Act (1921), Cooperative Marketing Act (1922), Grain Futures Act (1922), Intermediate Credit Act (1923), United States Cotton Standards Act (1923), Import Milk Act (1927), Agricultural Marketing Act (1929), Foreign Agricultural Service (1930), Perishable Agricultural Commodities Act (1930), The Agricultural Trade Development and Assistance Act (Food for Peace) or Public Law 480 (1954), The Agriculture Act of 1954 or Public Law 690 (School Milk Program), and Watershed Protection and Flood Prevention Act (1954). Added to this are legislative accomplishments under a Republican-controlled Congress, such as the Forest Pest Control Act (1947), Federal Insecticide, Fungicide, and Rodenticide Act (1947), Sugar Act (1948), Agricultural Act (1948), and the Commodity Credit Corporation Charter Act (1948), as well as numerous other conservation programs and legislative enactments.

It is the combination of these varied agricultural programs designed to accomplish high production levels and to sustain the production capacity of our soils through conservation practices that constitutes a great heritage for the American people today.

U. S. AGRICULTURAL ACCOMPLISHMENTS

It isn't just by chance that the American consumer enjoys the privilege of spending less of his income dollar (18.3 percent) for food than does the consumer in any other country in the world. It is of interest to note that in the United Kingdom, the consumer spends about 26 percent of his income for food; in France, 29 percent; Austria, 32 percent; Italy, 42 percent; and it is even higher in the Communist bloc countries.

The American consumer finds readily available the highest quality, the best packaged, the greatest variety of food in the world. These are the results of research by land grant colleges in every field of production and marketing, together with the most efficient production from a highly mechanized and efficient operation.

We have mentioned government's contributions in these respects, and surely they have been most noteworthy. But the accomplishments would have been impossible without the great contributions made by the industrial community, the free enterprise system, and the independence of American farmers as individuals.

Industry has produced not only great scientific contributions to mechanization, but, of equal import, comparable achievements in the use of fertilizers, chemicals, and other innovations.

The farmer, himself, because of his independence and freedom to exercise his every ingenuity and ability, has taken full advantage of the resources available to him through nature, plus the combination of contributions from government and a skilled, knowledgeable nonfarm populace. These accomplishments have brought noteworthy advances to the American people, and to people in foreign countries, wherever they have been implemented.

The fact that one farmer-worker in this country is able to feed nearly forty people with his productive capacity, has released more than 90 percent of the populace to produce the many other conveniences and comforts that only this nation has to offer in world-envied quantity.

There are some rather impressive figures that substantiate these accomplishments by American agriculture. For instance, the production per acre has increased by 84 percent since the 1919–21 period, and the output per man-hour has increased by 500 percent. The productivity of the American farm worker has increased at more than double the rate of the nonagricultural worker. It is these accomplishments—which have reduced the total number of man-hours of our populace being spent to feed and clothe the nation—that have enabled the rest of the populace to produce the wealth of other items that identifies this nation with the highest standard of living that man has ever known.

The history of every country in the world substantiates that without such food and fiber producing capacity, the other advances in domestic comforts and conveniences have not been achieved, either.

Major areas of the world share the benefits of our agricultural ability, as evidenced by our exports each year of nearly $7 billion in products. But those nations receiving our abundance still have grave problems because of a lack of development of their own abilities to produce even in small comparison to American agriculture.

THE CHALLENGE AND THE FUTURE ROLE OF U. S. AGRICULTURE

It is essential that we now look to the future, contemplating the role of the United States and the American farmer. To do so, we must be astutely aware of the many historical facts as related to our progress. A student of history will immediately detect that in dealing with the present and future food problems in the United States and throughout the world, progress and development will be substantially dependent upon the great foundation of achievement forged here in America.

Let us now consider the challenge as it exists today. It might well be classified into two specific, but related, categories, namely, that the world is now faced with a major food shortage for an ever-increasing world population, and that the American farmer and producer is again faced, as he has been so many times in the past, with an inadequate economic return for his most successful effort.

What are the future responsibilities of government? And how will the same Republican vision and direction of the past apply in establishing the agricultural policies of this nation in the immediate years ahead?

The world food problem is of gigantic proportion. Books have been written, many studies have been completed and publicized, emphasizing the dangers of a great famine that could confront the world within the next decade.

This writer had occasion to visit recently with Dr. and Mrs. William Paddock. He co-authored the book *Famine—1975!* Anyone who reads this book, and has occasion to benefit from the author's exposure to and knowledge of world food conditions, can only be alarmed when alerted to the great demands that will accrue to American agricultural know-how in attempting to overcome or minimize this great threat to humanity.

This is a problem that will demand the full extent of our knowledge and understanding, as evidenced by the predictions of a world population of more than five billion people by 1985—an increase of more than 2.7 billion over the world's present population during the next eighteen years. It immediately raises the question of what role this nation, and the American farmer, will play in meeting the food demands of such population proportions.

The Republican-instigated Morrill Land Grant College Act will increase in value, supplying knowledge that can be applied to the development of agricultural techniques in countries that are experiencing food shortages now because of an inability to best utilize their natural resources for the production of food.

This knowledge is already bearing fruit in foreign countries. A recent newspaper article referred to the increased production of wheat in India, with a new variety of wheat that had been developed in Mexico now doubling the per acre yield in the wheat producing area of India. It should be noted that new varieties, produced in Mexico, were accomplished by importing knowledge and personnel from American universities, with results that have more than tripled the acreage production capacity in Mexico.

This involved the coordinated efforts of many interests within the United States. The experience in Mexico is one example of accomplishment achieved through the efforts of government-inspired research, supplemented by private American interests such as the Rockefeller and Ford Foundations that have provided the organizational push, and American industry that provided new and modern machines to implement the operations.

This writer recalls Dr. Norman E. Borlaug, the leading research specialist from the State of Iowa and the University of Minnesota, saying: "We can duplicate this accomplishment in India and Pakistan in ten to twelve years if provided the means."

The Agricultural Trade Development and Assistance Act, Public Law 480, commonly called Food for Peace, is a Republican-instigated program. It authorizes the President to carry out a program of sale and distribution of American agricultural surpluses by means of accepting foreign currency as well as through a barter system. This has brought relief from hunger to millions and millions of people in underdeveloped countries. We must never assume that it is within the realm of possibility for the production capacity of the United States to begin to feed all, or even a major percentage, of the food-deficient people of the world. But this program has made a great contribution during recent years to many famine-stricken and needy countries. Recent amendments offered by

Republican Members of Congress, such as the Bread and Butter Corps Amendment offered by Congressman Robert Dole of Kansas, add even further potential and hope that millions more of the world's hungry people will be provided for by this program.

The National Reclamation Act of 1902, enacted during the administration of Theodore Roosevelt, is another program that has given us knowledge for development of food production in arid areas throughout the world.

It must also be recognized that American accomplishment in the production and distribution of food has not only been a major tool in the pursuit of peace, but has also been our major weapon in deterring aggression, and maintaining our superior defensive posture.

World Food Study Commission. Republicans have long since begun preparing for the needs of tomorrow by recommendations and proposed legislation to establish a United States World Food Study and Coordinating Commission. The purposes and duties of the Commission are identified as a complete review of past and present U.S. policies and programs of foreign agricultural assistance in their various forms. They will also include a comprehensive study of all aspects of the present and predicted world food and population situation. The Commission will then relate their findings to the future growth and domestic needs of the U.S. and to the U.S. potential for contributing to the solution of world food and population problems.

The legislation proposes fifteen separate areas where such review and study would be both essential and beneficial. It further provides that the Commission should make recommendations for the development of future U.S. policies and programs in regard to world food needs, with a final report of its findings and recommendations being submitted to the President and the Congress.

It is worthwhile to note that the eighteen-member Commission would be made up of representatives from the Congress, the Departments of State and Agriculture, with eight members from outside the federal government to represent various farm organizations, private agricultural trade, U.S. land grant and state colleges and universities, and other agricultural organizations. This would bring together the views, knowledge and experience from each of these departments and interests, and, most significantly, the interests of farm people.

It is self-evident that such a study and review should be completed at the earliest possible date.

The Farmer and the World. The world today is rapidly losing the race between an adequate food supply and a growing population. At the same time, the American farmer is fast losing his economic strength, and, as he does, his production capacity will be depleted in direct proportion. To respond to both of these needs, it is essential that we get the best minds together in a concentrated effort to grapple with these problems and come up with constructive and feasible programs and recommendations.

The entire area involving the movement of agricultural products from one country to another, and everything that might be classified as international agricultural trade, is equally in need of study and understanding. There is at this time a lack of evidence that the recent Geneva Conference provided any great recognition of the problems involved in the movement of agricultural products to satisfy the varied food needs. The availability of products is hampered by very complex tariffs, duties, restrictions, and complicated price structures in the many nations and governments involved.

Too often has the economic welfare of farmers been ignored in a variety of trade agreements and establishment of trade restrictions in all of their many applications. There are too many examples in recent years where exporting and importing of agricultural products have served to the detriment of the producer at both ends of the transaction.

An example would be wheat produced in this country, bought from the farmers at a price that did not provide them a reasonable return on their investment and production cost, and then sold in a foreign country at a price so low that it discouraged the producers of wheat in that country as well.

If we are to meet the future food demands, that trend should rather be reversed, so there would be an incentive for expanded production by the farmers in both countries involved. Such transactions would have a further salutary effect on world markets that in turn would encourage production investments and entice the industrial interests to lend their promotional efforts to the cause.

The U. S. Farm Role. Republicans have continuously advocated the proper and appropriate attention of government to the world food scene. Our concern becomes even more important in the future as the role of American agriculture expands to play an even larger part in the scene of world food production.

Such concern is particularly acute when we recognize the present plight of the American farmer. Even a hasty glance at the economic returns to the varied American occupations shows that the American farmer—at a time of general economic prosperity—is at the very bottom of the economic ladder when compared to the others.

The present problem of farmers is not new to our history, nor is it much different from the experience of the agricultural history in other developed countries of the world. It has proven to be a perplexing problem to every form of government, to economists, to architects of marketing procedures, and has usually baffled every attempt of man to correct it.

A brief review of our own history quickly reveals that the times of agricultural prosperity have come mainly during times of war, when food became strategic to our military effort and strength. It has been during times of war that farm prices have risen to such levels that mortgages could be paid off, buildings and equipment could be modernized, with an opportunity to achieve the rightful place for the producers of food and fiber within our economic and social structure.

The years between the wars have just as consistently brought price declines that created great economic hardships and, in far too many instances, bankruptcy and a necessity to leave farms for other more lucrative occupations. Such experience is repeating itself today, and so we have an enigma. While engagement in a war as a rule has brought better farm prices, we now find prices deplorable and getting worse every day.

Thus we come to the second and most important problem that confronts agriculture at the present time, and will in the future. This problem is worthy of attention not only by government, but by taxpayers and everyone who is concerned with an equal economic opportunity for all segments of the populace in a prosperous and wealthy nation. Last, but not least, the American consumer would be the real victim of tremendously higher food costs, if the United States should lose its productive capacity and find itself at the mercy of foreign food producers.

The future will demand an even greater need for the commendable efforts and judgments of the American farmer. But the farmer must have some reliable indication that he will be rewarded for investment and endeavor in a manner that is comparable to the rewards of industry and other occupations.

This is not true today, as evidenced by the fact that the past six years have shown a continuous decline of farm income, with ever-increasing costs of production and investment to make full use of mechanization and scientific research.

U.S. agriculture carries a mortgage in excess of $50 billion —almost equal the gross income. This debt has been increasing at a rate of nearly 10 percent a year of late. When associated with the increased interest rates, the farm mortgage debt constitutes a burden that is out of step with farm income, currently at a parity rate of 73 to 75 percent, a level so low that it finds comparison only in the depression years.

Total farm debt has increased by 50 percent since 1960, and is now greater than the total Federal Budget in 1951. These alarming statistics point out the complete failure of the present administration's farm programs.

It has come to the attention of this writer that government policies in areas other than agriculture have created problems for the American farmer. Witness, the choking off of transportation and communication by removal of railway mail and

passenger service in many rural areas throughout the country—actions that gain in momentum every day.

General living costs have also gone up on the farm, in the
same proportion as they have gone up for every other area
and sector of our population. It can not be disputed that farm
folks should have the same modern and scientific benefits in
living standards that are available to everyone else.

The Farmer as a Good Customer. The aggregate problems of farmers, in turn, have a direct effect on rural communities. As the farmer's net income, which is the equivalent
of take-home pay for other citizens, goes down, the local
businesses that serve him all find themselves in comparable
economic distress. These factors also reach the industrial and
other sectors of the nation.

Farmers in the U.S. spend more than $33 billion a year
for goods and services to produce crops and livestock, as
documented by the House Agriculture Committee Report
entitled "Food Costs-Farm Prices" issued in September 1967.
The Report says our farmers spend another $12 billion in
farm equipment; $3.4 billion a year for fuel and maintenance
as the nation's largest industrial petroleum user; almost $2
billion in fertilizer and lime; enough rubber to put tires on
nearly 6 million automobiles; enough electricity a year to supply the cities of Baltimore, Chicago, Boston, Detroit, Houston,
and Washington, D.C.; and 5 million tons of steel.

Government on all levels is equally indebted to American
agriculture, currently collecting many billions of dollars annually in real estate, personal property, federal and state income, motor fuel, vehicle license and sales taxes. A healthy
agriculture would benefit government even more.

The Farmer and the Consumer. The relationship of what a
farmer receives for his produce to what the consumer pays
for a finished product is often not understood. The farmer
receives little of the increase in the cost of the food he produces, sometimes nothing. The return from the foods in the
family market basket was the same in 1966 as it was in
1947–49, although the retail cost of this market basket rose
24 percent.

The cost of processing and marketing these foods increased 47 percent since 1947–49, according to the Office of Information, U. S. Department of Agriculture, in April of 1966.

The farmer actually receives only 2.8 cents for the corn in a 30-cent box of cornflakes, and 3 cents for the wheat in a 22-cent loaf of white bread. He gets about 23 cents for the cotton in a man's $4 business shirt. It is the same story in other commodities where packaging and manufacturing are factors.

Consumers must be alerted and made aware of the fact that adequate farm prices could easily be attained with very minor increases to them in the cost of the processed product. For instance, a 20 percent increase in the cost of corn would mean only an increase of slightly more than half a cent in the price of that box of cornflakes. This would significantly improve the farmer's income, yet would be only a very minor factor in the cost of the cornflakes.

There is no justification for any quarrel between farmers and consumers in the price of food, for actually it would serve the best interests of both to have the marketplace provide an adequate price in the first instance. The additional tax cost of government subsidies could then be eliminated, which would reduce the combined tax and food cost to the consumer and at the same time improve the return to the farmer.

It is important that not only the farmer but all consumers, taxpayers and anyone interested in the food and economic stability of this nation should consider all of these facts with the highest priority. To do so would lend greater assurance to everyone of a sufficient quantity and quality of food being available with which to meet greatly expanding demands and to use this added strength in continuing U.S. contributions to the possibilities of world peace and tranquility.

THE FARMER QUESTIONS HIS FUTURE

It is not only logical, but in the best interests of everyone, that farmers throughout the country today are raising the question: What will be our position in satisfying the world needs for food in the years ahead? And will our investment and effort bring sufficient economic return to warrant our best endeavors?

The future policy on the part of government must be continuously cognizant of the history and experience that we have had over the years, and to attempt to apply that knowledge and understanding more effectively and with greater vision and reality than we have been able to do in the past.

The farmer has provided and must continue to provide humanity with its basic needs of food and fiber. Government can do no less than cooperate with him in creating a new day in which he can, with a sense of pride, receive rewards appropriate to his labors and his importance to the future strength of this nation.

Past Republican efforts serve as an excellent background from which to begin.

While government participation and contribution is, and will be, necessary, we must not lose sight of the fact that the greater contributing factor will be the farmer's continuing independence, with every opportunity to exercise and develop his ingenuity and ability, encouraged by a sufficient economic incentive. Then it will naturally follow that the contributions of industry will find the same incentive for their best efforts. Processor-packaging firms must be given encouragement to locate plants near the source of the agriculture crop. The location of these plants would provide a lower cost of production for the processor, and on the other hand, job opportunities, taxes, and income for rural areas.

World history has, beyond question, proved that where the greatest amount of government intervention and participation has existed, such as in the Communist nations, food shortages from inefficient production management have invariably resulted.

Republicans have consistently directed their attention to the continued development of freedom for individuals to grow and adapt to a modern, mechanized agriculture, with the greatest possible use of the law of supply and demand, coordinated with government programs, to provide a desirable price structure. The years ahead will demand even more wisdom and vision to implement that objective.

NEW POLICIES FOR CHANGING TIMES

It becomes essential that we have a far greater understanding and a more realistic response to the development of international trade and world markets. We can no longer afford the fallacies of present policy. In far too many instances have producers of essential commodities here and elsewhere experienced economic hardships, and even bankruptcy, because of detrimental trade policies.

In our own nation, this has been evidenced by the great setback experienced in the production of dairy products, beef, hides, honey, mink and other products, due to imports that have found their way into this country because of price differentials and other inequities in the implementation of trade restrictions.

The very same thing has been true in many foreign countries as we disposed of surpluses on the world market at a price and under conditions detrimental to the producers of the same commodities in other nations. The net effect has been a distorted world market and price.

There is a first essential which must be part of any policy evolving from our Republican-proposed World Food Study and Coordinating Commission. This would be to assure that all international trade in agricultural commodities completed by an exchange of monetary values be done on the basis of a world price that adequately provides producers in all nations with equitable returns for their investments and efforts.

The more complex phase of this exchange of goods involves the supply of food to food-deficient nations without an economic structure that will permit them to participate on the same basis in the world market. It should be dealt with on a separate basis, with the Republican-initiated Food for Peace program as a background.

It is also in this area that it becomes essential that we put ourselves in a better position to export the scientific production knowledge that has proven to be one of the great riches of the United States. That such endeavor can be productive in areas of the world in need is in evidence in many nations, such as Mexico and India previously referred to. The results of such development of agriculture in the deficit nations would not only provide food for the millions of additional people, but would add stability and improvement to world markets as well. A far greater degree of international trade would result, with each nation adjusting to the production of food which it is by nature best suited to produce.

It is just as essential that we direct equal consideration to the distribution and availability of the variety of foods produced. Directing such foods to the areas of the world where food deficiencies exist would add energies that would enhance the growth of their own industrial and social improvement. But anyone who believes in the private enterprise system will immediately recognize that a reasonable profit to everyone concerned is essential if the desirable changes are to take place.

We must maintain our own price structure so that it will be dependable and responsive to the obvious demands. It seems apparent that this would require better coordination of government policy with freedom in the market place. It is in this area that we have found past endeavors to be completely inadequate. The many attempts to establish minimum prices, by price supports, have too often resulted in the *minimum* price becoming the *maximum* price.

This, in turn, resulted in a price structure that was unrelated to, and out of adjustment with, the cost of production, and added further to the economic plight of the producer, because he was restricted by government in making the best use of the production capacity of his farm operation. The inadequate return to the farmer has far too often been the result of a government restriction on his production capacity.

A simple example would be a farmer with a $20,000 investment in equipment, who could easily have planted and harvested an additional fifty to one hundred acres of grain on his farm without any additional investment. This would have greatly reduced his per bushel production cost, but he was prevented from doing so by a government acreage limitation. If the government limitation was necessary, then it was just as necessary to adjust the price available accordingly, because the government restriction actually caused the increase in the per unit cost of production.

There have been too many examples of government actions, or lack of action, moving prices downward sufficiently to wipe out the profit that might have been.

One of the many examples has been the use by the Commodity Credit Corporation of surpluses acquired for purposes of improving the price, which were later sold on the market to depress the same price that the first action was designed to correct. Such results often followed the mere announcement by the Corporation that they would place substantial quantities of a given product on the market. Such practices can only work to the detriment of both agriculture and government by a loss of farm income and an added expense to government. It was the consumer as a taxpayer who, in reality, paid for both losses.

It should not be beyond our ability to maintain all of the desirable qualities of the free enterprise and market system. It is the opinion and desire of Republicans that we seek that goal by, first, eliminating all of the adverse actions of government that have had a price-depressing effect.

These include: dumping large quantities of surpluses on the market at inappropriate times; limiting exports such as was done with cattle hides after the foreign markets had been developed by the producers; failure to use import limitations as provided for in Section 22 of the Agricultural Act, when it was obvious that markets had been depressed by excessive imports; limiting the use of dairy products and pork by the Armed Services, as was recommended and practiced within the last several years; and implementing trade agreements that sacrificed the economic benefits of the farmer in order to gain industrial advantage. We need rather to develop trade policies to encourage and provide a reasonable return to the producers of agricultural products in all countries. These would serve to eliminate market hazards and would involve no cost to either government or taxpayer, while providing a great asset to the entire national economy.

To realize additional reliability of price and security of investment, it is just as imperative that we give every thought and long-range planning to the establishment of government programs that would provide completely voluntary participation, but with ample bargaining opportunity for the individual farmer. Such bargaining provisions should be readily adapted to the sustenance of family farm operating units. History tells us that the maximum and most efficient production can be achieved only by encouraging the individual freedom of ingenuity that such units readily accommodate. While scientific research and mechanization will obviously promote such units to grow somewhat in size, they should still, as a management concept, be fully recognized for their ability to maintain the desirable qualities of proficiency. This has been well documented by the complete control of agriculture in highly socialized and communistic governments, who now find themselves reverting to policies which encourage the family farm and individual incentives.

It has been this writer's opinion that, in compliance with Republican principle and policy, we should do well to establish programs to satisfy the desire for independence and yet provide the opportunity for a price return that is adequate. The parity concept, if used to identify what the return should be, indicates an obligation of government to reward producers with a full parity of income, when that same government dictates the necessity of reducing production capacity.

Programs can be designed to sustain that principle.

I have always felt, and practical experience has taught me, that it would be most desirable that there be two new provisions incorporated in any farm program. A part of the responsibility for necessary production adjustments should rest with the producers themselves; and, when they fulfill that responsibility, they should have the assurance that the desired returns would be forthcoming.

Such a program and policy could provide benefits to farmers, consumers, and taxpayers alike. It would offer simplicity of administration with an achievable objective, that would generate both response and gratitude on the part of the American farmer.

The normal process of marketing would be substantially improved, if it were known that all of the usual factors which govern price changes were free to function without interference, and the danger of large government stocks being used to interrupt the normal movement of grains and prices were eliminated.

It is essential that any program be versatile enough to meet the many changing conditions. It would be wrong to assume that any given policy which might provide relief for the existing conditions at any given time would be adequate under another combination of circumstances that might develop. I am sure that as we look to the future, there will be agricultural problems consistently prevalent and that many years from now, even with the best attempts and substantial success on the part of government, there will still be problems confronting agriculture. They undoubtedly would be of a different nature and require a different approach from those we can envision today.

It is in recognition of these continuous demands and factors that Republican endeavors to date have been most responsive, as has been evidenced by this far too brief discussion of agriculture's complex problems. The many programs to which I have referred as Republican-oriented have characteristically provided a foundation for the growth, progress and development of American agriculture for more than one hundred years. They are of even greater need and importance today than at the time of their enactment.

Possibly the greatest contribution we can make today is an expressed dedication to the preservation and development of all the known factors that have been instrumental in the phenomenal achievements that constitute the great heritage of every living person in the world today.

Surely the demands of tomorrow for food and fiber would be in a far more precarious position, were it not for the assurance that these challenges can be, and have been, mastered in America. Let us then, no matter how tempting the situation may be, not sacrifice or deter a single one of the elements that have been responsible for this rewarding achievement.

All new government programs should be coordinated with individual freedom, free enterprise, with free and open markets, to accomplish the objective that investment and maximum endeavor in agriculture should receive its just and equitable share of our gross national product.

This has continuously been the principle, policy and philosophy of the Republican Party. America and the world are demanding the continuing interest in and reliance on those principles today.

I recall the words of a greatly respected president of Concordia College at Moorhead, Minnesota, stated in an article in the *Lutheran Standard*—words which we might do well to adopt, in view of what has happened in recent years: "If we are sincere in praying for daily bread, we dare not forget the farmer any longer."

Chapter 7

STRENGTHENING SOCIAL SECURITY

SOCIAL SECURITY: THE PAST THIRTY YEARS
by Colin D. Campbell

COLIN D. CAMPBELL is Professor of Economics at Dartmouth College, where he has taught since 1956. Professor Campbell was graduated from Harvard College, and received his Ph.D. from the University of Chicago. He served as an economist with the CIA in 1952–54 and later as an economist with the Government Finance Section, Division of Research and Statistics of the Board of Governors of the Federal Reserve System in Washington, D.C.

During the past thirty years, social security—and particularly the federal old-age, survivors, and disability insurance program—has grown to very large proportions. Benefit payments have increased from $35 million in 1940 to $21.7 billion for OASDHI in fiscal 1967. Payroll tax collections for OASDHI have increased to $25.6 billion, 17 percent of total federal tax collections. Over 23 million persons are currently receiving federal old-age, survivors, or disability pensions. Over 80 million persons are currently paying taxes into the social security fund.

The rise in social security benefits and tax revenues has resulted in considerable part from higher rates on taxpayers. The employment tax was 2 percent—1 percent on both the employer and the employee—from 1937 to 1949. By 1967, the tax rate for OASDHI had become 8.8 percent—4.4 percent on both the worker and his employer. The maximum wage base subject to the tax has also been increased. From 1937 to 1949, it was $3000; in 1968, it was increased to $7800. The tax payment for persons with the maximum wage base was $686 per year in 1968. Both the maximum wage base and the maximum tax payment per worker were increased by the 1967 amendments to the social security act.

Federal old-age insurance has become a significant part of the average American's provision for old age. A person retiring in 1968 with an average annual income in recent years equal to the maximum wage base is entitled to a social security pension for himself and his wife of $2828. This is approximately 36 percent of his pre-retirement income. Persons with lower annual incomes receive larger pensions relative to their pre-retirement income. A person retiring in 1968 who has earned an average annual income equal to only one-half the maximum wage base is entitled to a pension for himself and his wife of $1852 per year, 47 percent of his pre-retirement income. In 1968, the minimum pension for a man and wife was raised to approximately $1000 per year.

When the social security system was set up in 1937, federal old-age insurance was intended to be an insurance program. The benefits were referred to as annuities. The tax payments were often called premiums. The Social Security Administration expected to accumulate a large trust fund. At that time, financing social security by payroll taxes—even though they are regressive—was justified on the basis that it was an insurance system. Though the tax would be a much larger percentage of the income of the poor than of the rich, both would be paying for an annuity to be received during their old age. Such taxes would be in accordance with the benefit principle of taxation.

Important features of the federal old-age insurance program still give the impression that persons are purchasing insurance for themselves. Retired persons may receive benefits regardless of need if they have contributed to the fund. A worker must pay in for a certain length of time in order to be eligible for benefits. If a person wishes to retire at sixty-two, or if his widow wishes to receive benefits at sixty, they may do so if willing to take a smaller pension.

Despite the early intentions of the system and certain features that have been retained, from the start, the federal old-age insurance program departed in practice from the insurance concept. From 1937 to 1950, planned tax increases from the original 2 percent were continuously postponed. Then, over the years, new types of contingencies, such as allowances for dependents, were added. Also, the method of computing the average wage, on which benefits are based, was liberalized, permitting persons to use high-income years and shorter periods as the basis for benefits. There have been eight amendments increasing benefits, including the benefits of those already retired. Also, the coverage has been expanded several times, bringing in additional beneficiaries who have contributed little to the fund. The 1965 amendment extends coverage to self-employed physicians and provides more liberal treatment for divorced wives, widows who remarry, and persons already over seventy-two who worked in covered employment only a short time. Today, the federal old-age insurance program has drifted so far from its original intentions that some persons are referring to the insurance concept as applied to social security as a "myth."

If the federal old-age insurance system were a real insurance program, the average person would pay for his benefits. Actually, for almost thirty years, benefit payments to the retired have been much larger than could be justified on the basis of their tax payments or the actuarially determined risks involved. For a person retiring in 1968, for example, the value of his OASDI taxes accumulated at current rates of interest is at most $7357–$5235 in tax payments and $2122 in interest. A person retiring in 1968 could have paid social security taxes for no longer than thirty-one years. Up to 1950 the maximum tax payment per year for old-age and survivors' insurance was only $60, although since then, the tax rate and the wage base have been gradually raised. By 1966, the maximum tax payment per worker was over $500 per year, but recently retired persons have paid tax payments of this amount for only a few years.

A person retiring in 1968 has had, since 1939, survivors' insurance for his wife and young children in case he died early. Since 1956, he has also had disability insurance. If it is

TABLE 1

Cost-Benefit Ratios for Persons Already Retired Under the Federal Old-age Insurance Program

Age and starting date under OASI (1)	Retirement date (2)	Average annual wage (3)	Total value of OASDI taxes[a] (4)	Total value of taxes for old-age insurance[b] (5)	Current annual pension for man and wife (6)	Value of pension for 14 years[c] (7)	Cost-benefit ratio (Col. 5 ÷ Col. 7) (8)
Married Man							
40 in 1937	1962	Maximum base	$3,782	$3,026	$2,633	$26,572	11%
37 in 1937	1965	Maximum base	5,200	4,160	2,765	29,176	14
34 in 1937	1968	Maximum base	7,357	5,886	2,828	30,778	19
34 in 1937	1968	¾ Maximum base	5,518	4,415	2,353	25,608	17
34 in 1937	1968	½ Maximum base	3,679	2,943	1,852	20,156	15
Married Man, With Tax Payments Computed in Terms of Constant Dollars							
34 in 1937	1968	Maximum base	9,578	7,662	2,828	30,778	25
Married Man With Working Wife							
34 in 1937	1968	Maximum base	14,714	11,772	3,770	41,030	29
Single Person							
34 in 1937	1968	Maximum base	7,357	5,886	1,885	20,515	29
Self-employed, Married Man							
48 in 1951[d]	1968	Maximum base	4,168	3,334	2,828	30,778	11

[a] Compounded at E-bond rates until 1963 and 4 percent thereafter.
[b] Eighty percent of Column 4.
[c] Discounted at 4 percent interest.
[d] First covered in 1951.

assumed that 20 percent of the tax payments of the worker who lives to retirement has gone to pay for these other forms of insurance, this person has paid a maximum of $5886 for old-age insurance alone.

A worker retiring in 1968 who has paid in the maximum is entitled to an annual pension of $1885 plus $943 for an aged wife, a total of $2828. As shown in Table 1, a pension of this amount, discounted at 4 percent for the average length of life that they can expect—fourteen more years—is worth $30,778. His social security benefits are worth five times the value of the payroll taxes he has paid in.

Many retired workers have had an even more attractive bargain. Social security pensions may now be based on covered wages only since 1951, and the lowest five years in wages may be excluded. It is possible for a worker retiring in 1968 to obtain a pension worth $30,778 even if he paid no taxes before 1956, but maximum taxes since then. At age sixty-five, the value of such a person's tax payments for old-age insurance would be only $3556. He would receive almost eight times what he has paid in. Most workers who have been "blanketed" into the system since it began have received similar bargains, although over time the low cost-benefit ratios of these groups will disappear. Coverage was extended to domestic workers, farm wage workers, and the self-employed in 1951; self-employed farmers in 1955; dentists and military servicemen in 1956; and self-employed physicians in 1965. In 1950 only 62 percent of the labor force was covered compared with over 90 percent in 1967.

A group that has not had such a good bargain is those who are single at retirement—whether a bachelor, widower, or, in some cases, divorced. A single worker who has paid maximum taxes since 1937 and retires in 1968 is entitled to receive a pension of only $1885 per year. This is because he does not receive a secondary benefit for an aged wife. Single persons are not supposed to need as large a pension as married couples—although this is not always the case. This pension is worth $20,500, compared to the total value of his taxes for old-age insurance of $5886. His cost-benefit ratio is 29 percent (see Table 1).

The cost-benefit ratios of working couples are also relatively high. Married women workers are a significant group in the total labor force, and their numbers have been growing rapidly. In 1940 there were only 7 million married women workers in a labor force of approximately 56 million persons. In 1964 there were about 20 million married women workers (including widows) out of a total labor force of some 74 million. If a man and his wife, retiring in 1968, have both been employed and paid maximum taxes since 1937, together they will have paid in taxes worth $11,772. But, a wife cannot receive both the pension she is entitled to as a wife and the pension she herself has earned. She receives only the larger of the two. A working wife is not supposed to need both the wife's portion of her husband's pension and the pension she herself would be entitled to through her own tax payments. The maximum amount that this retired couple may receive is $1885 each, a total pension of $3770 per year, on the assumption that both husband and wife have worked long enough at the maximum wage base to earn the maximum pension. A pension of this amount, discounted at 4 percent to age sixty-five, is worth $41,030, and their cost-benefit ratio is 29 percent.

Actually, in most cases, a married woman worker will not have worked long enough or at high enough wages to earn an old-age pension that is larger than the amount she would automatically be entitled to as a wife (either half her husband's benefit or a maximum of $105 a month). As a result, she receives no additional pension over the amount she would in any case be entitled to as a wife in return for the taxes she has paid in. A woman worker retiring in 1968 must be employed at least 3½ years in order to be eligible for benefits of her own, and 9 years' wages must be averaged to compute benefits. In the future, the law provides that a woman born after 1928 be employed at least ten years in order to be eligible for benefits on reaching age sixty-five and that wages for thirty-five years be averaged as a basis for her benefits.

How have retired persons who have earned less than the maximum wage base fared under the federal old-age insurance program? A worker, retiring in 1968, who has paid taxes on three-quarters of the maximum base since 1937 has paid old-age taxes worth $4415. He and his wife would be eligible for an annual pension of $2353. Such a pension is worth $25,600 and his cost-benefit ratio is 17 percent, as compared with 19 percent for the worker who has paid the maximum tax. If he has paid one-half the maximum tax since 1937, the cost-benefit ratio would be 15 percent. The lower cost-benefit ratios for persons with wages below the maximum wage base are intentional. The social security law does not reduce their benefits in proportion to the taxes paid in.

Self-employed persons, another distinct group under the social security program, have relatively low cost-benefit ratios because their tax rate is approximately one and a half times the employee's tax rate (or three-fourths the combined employee-employer tax rate). Also, they were first included in 1951. Table 1 shows that the maximum accumulated tax payments for old-age insurance of a self-employed person retiring in 1968 is $3334, compared with benefits for himself and his wife worth $30,778. This is a cost-benefit ratio of only 11 percent. In 1965, 6.6 million persons out of 62.7 million— 11 percent of civilian employees covered by OASDI—were self-employed.

Because of the inflation between 1937 and 1968, the real value of the taxes paid in is larger than the nominal amount. Table 1 shows that in terms of 1966 dollars, the total value of tax payments for old-age insurance for the man contributing the maximum from 1937 through 1967 is $7662, approximately 30 percent more than the nominal value. Even so, the value of his tax payments for old-age insurance alone would be worth only 25 percent of the value of the pension he is entitled to for himself and his wife.

Table 1 also shows that cost-benefit ratios for persons retiring in recent years have been increasing. The married man who retired six years ago, in 1962, paid in, at most, only 11 percent of the value of the pension he has already received and is scheduled to receive in the future. Three years ago it was 14 percent. Today, it is 19 percent. The federal old-age insurance system attempts to collect each year just enough through the payroll tax and through interest on the trust fund to cover benefit disbursements. The system has become more costly as larger numbers of persons have retired who are eligible for higher benefits, and as benefits for those already retired have been increased to keep up with the cost of living or to provide larger minimum benefits.

The fact that persons who have retired thus far under the federal old-age insurance program have received a bargain is one reason why the program is so popular. But, will persons retiring in the future continue to have such a bargain? The cost-benefit ratios as provided in the current law for young persons entering the system are shown in Table 2. It should be kept in mind that the actual cost-benefit ratios for young persons may turn out to be very different from these. The tax rates on payrolls, the maximum wage base, and the benefit levels will undoubtedly be raised in the future. Nevertheless, an examination of these ratios shows some of the problems ahead.

A young person starting work in 1968 at the age of twenty-two and earning at least $7800 per year for the next forty-three years is scheduled to pay OASDI taxes (excluding medicare) worth $83,053, if 4 percent interest is assumed. In 1968, the rate of tax for old-age, survivors', and disability insurance was 7.6 percent, and the maximum tax per worker was approximately $593 per year. This total will be gradually increased until it reaches $780 in 1973. The tax payments over his lifetime amount to approximately $30,600, and the accumulated interest to $52,400. After deducting 20 percent of the total value of his taxes for survivors' and disability insurance, the amount paid in for old-age insurance alone would be $66,442.

The maximum retirement benefit that this young worker is scheduled to receive is $3876 per year—$2616 for himself and $1260 for his aged wife. A pension of this amount could be financed at age sixty-five with accumulated tax payments

TABLE 2

COST-BENEFIT RATIOS FOR YOUNG PERSONS UNDER
THE CURRENT FEDERAL OLD-AGE INSURANCE PROGRAM

Age and starting date (1)	Retire-ment date (2)	Average annual wage (3)	Total value of OASDI taxes[a] (4)	Total value of taxes for old-age insurance alone[b] (5)	Annual pension (6)	Value of pension for 14 years[c] (7)	Cost-benefit ratio (Col. 5 ÷ Col. 7) (8)
Married Man							
22 in 1968	2011	$7,800 or more	$83,053	$66,442	$3,876	$42,183	158%
22 in 1968	2011	5,850	62,290	49,832	3,154	34,326	145
22 in 1968	2011	3,900	41,526	33,221	2,417	26,305	126
Married Man with Working Wife							
22 in 1968	2011	7,800 or more each	166,106	132,884	5,232	56,941	233
Single Person							
22 in 1968	2011	7,800 or more	83,053	66,442	2,616	28,470	233
Self-employed, Married Man							
22 in 1968	2011	7,800 or more	58,975	47,180	3,876	42,183	112

[a] Compounded at 4 percent interest.
[b] Eighty percent of Column 4.
[c] Discounted at 4 percent interest.

of only $42,183—much less than the value of the taxes he is scheduled to pay in. This young worker's cost-benefit ratio is 158 percent. As an insurance policy, the explicit terms offered to a young worker under the federal old-age insurance program are not attractive. What is significant for the future is that benefits must be increased if young persons today are going to get their money's worth, and this will result in additional pressure to raise tax revenues for this purpose.

Some persons object to these calculations because I have assumed that the half of the old-age insurance tax that is paid by the employer is a cost to the employee. They doubt whether the payroll tax on the employer is shifted to the employee rather than the consumer. As a result, their estimates of the cost to the employee are approximately one-half mine. The problem of tax shifting is a difficult one; nevertheless, to my knowledge, most tax economists believe that payroll taxes on an employer are eventually shifted to their employees. This is because the tax increases the employer's labor costs and decreases his demand for labor. This spread over all firms causes the rise in money wages to slow down, so that the wage earner, in effect, usually pays this employer part of the tax as well as that nominally levied on himself.

Even if it is assumed that not all of the payroll tax on the employer is shifted to the employee, the examples in Table 1 show that there is a very loose relationship between the cost of one's social security pension and the value of the benefits that one can expect to receive. This raises questions as to the nature of the program as an insurance system.

Some persons who admit that the social security system has shortcomings as an insurance program defend it as a welfare program, although it is not really a welfare program because a needs test is not necessary to qualify for benefits. In recent years, the social security program has been attacked even as a welfare program. What are the reasons for these criticisms?

First, it is said that the social security system is extremely inefficient as a welfare program. It has been estimated that for every additional dollar paid out in larger benefits to persons who need welfare, four dollars are paid out to persons who could not qualify for welfare. It is not known just how much of the $20 billion per year currently paid out in social security pensions goes to persons in need and how much goes to those who are not in need. But, the amount going to those who are not in need may be a sizable figure. As we have seen, all retired persons have paid such a small portion of the cost of their pensions that most of their pensions should be considered a welfare payment.

The federal old-age insurance program is also being criticized as inequitable. It is widely believed that under this program the federal government—like Robin Hood—is taxing the rich to benefit the poor. Actually, it is not at all certain that this is what is taking place, even though we need to know a lot more about the effects of this program on the distribution of income. Several features of the social security system as it now operates, suggest that it may be hard on the poor, though it need not be.

In the first place, because this program is financed by payroll taxes, persons with incomes from rent, interest and dividends are able to avoid paying for the vast bulk of the welfare costs associated with old age. In addition, the payroll taxes used to finance the system are regressive for all incomes above the maximum wage base. Currently, for example, the effective tax rate is 8.8 percent on all incomes up to $7800, but is 4.4 percent of an income of $15,600, and only 2.2 percent of an income of $31,200.

Another reason why the old-age insurance program may be disadvantageous to the lower income groups is that federal old-age pensions are not subject to the federal income tax. To persons in high income tax brackets, social security benefits are worth more than their face value. For example, a person in the 50 percent tax bracket who receives additional taxable income of $5656 is allowed to keep for his own use $2828 of this amount. Consequently, a tax-free social security pension of $2828 is worth twice as much, or $5656.

A third reason why federal old-age insurance may not be helping to narrow the gap between the poor and the well-off is that a person between sixty-five and seventy-two years of age receiving $5000 a year from income from investments can still collect his entire social security benefits; but an older person getting $5000 by taking a job is not entitled to any old-age pension because of the work-income test. This obviously works to the advantage of those who are better off as compared with the poor.

A fourth built-in bias has to do with the fact that the average length of life varies among different economic and social groups. High-income professional men, on the whole, probably have a longer average life than the unskilled. A white man twenty years old has a 69 percent chance of living to age sixty-five compared with only a 55 percent chance for a nonwhite man of the same age. Under federal old-age insurance, low-income groups whose average life expectancy is relatively short are charged just as much for their old-age coverage as high-income groups whose average life expectancy is relatively long.

As soon as the social security system matures and persons will have paid taxes into the program for their entire working lives, a fifth source of bias will result from the fact that the lower income groups who do not go to college typically start to work at a younger age and will thus pay in taxes for a larger number of years. Recent studies indicate that the effect of this source of bias will be substantial.

The shortcomings of the social security system both as an insurance system and as a welfare program have resulted in a sudden rebirth of interest in reforming the program. The Joint Economic Committee of Congress has recently published a compendium of studies on old-age income assurance. The Brookings Institution in Washington, D.C., has also published several research monographs in this area and is planning some more.

Future reform of the social security program will probably involve unravelling its current insurance and welfare objectives. The major question to be decided is whether the program should be revitalized as a bona-fide insurance system or whether it should be developed further as a general welfare program designed to eliminate poverty. In order to strengthen the program as an insurance system, it would be necessary to establish a closer relationship for each insured worker between the cost of his insurance and the value of his expected benefits. Financing such a program by payroll taxes would be equitable because it would be based on the benefit principle of taxation. On the other hand, if the social security system is to develop further into a general welfare program, reliance on the payroll tax would appear to be both inadequate and inequitable. For the past thirty years, because the Federal Old-age and Survivors Trust Fund has been self-financing and independent from the federal government's administrative budget, the pension benefits that elderly persons receive in excess of what they have paid for have been financed by contributions from young workers. But, should not the general taxpayer rather than young workers pay for the cost of these welfare payments? The further development of the social security system as a welfare program would probably require general revenue financing and result in the eventual demise of the Federal Old-age and Survivors Trust Fund as an independent and self-financing unit of the federal government.

SOCIAL SECURITY: THE NEXT THIRTY YEARS
by James F. Battin

JAMES FRANKLIN BATTIN, elected Congressman for the Second Congressional District of Montana in November, 1960, is now serving his fourth consecutive term. A graduate of Eastern Montana College at Billings and George Washington University, Mr. Battin served as deputy county attorney and city attorney in Billings before serving in the Montana State House of Representatives in 1959. Since entering Congress, Congressman Battin has been a member of the Judiciary Committee, the Foreign Affairs Committee and the Subcommittees on Europe and Foreign Economic Policy. He has also represented the Congress at the Intergovernmental Committee on European Migration in Geneva in 1962 and was Chairman of the Republican Task Force on Cuba and Subversion in the Western Hemisphere. Presently he serves on the Ways and Means Committee, the Executive Committee of the Republican Congressional Campaign Committee, and the Joint Commission on Coinage.

INTRODUCTION

In a little more than thirty years, our social security system has grown into a program significantly affecting the lives of virtually every American. Our citizens are probably more familiar, in a general way, with the social security program than any other program of the federal government.

In speaking of the social security program, I would like to emphasize certain points made in the preceding paper. I will be referring to the Old Age, Survivors, and Disability

Insurance Program—commonly referred to as the OASDI program. The hospital insurance (H.I.) program enacted by Congress in 1965 has stretched out the letters OASDI to OASDHI. However, the hospital insurance program has only been operating for a little over one year and any over-all evaluation of the hospital insurance program at this time would be premature.

As its name indicates, the OASDI program provides cash benefits to workers and their families when wages are lost due to retirement, death, or disability of the wage earner. These benefits are financed by a payroll tax imposed on workers and their employers, as well as on the self-employed. While a small contingency is maintained in the OASDI trust funds, current contributions are primarily used to pay benefits to current beneficiaries.

In 1967, 86 million workers will contribute 26 billion dollars to the OASDI trust funds; over 23 million individuals will receive benefits totaling 21.6 billion dollars. Approximately nine out of ten Americans currently have protection under OASDI against the loss of wages resulting from old age, death, and disability. It is obvious that the social security program has a profound economic, sociological, and psychological impact on the lives of our citizens and our country.

Our social security program is a pragmatic solution to the problems of economic insecurity occasioned by old age and misfortune. The history of the program reflects both the practical character of our people and the pluralistic nature of our society. The program provides a measure of economic security to nearly all of our people in a framework consistent with the American philosophy that each individual has the right to chart his own life course. In the future, social security will surely have to be adapted to the changing social order, but amendments to the program will not represent progress unless the program continues to eliminate the hazards of economic insecurity within a framework preserving individual choice.

FRAMEWORK OF THE PROGRAM

Closer inspection of this social security framework must necessarily precede any analysis of the direction that the program should take in the future. The level of social security benefits has traditionally been based on two concepts—"individual equity" and "social adequacy." The individual equity principle emphasizes the insurance aspects of the system and is designed to insure that an individual who supports the system during his working years receives retirement benefits reasonably commensurate with his contributions. The social adequacy principle emphasizes the social aspect of the system, recognizing that minimum basic living expenses must be considered in establishing a benefit level. It has been necessary to make many adjustments through the years in applying these conflicting criteria because the benefit level is limited by available resources.

Several characteristics of the social security law illustrate the "social adequacy" principle. The benefit formula is weighted in favor of employees with lower earnings, and an absolute floor is provided in the form of the "minimum benefit." Due to the provision of a wife's benefit, a married worker's benefits will be about 50 percent higher than a single individual's, even though they have identical earnings records. It is largely on the grounds of "social adequacy" that individuals who did not have an opportunity to earn adequate benefits under the system before retiring—"the short-term workers"—are paid benefits disproportionately large in relation to their contributions. The short-term worker problem will disappear as the system fully matures in the future.

Although social adequacy plays a significant role in our social security system, it is fair to say that individual equity is still given primary emphasis. This is so because the most pronounced characteristic of the benefit formula is that it provides wage-related benefits. When a worker retires, the average wage on which he and his employer paid taxes is computed and he is paid benefits equal to a percentage of this average wage. This important characteristic is the foundation of the system, for it means that benefits are payable as a matter of right.

Although it is legally true—and the Supreme Court has so ruled—that individuals have no contractual right to benefits analogous to a private annuity, there is a strong moral obligation to continue to pay benefits in accordance with the expectations that those supporting the system have reasonably formed. Additionally, the phrase "benefits payable as a matter of right" does not necessarily imply a contractual right. During the history of the program wage-related benefits have been payable pursuant to a statutory formula applicable to all individuals qualifying on the basis of their work record. There is no means test applied, and this is what is meant by the phrase "benefits payable as a matter of right."

This represents the framework of our social security system. It suggests three important questions relating to the future character of the program, the future scope of the program, and future amendments to the program, which will be of paramount importance in the future.

Future Character of the System

The first question we must deal with is this: Will the principle of benefits "payable as a matter of right" be maintained, or will social adequacy criteria continue to erode the foundation of individual equity on which the principle rests? I am convinced that the American people would be strongly opposed to any proposal to eliminate the principle of benefits payable as a matter of right, and I share this opposition. However, the heavy reliance on social adequacy in recent years has been chipping away at the foundation on which the principle rests. It cannot endure many more nicks without causing the entire structure to tumble down. Unless we maintain payroll tax financing and wage-related benefits, benefits payable as a matter of right—the cornerstone of the system—will be jeopardized.

A more careful analysis of the social security tax and the wage-related benefit principle will demonstrate the basis of this contention. Our income tax imposes progressive tax rates on a relatively wide income base, which includes dividends, rent, interest, and other forms of investment income. The social security tax (OASDHI) imposes a flat rate—currently 4.4 percent—on the employee and employer each. Additionally, the tax is not imposed on all income, but only on the first $7800 of a worker's wages. Specifically limiting the base to "earned income" means that no tax is imposed on dividends, interest, rents, and other forms of investment income. The social security tax base is thus limited with respect to both dollar amount and type of income included. A skilled laborer working in a General Motors' factory pays the same tax —currently $343.20 (which is matched by his employer)—as the president of General Motors.

If the social security tax were used for general governmental purposes—for example, for defense, for the administration of justice, or for public welfare—the tax would surely be condemned as regressive, and the widespread support for the social security program soon would turn to hostility. However, the tax proceeds are not used for general governmental purposes, but can be used only to pay social security benefits and the cost of administering the system. Although the tax imposes a flat rate on a wage base of earned income that is limited with respect to dollar amount, the benefits are based on this same wage base—they are wage-related. The individual is legally paying a tax, but in one sense he is contributing towards his retirement benefits by supporting the system during his working years. The tax has been considered by some to be analogous to a premium, and this thinking is partly reflected in the attitude of the public toward social security.

If we continue to undermine the wage-related benefit structure by expanding the benefits on the basis of social adequacy rather than individual equity, we will soon be paying benefits that bear very little relation to the wages that taxes are paid on. Benefits will be paid on a pre-determined welfare standard written into the social security law. In effect, we will be using the social security tax to meet a general governmental expense—public welfare. When this occurs, the social security tax will be condemned as regressive, and the hue and cry for general revenue financing through the graduated income tax will be heard.

But general revenue financing on a permanent basis poses a danger to benefits payable as a matter of right. Benefits paid on the basis of a payroll tax on wages can be related to wages. What can benefits paid with general governmental funds be related to, except demonstrated "need"—that is, some form of means test? General revenue financing might result in pressure to expand the weight given to "need," that is social adequacy, in the benefit formula, which in turn could result in resort to further general revenue financing. At some point, we can anticipate recommendations for taking the final step towards converting the system into a welfare program.

It should not surprise anyone that general revenue financing on a permanent basis involves these dangers. The government does not meet a public welfare goal by simply taxing one average citizen to pay cash benefits to another average citizen. Historically, welfare payments have been based on need, and even the income maintenance plans currently being discussed, such as the negative income tax and the guaranteed annual income, are based on some standard of individual need.

But even aside from the dangers posed by a drift towards general revenue financing, the further erosion of individual equity at the expense of social adequacy may undermine public support for the program. The income that a worker can currently devote to future contingencies is limited by his ability to meet the immediate needs of his family. If the cost of social security cuts too deeply into daily living requirements, people will begin to make unfavorable comparisons between current costs and distant benefits that provide little individual equity. If the time ever comes that current workers are unwilling to bear the cost of providing benefits to current retirees, the social security system will be in real danger and may be unable to survive. Those who will stand to lose most will be the current beneficiaries—those receiving retirement, survivors, disability, and health insurance benefits.

A recent article by Social Security Commissioner Robert Ball indicates that it is none too early to worry about this danger. Commissioner Ball wrote:

> Future generations of covered workers will get protection that is worth less than the combined employer-employee contributions with respect to their earnings, since some part of these combined contributions will necessarily go to meet part of the cost of paying full benefits in the early years. It is true that future generations of workers will get protection that is worth *their own* contribution.[1]

Two points need to be made about this statement. The first point is that some workers will not get benefits worth the value of *their own* contribution. A young worker who begins work tomorrow and who pays the maximum tax until retiring, unmarried, at age sixty-five will get significantly less in benefits than the value of his own contribution. He will not benefit from the minimum benefit provision, the weighted benefit schedule, or from the wife's benefit.

It seems somewhat artificial to say, as Commissioner Ball has, that in computing the value of this individual's benefit we must assign an actuarial value to the possibility that he might have married and had a wife at age sixty-five, even though he did not. Candor requires, I believe, that we recognize that the wife's benefit is grounded in social adequacy criteria and has little or no relation to individual equity.

The second point that should be noticed is that economic reality and the expectations of our citizens require that we look somewhat beyond the individual's own contribution in determining whether individual equity is provided. For as Commissioner Ball pointed out in the same article, "the employer

[1] Ball, Policy Issues in Social Security, 29 Soc. Sec. Bull. 3, 8 (1966).

contribution in part, at least, is shifted to workers in the form of lower wages . . ."[2]

Rather than attempting to find solutions that will change the character of the program or justifying on grounds of individual equity provisions that are based on "social adequacy," we should face the issue squarely. We need to strengthen the benefit formula at all levels to provide more individual equity. The Congress passed legislation earlier this year that strengthens the entire benefit formula to insure more individual equity for all beneficiaries. Amendments were also included that will eventually improve the relative position of single men and women and also of working wives. Enactment of these provisions will not be a panacea, but they will be a step in the right direction.

This re-emphasis on the insurance basis of the system does not mean that we are ignoring the problems of the poor. In establishing the benefit formula, we can consider social adequacy within reasonable bounds consistent with maintaining the insurance basis of the system. But social security is primarily designed to prevent poverty. It can have a significant effect on poverty due to existing conditions, but this must be incidental to its primary goal of preventing economic dependence. Manpower training, vocational education, and other programs must be relied on to provide our disadvantaged citizens with the skills and opportunities to earn wages qualifying them for social security benefits payable as a matter of right. The original architects of the Social Security Act recognized this by including public assistance programs in the legislation that created the social security system. Those who have administered the social security program during its thirty-year history have recognized this distinction, and we must recognize it today.

If we continue to confuse the goals of social security with those of other programs, we will impair the principle of benefits payable as a matter of right. I believe it is this principle that gives social security its distinctive character, and has resulted in widespread acceptance of the program.

[2] Ibid.

FUTURE SCOPE OF THE PROGRAM

The second question we should be concerned about is this
Will the scope of the social security program be adequate t
fully meet the goals of guarding against economic insecurit
while preserving individual preferences, or will the progran
be expanded to consume nearly all of the average citizen
dollars available for savings?

Social security has often been spoken of as a "floor c
protection" on which an individual can build an adequate re
tirement program in accordance with his own preferences i
the form of savings accounts, savings bonds, annuities, pr
vate pensions, or other forms of investment. Another vie
holds that social security benefits should be adequate to mee
the minimum basic living expenses of an individual who work
under the system during his entire working life. While th
former view may still be correct in theory, it must be ac
mitted that the trend of the program in recent years has bee
towards the latter view. Under legislation enacted by the 90t
Congress, maximum retirement benefits payable to a man an
his family, based on a single earnings record is $434.40,
month and these benefits are not subject to income tax.

There is certainly room for reasonable disagreement ove
the appropriate scope of the program—i.e. to provide a floc
of protection or to provide minimum basic living expense
However, I feel quite certain that many who advocate ex
panding the system will not be satisfied until the scope of th
program is so broad that it consumes nearly all of the averag
citizen's dollars available for savings and represents virtuall
his only programs for building retirement income.

It has been contended that the scope of the program alread
leaves little leeway for the average man to save outside c
the social security program. In opposing legislation in the 89t
Congress to provide further incentives to self-employed in
dividuals to establish private pension plans for themselves an
their employees, the Treasury Department contended:

For middle and lower income people, social security tax payments represent a significant financial outlay toward retirement. For example, a self-employed person with earnings of $6600 must in 1967 and 1968 pay 6.4 percent of his income toward social security and medicare. A $10,000 a year man must devote 4.2 percent of his income for this purpose. These percentages will rise to 7.1 and 4.7, respectively, in 1969. It is doubtful that many individuals at these income levels can afford to devote appreciably more to their retirement in the form of a long-term program.[3]

By the end of the 90th Congress an even higher proportion of the average individual's dollars available for savings will be consumed by the social security program, for legislation has been enacted increasing the wage base.

But many individuals will be calling for still larger increases in the scope of the program. This year the administration recommended raising the tax base to $10,800 in three steps. At least one U. S. Senator has recommended a wage base of $15,000. It is argued in support of these proposals that the 1938 wage base of $3000 covered all of the wages of 97.1 percent of the covered workers and 93 percent of the wages in covered employment. Due to the tremendous increase in earnings over the years, it would now require a wage base of $15,000 to provide similar coverage.[4] Therefore, we must "update" the program—according to "1938" standards—by raising the wage base to $15,000.

Instead, I suggest we need to carefully consider the purposes of our social security program in the light of the extensive change our society has experienced. As we have seen, social security is intended to prevent economic dependency by protecting against wages lost through death, disability, or retirement. Since about three-quarters of an individual's OASDI taxes are attributable to his retirement benefits, pri-

[3] *H. Rept.* 1557, 89th Congress, 2nd Sess., 16 (1966).
[4] Resnick, *Annual Earnings and the Taxable Maximum for OASDHI*, 29 *Soc. Sec. Bull.* 38, 40 (1966).

mary emphasis is placed on the retirement aspects of the program.

It seems to me that once the program has required our citizens to contribute a sufficient proportion of their earnings to insure that they will not become economically dependent —that they will be able to meet their minimum basic living expenses in the event of misfortune or old age—we can permit them to use the remainder of their resources as they see fit.

When wages were very low, as in 1938, a high wage replacement level was required to meet this goal. As our citizens become better off, the same wage replacement level is neither necessary nor desirable. This philosophy is built right into the benefit structure of the system. The minimum benefit, and the weighted benefit schedule reflect the judgment that a higher wage replacement percentage is necessary at lower wage levels in order to prevent economic dependence. Conversely, it follows logically that at some higher wage level little or no wage replacement is required to avoid economic dependence. An individual in these circumstances can exercise his own preferences, saving in the manner he pleases, or not saving at all if he so chooses. "To give any fair play to the nature of each," said John Stuart Mill, "it is essential that different persons should be allowed to lead different lives. In proportion as this latitude has been exercised in any age has that age been noteworthy to posterity."

What specific wage replacement level is appropriate at any time is admittedly a difficult question, but we need not speculate about specifics here because it is the principle that we are concerned with. And the principle is quite consistent with our philosophy of government, although it requires a little more faith in the common man than some are willing to profess.

But I feel that this faith is justified by the American experience. Our citizens have not been a profligate people when left to their own devices; on the contrary, thrift has been a basic American characteristic and frugality an essential ingredient in our recipe for success.

Although the discipline of necessitous circumstances has been eased by relative affluence, these basic American traits are still much in evidence. In addition to the growth in recent years of personal savings, annuities, life insurance, and other forms of investment, private pension systems have been expanding. As evidence of "the tremendous strides in private economic security measures in the last 15 years" experienced by employee-benefit plans, a recent study by the Social Security Administration points out:

> Benefit payments [in 1965] amounted to $13.0 billion (10.5 percent more than in 1964), and contributions reached the level of $19.1 billion (about 11 percent more than a year earlier).

> As 1965 ended, 122 million persons had hospital expense coverage, 47 million had life insurance protection, 28 million had temporary disability protection, and over 25 million had retirement coverage.[5]

Recognizing the value of this growth, the 1965 report by the President's Cabinet Committee on Corporate Pensions and other Retirement and Welfare Programs, entitled *Public Policy and Private Pension Programs,* concluded that private pension plans "should continue as a major element in the nation's total security program."

We must, therefore, carefully consider all the ramifications of any proposed increase in the scope of the social security program. For if the governmental program becomes virtually the only system providing income protection to our workers, we will have nothing with which to compare its performance. Private initiative and creative ideas are characteristic of our system because we allow diversity, encourage individual participation, and foster spontaneity. This is essential if we are to continue to hold our social security system to high levels of performance, and to insure that it can continue to serve our citizens in accordance with our traditions.

[5] Kolodrubetz, *Growth in Employee-Benefit Plans, 1950–65,* 30 *Soc. Sec. Bull.* 10 (1967).

FUTURE AMENDMENTS TO THE PROGRAM

The fundamental philosophy of the social security program has been the focal point of this paper about the future course of the program. It seems appropriate to conclude by briefly discussing the extent to which potential amendments to the program are in accord with this fundamental philosophy, will achieve the goals of the program, and will respond to the changing social order.

The number one problem of the aged in our society has traditionally been securing an adequate income; the number one threat to this goal is inflation. An increase in prices is, in effect, a diminution of income to people living on fixed incomes. Congress has increased benefits through the years to compensate for inflation and to expand the scope of the program. But the need to adjust benefits to increased living costs —upon which there is general agreement—has sometimes been caught up with other more controversial amendments to the program, causing needless delay in restoring the purchasing power of social security benefits.

Congress should consider providing a mechanism for periodically adjusting benefits to increases in the cost of living. The civil service and military retirement programs of the federal government already have such mechanisms—commonly called "escalator provisions." Providing similar treatment to our social security beneficiaries would assure them prompt justice when benefits are eroded by severe inflation such as we have had in the past couple of years.

Another amendment concerns extending coverage to the remaining workers not now protected by the social security system. The principal group not now covered are the federal employees, a group of approximately 2.5 million workers. This leave gaps in the survivorship, disability, and retirement protection federal employees have against economic security. Some means for including these employees in the national program of social insurance on a basis both fair to themselves and fair to other workers supporting the program must be found.

One of the most profound changes in American life is the number of women who work under social security. Under present law a woman is entitled to either one half of her husband's benefit or a benefit based on her own earnings record, whichever is higher. Since a woman's average wage is usually less than her husband's, she generally gets very little, if any, additional social security benefits by working under social security all of her life. Congress should consider amendments to the program, in addition to those passed by the House earlier this year, to insure working women a fairer return on their contributions to the system.

Many social security beneficiaries are concerned about the earnings limitation, which reduces benefits when earned income exceeds certain levels. The essential purpose of this often misunderstood provision is to measure the extent to which an individual is retired. An individual generally does not receive pension benefits until he terminates his employment connections with his employer. This is easy enough for a particular employer to determine for purposes of an employee-benefit plan, but social security is a nationwide retirement system covering nearly all of our workers. This presents problems in determining when an individual is retired, and these problems are resolved by the earnings limitation.[6] Unless we are to turn retirement benefits into an annuity automatically payable at a certain age, at a cost of over two billion dollars the first year, some such test as the earnings limitation must be retained.

However, the earnings limitation can and should be liberalized periodically, particularly when we are experiencing heavy inflation, as in recent years. Additionally, if a general sentiment develops for completely removing the limitation, and this can be done consistent with sound financing of the program, Congress should give favorable consideration to such

[6] There is a "substantial services" test for self-employed individuals in addition to the earnings limitations, but it is not necessary to develop this concept here.

an amendment. It is certainly consistent with the American ethic to avoid discouraging citizens from working who both want to work and are able to do so.

Another amendment Congress might consider is illustrated by individuals who, from necessity or personal choice, continue in their regular job for a few years after reaching age sixty-five. These individuals not only save the program money by drawing benefits for a shorter period of time, but continue to pay taxes into the social security fund. It is obvious that this also occurs on a lesser scale when individuals lose benefits due to the earnings limitation, and to some extent the problems are related. Some consideration should be given to providing benefits that reflect both the greater number of years that an individual works under the system, and the fact that he continues to pay social security taxes after reaching age sixty-five. While I am aware of the costs and administrative difficulties in framing appropriate amendments, I think that the issues merit serious attention.

An issue that has been receiving attention recently is the tax-free status of social security benefits. Although last year the administration proposed a formula for taxing social security benefits, it was rejected by the Congress.

I feel it would be a mistake to tax social security benefits. Since an individual has already paid an income tax on the money he contributed to the fund during his working years, he would have to be permitted to recover benefits at least equal to his contributions before being subject to the income tax. Aside from the difficult administrative problems associated with determining "cost," imposing a tax on benefits above cost would work against the weighted benefit schedule favorable to workers with lower average wages. This is because these workers get a larger return on their contributions —a larger benefit above cost—than more affluent workers.

Additionally, any diminution in benefits resulting from the imposition of income tax would probably require an increase in social security benefits, resulting in the imposition of higher payroll taxes. To the extent this occurs, we would in effect simply be transferring payroll tax receipts to the general funds of the Treasury.

There are other considerations relating to this issue, I realize, and the issues are too complex to explore in depth here. I also realize that in the future there will be a marked increase in the economic well-being of the aged. We can therefore preserve an objective attitude towards this question in anticipation of eventually reaching that happy state of prosperity for our senior citizens.

Finally—although this does not by any means exhaust potential changes in the program—the future should bring about further improvements in services to our beneficiaries as technological advances are made in the field of automatic data processing equipment. More sophisticated equipment and improved procedures that have characterized the past will surely be a trait of the future. These advances should reduce operational costs and serve the convenience of our 23 million beneficiaries, and the 86 million workers and their employers who are contributing to the social security trust funds.

CONCLUSION

A program as broad, pervasive, and complex as social security does not permit easy answers or instant solutions. Based on my experience with the program, I have attempted to outline the general direction the program should take, rather than to advance a bill of particulars.

I have attempted to advance a philosophy of social insurance which may be reduced to the following: As a nation we need and want a soundly financed, efficiently administered social security program with benefits adequate to fully insure our citizens against the economic insecurity and indigency accompanying loss of wages through death, disability, or retirement. For without some measure of security, man cannot be truly free.

But the converse is also true: Without freedom, no man

can truly be secure. Social security should accomplish its
worthwhile goals within a framework permitting diversity and
individual preferences. Like the government itself, the program doesn't exist for its own ends but exists solely to serve
the people, and it must, therefore, continue to respond to human nature. In this day of the "organization man" it may pay
to recall John Stuart Mill's definition of human nature, which
is not likely to be improved upon:

> Human nature is not a machine to be built after a model,
> and set to do exactly the work prescribed for it, but a
> tree, which requires to grow and develop itself on all
> sides, according to the tendency of the inward forces
> which make it a living thing.

Chapter 8

FULL EMPLOYMENT
AND ECONOMIC STABILITY

THE EMPLOYMENT ACT OBJECTIVES:
RETROSPECT AND PROSPECT
by Henry C. Wallich

HENRY C. WALLICH is Professor of Economics at Yale University. He studied at Oxford University and later received the M.A. and Ph.D. degrees from Harvard University. Professor Wallich was Chief of the Foreign Research Division of the Federal Reserve Bank of New York from 1946 to 1951. In 1958–59, he served as Assistant to the Secretary of the Treasury, and from 1959 to 1961 he was a member of the President's Council of Economic Advisers. Professor Wallich is the author of *Monetary Problems of an Export Economy* (1950), *Public Finances of a Developing Country* (with John Adler) (1951), *Mainsprings of the German Revival* (1955), and *The Cost of Freedom* (1960).

In February 1946 Congress passed, with strong bipartisan support, the "Employment Act." The vote had been preceded by a long legislative battle. At the end of World War II, with war production ceasing and millions of men and women coming home from the services looking for jobs, fears of a big depression were widespread. There was agreement among Democrats and Republicans that the depression of the 1930s must not be allowed to repeat itself. There was no agreement, however, as to how this objective could best be achieved. One side argued that the government must play the principal role, spending money freely and if necessary offering employment directly. The other side favored reliance on private enterprise, within a framework of government policies that would help enterprise do the job.

A COMPROMISE ACT

The proponents of massive government action produced the so-called Full Employment Bill. The opposition, ably led by Senator Taft, defeated the proposal. Instead the Congress adopted the Employment Act, which took a balanced approach to the respective functions of government and the private sector.

The legislation was couched in very general terms. The marching orders, as expressed in section 2 of the Act, read as follows:

"The Congress declares that it is the continuing policy and responsibility of the Federal Government to use all practicable means consistent with its needs and obligations and other essential considerations of national policy, with the assistance and cooperation of industry, agriculture, labor, and State and local governments, to coordinate and utilize all its plans, functions, and resources for the purpose of creating and maintaining, in a manner calculated to foster and promote free competitive enterprise and the general welfare, conditions under which there will be afforded useful employment opportunities, including self-employment, for those able, willing and seeking to work, and to promote maximum employment, production, and purchasing power."

Evidently a good many different meanings could be read into this language. This is due partly to the legislative struggle that preceded enactment. It also reflects, however, the good sense of the American legislative system. In passing a law whose ultimate consequences were hard to foresee, Congress provided for maximum flexibility. Future generations of legislators and administrators would have an opportunity to give contemporary meaning to the generalities of the legislation.

Flexible Interpretation

This flexibility has turned out to be a blessing for more than one reason. To begin with, the needs of political compromise had led to language that is quite at variance with the concepts of economics. Take the phrase "maximum employment, production, and purchasing power." The first two objectives largely duplicate each other. Employment and production are broadly coextensive—high employment and low production are unlikely to go hand in hand. "Purchasing power" is not a well-defined term. If it were to be interpreted as "income," it would once more repeat the essential content of employment and production.

Moreover, a maximum of three different variables at once is something at which a mathematician would wince—one cannot stand on three hilltops at the same time. This terminology becomes understandable only from the legislative history of the Act, which shows that "maximum" was substituted for "full" in order to render the language, as its sponsors thought, less extreme. "Maximum" in the language of the Employment (not "Full Employment") Act means "less than full."

The three goals, spelled out in the Act, moreover, are tied to the preceding part of the sentence in a manner that leaves uncertain whether "the continuing policy and responsibility of the federal government" is to promote the three goals unqualifiedly or whether the goals are to be promoted subject to all the considerations and qualifications that make up the bulk of the context. The statement, however, would lack internal consistency if the qualifications relating to "free competitive enterprise" and "employment opportunities" were not to apply to the manner in which "maximum employment, production and purchasing power" are to be pursued. The most plausible interpretation, therefore, is that the promotion of the three goals is to remain subject to these qualifications.

358 FULL EMPLOYMENT AND ECONOMIC STABILITY

Unexpected Developments

The wisdom of choosing very general language became apparent soon after the passage of the Act. The fears of those who had questioned the ability of the private sector to provide full employment revealed themselves as groundless. Transition to a peacetime economy proceeded smoothly. Not unemployment, but inflation became the chief problem of the immediate postwar period. Price stability had not even been mentioned specifically among the objectives of the Act. Moreover, as avoidance of large-scale unemployment came to be taken for granted, the interest of the nation increasingly shifted to the objectives of economic growth. This, too, did not appear as such in the Act.

The language of the Act, however, allowed these shifting goals to be accommodated. It has become the custom to integrate the new concerns of price stability and growth into the Act by identifying "maximum production" with growth and "maximum purchasing power" with stable prices. Employment has remained employment. Further degrees of freedom were provided because "maximum" did not spell out any particular rate of growth or employment. Such growth or employment targets as have since been advocated have standing only as administrative decisions.

Even the problem of the balance of payments deficit can be accommodated within the meaning of the Act. Such a condition was of course unheard of in the early postwar years. Had a reference to the balance of payments been made at all, it presumably would have pointed to the need to end the tendency toward a heavy U.S. surplus in international transactions which was interfering with the unfettering of world trade. But the phrase "other essential considerations of national policy" admirably allows for emerging new problems to be dealt with in the context of the Employment Act.

COMPETITIVE ENTERPRISE A GOAL

As of today, therefore, it seems fair to say that the contemporary meaning given to the goals of the Employment Act comprises full employment, adequate growth, reasonable price stability, and a satisfactory balance of payments. This common interpretation, however, may still be inadequate in view of the injunction upon the Government to perform its obligations under the Act "in a manner calculated to foster and promote the competitive enterprise and the general welfare." Promotion of the general welfare seems already inherent in the pursuit of the four other goals. Still, one may read into it an instruction to promote a fair distribution of income, although hardly a welfare state. More explicit than this injunction, however, and more generally overlooked, is the reference to free competitive enterprise. It seems clear that, as a condition of its other obligations under the Act, the government here is instructed to work on behalf of the freedom and competitiveness of American enterprise. Without elevating welfare and enterprise to the same level of importance as the other four goals, their presence among the objectives of the Act deserves to be noted.

GOALS COMPATIBLE IN LONG RUN

What the Act does not clearly consider is the degree to which its objectives are compatible with each other. I shall argue here that in the long run the major goals are largely compatible. Conflicts are likely to exist only in the short run. Because they obtrude themselves when we view them within a short time horizon, these conflicts have received a good deal of publicity. They are indeed important in this sense, and need to be explored carefully. But the trade-offs that thus may be found to exist among various goals, the possibility of getting a little more employment and growth by sacrificing a little more price and balance of payments stability, are short run indeed. They have little long-run validity.

Employment and growth are generally adjudged broadly compatible. Employment could be raised at the expense of growth, to be sure, by inhibiting automation and other productivity advances. But that is a foolish procedure. In the long run, the advance of technology creates new and better jobs. By raising the rate of investment, moreover, it is always possible to raise employment. Growth of course will accelerate if the rate of investment is raised. That is the sensible way of dealing with automation.

UNEMPLOYMENT VS. INFLATION

The principal conflict is believed to occur between employment and growth on one side and price stability and, in some circumstances, payments balance on the other. Economists' efforts to measure the trade-off involved in trying to reduce unemployment at the expense of inflation have been embodied in the so-called Phillips curve. This device shows by how much the rate of wage increases accelerates as the rate of unemployment falls. Our recent experience with rising union wage settlements as the economy moved from the unemployment of the early sixties to the overfull employment of 1966 illustrates the issue. Estimates made for the American economy are not as firm as those available for the United Kingdom, where these studies were first made. The American data seem to show, however, that it would take unemployment well in excess of 4 percent to achieve full stability of the consumer price index.

This approach, nevertheless, seems valid only in the short run. It seems to rest on the assumption that people will never learn to discount inflation. If labor really continues to believe that a 6 percent wage increase accompanied by 3 percent inflation is more than a 3 percent increase with no inflation, if businessmen continue to believe that the former increase is more costly to give than the latter, then unemployment can be permanently reduced by accepting more inflation. I doubt that people are incurably afflicted with this kind of money illusion.

If inflation can be predicted, it can be discounted. Labor, business, consumers, investors will think in "real" terms, that is, in terms of constant purchasing power. To achieve the same employment effect, inflation would have to be accelerated beyond the expected rate, and when that new rate became expected, more acceleration would be needed. Few people believe that constantly accelerating inflation is a feasible policy. I conclude that the possibility of raising employment by accepting inflation exists only in the short run, until people have caught onto the game. If that is true, the cost of price stability in terms of unemployment is very much lower than is commonly thought. Just how large the level of unemployment compatible with price stability is, and what can be done to lower it, is an important matter to which I shall return presently.

PRICE STABILITY VS. GROWTH

Next, let us contemplate the likewise much publicized conflict between price stability and economic growth. Some see a conflict because they equate growth with pushing employment to very high levels. That is a palpable misinterpretation of the meaning of growth, although a frequent one. Raising the rate at which existing productive capacity is utilized is not growth. True growth consists in increasing productive capacity itself. But a little reflection will show that growth in productive capacity is not closely dependent upon the rate of unemployment.

The principal factors through which a free market promotes growth are investment in plant and equipment, and research leading to technological advance. These are importantly influenced by the rate of growth of demand, by the pressure of demand upon plant and equipment capacity, and by the level of profits, both as incentive and as source of funds. Among these three stimulants to investment and research, the rate of growth of demand and the operating rate of equipment are not dependent upon the level of unemployment. GNP can be rising rapidly at lower as well as at higher rates of unemployment. Demand can press closely on plant and equipment capacity without pressing equally hard on labor capacity. Only profits may be dependent upon the level of unemployment —they are likely to be higher when there is some amount of inflation. But if inflation is of the cost push variety, even that ceases to be probable.

It is clear that heavy unemployment would act as a disincentive to investment and research in many ways. But the issue is not whether heavy unemployment should be tolerated—it obviously should not. The issue is whether growth could be promoted by reducing unemployment to the point where significant inflation occurs. The facts I have cited suggest that growth would benefit little from such policy.

Growth would suffer if inflationary pressures are combatted mainly with high interest rates. The experience of 1966 and 1967 has illustrated this point. Mounting government spending brought on inflationary pressures. The Federal Reserve responded to these with very high interest rates. This severely reduced investment in housing, which is an important source of growth. It also affected business investment, although to a lesser degree. Excessive demands by the public sector, leading to a squeeze upon the private sector via tight money, are clearly at odds with growth. This is very different from saying that price stability and growth are in conflict with each other. I conclude that the conflict between price stability and growth is no deeper, and perhaps less so, than that between price stability and full employment.

PAYMENTS BALANCE AT STABLE EXCHANGE RATES

Similar conclusions follow when we examine the frequently mentioned antagonism between balance of payments equilibrium on one side and full employment and growth on the other. Payments balance requires, broadly speaking, that the United States inflate no faster than other countries. If our capital exports, foreign aid, or military expenditures abroad are rising rapidly, we shall have to do better than others to keep our international accounts from deteriorating. We must then inflate less than other countries.

Advocates of high inflation tolerance argue that this competition-imposed quasi-stability of prices may be a drag on full employment and growth. Many, therefore, propose flexible exchange rates. That would mean that the link between the dollar and gold would be cut, and the dollar allowed to fluctuate freely in international exchange markets. So long as the American balance of payments was in deficit, the dollar would float downwards, making it cheaper for foreigners to buy, travel, and invest abroad. Thus, in the view of the advocates of flexible exchange rates, our balance of payments could be kept in equilibrium no matter how rapid our rate of inflation.

My own view, which I would like to note parenthetically, is that flexible rates would get us from the frying pan of payments imbalance into the fire of trade wars, exchange speculation, and accelerated inflation. But in any event, the dilemma that flexible exchange rates supposedly would solve is itself more apparent than real. If price stability is not, in the long run, severely at odds with full employment and growth, neither is payments equilibrium. Moreover, the price restraint that needs to be applied in order to end a payments deficit is non-recurring: once domestic prices have become more competitive, we can live happily ever after with a strong balance of payments.

Growth could be hurt by balance-of-payments policies that take the form of high interest rates to restrain capital outflows instead of fundamental improvement in competitiveness. Defensively high interest rates must remain a temporary measure. Aside from this, I believe in the long-run compatibility of payments balance with employment and growth.

It may reasonably be asked whether precise equilibrium in our balance of payments is in the national interest. A small deficit may be preferable, as a means of supplying the rest of the world with the dollars that part of the world likes to hold as international reserves. Under some circumstances, a surplus might be desirable, if our own reserves had been depleted below the danger point. The goal of "balance of payments equilibrium" therefore is a shorthand way of referring to a viable balance of payments, that in any event however, should not be very far removed from equilibrium.

It may be surprising to arrive at this happy conclusion about the possibility of peaceful coexistence among our goals, at least in the long run. It should not be. Truly competing objectives are those that make demands upon resources—more investment for growth versus more output for current consumption, moonshot versus poverty programs, public versus private use of resources. Full employment, growth, and price stability are not of this sort. Each moves in a different dimension. A rational society should have no permanent difficulty in reconciling them, though the learning period may be painful.

New Goals?

I have tried to show how the flexibility which the founding fathers introduced into the Employment Act has permitted a reinterpretation of its goals in the light of contemporary needs. Beyond that, I have argued that while there are serious short-run conflicts among some of the goals that we now read into the act, these conflicts diminish in the long run. Next, I shall proceed to raise questions about the present explicit and implicit goals. Are they adequate as statements of our purposes, or should the act be amended, be it by making implicit goals explicit, or by defining targets more precisely, or by adding new goals?

In undertaking this assessment, I should like first to raise some general questions about the propriety of setting national goals in a democratic society.

There are pitfalls that the goal setter must avoid. First,

the goal setter must bear in mind clearly that the nation is
nothing but the sum of its citizens, and that a nation's goals
cannot be anything but the totality of their enlightened self-
interest. To argue differently is to place democracy itself in
jeopardy. For if the citizens' goals do not exhaust the national interest, then there must be somebody who knows
better than the citizens what decisions to make. Totalitarian
governments exalt the state and its goals against those of its
people. A democracy cannot.

Second, the goal setter must remember that his activity
involves certain logical perplexities that have never been satisfactorily resolved. It seems fair to demand that the process of
democratic decision-making meet certain criteria of reason-
ableness. Yet it has been shown that the process often cannot
meet these criteria. In other words, public decision-making
may either violate democratic standards, or fail to demonstrate
that it makes even the majority of voters better off. To illustrate, if three Members of Congress were to rank the priorities
of spending an added billion dollars on the poverty program,
the moonshot and defense, each in different order, there
would turn out to be a majority of 2 to 1 favoring the poverty
program over the moonshot, the moonshot over defense, and
defense over the poverty program.

Finally, even when it is clear that a majority is made better
off by implementing a public goal, there is a question how
far it can properly go in imposing its will upon the minority.
In our system of checks and balances, this question is less
serious than in a parliamentary system where even a small
majority wields great power while it remains in office. In our
system a narrow majority rarely can impose anything very
serious upon the minority. The latter can usually bid away
enough votes from the other side to block a proposal. Nevertheless, it should give the goal setter pause to think that, as
broad goals are reduced to specific decisions, what makes
the majority better off makes the minority worse off.

These thoughts, abstract as they are, counsel caution in
setting national goals. The need for caution is underscored
by the experience of the Employment Act goals. If the goals

of maximum employment, production, and purchasing power were taken literally, they would long be out of date. They would have failed to anticipate the problem of inflation, the problem of growth as contrasted with mere "production," and the problem of the balance of payments. Interpreted in this sense, the lesson of experience is that goals date very quickly and that, raised to a high legal pedestal, they will be bypassed by the future. If the goals of the Employment Act are to be reinterpreted in the light of contemporary problems, as I have argued they should be, they demonstrate the virtue of flexibility. The lesson of experience, then, is that this flexibility should be preserved. We should not, by crystallizing the lessons of twenty-two years, try to freeze the wave of the future.

Lessons of Experience

In addition to these warning signals, however, the lessons of the last twenty-two years also contain many positive hints. Economic experience does not necessarily lead to economic agnosticism. We have learned much about the goals that are explicit in the Act, and about those that are implicit.

About employment we now know, what we did not know in 1946, that it can readily reach a 96 percent level and, what few would have believed then, can reach this level quite possibly without massive budget deficits. There is every reason to think that enough aggregate demand can push unemployment still lower. The experience of continental Europe, if not our own, shows that peacetime economics can achieve less than 1 percent unemployment, although differences in definitions may enter here.

At the same time we have observed, in the course of the past year, that below 5 percent unemployment, significant price and wage pressures develop. "Full employment unemployment" seems to lie somewhere in the 4 to 5 percent range. As I have argued earlier, the relation between unemployment and prices probably is not a stable one. A small stable rate of inflation will help to keep unemployment down only so long as labor, business and investors have not learned to discount it. But before this discounting becomes general, there is a trade-off between unemployment and inflation, and we are now discovering what it is.

To improve this trade-off is an urgent policy goal. Two approaches are available: to match the skill structure of the labor force to the skill structure of jobs, by education and retraining, and to modify wage and price setting habits of labor and business through guideposts on wages and prices or some other form of incomes policy. Needless to say, any such devices must be kept compatible with a free market economy and must not be misused as a pretext for arbitrary intervention in wage and price setting.

In time, we must succeed in reducing the level of "full employment unemployment" well below the 4 to 5 percent range. The experience of 1965–67 has shown that we cannot do it yet. With our employment goals thus in a state of flux, I conclude that it would not be advisable to write a precise employment target into the Employment Act.

Experience also has taught us something about economic growth. We now know that the rate that has prevailed in the United States for so long as we have data is not easy to speed up. We did not know this during the first fine flurry of growth enthusiasm during the late fifties, when the sky was just an interim goal. We also have learned that we are still quite uncertain about the quantitative effect of particular actions to strengthen investment, research, and education. We know enough to be able to say that measures in these areas will accelerate growth. It would seem entirely reasonable for the voters and the Congress to decide that, in the light of international and domestic needs, we should accelerate growth. We can then adopt particular measures and see how far they take us. But the lessons of experience provide no basis for writing a particular growth rate into the law. We do not know the measures required to reach that rate, and we might not like them once we did know.

On the subject of price stability, experience has taught us

that perfect stability is very hard to achieve. We have also learned that inflation, once it exceeds the 1 to 2 percent rate and becomes widely expected, can be kept from accelerating and reduced to a slower rate only at great cost. Even so, I am unable to share the view that a low rate of inflation, of 1 to 2 percent, is only a minor nuisance and a cheap price to pay for gains in employment and growth that, to boot, I believe to be transitory. A good monetary system is part of our social fabric, like our system of laws. Lack of trust in stable money means lack of trust in all economic relationships. It has been well said that an inflationary economy is like a country where nobody speaks the truth.

A government that inflates while professing to aim at stability, thus denying its people the opportunity to anticipate inflation correctly, may be acting in their interest in terms of employment and growth. But if such benevolent deceit is justified in economic matters, why not also in matters of war and peace, or any other? I prefer truth.

Our balance-of-payments experience of the last 8 years has taught us another lesson about inflation. If the international value of the dollar is to be maintained, and all that goes with it economically, politically, and militarily, we must keep our international payments in reasonable balance and hence inflation under control.

Payments equilibrium has become a major objective of policy in its own right. It is the only objective where a fairly precise target must be achieved. We can choose our way of achieving balance, beyond the deficit justified by amount of dollars the world wants, by exporting more, or investing less, or by borrowing abroad. But we cannot afford to run out of international reserves.

Since stable prices as a goal can be found in the Employment Act only by interpretation, and payments balance only under the catchall "needs and obligations and other essential considerations of national policy," there is a good case for writing both into the act. I would favor this amendment. However, I doubt that, up to the present, inflation and the payments deficit would have been fought any less energetically had the two new goals always been set forth clearly in the act. To amend the act, therefore, would not mean much without a new resolve on the part of the people and the Congress to hold the line hereafter.

MORE QUALITATIVE GOALS

Inclusion of price stability and payments balance would advance the Employment Act in a direction that strikes me as desirable: toward more qualitative goals. I use the term not in contrast to target goals, but as focusing on the content rather than the amount of things. The basic English of the Employment Act is heavily quantitative: a maximum of everything. But employment, too, has qualitative aspects. A job is not only a source of income, but the foundation of human dignity. Stability and balance, which a poet once equated, are qualitative concepts. As we become richer, it seems increasingly appropriate to concern ourselves not only with "How much?" but also with "How good?"

The trend of recent government programs seems increasingly designed to improve our life qualitatively as well as quantitatively—through medicare, education, the ending of poverty, pollution control, a more beautiful America. These endeavors go in the right direction, although the means adopted often are faulty. In particular, while they correctly reflect the increasingly collective nature of our needs,—no single individual can purchase cleaner air and water, nor pay for reduction in scenic blight—they err in identifying collective with public. Much of what is proposed today as public sector activities could be done privately. This is particularly true of health insurance, old age provision, and some phases of education. Subject to a proper balance being struck between public and private activity, assigning to the public sector only what demonstrably cannot be done through the private, the move toward more qualitative goals is in keeping with the increasing wealth of Americans.

In time, I expect, our goals will become more social and

less purely economic. As new aspirations acquire the status of national goals, they should be given greater force by embodiment in the Employment Act. Legislative pronouncements will have to reflect a broadly felt need, however, if they are to amount to more than economic New Year's resolutions.

IMPLEMENTATION THROUGH THE PRIVATE SECTOR

Care must be had, too, lest the multiplication of seemingly worthwhile ends leads to a proliferation of more questionable means. A respectable doctrine of economists has it that in order to achieve several goals at once, the number of policy instruments must equal the number of objectives. Technicians may argue over the qualifications to be attached to this general rule. To the extent that goals are in harmony with each other rather than conflicting, they can certainly be pursued by means of one rather than several policy instruments. Nevertheless there remains the strong probability that, as the government establishes new goals, it will create for itself new instruments to attain them. These instruments are bound to circumscribe economic and other freedoms, whatever desirable results might otherwise flow from them.

It is far preferable, therefore, to seek out arrangements that allow new goals, qualitative or otherwise, to be pursued within the confines of the free market. The government may create the framework, by establishing rules and incentives. But implementation, wherever possible, should be through the voluntary action of individuals or businesses.

ROLE OF MINORITY PARTY

A minority party, even though in opposition, can make a great contribution to evolution in these directions. It has been said that the business of the opposition is to oppose. Constructive opposition will perform this function best, however, if it opposes, to the proposals of the majority, counter proposals of its own designed to achieve the same objective by more effective means. The legislative proposals of the majority inevitably are encumbered by compromises and expediencies that have little to do with the real issue. Bargains must be struck to obtain legislative support. Quick results must be sought in order to make what looks like a record before the next election. An opposition party is not bound by these constraints. It can analyze programs on their true merits. It can expose the compromises, the bargains, the expediencies. Being less under the pressure of election deadlines than those who stand to be turned out of office, the opposition can afford to take a long-run point of view.

The long-run point of view is not a popular one. It requires eschewing the quick and facile solution, the shot in the arm, the plastering over of basic problems with hasty expedients. The political cynic may reject the farsighted approach by saying that in the long run we are all dead, and that the long run in any event is only a succession of short runs. This is not a responsible position. If not we ourselves, our children will live to see and feel the long run consequences of the mistakes we make today.

A reasonable attitude toward the future of our nation requires us to take a long-run view. It requires us to reject proposals for solving all problems by spending a little more money, or inventing some new form of control. It requires us not to create problems that future generations will have to meet.

An opposition party, not having to elaborate every last legislative detail, can insist on fundamentals. It can concentrate on proposals that will wear well over decades, not just to the next election. It can point up the need for major changes which an entrenched majority, immobilized by conflicting interests, can never contemplate. Basic reforms are rarely undertaken by a party that has grown old in office. They require the fresh ideas that germinate in adversity, and the change in leadership that only a change in administration can bring.

ECONOMIC POLICY AND
THE LESSONS OF EXPERIENCE

by Paul W. McCracken

PAUL W. McCRACKEN is Edmund Ezra Day University
Professor of Business Administration at the Graduate
School of Business Administration at the University of
Michigan. Professor McCracken received his doctorate
from Harvard University and, prior to joining the faculty
of the University of Michigan in 1948, was an economist
with the U. S. Department of Commerce and later a
Financial Economist and Director of Research of the
Federal Reserve Bank of Minneapolis. From 1956 to
1959, Professor McCracken served as a Member of the
President's Council of Economic Advisers. Professor Mc-
Cracken is the author of numerous articles and monographs on economic and financial policy. Among his
many activities, Professor McCracken was in 1961 a
member of the Task Force Reporting to President Kennedy on the Domestic Economic Situation and the Balance of Payments, and in 1966 he was a member of the
President's Commission on Budget Concepts.

High on the list of deficiencies which economists share with
Americans generally is inattention to the lessons of history.
While we use statistics and other raw material of experience
prodigiously, we are not much inclined to read the minutes

NOTE: Adapted from a paper presented to the Symposium on
Fiscal Policy and Business Capital Formation, American Enterprise Institute for Public Policy Research, Washington, D.C.,
April 21, 1967. Mark Riedy was most helpful in assembling materials for this paper.

of earlier meetings in order to gain some historical perspective about how we got to where we are. This is a pity because the record of our experience with the operation of economic policy provides us with some useful, and even surprising, lessons.

As we examine this record, one conclusion stands out sharply. Fiscal and monetary policies have themselves been a major source of erratic movements in the economy, and the first requirement for improving our economic performance is that these policies themselves be operated in a more even-handed and steady manner. Far from automating fiscal policy, this view of the problem will, if it is correct, require considerably more sophistication and precision than we have yet applied to the task.

I

The prevailing concept about the nature of the problem of economic instability is itself a manifestation of our disinclination to examine history. We have tended to assume that ours is an economy with strong indigenous tendencies to ricochet from boom to bust, from overheating to unemployment, unless these inherent tendencies are neutralized by stabilizing economic policies. Our strategy, then, would be for these policies to zig or zag vigorously as the economy zags and zigs.

There is a good deal of historical evidence to suggest that this conception of the problem is close to being 180 degrees off course. It would be more in accord with the evidence of history to say that we have had an economy with an impressive capacity to follow a course of vigorous and orderly expansion—except when it has been deflated by a miscarriage of economic policy. Suppose that we explore this a bit to see whether it seems to square with the facts of history.

For several reasons it is useful here to begin with the pre-1929 era, specifically the four decades from 1889 to 1929. The period has certain natural advantages for our point. Annual data are reasonably available. We did not even have a central banking system for two-thirds of these years. During most of these four decades the federal budget was equal in magnitude to about 3 percent of GNP, so its inherent capacity to keep an erratic economy on a short leash would have been severely limited. In any case the concept of fiscal policy had not even been invented at this time. Thus we have here a segment of history during which we should be able to observe the private economy "in the raw" before the instruments of economic stabilization were really available to exert their "restraining" effects on its natural instability.

The National Bureau of Economic Research has decreed that there were twelve identifiable cyclical swings in this span of four decades. And there were eight years during which real output fell below that of the previous year.[1] When we examine the data more closely, however, we discover some interesting things. The median decline for the recedence years was only 2.6 percent in real output. And in eight of the twelve recessions real output in the year containing the low point of the recession was higher than that for the year containing the previous peak.

The four more serious recessions were 1894, 1908, 1914, and 1921. The recession of 1908 was clearly associated with a major monetary panic, and the collapse of 1921 arose out of an overly expansionist set of policies through 1919, followed in 1920 by a drastic reversal of both monetary and fiscal policies. The $13.7 billion swing from a large deficit in FY 1919 to a small surplus in FY 1920 was equal to 16 percent of GNP in 1919 (the equivalent of a $120 billion year-to-year restrictive budgetary swing today). And in three moves the Federal Reserve pushed the discount rate to an all-time high of 7 percent by mid-1920, forcing a 5.2 percent contraction in the money supply from mid-1920 to mid-1921. The remarkable thing here is not that there was a 1921 recession but that our economic system even survived this massive fiscal and monetary whipsaw.

[1] Cf. "Long-term Economic Growth, 1860–1965" (Bureau of the Census, 1966), pp. 166–67.

Here clearly what we are observing is not an economy with some endemic case of the shakes, inherently tending to dash from the cellar to the penthouse. It is a record of surprisingly orderly and sustained expansion, except when our foot was pressed too heavily on the accelerator or on the brake (often in quick succession).

The final decade of this period (i.e., 1922 to 1929) is particularly instructive here. Indeed, it is one of the ironies of history that this vastly underrated economic performance tends so often to be characterized as the era that landed us in the ditch of the Great Depression. Actually it was a period that lived up well to Section 2 of the Employment Act of 1946.[2] Real output rose at the average rate of 4.7 percent per year, and each year saw a rise. The price level was steady. And the unemployment rate averaged 3.6 percent.

This good economic performance was no accident. The money supply rose quite steadily at the average rate of 5.1 percent per year, and fiscal policy was also turning in an impressive performance. The full employment surplus (the difference between federal outlays and the receipts that the revenue system would produce at full employment) for fiscal years 1923 to 1930 apparently ranged from a low of about $0.7 billion in 1926 and 1929 to a high of just under $1 billion in 1930. The full employment surplus, in short, varied within a narrow range that was equal to roughly 0.3 percent of GNP. Thus this calibration of fiscal policy (which is, of course, analytically superior to actual surpluses as a measure of fiscal policy) shows a remarkable stability, with a full employment surplus of somewhat less than 1 percent of GNP during this period.

Though it has required about three decades to get the point in focus, we do now see that the Great Depression itself was also the result, particularly in the critical 1931 to 1933 phase, of our doing things wrong in the field of public policy virtually whenever there was an opportunity to do so. And we also now see that the catastrophe had nothing to do with any inherent

2 See page 356.

or natural tendency of our economic system to operate at underemployment levels. What we had here was a massive monetary blood-letting. By 1933 the full-employment money supply would have been roughly 50 percent above actual

FULL EMPLOYMENT SURPLUS
(IN BILLIONS)

Fiscal Year	Amount
1923	$0.7
1924	0.8
1925	0.7
1926	0.6
1927	1.0
1928	1.0
1929	0.7
1930	0.9

SOURCE: Estimates for potential GNP were interpolated from James W. Knowles, "The Potential Economic Growth of the United States," Joint Economic Committee, 86th Congress, 2nd Session, 1960, p. 37. Annual Commerce estimates of GNP were converted to quarterly data using the quarterly pattern of Harold Barges, "Outlay and Income in the United States, 1921 to 1928," (N.B.E.R., 1942), pp. 114–19. The ratio of actual GNP to potential was then applied to each fiscal year's revenues. This figure minus actual expenditures is the derived full employment surplus estimate. These data pertain to the administrative budget.

levels, and our zeal for economic masochism had enabled us to accomplish the extraordinary feat of extinguishing 40 percent of our banks. (We had 25,000 banks in 1929, and we emerged in 1933 with about 15,000.)

Fiscal policy was also afflicted with its full share of gremlins in this unhappy period. The full employment surplus moved from a deficit to a modest surplus in the critical 1932–33 period, a "wrong" swing of close to 2 percent of GNP. And the swing in the full employment surplus from a deficit of roughly $2½ billion in 1936 to a surplus of less than $1 billion in 1937 (a perverse swing equal to about 4 percent of GNP) was certainly a major source of the downturn in 1937 that began before we had regained full employment—a downturn of great conceptual significance because it raised questions about the ability of our economy to sustain reasonably full employment.

The long-sustained period of abnormally high unemployment from late 1957 to mid-1965 is, of course, another illustration of an aberration in our economic performance whose sources can be traced to economic policy. The glacial pace of monetary expansion from 1956 through 1959 (excluding a brief interlude early in 1958) was certainly a major factor. The money supply (including time deposits) from the end of 1955 to the end of 1959 was allowed to increase at the rate of 3.1 percent per year, considerably short of that required for the economy to keep on a growth path consistent with reasonably full utilization of our productive resources.

Fiscal policy also was allowed to wander off course in a major way. In the recedence phase fiscal policy actually was working well. The full employment surplus was declining rapidly to a $1–2 billion level by the end of 1958, and this contributed to the brevity of the decline and the strong subsequent upswing. At this point things began to develop less favorably. The full employment surplus then rose from this $1–2 billion annual rate at the end of 1958 to the $14 billion zone two years later. Monetary policy also turned severely restrictive as the money supply, from mid-1958 to mid-1960 was permitted to increase at the rate of 2.4 percent per year —wholly inadequate for an economy whose basic capacity was rising then 3½–4 percent each year. Subjected to these fiscal and monetary drags, the economy faltered in 1960 before it achieved full employment. The administration's failure to provide leadership for a 1958 tax reduction cost the economy another recession (and its own party the White House in

1960). Here is a major lesson for the Republicans in the realities of political economy.

At the same time it must be remembered that this was an era of inflation-mindedness. The price level was rising at the rate of more than 3 percent per year. Of even greater significance was the surge of inflationary expectations, and decisions about things ranging from investments to the size of wage increases were being distorted accordingly. While fiscal and monetary policies did become too restrictive, a stern disinflationary policy was then in order, and it made a major (and underappreciated) contribution to the orderly subsequent expansion.

So much for a history that to some must seem ancient. Fortunately in recent years, some feel, the forces of darkness that produced these aberrant results have been dispersed. With the new economics we have ushered in an age of enlightenment. Since 1961, we have been told (about as often in lyric poetry as in prose) that the economic performance has been truly remarkable. Now it has been a better performance than we saw in the late 1950s. From 1960 to 1966 real output grew at the average annual rate of 4.8 percent per year—quite impressive for an economy whose long-run growth rate has been about 3½ percent. Moreover, there has been no recession since 1961 (though the expansion suffered a prolonged interruption in late 1962 and early 1963, and a recedence in the first half of 1967). And we had a major tax decrease in 1964 that clearly helped the economy to regain full employment somewhat over a year later.

Now it is not easy to gain perspective on the new economics. For one thing the precise substantive content of the phrase is astonishingly difficult to identify. There is certainly very little in its literature about objectives of economic policy that is new. Let me quote a sentence: "Government must use all practicable means to promote high levels of production and employment, and to contribute toward achieving an expanding and widely shared national income earned in dollars of stable buying power." The author of this sentence, which might have come even from New York's junior senator, was actually a spokesman seemingly more benevolently disposed toward the Johnson administration—namely, the last Republican President in his 1957 Economic Report.

Nor have there been major innovations in the instruments of economic policy. The guidelines were a logical extension of increasing official attention before 1962 to the wage-price problem, but by 1967 they seemed to have a tenuous hold on official affection. There was a large tax reduction in 1964 that was needed and effective, equal in magnitude to 2.1 percent of 1965's GNP (the year in which the full reduction became effective). We have had, however, other tax cuts of similar relative magnitude. A decade earlier the $7.4 billion tax reduction was equal to 2.0 percent of 1954's GNP, and it was in the face of a substantial deficit in the budget. Moreover, it was made with the economic situation in mind—this according to no less a "new economist" than Secretary of the Treasury George M. Humphrey. Indeed, one of the best performances in tax reductions (or for fiscal policy generally) was in the mid-1920s when in three steps the revenue producing capability of the federal tax structure was reduced by $1.6 billion.[3] This was equal again to roughly 2 percent of GNP. Moreover, the full employment surplus from 1922 to 1929 was kept remarkably steady, moving within a quite narrow range. Indeed, by this important measure fiscal policy was operated more expertly in the 1920s than in the 1960s.

For a time the main basis for claiming that our capacity to execute policy has improved dramatically in recent years has been simply the improved performance of the economy. This better performance must mean that policies have also been different and better. Undoubtedly our policy capabilities have improved. Hopefully we learn a few things as we go along. What needs far more critical evaluation, however, is precisely this basic premise that our performance in recent years has been so superior that it is out of context with our historical experience. This is not so obvious as it may seem.

[3] Annual Report, Secretary of the Treasury, Fiscal Year 1926, p. 24.

The average annual rate of growth in the 1920s was equal to that since 1960—4¾ percent per year in both cases. And we did at least that well for a period that was twice as long from 1895 to 1907 (both cyclical "peak" years).

The real point here, however, is something more fundamental than a crude comparison of growth rates. That the growth capability of the economy was going to be unusually high in the 1960s was determined less by the new economics than by the birth statistics following the war that made a rapid subsequent rise in the labor force ineluctably certain. We are now in a period when the annual increments to the labor force are almost double their numbers in the 1950s, and there is

AVERAGE ANNUAL INCREASE IN THE LABOR FORCE
(IN THOUSANDS)

Period	Number
1950–60	810
1960–65	1,010
1965–75*	1,520

* Cf. "U. S. Economic Growth to 1975: Potentials and Problems," Joint Economic Committee (89th Congress, 2d Session, 1966), p. 11.
SOURCE: Basic data from Department of Labor.

some evidence that the rate of growth in productivity is also favorably affected by the higher rate of growth in output made possible by the more rapidly enlarging labor force.[4] The test of policy is how the economy operated relative to this more rapidly rising potential. And here the record since 1960 is simply not superior. In the low quarter of 1961, according to the Wharton index of capacity, the economy's operating rate was 80.5 percent.[5] This was within a percentage point of the figure at the low point in 1949 and again in 1958, but it was below the 85.2 percent in the third quarter of 1954. The 1961 recession, in short, did not bring the economy's

[4] Cf. Nicholas Kaldor, "Causes of the Slow Rate of Economic Growth of the United Kingdom" (Cambridge, 1966).

[5] Release of September 12, 1967. This is the combined index of industrial and service capacity.

operating rate to a level unusually low by historical standards. In the year following the 1961 low point, the operating rate increased 6.2 percent. This is far less than the 13.4 percent improvement during the comparable period after the low point in 1958, or even the 9.4 percent after 1954. (There was a 15.8 percent gain after the 1949 low quarter, but this was influenced by the Korean Conflict.) Moreover, after the first year's improvement of the operating rate into early 1962, there was no further gain until the second quarter of 1964. Or, to put it somewhat differently, after the low point in 1961 the economy required sixteen quarters to accomplish a gain in its operating rate that required only four quarters in the post-1958 period—in both cases starting with about the same relative shortfall from par.

When we realize this, the absence of a recession in the 1960s also takes on a somewhat different meaning. It arose in part out of the unusually long, drawn-out path of the return to full employment, and when full employment was finally achieved in the final quarter of 1965, some of the old problems again became visible. And they have been exacerbated by an unusually erratic course of policy in 1966 and 1967. In 1965 as the economy was re-entering the zone of full employment fiscal and monetary policies should have become less expansive. Instead, they became more so. The rate of monetary expansion in 1965 accelerated from an 8.4 percent annual pace in the first half to a 10.6 percent rate in the second half. And the $8.6 billion full employment surplus (at an annual rate) in the first half of 1965 shifted to a small deficit in the second half—a $9 billion swing in the wrong direction.

Then came the ill-fated January 1966 Budget Message, with its egregious underestimate of outlays for FY 1967, which immobilized fiscal policy and made it impossible to establish the case for a 1966 tax increase. Faced with an accelerating economy, the Federal Reserve panicked in 1966 and jammed hard on the brakes. There was an almost classic response. With the usual lag of two or three quarters, the economy in early 1967 faltered—with enough weaknesses to have produced a recession except for rapidly rising federal outlays (heavily for national security). During 1967, as if to cancel one error with another, the Federal Reserve has allowed the money supply to increase at a 12–14 percent rate—twice the economy's growth capability. And we now confront a budget for FY 1968 in a state of fundamental disequilibrium—with a prospective deficit that may be in the $20 billion range. These policies now expose us to a baleful combination of upward pressures on the price level, floundering credit markets, a major disequilibrium in our balance of payments and demands for direct controls. Some may be tempted to conclude that those now in charge of policy are simply less expert practitioners of economic policy than their predecessors in the early 1960s. Not necessarily. Those in the early 1960s had a far easier task than they readily admit. The disinflation of 1958–60 had established the basis for an orderly expansion. What then happened to be needed were expansive policies—which are also popular.

The real point is more fundamental. Departures from the full employment growth path have had their origins primarily in the erratic management of economic policy, and this has its manifestations in the era of the new economics as well as earlier. The first great hope for a steadier course of economic expansion is, therefore, a steadier and more even-handed management of economic policy.

What, more precisely, does this mean?

II

Monetary and fiscal policy have a synergetic relationship with each other, and a few quick comments about the nature of this relationship may be in order. The usual conception is of two relatively separate and distinct instruments of policy, either of which can be used to achieve a certain effect on the level of business activity. We can, then, pursue an easier fiscal policy and a tighter monetary policy with a neutral effect on the level of business activity—making these off-setting adjustments in order to achieve certain subsidiary objectives such as a stronger balance of payments. The 1966 problem has occasionally been described as a condition where the brakes on the monetary wheel were set hard and the brakes on the fiscal wheel were not used—causing the economy to swerve.

Part of the trouble here is the use of some terms that have less than precise meaning. What do we mean by an easier or tighter fiscal policy? We now know that this must be measured by something other than the size of the actual surplus or deficit, because this with no fiscal actions at all can change simply as the level of business activity changes. We have solved this ambiguity, in principle, by the use of the full-employment surplus concept (expenditures less the receipts the tax system would produce at full-employment). Apart from secular economic growth this changes only when the "fiscal functions" of the economy are changed—only when expenditure *programs* or tax *rates* are altered.

What, however, do we mean by an easier or tighter monetary policy? Clearly these phrases have little meaning if we are thinking in terms of whether credit markets are under pressure or whether interest rates are high or rising. We could, in that case, get "easier money" by a further decline in an already depressed demand for output, but this "easing" would be the harbinger of further economic deterioration rather than expansion. Or we could get "tighter money" in credit markets with accelerating demand, but "tight money" here would be an augury of further economic expansion rather than contraction.

Now, fortunately, there is a way out of this problem. It is opened up by the fact that the relationship between the money supply and GNP is fairly stable through time. During the last decade the ratio of the money supply to GNP averaged 43.3 percent, and only 1958 of the eleven years from 1957 to 1967 turned in a ratio deviating from this average by more than one percentage point.[6] If we calibrate monetary ease

---

[6] Even on a first difference basis, lagged quarterly changes in the money supply explain statistically about 44 percent of the changes in GNP.

or tightness by the rate of monetary expansion, we have an unambiguous measure. A more rapid rate of monetary expansion is an easier monetary policy than a policy permitting a slower expansion. Thus monetary policy was tightening in 1966 because the rate of monetary expansion was reduced, not because interest rates were rising. And monetary policy became easier in the second half of 1965 because the rate of monetary expansion was allowed to accelerate, even though interest rates were also rising.

GNP AND THE MONEY SUPPLY
(DOLLAR AMOUNTS IN BILLIONS)

Year	GNP	Money Supply* Amount	% GNP
1957	$441.1	$191.1	43.3%
1958	447.3	199.9	44.7
1959	483.7	207.9	43.0
1960	503.7	211.6	42.0
1961	520.1	221.1	42.5
1962	560.3	236.6	42.3
1963	590.5	255.3	43.2
1964	632.4	275.5	43.5
1965	683.9	299.8	43.9
1966	743.3	321.3	43.2
1967	785.1	347.1	44.2

* Time deposits are included. Each figure is the average of year-end figures bracketing the year (based on seasonally adjusted data).
SOURCE: Department of Commerce & Federal Reserve.

Since the economy is not apt to stray far from the trail being blazed earlier by the pace of monetary expansion, we must then be careful in our use of such concepts as "easier fiscal policy and tighter credit policy." A tighter monetary policy in the sense of a reduced pace of monetary expansion is apt to slow the economy even if fiscal policy is eased in the sense of reducing the full employment surplus. Indeed, we could almost say that monetary policy establishes the level of business activity, and fiscal policy influences such financial matters as money and capital market conditions and the level of interest rates.

Now this is not to say that a change in fiscal policy has no effect on the level of business activity. It can help to activate an expansion or to cool off an overheated economy. The effect of, for example, an easier fiscal policy may work itself out through a reduced propensity to hold money (though the ongoing tolerances here are small), or it may force or enable the pursuit of a more rapid monetary expansion. In any case we do well to keep in mind the complex and subtle nature of the relationship between monetary policy and fiscal policy as we turn to the latter.

III

It is well for us to remember, as we come to fiscal policy, that we want the fiscal operations of government to accomplish more for us than to help the economy pursue a stable growth path. Through government budgets we want to arrange for collectivized consumption and investment. And we also want these fiscal operations to redistribute the national income more equitably. Some of the most urgent work in budget policy must be concerned with these matters.

How can we assure that our budget procedures give effective expression to the preferences of people about the allocation of their incomes between public and private consumption and investment? There are major problems posed by our fiscal procedures here. For one thing the decision-making process that finally determines actual outlays is not subjected to the discipline of a total. Each appropriation bill must be decided "on its merits" and with whatever guesses and hunches can be mustered about what it will all probably add up to. Yet the aggregate of spending requests that have merit in themselves is bound to exceed a viable total. This is what the discipline of economics is all about. The budget hiatus at the end of 1967 points up the urgency of making progress on expenditure policy.

It would, of course, be helpful if we could inject more market-place disciplines into the public sector. Surface area devoted to street-side parking, for example, might suffer from less excess demand if its prices bore some relationship to its scarcity. The post office problem of junk mail is not that this mail is junky (a matter of definition) but that the post office offers to carry it at bargain-basement rates. Yet prospects here are not bright. New York could not muster enough political courage to meter water use even in the face of a crisis. The post office will continue to wallow in a rising volume that it is ill-prepared to handle. If we cannot find ways to use market disciplines more, the case for an expansion of activities in the public sector is correspondingly weakened.

The objective of redistributing income through the government's fiscal operations also needs to be brought into better balance and focus. What are the criteria for deciding how far the budget should attempt to go in income redistribution? Should we look only at the incidence of taxes, as is usually done, or should we look also at benefits received by income levels? While the total tax system does not seem to be highly progressive until we get to upper income groups, the total fiscal operations of government are redistributing the national income in favor of low income groups in a massive way. In 1965, according to one estimate, those with incomes under $2000 received net benefits (benefits received less taxes paid) of 80 percent of their income. We can safely take into account other considerations than whether each tax change makes the tax system more progressive, secure in the knowledge that the nation's total fiscal system is heavily redistributing incomes toward lower income groups.

In these non-stabilization areas are to be found some of the least satisfactory aspects of budgetry, and it is good that they are now beginning to receive more attention. Our specific concern here, however, has to do with the contribution of fiscal policy to stable economic growth, and it is to this that we now turn.

Clearly the most fundamental contribution that fiscal policy can make to orderly and vigorous economic progress is that the budget itself pursue a more even-handed and steady course. The blunt truth is that prospects for the budget are a

GOVERNMENT TAXES AND BENEFITS RECEIVED AS A PERCENTAGE
OF TOTAL INCOME, 1965

Income class	Taxes paid	Benefits received	Benefits received per dollar of taxes
Under $2,000	28.1%	109.0%	3.88
$2,000–$2,999	26.7	65.0	2.43
$3,000–$3,999	29.7	46.0	1.55
$4,000–$4,999	29.1	33.7	1.16
$5,000–$5,999	29.4	29.5	1.00
$6,000–$7,499	28.5	25.4	.89
$7,500–$9,999	28.5	22.1	.78
$10,000–$14,999	30.6	20.0	.65
$15,000 and over	44.0	16.3	.37
Average	30.4	29.9	.98

SOURCE: "Tax Burdens and Benefits of Government Expenditures by Income Class, 1961 and 1965" (Tax Foundation, 1967).

major uncertainty in any appraisal of our economic prospects, and perverse swings in the budget have been an important source of instability. It is here that improvement must begin.

The flow of budget data is itself one of the more erratic and uncertain elements in our economic information system, and this must be remedied. Some of this is a simple matter of regular and prompt reporting. We particularly need more regularized and periodic estimates of where the whole budget seems to be going for a year ahead and what programs adopted now mean for outlays for several years ahead. If this cannot be done by a federal agency, and obviously no administration wants thus to predict Congressional defeat of any program, this gap must be filled by competent private estimates. While the budget is supposed to be a stabilizer, we have more information from the federal government about the number of cars that will be bought or changes in business outlays on plant and equipment than about where the federal budget itself will be going.

A review of the structure and format of our budget information system was long needed. The President himself provided the leadership here in 1967 with his Commission on

Budget Concepts. Its recommendations will help greatly to dispel murkiness surrounding budget information. And the President is to be commended for the prompt implementation of these recommendations in his January Budget Message.

Finally, we need a more explicit working concept of what constitutes the equilibrium relationship between receipts and expenditures that should be the navigation chart for fiscal policy. In the always-balanced-budget era, we had such a guideline. It was crude, but it was definite. Indeed, on the whole it worked surprisingly well, and its definitiveness did inject a wholly desirable fiscal discipline into the budgetary process. A major limitation of the new fiscal policy is that we have never really replaced the old rule with anything. This has created problems of its own. Our conception of the problem as one of countering instability endemic to the private economy has led us to adopt a strategy of policy that is itself a major source of instability. Fiscal policy now runs to this side of the ship and then to the other, but often in this process it becomes itself the source of the ship's wallowing course.

The full-employment surplus gives us the guideline here that we need. It is consistent with the requirements of fiscal discipline and also with the new fiscal policy. Each proposed budget should be shown on a full employment as well as an actual basis. Moreover, our on-going operating rule should be that proposed expenditures be reasonably in balance with the receipts that our tax structure would produce at full employment. With such a rule a larger proportion of the years will have budgets consistent with stable economic growth than if we try to *ad hoc* our way along—playing it all by ear, leaning against the wind, judging each situation on its merits, and employing all of the other Good Phrases that imply a wisdom too profound to be limited by guidelines. History, as we have found, has written its own record of the results of this strategy, and it suggests that we should try for something better.

Now it should be clear that what is proposed here is no passive or automatic fiscal policy. If our expenditure and tax programs are to be managed so that the full employment budget remains in reasonably close balance, a far more exacting and sophisticated management of fiscal policy will be required than we have had in the postwar period. We need to pass from the stage of the economic blacksmith to the narrower tolerances of economic engineering.

IV

Much of the discussion in recent years about strengthening the capability of policy to stabilize the economy has been in terms of introducing greater flexibility—e.g., giving the President limited power over tax rates. These proposals have merit. Most important ones would require approval of the Congress, however, and the Congress has seemed fully capable of restraining its enthusiasm about these suggestions. Moreover, the theory of strategy often implied here is that the primary task of policy is to dash about quelling uprisings whose origins are in the private economy. This is based on a faulty premise, and it is too crude and primitive a strategy for the modern economy.

Since a major source of departures from the path of vigorous and orderly growth and reasonably full employment has been the fitful and spasmodic behavior of fiscal and monetary policies, the most fundamental requirement for orderly movement along the full-employment growth path is that fiscal and monetary policies themselves pursue a more steadfast course. It is here that the greatest gains are to be had, and fortunately this does not involve colliding with any great constitutional issues such as the doctrine of the separation of powers. Moreover, it is worth repeating that this is not a recommendation for abdication to automaticity. It is a call for learning to operate these instruments of policy with more sophistication and exactitude, and within substantially narrower tolerances, than in the past.

If we can keep expenditures in reasonably close balance with revenues that the tax system will generate at full employment, and if the course of monetary expansion also moves more steadily along the full employment growth path, we can reasonably expect that the economy will come even closer to a course broadly consistent with utilizing all of our "plans, functions, and resources . . . to promote maximum employment, production, and purchasing power."[7]

[7] From section 2, Employment Act of 1946.

ESSENTIAL INGREDIENTS OF FUTURE POLICY

by John B. Anderson

REPRESENTATIVE JOHN B. ANDERSON was first elected to Congress in 1960 and is now serving in his fourth term as Representative of the 16th Illinois District. He was educated at the University of Illinois and received a Master of Law Degree from Harvard University Law School. In 1952, as a member of the Career Diplomatic Service of the U. S. Department of State, Mr. Anderson went to West Germany to serve two and one half years as an adviser on the staff of the U. S. High Commissioner for Germany. After practicing law in Rockford, Illinois, Mr. Anderson was elected to the Office of State's Attorney of Winnebago County in November of 1956 and served four years in that position prior to his election to the House of Representatives. Congressman Anderson is currently serving on the Rules Committee and the Joint Committee on Atomic Energy.

We cannot achieve the goals of the Employment Act of 1946 by simple legislative fiat. Those goals will elude us unless the fiscal, monetary and economic policies of the federal government foster a climate in which the American free enterprise system can make its maximum contribution toward their attainment. It is noteworthy that even the most devoted disciples of the New Economics, those who regard the Federal Budget as a mighty fiscal engine to be "revved up" when it is necessary to stimulate the economy and to be decelerated in the cyclical upswing, are now changing their emphasis. More and more they and other members of the liberal community refer to the urgent necessity for enlisting all of the resources of the private sector to solve such problems as unemployment, poverty, and the other social ills that have been compounded into the crisis of our cities. Urban expert and self-professed liberal, Daniel Moynihan, put it as succinctly as anyone when he addressed a meeting of fellow liberals, Americans for Democratic Action, and said:

> "Liberals must divest themselves of the notion that the nation, especially the cities of the nation can be run from agencies in Washington. We must attend to what the Federal Government is good at . . . it is good at collecting revenues, rather bad at disbursing services."

Former Secretary of Health, Education, and Welfare, John W. Gardner, has called for the "regeneration of a spirit of individual creativity and responsibility vis-à-vis public problems," his call is by definition a summons directed to the private sector of society. This is not to assert that government need not play both a direct and a cooperative role in the evaluation and solution of the problems of today's highly technological and urbanized society. For this perforce is must do. However, the thesis to which we are here directing our attention is that government should serve as the catalyst which will bring to bear the forces of our free enterprise system in waging the battle for maximum employment, production and purchasing power, the announced goals of the Employment Act of 1946. To take our analogy of government as a catalytic agent one step further—the success of an experimental reaction in the laboratory depends upon more than the selection of the proper catalyst. The other necessary factors in the equation must also be present along with such carefully controlled laboratory conditions as the proper temperature, pressure, etc. Thus it is the total environment which will determine the success of the experiment. I would like in this paper to consider briefly some of the conditions that we must necessarily obtain in our politico-economic environment if we are to look forward to a successful reaction between the forces of government and the forces of a free economic system to achieve the desired compound of maximum employment, production and purchasing power. For it is truly in the attainment of these goals that we stand the best chance of avoiding the chaos and violence and the bitterness and despair that has characterized life in our great population centers in the recent past.

I believe that when the history of this decade is written it will reveal that one very important reason why the promise of the "soaring sixties" which was seemingly so evident in the first half of the decade soured to become instead the sobering saga of the post-1965 period was the explosion in federal expenditures and its corollary effects.

In the last complete fiscal year under the Eisenhower administration the Administrative or Cash Budget showed a surplus of 3.6 billion dollars. In fiscal 1961 the Federal Administrative Budget reflected a 6.8 billion dollar deficit, and every annual budget since that time has required the use of red ink to show our financial condition. Through the fiscal year which ended on June 30, 1967, the cumulative total of these deficits was over 40 billion dollars. The fear of a 30 billion dollar deficit piled on top of this mountain of debt finally led the Johnson administration to call for a tax increase in 1967.

It is quite clear that the insatiable appetite of the federal government for more and more revenue has been greatly stimulated by the cost of the war in Vietnam. However, it is equally clear that it would be an error of the first magnitude to label the Vietnam conflict as the sole villain in the piece. It is also evident that, even though the United States passed an historic milestone in November 1967 when the census clock in the U. S. Department of Commerce recorded the fact that our population had reached 200 million, this growth factor was not solely responsible for the explosion in federal expenditures. In the decade between 1956–66, the population increase in this country averaged about 1.6 percent annually. During this same period, all non-defense outlays were going up from 23.7 billion to 49.3 billion for an increase of around 108 percent. Even when allowance is made for changes in the price level, and we will have more to say about that, it is pre-eminently clear that the price-growth factor has played only a relatively minor part in the buildup of federal debt on which the interest charges alone were budgeted at almost 14 billion during the last fiscal year. The federal expenditure explosion can be traced to the fact that between 1961 and 1966 a total of seventy-eight new programs were placed on the statute books. In the President's Budget Message last year he advocated a total of sixteen additional federal programs. This proliferation of programs during a time of escalating expenditures for the war in Vietnam has produced budgetary stresses of a magnitude not seen since World War II. In my judgment, the refusal of the Johnson administration to discipline its demands to the conditions created by the war, and its refusal to establish any spending priorities have served to exacerbate the very symptoms of economic distress which the President outlined as the rationale for his demand for a 10 percent surcharge on corporate and personal income on August 3, 1967.

At that time he warned that without a tax increase and tight expenditure control a federal deficit in excess of 28 billion could result. He proceeded to point out that a deficit of this size would spark a ruinous cycle of inflation. Despite this dire prediction it was not until the dying days of the first session of the 90th Congress that the President indicated any willingness to yield to Congressional demands that any tax increase be accompanied by significant reductions in federal expenditures. By the time the President made this concession inflation had already become a reality rather than merely a small dark cloud on the far horizon. For the third quarter of 1967, the very period that this violent tug of war over federal spending was going on between the President and the Congress, fully one half of the gain in our gross national product was accounted for by higher prices.

It seems to me that the great underlying fallacy of this tremendous increase in government expenditures is that it has made it more rather than less difficult to attain the goals of maximum employment, production and purchasing power. For government does not create jobs in a free enterprise system other than those which are associated with its own payrolls. We realized this as long ago as 1939 when after a half dozen years of various federal programs there was still a vast army of unemployed in the United States. There are, of course, some today who still urge that the government must be the "employer of last resort." But I feel that something else should be tried first. We should seek to reduce the level of government expenditures and thereby make it possible to offer sufficient incentives to the private sector in the form of tax relief so that it will be feasible for our system of private enterprise to entertain social goals as well as to pursue purely economic goals.

Let me be somewhat more specific. In a plethora of programs that have grown up largely since 1961 the federal government today spends in excess of 2 billion dollars annually on manpower retraining and development programs that are spread throughout more than a half dozen federal agencies. We have a Job Corps where originally the average annual cost per enrollee was in excess of $10,000. Despite reductions that have been achieved in this figure the first session of the 90th Congress felt obliged to place a ceiling at $6500 per enrollee on this type of government financed training. An alternative that has never been tried although it has been sponsored by more than one hundred Republican members of the Senate and House of Representatives is the Human Investment Act.[1] The principle of this proposed legislation is already embodied in the 7 percent investment tax credit which is allowed those who invest in new capital facilities such as buildings and machinery. The Human Investment Act would make a similar tax credit available to those employers who would undertake to train the unskilled or retrain those who are unemployed or perhaps underemployed due to technological change.

Other proposals in this area would provide similar tax incentives and favorable tax treatment to business firms willing to locate in slum areas with particularly difficult unemploy-

[1] See Chapter 3.

ment problems. There is a tendency to forget that although we have for some months past had an overall unemployment rate hovering around 4 percent, this figure by no means accurately reflects the true unemployment rate in many so-called ghetto areas where among Negro teenagers the rate has been as high as 40 or 50 percent.

Although the subject of housing is not directly related to the goals of the Employment Act of 1946, one of the most important social goals confronting our nation today is the provision of decent housing for all of our citizens. It also provides an example of how imaginative proposals involving the private sector can be offered to meet this basic human need of adequate shelter. The federal government has, of course, been in the business of constructing and operating public housing ever since the Housing Act of 1937. The program has certainly not been an unqualified success. On the contrary in some quarters giant metropolitan public housing projects have been referred to as "vertical slums." In 1967 more than one hundred Republican Senators and Representatives joined in introducing legislation to establish a National Home Ownership Foundation. The germ of the idea is to encourage home ownership among lower and lower-middle income groups by making loans available through a federally chartered cooperation which would obtain its funds from the sale of debentures to the public rather than from Congressional appropriations. The government would back these obligations and would also pay part of the interest on those loans made to borrowers who were unable to afford financing at conventional rates. In all other respects the Home Ownership Foundation would operate without direct government financing or control.

These proposals, the Human Investment Act and the National Home Ownership Foundation Act, are specific examples of ways in which the resources of private capital know-how and initiative could be employed in lieu of a purely governmental approach in order to build the bases for a sound and healthy economy.

It is quite true that the Employment Act of 1946 as finally enacted sought to take the road of a balanced approach to the respective functions of the public and the private sectors of the economy in providing jobs for the American labor force. However, it is my conviction that with the expenditure explosion and the proliferation of federal programs mentioned earlier that balance has shifted preponderantly in favor of a purely governmental approach. This distortion poses not only a serious threat in the long run to the maintenance of a free enterprise system but over the much shorter term it unleashes inflationary forces which impair the economic health of the nation as a whole. Unless we can achieve better expenditure control at the federal level we simply cannot pursue the kind of fiscal policy which will make it possible for us to restore that proper balance between public and private effort. It does very little good to recommend programs involving tax credits and similar concessions or even to talk in terms of revenue sharing with state and local governments when the federal government is running deficits of the proportions currently confronting us.

The pathway to expenditure reform and control will not be easy. However, at the very least it will entail the mandatory requirement that proposed new programs be viewed not simply in terms of their initial cost but in the light of projections covering a period of a number of years into the future. It will require the careful scrutiny and re-examination of existing programs to see if they are truly effective by objective standards. New programs that may be enacted should be subject to a periodic mandatory review.[2] If we are willing to apply a rigid cost-benefit ratio to public works projects, we should be willing to employ a similar set of standards in reviewing and assessing the accomplishments under a particular program whether it is administered by the Corps of Engineers or some other federal agency. If cost-effectiveness is a valid tool in the Department of Defense it ought to possess comparable utility if employed in other departments of the executive branch. Finally, on this point of seeking to achieve expenditure control I agree with the recommendation of the

[2] See Chapter 11. "Oversight and the Need for Congressional Reform."

President's Commission on Budget Concepts that any presidential request to Congress for new appropriations should be accompanied in every instance with detailed and specific recommendations as to the means of financing them. This would serve not only to restrain the President in making such requests, but it would surely give the Congress considerable food for thought before proceeding to enact them.

If we are ever effectively going to use the resources and ingenuity of American business to expand job opportunities and train, retrain, and upgrade the skills of the poor and disadvantaged, we must first recognize that this imbalance between the efforts being expanded by the public and the private sectors exists and then reallocate the necessary resources to the private sector through an enlightened tax policy so that it may be redressed.

The second major condition which must exist if we would truly be successful in implementing the goals of the Employment Act of 1946, is wage-price stability. The notion that a little bit of inflation is a tolerable thing suffers from several defects. Inflation tends to become a way of life for governments—a fixed habit which is difficult to break. It is in effect a self-sustaining reaction which feeds on itself. Like the Breeder Reactor which we are striving to develop in the field of nuclear energy and which will produce more atomic fuel than it consumes, government-sponsored inflation leads to increases in prices and wages which beget still more increases as the cycle continues. The expectation of still further wage rate rises will eventually produce unemployment. It will lead to a decline in production as demand then decreases. Finally it will exact the cruelest tax of all from the consumer by robbing him of his purchasing power. In the words of the Joint Economic Committee in a 1967 report on the "Economic Effect of Vietnam Spending" wherein reference is made to the goals enunciated in section 2 of the Employment Act of 1946:

"... as the Committee construes this mandate it incorporates policies for optimum growth and also for relative

stability of prices and wages. A shortfall under either of
these objectives would detract from the accomplishment
of the act's major purposes . . . objectives of growth, full
employment and stability can only be served by timely
and adequate action to prepare policies that are carefully
designed to avoid dislocation *and particularly wage-price
dislocations.*" (emphasis supplied)

Just as there are no policies which will put an end to inflation without inflicting some harm or economic disadvan-
tage on someone, there are no guaranteed painless methods
to head off inflation. Economic statesmanship requires the
same kind of vision combined with the courage to make painful decisions that characterizes political statesmanship. However, this provides no justification for the lack of any adequate
anti-inflation policy since the complete collapse of the Johnson
administration's ill-fated wage-price guidelines. Neither big
labor nor big business has proved amenable to the jawbone
treatment which has emanated fitfully from the White House
or the President's Council of Economic Advisors. Even before the round of wage settlements in the automobile industry
commencing in the fall of 1967 which ran between 6 and 7
percent, one of the governors of the Federal Reserve System,
Andrew F. Brimmer, in a speech in Seattle, Washington, on
August 23, 1967, offered this gloomy prognosis:

"From the view point of national stabilization policies,
the outlook for wage developments is no more optimistic
than it is for prices. One calculation shows that recently
negotiated wage and fringe benefit packages have involved
an increase of about 5½ to 6 percent in total labor cost.
Moreover, this range of increases seems most likely to
persist in the near future.
The consequences of negotiated wage settlements in
manufacturing have been particularly striking. Straight-
time hourly earnings in the first half of 1967 were 4½
percent above a year earlier. This was the largest increase
in the first half of any year in the last decade. The rise in
the cost of fringe benefits has also been substantial. Sup-

plements per man-hour (including legally required social security taxes and other employer contributions to public as well as private programs) recently have been rising at an annual rate of roughly 11 or 12 percent. In contrast, during the period 1960–65, the rate of increase averaged about 6½ percent per year. Although the funding of some of these added costs sometimes can be postponed, this rapid increase must necessarily mean a significant boost to current labor costs."

The pressures which have led to inflated wage settlements with their concomitant destabilizing effects can be traced directly, of course, to steadily rising consumer prices and a corresponding decrease in real wages for American workers. As a result the bitter medicine of higher taxes is the remedy which the government feels obliged to prescribe. It could be observed here that from the standpoint of dampening consumer demand in order to relieve inflationary pressures a dollar of expenditure reduction by the government could have a far greater impact than a dollar of increased taxes. Even though the government takes a bigger bite out of a worker's paycheck, he may still have recourse to savings to sustain his demand. The government agency which is cut back in its expenditures has no similar option.

In retrospect it seems abundantly clear that with the acceleration of war expenditures that began as the American commitment in Vietnam was enlarged commencing in mid-1965 the administration committed an egregious blunder in not establishing a rigid system of priorities to reduce non-defense spending. Moreover its mistake, if it can be called that, in underestimating the cost of the war in fiscal 1967 by more than one-half or twelve billion dollars contributed to the failure of fiscal policy as an anti-inflationary weapon. Rather than the much vaunted fine tuning of the economy—which the New Economists had promised—the nation watched the dials spin until the unwelcome static of inflationary rumbling began to interfere with the reception of good economic news. The severe credit crunch in the early fall of 1966 signaled serious trouble, and the administration shortly thereafter scrambled to seek Congressional reinstatement of the investment tax credit.

One of the leading New Economists, Professor Paul A. Samuelson, has said that economics is "how men and society choose to employ scarce productive resources . . ." Maybe this is the reason why an earlier writer, Carlyle, referred to economics as "the dismal science." For a nation beset with as many crises both foreign and domestic as the United States faces today in this affluent yet anxious age, the choices are extremely difficult to make. We have learned, and this to the apparent astonishment of some, that our resources are not unlimited. In allocating those resources so that we may achieve the particular goals of economic well-being that we have been discussing it is imperative that we pay attention not only to "how" but "by whom" we undertake this task. I believe that we need to enlarge rather than to contract the role that the private sector should play in this decision making process.

Finally there is a third basic condition which must exist if we expect to maintain the kind of economic climate which will foster the achievement of full employment, production and purchasing power. We need a tax policy which is certain, definite, and committed to long range goals which are compatible in an economic sense with what we spoke of earlier—a balanced approach to the respective functions of government and our free enterprise system in achieving the objectives of the Employment Act of 1946.

Let us go back for just a moment to the passage of the Revenue Act of 1964 and the prolonged debate that preceded the enactment of this eleven billion dollar tax cut.

The Chairman of the House Ways and Means Committee, Wilbur D. Mills of Arkansas, in his remarks during the Floor debate on September 24, 1963, referred to the fact that there were two roads the government could follow toward the achievement of a larger and more prosperous economy. One road consisted of ever increasing government expenditures; the other was the road of tax reduction. Section one of the

Bill contained a positive assertion that the nation was embarking upon the latter route while rejecting the former. The nation was assured that by removing the fiscal drag on our economy created by excessively high tax rates we would inaugurate an era of fiscal responsibility. The Chairman said of the phrase "fiscal responsibility":

> "It means conducting the finances of the federal government in such a way that a balanced budget can be and is achieved in an economy which is growing rapidly, providing adequate employment and investment opportunities, making full use of its capital and human resources, and giving the fullest possible play to the initiative and venturesomeness of the private sector."

One could scarcely quarrel with these objectives. Indeed if carried out, they would have represented the fulfillment of the goals of the Employment Act of 1946. However, no one needs to be reminded that we have not succeeded in balancing the budget. Neither have we succeeded in my judgment in making the fullest use of our capital and human resources within the framework described; namely, the private sector. Instead we have steadily compounded the imbalance in the respective roles of the public and private sectors which existed when this act was passed. We have attempted to travel both roads at the same time with results that should have been foreseeable.

The President's request for a 10 percent surcharge on individual and corporate income in August of 1967 came at a time when business activity was still high. However, unless government's insatiable appetite for additional revenue can be curbed, tax increases will be necessary in the future, notwithstanding the business barometer. There were many economists in 1967 who believed we were suffering from a cost-push type of inflation for which a tax reduction would have been a better remedy than the suggestion of a tax increase. It can certainly be argued with great force that when unit labor costs are advancing more rapidly than increases in productivity, one most effective way of absorbing those increased costs is to obtain a more rational and efficient production by modernizing. This obviously requires capital investment in the form of new plant and equipment. A tax increase which makes it impossible to carry out such needed investment can well be inflationary, therefore, in the sense that it becomes difficult or perhaps even impossible to combat these rising costs of labor per unit of output.

Another very definite problem in employing a tax increase to combat inflation is the factor of the time lag that is involved. The Machinery and Allied Products Institute in a study entitled "Lead Time and Contracyclical Tax Policy," Capital Goods Review No. 68, December 1966, points this out. It would take around five months for a corporate tax increase, even if reflected immediately and completely in reduction of fixed-asset commitments, to build up a production response one-half as large as the increase itself. In other words in the durable or capital goods industries a tax increase does not suddenly dampen demand because of the lead time involved. Indeed we had confirmation of this in the experience in 1966 and 1967 with the repeal and reinstatement of the investment tax credit.

If tax policy is to be successful in creating a climate that is conducive to sustained economic growth, it should be definite and certain and not quixotic. Business and industry require time to adjust investment plans. Frequent and sudden changes in tax policy inhibit economic growth, and over-adjustment of fiscal policy as a contracyclical device can be self-defeating. Our long range goal must certainly continue to be the reduction of the tax burden for both individuals and business enterprises if we would maximize the opportunities to involve the private sector of our nation's economy in achieving full employment, production and purchasing power.

In summary, and conclusion there are three essential conditions which should be maintained if we hope to attain our economic objectives. They are first of all that we regain control of federal expenditures and insist that our government establish spending priorities and then accept this type of fiscal discipline. We must give renewed attention to the importance of maintaining wage-price stability and avoid those policies by government that foster inflation. We should pursue a course of expenditure control with the view in mind that this will make it possible ultimately to reduce rather than constantly raise the level of taxation. To accomplish these ends without abdicating our responsibility to find solutions to a host of social problems which are of mounting concern means that the private sector of our economy must become involved with social goals in a far more meaningful and extensive way. The economic conditions and climate outlined above should make that involvement possible if they are fostered and maintained. The failure of the Great Society lies in its inability to solve the monumental problems of our times with the resources available within the public sector. At the same time it has failed to provide the incentives that would challenge the private sector to seek and find the solutions that have thus far eluded us. It is the responsibility of the Republican Party to oppose with all possible vigor the drift toward bigger and bigger government and a smaller and smaller private sector. But its responsibility goes far beyond merely sounding the alarm. It must also continue with all of the ingenuity and resourcefulness that it can muster to seek to develop new methods, new approaches and new institutions which will provide the alternative to the welfare state.

Chapter 9

BUDGETARY PROBLEMS

———————◆▶———————

THE NEED FOR BUDGETARY REFORM
by Murray L. Weidenbaum

DR. MURRAY L. WEIDENBAUM is Professor of Economics
and Chairman of the Department of Economics at Washington University, St. Louis, Missouri. He served as economist with the U. S. Bureau of the Budget for several
years and has written widely on the subject of government
expenditures. His most recent work includes *Federal
Budgeting: The Choice of Government Programs* (1964)
and *Prospects for Reallocating Public Resources* (1967).

Discussions of budgeting usually conjure up visions of
Ebenezer Scrooge, green eye shades, detailed accounting reports, boring routine, and trivia. Contrary to this often popular conception, budgetary decisions affect basic aspects of
our national life. As the nineteenth century British Prime
Minister William Gladstone stated, "Budgets are not mere
matters of arithmetic, but in a thousand ways go to the root
of prosperity of individuals, and relation of classes, and the
strength of kingdoms."

Any objective examination of federal government budgeting
in modern day America reveals that Gladstone is still right.
Despite, or perhaps because of, the focus on detail and dollars,
the preparation and approval of the Federal Budget is the fundamental mechanism for making public decisions on important questions of substance. Some of these basic issues are the
following:

What should be the role and size of the federal government?

Where should we draw the dividing line between the public and private sectors?

Should taxes be raised or lowered?

Are existing government programs adequate?

How can their efficiency be improved?

The fact that these important decisions are made via the budget does not necessarily mean that the budget, as now prepared, is properly designed for effective decision-making. On the contrary, every appraisal of federal budgeting—whether made by government officials or private experts, by economists, accountants, or other specialists, by Republicans, Democrats or Independents—has concluded that fundamental shortcomings exist.[1] The disagreement, of course, arises in selecting the specific improvements to be adopted.

In part as the cumulative effect of more specific defects, the overriding shortcoming of the budget at the present time is the lack of public confidence in the basic information issued on budget matters by the federal government itself. For example, in commenting on the January 1967 Budget Message, Walter Lippmann gave it a backhanded compliment, "Compared with last year's budget, the present one is a refreshingly straightforward piece of estimating and accounting." In describing the prior budget, Lippmann used the terms, "absurd assumption," "false estimate," "credibility gap," and "phoneyness." Such an attitude unfortunately is not unique.

In part this situation results from the tremendous amount of information made available by modern statistical systems and data processing equipment. The availability of a multiplicity of ways in which to report on the results of the budget lends itself to selecting that method which, at the time, yields the most favorable results to the person making the analysis.

In general, the party in power has an incentive to make these technical choices on whichever basis shows the smallest deficit (or on rare occasion, the largest surplus) in

---

[1] See U. S. Commission on Organization of the Executive Branch of the Government, *Budgeting and Accounting*, 1949; Joseph P. Harris, "Needed Reforms in the Federal Budget System," *Public Administration Review*, Autumn 1952; Arthur Smithies, *The Budgetary Process in the United States*, McGraw-Hill, 1955; American Enterprise Institute, *Congress and the Federal Budget*, 1965.

the budget. Conversely, the party out of power would be expected to prefer that budget reporting method which shows the poorest results which can be attributed to the "ins." This hardly makes for public confidence in the budget figures or for a high level of public discussion on issues of government spending and taxation.

To muddy the water further, the party in power often finds it convenient to shift from one budget basis to another, as events change. For example, in January 1967, the emphasis in the Presidential Budget Message was on extolling the effectiveness of the federal government in reducing inflationary pressures. Hence, the emphasis was given to a relatively new budget concept which showed the smallest deficit. Page 9 of the Message stated: "I am emphasizing the national income accounts as a measure of federal fiscal activity because the traditional administrative budget is becoming an increasingly less complete and less reliable measure of the government's activities and their economic impact."

However, by August 1967 inflationary pressures were considered to be sufficiently strong that the administration recommended a substantial tax increase. In order to bolster the case—by showing a very large impending deficit—the administration abandoned the budget concept favored in January 1967 and used once again the administrative budget which it had attacked six months previously because of lack of completeness and reliability.

Although identifying past errors and inconsistencies may be useful and provide some satisfaction, improvements will only be forthcoming as the basic problems are identified and alternative solutions examined. In the studies to date, four basic shortcomings of federal budgeting have been identified:

1. The existence of at least three different "budgets." Hence, there are several different ways of reporting the total amounts that the federal government taxes and spends in a given period and the size of the resulting deficit or surplus.

2. The repeated changes in the ground rules determining which government programs are "in" or "out" of any of these budgets.

3. The unpredictability of the release of information on the state of the budget.

4. The lack of an effective and objective way of making budget decisions.

THE THREE BUDGETS

The January 1967 Budget Message reports figures on three bases: (1) the administrative budget, (2) the cash budget, and (3) the so-called national income accounts budget. None of the three is identified as "the" budget, and the text of the message jumps back and forth from one basis to another. A brief examination shows that the three budgets are hardly interchangeable. The "cash" budget shows expenditures in 1968 to be $37 billion higher than the "administrative" budget. The "national income accounts" budget shows up in between these two. However, in terms of the anticipated deficit, the latter shows the smallest excess of outgo over income—$2 billion—while the administrative budget basis yields a deficit four times as great for the same period ($8 billion). The cash budget here occupies an intermediate position, with a projected deficit of a little over $4 billion. It seems to be a great game.

Resort to the accompanying budget document yields a substantial amount of explanatory material on how each of the three budgets is developed and on the differences among them. However, the explanations are so full of technical jargon as to be almost unintelligible to the layman, dealing with "excess of accruals (+) over collections (−)," "miscellaneous netting, grossing, and related adjustments," "debt issued in lieu of checks and other adjustments," "excess of deliveries or accruals (+) over payments (−)," etc., etc.

In their fundamentals, the differences among the three budgets are simple, clear, and important. The differences can be visualized by dividing government financial transactions into three categories:

Category A comprises general tax revenues, on the one

hand, and the disbursements of the traditional cabinet departments and government agencies on the other. Category A covers, for example, income tax receipts and defense expenditures. In recent years, total expenditures in this category have exceeded revenues, and the resulting deficit has been substantial.

Category B contains the special trust funds which have been set up primarily to handle large benefit programs of a quasi-insurance nature. Social security, unemployment compensation, and medicare are the most important examples here. In general, the receipts of these trust funds (such as social security contributions withheld from paychecks) exceed the current disbursements, as the assets of the funds are built up to pay future benefits.

Category C is the banking operations of the federal government, where it is lending money and obtaining repayments on outstanding loans. The Export-Import Bank and the Federal Land Banks are typical cases in point. The financial flows in this category are very erratic; sometimes on balance they contribute to surpluses and often to deficits.

The major differences among the three budgets then boil down to these: the administrative budget covers category A and part of C, and thus tends to show a large deficit. The national income accounts budget covers categories A and B, and thus tends to yield a much smaller deficit. Only the cash budget covers all three categories of governmental transactions and usually, but not always, results in a budget deficit of a size in between the other two concepts.

No single budget concept satisfactorily meets the needs of the various users. The budget, alternatively and simultaneously, is a basic document of public policy, a mechanism for Congressional review of the executive branch, a tool for executive management of governmental resources, and a means of governmental communication to the public.

However, because so many of these uses involve either political forces or persons not expert in budgetary concepts and terminology, many observers believe that a single budgetary statement should be adopted as the common meeting ground for all of the users. This might reduce confusion and the lack of confidence in the budgetary process. However, even the experts do not agree on which budget concept to choose. The administrative budget has strong support on the part of legislators who are primarily concerned with the use of funds appropriated from the general revenues (category A transactions), rather than insurance and lending operations. Many persons support the cash budget because of its great comprehensiveness as being the only one to cover all three categories of transactions. Many economists in recent years, however, favor the national income accounts method because it ties in directly to Gross National Product, National Income, and other indicators of the performance of the American economy.

The desirability of budgetary "unity" is considered sufficiently important by many students of government budgeting to merit the compromises which are required to agree upon one concept. Of course, subsidiary budgetary statements could and undoubtedly would continue to be prepared and presented in the details of the President's budget document. However, public discussions on the budget would—under the unitary approach—be based on a single way of arriving at the budget totals and the resulting surplus or deficit. Thus public debates on government spending and taxation could shift away from emphasis on "gimmicks" and "tricks" in budgeting and to matters of substance.

THE CHANGES IN THE GROUND RULES

In a fascinating novel written some twenty years ago, George Orwell described a world of 1984 where history was continually being rewritten to suit the purposes at hand. During these past two decades, budgetary history has continually been rewritten, also serving to reduce public confidence in the results. Between 1948 and 1967, the federal government was constantly redefining what items should be included in the budget and which should not. This was not a partisan matter, as the changes occurred in Democratic and Republican administrations alike. Moreover, virtually all the changes followed a simple pattern—items which formerly were included in the budget total were gradually eliminated.

One result of this development was clear. During periods of concern that the annual budget stay within some desired "ceiling," such as $100 billion, the redefinitions at a constantly lower level meant that real increases in government spending could continue to take place without the budget total bumping against the ceiling.

Viewed in isolation, some of the changes seemed reasonable enough, if not desirable. Tax refunds, which hitherto had been an item of expenditure, were deducted from revenues and only the net amount retained by the government was shown beginning in 1949. However, in the year of the change, budget expenditures were $2 billion lower than they otherwise would be, because of the shift.

However, other changes had the effect of removing important government activities from the close scrutiny of budget review. For example, motorists have been paying various highway user taxes to the Treasury for years, notably the excise on gasoline. Simultaneously, the federal government has been spending several billion dollars a year on building national highways. During the 1950s, both the highway taxes and the highway expenditures were "moved" out of the budget and put into a special so-called trust fund. Little substantive change was made. Motorists continued to pay their gasoline taxes and the U. S. Bureau of Public Roads continued to disburse highway grants. However, the administrative budget became a less meaningful document, as it no longer included this major governmental function. Over the years, many government programs have been "moved" out of the administrative budget—although the expenditures by no means have been eliminated. Other examples include the social security program, medicare, railroad retirement, veterans' life insurance, unemployment compensation, mortgage assistance, a portion of the foreign aid program, etc., etc.

The cumulative impact of these changes has been substantial. As shown in Table 1, administrative budget expenditures in the fiscal 1966 would have been $119.8 billion or $12.8 billion above the figure actually reported if the concepts employed in 1948 were still utilized today.

TABLE 1

AN ANALYSIS OF ADMINISTRATIVE BUDGET EXPENDITURES IN 1966
(FISCAL YEAR. IN MILLIONS)

Item	Amount
Total, per January 1967 Budget Message	$106,978
Add: Items Formerly included	
Refunds of receipts	6,902
Highway expenditures	3,966
Railroad retirement program	677
Unemployment insurance administration	494
Interfund transactions	635
Capital transfers (investments in treasury issuances)	158
Equals: Total Budget Expenditures (Prior to Deductions)	$119,810

SOURCE: Budget of the United States Government for the Fiscal Year Ending June 30, 1968.

The many changes in the coverage of the budget point up the need for consistent treatment over time. Certainly, no one can state with confidence that the present "net" treatment of tax refunds is correct and the earlier "gross" treatment was wrong. Rather the need is for a consistent use of either a gross or a net concept over a sustained period of time.

In its essence, the problem boils down to the simple fact that a standard way of reporting budget results may be more important for public acceptance and confidence than a succession of refinements, some of which may be considered to be politically inspired.

THE RELEASE OF BUDGET INFORMATION

During a period of major change in government spending patterns, such as is characteristic of the Vietnam War, the information in the January Budget soon gets out of date.

Until recently, the Bureau of the Budget had issued a Midyear Review of the Budget each Fall which updates the figures on the basis of more recent developments, including Congressional action on the President's recommendations.

The traditional midyear budget review has not been issued during the last few years. The reasons given were the uncertainties in Vietnam and the delay of Congressional action on budgetary legislation. The discussion of this point between Congressman John W. Byrnes and Budget Director Charles L. Schultze, as published in the January 1967 Hearings of the House Ways and Means Committee, is quite fascinating.

At first the Budget Director stated that in no year when the Congress adjourned as late as it did in 1966 was a midyear review issued. In the face of numerous citations to the contrary, the Budget Director then modified his position to the effect that in no year that the budget legislation was enacted as late as it was in 1966 was a review issued.

This reluctance to provide detailed, timely information on public sector activities is in marked contrast to the wealth of information that the federal government regularly publishes on the activities in the private sector of the economy. Federal agencies issue every few months historical information and forecasts of consumer spending and business investment, detailed by various categories. It has been suggested that similar information should be provided on the government's own operation.[2]

How to Make Budget Decisions

One of the most frequently encountered criticisms of Federal Budgeting is the lack of a mechanism for reviewing an individual expenditure decision in the light of the total budget picture. Similarly, it has been stated that the Congress never has an opportunity to consider the budget as a whole and

[2] See U. S. Congress, Joint Economic Committee, *Economic Effect of Vietnam Spending*, Volume 1, 1967, p. 178.

weigh the relative needs of all programs. "Thus the central purpose of the budget process is largely defeated."[3] Also, public interest in budgeting is diminished, to the extent that it is viewed as an arcane art or an exercise in futility.

Numerous suggestions have been made over the years for dealing with the problem of improving budget decision-making. Although the details vary, most recommendations fall in one of the following groups: (1) changes in Congressional organization, (2) changes in legislative procedures, (3) systematic analysis of individual programs, and (4) examining the basic choices available in allocating government funds among the major programs.

Most of the specific suggestions for improved budgeting have related, over the years, to changing the Congressional organization for budgetary review. The Legislative Reorganization Act of 1946 made one of the most ambitious efforts along these lines. It created a joint committee composed of all members of the four taxation and appropriation committees of the two houses of the Congress. It also directed the committee to compare the estimated total receipts and the total expenditures in the budget for the coming year, and then recommend a ceiling on total expenditures to serve as some sort of control over the total amount of appropriations to be enacted.

The 1946 effort at a joint budget committee and effective ceilings on spending proved unworkable and was soon abandoned. More recent suggestions for new Congressional committees have failed to win approval of either or both houses of Congress. The proposed joint committees generally have been turned down in the House of Representatives, which is concerned with maintaining its primacy in financial matters. Attempts to establish new committees in either House have failed in good measure because they have been interpreted as diluting the powers of the respective appropriations committees.

[3] Joseph P. Harris, "Needed Reforms in the Federal Budget System," *Public Administration Review*, Autumn 1952.

Another family of suggested budgetary improvements covers omnibus appropriation bills, special sessions, joint hearings, and similar procedural changes. Although not involving changes in Congressional committee structure, these proposals do require significant departures from either the way in which the Congress meets to consider the budget or in the nature of appropriation legislation.

An example was the one-package or omnibus appropriation bill passed in 1950, covering all nondefense programs. This method was abandoned after one try, because it delayed the passage of appropriations and lent itself to the addition of legislative riders.

Other procedural suggestions have included joint hearings by the appropriation committees of both Houses, a regular budget session of the Congress to be held separately from the session on other legislative matters, and a requirement that the Congress stay in session until it balances the budget. The last one conjures up visions of perpetual national rule by lame duck legislators.

The third family of suggested budget improvements focuses at the level of the individual bureau and appropriation account. Specific techniques which can be applied include benefit-cost analysis and cost-effectiveness analysis. In general, these techniques aim to answer the question: given the funds available for an individual program, what is the most effective way of spending them—that is, how can the public receive the maximum amount of benefit from a given expenditure?[4]

Despite its advantages, such program analysis or program budgeting fails to come to grips with the basic question of budgeting, "Would an extra dollar (a billion, in the case of the government) be more wisely spent for Program A or for Program B?" This is the fundamental question implicit in the allocation of budgetary funds. The literally thousands of pages of budget justifications and Congressional hearings which are published each year fail to show even any awareness of the problem, much less any attempt to an answer.

[4] See U. S. Bureau of the Budget, *Planning-Programming-Budgeting*, Bulletin No. 68–2, July 18, 1967.

The last category of budget reforms suggested is the revamping of the federal budget so as to enable the users of
the budget document clearly to see what the major alternatives are. Such a government-wide program analysis would
compare alternative programs of different agencies for fulfilling basic national goals, rather than merely examining as
at present the alternatives available to a single federal
agency.

A program budget for the entire federal government can
be developed by basing it on the fundamental end purposes
for which the various government programs are carried on.
National Security, Public Welfare, Economic Development
and Government Operations. (See Table 2)

TABLE 2
A PROGRAM BUDGET FOR THE U. S. GOVERNMENT
(FISCAL YEAR 1967. NEW OBLIGATIONAL AUTHORITY)

Broad purpose	Amount (billions)	Percent
National Security	$68.1	41.4
Public Welfare	65.0	39.6
Economic Development	15.5	9.4
Government Operations	15.7	9.6
Total	164.3	100.0

It may come as no surprise that a large portion of the budget
—but less than one-half—is devoted to the promotion of the
national security, mainly the Department of Defense. In contrast, the fact that the great bulk of all nonmilitary spending
is devoted to the various welfare programs (social security,
unemployment compensation, public assistance) may not be
as widely known. A comparatively small portion is allocated
to economic development. These are activities which tend to
increase the growth of the national economy, such as investments in roads, airports, natural resources, education, and research.

It may be mere conjecture to conclude that, possibly, the
allocation would have been different if the appropriation re

quests and reviews had been approached from this viewpoint. Certainly the various programs in each of the four major categories are not now currently brought together and viewed as a totality anywhere in the budget process, nor are cross-comparisons made between programs in the various categories.[5]

The use of such a government-wide analysis might lend itself to first raising and then answering questions such as the following: Would the public welfare be improved if some funds were shifted from farm subsidies (in the Public Welfare category) to aid to education (under Economic Development)? From foreign aid (listed under National Security) to domestic research and training (under Economic Development)?

Raising these questions should not be taken as expressing value judgments, but rather as indicating a new pattern for governmental decision-making. Although this would be an innovation in the public sector, such types of choices are constantly being made in the private sector. They are no more novel than a family's decision to use the Christmas bonus for a new car rather than for a vacation, or a company's decision to use an increase in earnings to raise the dividend rate rather than to embark upon a new research program.

CONCLUSIONS

Basic reforms are needed in order to restore public confidence in the budgeting and financial operations of the federal government. There certainly is no shortage of suggestions for improvements. Although there is as yet no agreement on the specific changes to be initiated, four basic types of innovation appear to be highly desirable.

1. Selecting a single budget—a standard way of recording

[5] For a more detailed exploration of the uses of a government-wide program budget, see M. L. Weidenbaum, *Federal Budgeting: The Choice of Government Programs,* Washington, American Enterprise Institute for Public Policy Research, 1964, pp. 59–69.

the government's income and outgo in a given period, and the resultant deficit or surplus.

2. Stabilizing the ground rules for reporting government financial transactions so that each year's figures are comparable to the ones issued in previous years.

3. Releasing detailed information regularly on the government's current budget transactions and on its plans for the future.

4. Adopting an objective method of allocating government funds among the various programs.

THE FEDERAL BUDGET
by Frank T. Bow

FRANK T. BOW is the ranking Republican member of the House Committee on Appropriations, having been a member of that committee for fifteen of his seventeen years in Congress. A longtime critic of the federal budget process, he served as a member of the 1967 President's Commission on Budget Concepts. Mr. Bow first came to Washington in 1947 as general counsel of the Subcommittee on Expenditures in the Executive Departments. In 1950 he returned to Canton, Ohio, to win election as Representative of the 16th Congressional District and has been re-elected to each succeeding Congress. Prior to government service he engaged in the practice of law in Canton.

It is hard to imagine a more appropriate time than now to present the public with a Republican paper on budget policy. During the last five years the government's fiscal and budgetary policies and procedures have generated an extraordinary degree of public controversy. This controversy, with its attendant charges of gimmickry and delusion, led directly to the appointment of a Presidential commission to make, in the President's words, "a thorough study of the federal budget and the manner in which it is presented to the public." The appointment of this commission represented an extraordinary acknowledgment by the administration that misunderstanding and confusion concerning federal budget figures had become serious.

The current policy debate and the question of budget reform must be considered in the context of the five year period

which dates from President Kennedy's recommendation, i
January of 1963, that Congress enact a major tax reductio
to spur economic growth. In spite of the fact that the Pres
dent's administrative budget[1] projected a 12 billion dolla
deficit for fiscal 1964, Congress approved a tax cut; howeve
one important condition was set forth in section one of th
bill itself:

> Section 1. Declaration by Congress. It is the sense of
> Congress that the tax reduction provided by this Act
> through stimulation of the economy, will, after a brief
> transitional period, raise (rather than lower) revenues
> and that *such revenue increases should first be used to
> eliminate the deficits in the administrative budgets and
> then to reduce the public debt.* To further the objective
> of obtaining balanced budgets in the near future, Con-
> gress by this action, recognizes the importance of taking
> all reasonable means to restrain Government spending
> and urges the President to declare his accord with this
> objective. (emphasis added)

As an economic stimulant, the 1964 tax cut certainly fu
filled the expectations of its supporters. During the three fisc:
years (1965, 1966, 1967) following the tax cut the gross n:
tional product grew from $612 billion in fiscal 1964 to a
estimated $763 billion in fiscal 1967; an increase of 25 pe
cent producing $151 billion in additional GNP. Administr:
tive budget receipts, in turn, responded with a jump of 2
percent, which has increased receipts by some $26 billion.

Unfortunately, with pressure from a spendthrift admini
tration, Congress has disregarded its 1964 pledge to redu

---

[1] Much confusion stems from the fact that three budget concep
have been used in recent years. The *administrative budget* cove
the receipts and expenditures of government-owned funds. T
cash budget covers all receipts and payments to the public, an
includes the trust funds which finance such programs as soc:
security, highway construction, and medicare. The *national incon
accounts budget* estimates receipts and expenditures on an accru
basis, and includes the trust funds but excludes loan disbursemen
and receipts. (See p. 408.)

administrative budget deficits and the public debt. The deficits for fiscal years 1965, 1966, and 1967 total $15.6 billion, and the public debt increased by $14.5 billion between the end of fiscal 1964 and the end of fiscal 1967. The deficit was limited in 1965 by a reduction of defense spending, and in 1966 by a spurt in receipts. However, steady upward movement of spending, both for defense and nondefense, during 1966 and 1967 has brought the budget deficit to the same state as it was in 1964 before the tax cut. Here are the figures:

THE GNP AND THE ADMINISTRATIVE BUDGET
(IN BILLIONS)

Fiscal year	GNP	Total	Expenditures National defense	Non-defense	Receipts	Deficit
1964	$612.0	$97.7	$54.2	$43.5	$89.5	$8.2
1965	651.8	96.5	50.2	46.3	93.1	3.4
1966	712.0	107.0	57.7	49.3	104.7	2.3
1967	763.1	125.7	70.7	55.1	115.8	9.9
Increase 1964–67						
$	151.1	28.0	16.5	11.6	26.3	—
Pct.	24.6	28.7	30.4	26.6	29.4	—

The 1964 tax cut was related to the administrative budget because it did not directly affect the revenues of the trust funds, which are meant to be self-supporting and have, in most years, operated with a surplus. However, trust funds account for about 40 percent of the federal government's nondefense expenditures, and any comparison of defense versus nondefense priorities should be based on the cash budget, which includes the trust funds. On this basis, the comparison of defense and nondefense expenditures between 1964 and 1967 is shown on page 422.

These figures from both the administrative and cash budgets completely dispel any notion that nondefense spending has been "moderated" since the 1964 tax cut. The administration and the Democrat controlled Congress simply have not respected the sense of Congress resolution which was expressed

CASH BUDGET
(IN BILLIONS)

Fiscal year	Total	Expenditures National defense	Non-defense	Receipts	Deficit
1964	$120.3	$54.5	$65.8	$115.5	$4.8
1967	155.3	71.7	83.6	153.5	1.8
Increase 1964–67					
$	35.0	17.2	17.8	38.0	
Pct.	29.1	31.6	27.0	32.9	

in the 1964 tax bill. This failure is part of the explanation for the hostile reception which the administration's surtax proposal received in Congress.

The second factor which contributes materially to the present fiscal crisis is the understatement of Vietnam war costs in the budgets for fiscal 1966 and 1967. The original budget estimates for these years were so far off the mark that Congress and the public have no confidence in the data which the administration cites as supporting the need for a surtax.

The third factor in the "confidence gap" is the flagrant budget juggling which accompanied the administration's decision to seek a tax increase in 1967.

ADMINISTRATIVE BUDGET
ORIGINAL AND FINAL EXPENDITURE FIGURES
FISCAL YEARS 1966 AND 1967
(IN BILLIONS)

	Fiscal Year 1966 Original estimate January, 1965	Actual	Change	Fiscal Year 1967 Original estimate January, 1966	Actual	Change
Expenditures						
National defense	$51.6	$57.7	$+6.1	$60.5	$70.7	$+10.1
Nondefense	48.1	49.3	+1.2	52.3	55.1	+ 2.8
Total Expenditures	99.7	107.0	+7.3	112.8	125.7	+12.9
Receipts	94.4	104.7	+10.3	111.0	115.8	+4.8

Figures do not add because of rounding.

In his budget message submitted to Congress in January 1967 the President placed primary emphasis on the national income accounts budget, which is not really a budget but a set of economic accounts designed to show the aggregate impact of government finances within the framework of the national income and product accounts. The national income accounts budget is entirely unsuited for the analysis of programs and program priorities which a budget must provide. The explanation for this sudden new emphasis in January 1967 lay in a familiar place; the national income accounts budget showed a smaller anticipated deficit (−$2.1 billion) than the cash budget (−$4.3 billion) or the administrative budget (−$8.1 billion), and political strategy at that time dictated that the deficit be made to seem as small as possible. Several months later the President actively pursued a 10 percent surtax increase from Congress (anticipated in the January budget at 6 percent) and attention was shifted to the administrative budget which, with a newly estimated deficit ranging from $15 billion to $29 billion, gave more support to arguments that a tax increase was needed to prevent overheating of the economy.

These three developments largely explain the crisis of confidence over fiscal and budget policy which the administration is suffering with both Congress and the public. The President is to be commended for acknowledging the problem by his appointment of a commission to study the budget, but it should be clear that the loss of public confidence in budget figures lies not only in the mechanics of the budget, but also in the very natural inclination of the administration in power to present information in the most favorable light possible.

The President's Commission on Budget Concepts—of which I was a member—produced recommendations which were intended to make the budget less susceptible to flagrant juggling. First and foremost, the commission strongly urged reliance on a single budget which would show expenditures and receipts on an accrual basis. There is no question that the existence of three budgets made it very easy for the administration to pick whichever budget painted the most favorable picture. Unfortunately, the commission's new "unified budget" would permit—in fact, invite—budget juggling which would be more subtle (and thus more dangerous) than the very obvious changes in emphasis seen recently with respect to the three budgets now in use. I am referring to the commission's recommendations (1) that loan programs be shown separately from expenditure programs, and that the surplus or deficit be shown with and without net lending, and (2) that primary emphasis be placed on the federal debt held by the public. At present, emphasis is given equally to public debt held by the public and to debt held by government agencies. Both of these proposals could—and I believe may—be used to provide an unrealistically limited picture of government activities and their financing.

New spending programs may very well be classified, and old programs reclassified, as loans and kept apart from "regular" expenditures in exactly the same manner as trust fund expenditures are distinguished from the "regular" expenditures of the administrative budget—a practice the commission rightly deplored. By the absence of restraint, loan programs may grow to such a proportion that the usefulness of the commission's unified budget will be limited. It is noteworthy that a majority of the commission members opposed the recommendation that loan programs be listed separately in summary budget tables following the tabulation of a surplus or deficit in expenditure accounts, but deferred to the wishes of Treasury Secretary Fowler and Budget Director Schultze, both commission members.

It would be misleading if the public were led to believe that the total public debt is only that debt which is held by the public. After all, the debt held by the federal trust funds accrues interest costs just like the debt held by the public. Of the $326 billion in federal debt outstanding at the end of fiscal 1967, $266 billion (82 percent) was held by the public, and $60 billion (18 percent) was held by government agencies or international organizations. Between June 30, 1964, and June 30, 1967, the debt held by sources other than the public rose by \$9.1 billion, and the share of the debt so held increased from 16.4 percent to 18.4 percent.

I will not belabor the point, but it is vital to establish that the budget is still susceptible to a significant degree of manipulation by the executive branch. Moreover, this probably will always be the case because any attempt to redefine budget concepts—such as the report of the President's commission—will bear the marked influence of the top officials responsible for budget and fiscal policy. I doubt whether Congress or the public could, as a practical matter, impose on the executive a system which would assure complete and timely presentations of budget data.

Complete and timely information on federal finances will become available to the public only if Congress, and responsible and authoritative sources in the private sector, equip themselves to furnish the information and analysis which the executive is reluctant to provide. Congress, in particular, must acquire the capability to assess continually the over-all effect on the budget of the major steps in the process as they occur:

(1) the approval of authorizing legislation by the legislative committees;
(2) the approval of appropriations by the appropriations committee;
(3) the point at which obligations are incurred by the executive branch;
(4) the actual use of resources; and
(5) expenditure.

Congress has traditionally measured the budget in terms of appropriations requested by the President and approved by Congress. This is no longer an adequate basis for evaluating or controlling the complex activities of today's federal government. This point was driven home to many members of Congress by my introduction, during the 89th and 90th Congresses of the so-called "Bow amendment" which would have specifically limited expenditures by the executive. During these debates many House members came to appreciate fully the fact that Congress has in the past controlled only appropriations, and that timing of obligations and expenditures is made with very wide discretion by the executive. For example, of the $135 billion in administrative budget expenditures proposed for fiscal 1968, $39.3 billion (29 percent) was based on appropriations made in prior years. In short, Congress could effectively limit expenditures in fiscal 1968 only by directly restricting expenditures through a device such as the Bow amendment. Such a device should be adopted in the future to control the expenditures of individual agencies.

However, there are many areas in which Congress cannot exercise its powers effectively because it simply cannot compile and analyze, in detail and in depth, the complex financial statistics which describe the equally complex activities of the federal government. Congress has rightly refused to encumber itself with a staff bureaucracy; however, this limitation has kept Congress from effective utilization, in program analysis and control, of such important components of the budget as balances of appropriations from previous years, obligations incurred, and, the extensive spending authority which is approved outside the appropriations process.

This last point provides a perfect illustration of the relationship between the effectiveness of Congress, and the quality of information Congress possesses. The President's fiscal 1968 cash budget anticipated total appropriations of $194 billion for administrative budget and trust funds. Yet the executive actually anticipated total obligational authority of almost twice that amount—$378 billion. This authority consisted of:

New obligational authority	$194 billion
Authority granted in previous years	$127 billion
Authority to spend receipts	$ 57 billion

Figures such as these show how mistaken it is to speak of the "immense power" which Congress wields through the appropriations process. As a practical matter Congress is able to exercise but little control over authority granted in previous years and to control these funds it will be necessary to adopt some current and direct control over obligations and/or expenditures such as is provided by the Bow amendment. Second, the appropriations committees have inadequate control over authority to spend receipts granted by the legislative committees. Congress should avail itself of the advantages of modern data processing. The speed and capacity of present-day computers are especially suited to the mass of data which relates to the finances of the federal government. Preliminary work in computerized analysis of the federal budget has been undertaken by the American Enterprise Institute, a private nonprofit research institute based in Washington. It may well be that Congress is not yet prepared to acquire its own computer facility but successful demonstrations by the private sector may influence Congress to do so.

In any event, Congress needs access to detailed and authoritative alternatives to the information which flows from the executive. Its constitutional responsibilities require no less.

Chapter 10

MONETARY REFORM: NATIONAL AND INTERNATIONAL

――――◀◆▶――――

THE UNITED STATES BALANCE OF PAYMENTS
by Gottfried Haberler

GOTTFRIED HABERLER is Professor of Economics at Harvard University. Professor Haberler studied abroad and in the United States and was a professor of economics and statistics at the University of Vienna before coming to the United States in 1936. Professor Haberler has been associated with the Board of Governors of the Federal Reserve System and was President of the National Bureau of Economic Research in 1955, and President of the American Economic Association in 1963. Professor Haberler was a contributor to the volume *The Conservative Papers,* published by Doubleday in 1964.

AN OVERVIEW OF THE PROBLEM

The United States balance of payments has been in serious deficit for ten years in a row—1958 to 1967—not counting years with much smaller deficits before 1957. Very bad years were 1958, 1959, and 1960; the worst was 1959. After that there was a rapid improvement until 1964. Since 1965 further deterioration has taken place.

In 1959 the balance on goods and services showed no surplus—the only postwar year when that happened. In that year the Eisenhower administration took drastic action to curb inflation. The federal administrative budget swung from a deficit of $12.4 billion in fiscal 1959 to a surplus of $1.2 billion in fiscal 1960,[1] the largest peacetime turn around in the annals

[1] In the "Cash Budget" the swing was from a $13.1 billion deficit to a $0.8 billion surplus.

of American fiscal policy. Equally drastic action was taken on the monetary front. The effect on the balance of payments was quick and decisive. The balance on goods and services (excluding transfers under military grants) rose from almost zero in 1959 to $4 billion in 1960 and continued to rise to $8.5 billion in 1964. Since then it has rapidly declined to $5.1 billion in 1966 and to a still lower figure in the first two quarters of 1967.

The improvement after 1959 in the over-all balance (on the so-called "liquidity" basis as well as on "the official reserve transactions" basis) was less dramatic than the improvement in the balance on goods and services; in fact, the "liquidity" deficit in 1960 was slightly greater than in 1959 but declined by 1965 and 1966 to about half of what it was in 1959 and 1960. The reason is that the over-all balance, in addition to the balance of goods and services, reflects also the capital balance (private capital exports, net) and government transactions (largely grants and loans to foreign countries, and military expenditures). Private capital exports, especially direct investments and other long term investments, have increased since 1959 until they were restrained by special government controls (the "interest equalization tax" and the various so-called "voluntary" restriction schemes). Government grants and capital outflows, too, have risen sharply, largely as a consequence of the war in Vietnam. Private capital outflows, especially direct investments, soon produce a backflow of earnings and often stimulate exports of equipment, spare parts, and give rise to royalty and license payments from abroad. Income from private United States investment abroad increased from $2.7 billion in 1959 to $5.6 billion in 1966. Unfortunately, government grants do not usually return income flows.

The slower improvement in the over-all balance does not, however, make the improvement in the goods and services balance unimportant. An over-all deficit that is due mainly to capital exports (as it was in 1960) is less alarming than a deficit of equal size that reflects a weak goods and services balance (as in 1959), because it can be expected soon to produce a return flow for the reasons that were just explained.

There can, thus, be no doubt that the drastic action of the Eisenhower administration in 1959 was highly effective as far as the balance of payments was concerned. It was also effective in checking inflation. Without this action, it would not have been possible to have a period of stable wholesale prices which lasted through three years of cyclical expansion (1961 to early in 1965).[2] It is also true, however, that the anti-inflationary policy brought about the mild and very short recession from May 1960 to February 1961. This recession was greatly played up in the Presidential election of 1960 and, in view of the extremely small majority of the winning party, can be said to have had a decisive influence on the outcome of the election. Even those who felt at the time or who feel now that the anti-inflation medicine administered in 1959 was somewhat too strong or too abrupt cannot deny that it was a highly responsible approach to the problem; it was politically not opportune to do such a thing on the eve of an election. But economically it paid off in the years to come. If the sixth decade had started with a balance of payments no better than in 1959 and with prices rising as fast as they have been rising again since 1965, the longest peacetime expansion of the United States' economy which, not counting the mild slack last year, has now lasted uninterruptedly for seven years, would hardly have been possible.

Since 1965 the balance of payments situation has greatly deteriorated. This is most clearly shown by the continued erosion of the surplus on goods and services. The deterioration is not fully reflected in the official figures for the over-all balance. In fact, the (liquidity) deficit in 1966 has not been greater than in 1965.[3] This is, however, deceptive. Actually,

[2] Wholesale prices, in fact, remained stable from 1958 to 1965. Consumer prices rose by something like 1.5 percent per annum during the same period. Since 1965 both price indexes have gone up more sharply.

[3] That the "official settlements" balance for 1966 showed a small surplus is admittedly due to certain freakish developments. Concretely, it reflects shifts abroad of dollar balances between foreign official agencies and foreign private banks. These shifts were reversed in 1967, which put the official settlements balance sharply

there has been a substantial deterioration. The deficit in the over-all balance has been kept down by special restrictions on the outflow of American capital. In addition an inflow of short term funds in 1966 induced by the exceptionally high interest rates and monetary stringency then prevailing—the so-called "credit crunch"—temporarily relieved the pressure. Furthermore, on paper the over-all deficit is being kept smaller than it actually is by certain statistical manipulations. Thus, foreign official agencies and international and interregional organizations were induced to shift some of their dollar holdings from short term to long term deposits and securities. The latter, although just as liquid as the former, are not counted in the deficit; they are put "above the line" not below, as it is often expressed. These and similar "cosmetic" devices have reduced the deficit on paper in the last two years or so by something like one billion dollars a year.

MAGNITUDE OF THE PROBLEM

Before going into the question of causes and cures of the persistent deficit, let me say a word on the order of magnitude of the problem. When we compare the size of the deficit, under any definition or method of recording even in the worst years, with the relevant magnitudes of our economy— GNP topping the $800 billion mark, annual increase in GNP $40 to $50 billion, exports of goods and services $45 billion, merchandise exports $30 billion—we cannot fail to be struck by the small dimension of the real problem. A tiny tail threatens to wag a huge and rapidly growing dog! The true dimension of the problem should be pondered by foreign critics who complain that the role of the dollar as an international reserve currency enables the United States to "live beyond its

---

into the red during the first two quarters. These developments have nothing to do with the state of the United States balance of payments position, but they cast doubts on the usefulness of this particular measure, that is, the official settlements definition of deficit and surplus.

means" by extracting "involuntary loans" from other countries. In reality, the so-called "involuntary loans," as measured by the dollar holdings of the complaining foreign central banks—balances on which they earn a good interest—are a small fraction of the United States' transfers abroad for economic aid, government loans, military assistance, private capital investments abroad which contribute to the growth and development of the recipient countries. In fact, the net international investment position of the United States, that is to say, total U.S. assets and investment abroad minus total foreign assets and investment in the United States has increased from approximately $14 billion in 1950 to $51 billion in 1960 (or, if we deduct the decline of the gold stock during the same period, to $42 billion).

The true magnitude of the problem is quite small in the sense that if and when the problem is solved, as it must and will be in the end, by an increase in exports and/or a decrease in imports, the impact on our welfare will be negligible. (Contrary to what is popularly assumed, larger exports and smaller imports constitute a burden on the economy because it means that fewer goods are available for domestic use.[4] But in this case, the burden is negligible because of the small size of the deficit compared with GNP.) While this is true, we must live by the rules of the international monetary game which were laid down under American guidance in the Bretton Woods Charter of the International Monetary Fund and have been

---

[4] This statement has to be qualified, if there is much unemployment and excess capacity in the economy. Then it is possible, up to a point, to export more, import less and have more goods available for domestic use, and to provide butter and guns at the same time. No such miracles are feasible today because we have substantially though not literally full employment.

This is, of course, not to deny that in some sectors unemployment is shockingly high. For example, among Negro teenagers unemployment is over 20 percent. This is, however, due to special circumstances which cannot be dealt with by global monetary, financial or balance-of-payments measures. Minimum wage laws in particular operate powerfully to keep the lowest strata of unskilled labor out of work.

consistently upheld and reconfirmed by successive administrations. These rules are, in brief, a fixed rate of exchange between the dollar and other currencies and free convertibility of the dollar, in other words, absence of payments restrictions.

Under these rules our deficit, though small, is too large to be maintained much longer. I cannot accept (at least not fully although it obviously contains a grain of truth) the comforting theory of my friends Despres, Kindleberger, and Salant to the effect that the deficit is imaginary, that it is entirely the consequence of faulty methods of balance of payments accounting and lack of understanding of our role as the world's banker. Nor can I share friend Machlup's optimistic diagnosis that a restoration of confidence in the dollar "would all of itself" restore equilibrium in the United States balance of payments.[5]

CAUSES AND CURES

A complex phenomenon such as the deficit in the external accounts rarely has a single well-defined cause.[6] There is prac-

[5] One could argue that foreign central banks, if they had full confidence in the dollar, would hold much larger dollar balances than they hold now and that then the deficit could be financed at its present level, if not indefinitely at least for a long time. (It is another question whether foreign countries could not be induced by a gold guarantee to hold on to their dollars.) This is not, however, what Professor Machlup had in mind. He was referring to the lack of confidence in the dollar on the part of private investors which in his opinion explains at least a large part of private capital outflows. Apart from short periods, however, this factor—capital flight—does not seem to have been an important factor. This does not, of course, exclude that it may become one in the future. [Since this was written, the confidence in the Dollar has, in fact, been seriously shaken, first through the devaluation of the pound sterling then through the policy steps taken and proposed in the President's New Year's message on the balance of payments. See *Postscript,* February 1968 below.]

[6] I would not go so far as to say that there never can be a single cause. Suppose a country pursues highly inflationary policies and prices rise by 20 percent or more a year. (It would not be hard

tically always a combination of factors that can plausibly be held responsible for the existing state of affairs. Let me enumerate the more important factors that have been mentioned as the cause of our balance of payment troubles: If we had less inflation, other things being equal, our exports would be larger and imports smaller and there would be no deficit. If the European countries had more inflation, the result would be the same. But let us not forget that every country in the world has its share of inflation. There is not a single case of real deflation, either in the sense of falling prices or shrinking monetary circulation, on the record of the whole postwar period. (This was quite different during the interwar period.) If the major currencies had not been depreciated as much against the dollar as they were—the pound sterling and scores of others in 1949, the French franc several times, the last time in 1958—the United States' balance of payments would be better. If American capital exports and American government expenditures abroad were substantially smaller, the balance of payments position would be easier.

More doubtful is the relationship of the balance of payments to economic growth. In the early sixties it was popular to say, that if only the American economy grew faster, capital would stay at home, the current balance too would be better and the payments problem would be solved. Well, the growth rate did go up sharply but capital still went abroad and the current balance deteriorated again. More important than growth itself is how it is brought about. Growth stimulated by monetary expansion and accompanied by inflation is one thing. If it were possible to have growth without inflation, this would be an entirely different and healthier thing. If the rest of the world removed tariffs and other obstacles to our exports while we kept our tariffs, American exports would expand and the balance of payments improve.

There is some truth in all or most of these statements. But

---

to find concrete examples.) Then we can definitely say that inflation is "the" cause of the deficit if the exchange rate is fixed. In the United States the situation is not that simple and straightforward.

clearly some of the factors mentioned cannot be changed, others we would not like to change even if we could. We cannot well ask other countries to inflate faster, although in a veiled manner this is often done.[7] We would be reluctant to reduce our long run rate of growth for the sake of the balance of payments. (Whether very high growth rates in recent years are sustainable even apart from the balance of payments is another question.) We should not give up convertibility and introduce all sorts of restrictions on capital movements, tourist expenditures, etc. (To this question I shall return presently.)

To make a long story short, the strategically most important factor contributing to our balance of payments troubles is our inflation. That does not mean that inflation in the United States has been more rapid than elsewhere. On the contrary, in the long run as well as in the short, the purchasing power of the dollar has been better preserved than that of any other important currency, including the Swiss franc, German mark, French franc, not to mention the British pound and scores of others.[8] What it means is that our inflation has been a little too much, especially again since 1965, for the

[7] For example, when spokesmen of the administration reproach European countries for not "developing more efficient capital markets," it is tantamount to inviting them to have a little more inflation. The idea is that they then could finance the projects out of European sources that are now financed by American corporations. Since these countries had inflation and full employment all the time—apart from some pauses milder than ours—more investment would mean more inflation. Let me repeat, no country has pursued a really deflationary policy.

[8] If anybody doubts this in the heat of the argument over the current rate of inflation, he should take a look at the table in the July issue of the Monthly Economic Letter of the First National City Bank of New York. There he will find that the annual rate of depreciation of the U. S. Dollar from 1956 to 1966, as measured by the rise of the cost of living index, was substantially less than that of any other currency except that of Guatemala, Venezuela and Honduras. From 1965 to 1966 the U.S. performance was better than that of Switzerland, Germany and many other countries, but slightly worse than that of Austria, Taiwan and a few others. In 1967 the picture was less favorable.

equilibrium in the balance of payments, in view of the fact that foreign currencies have been devalued and that Europe and Japan have recovered from the war, thus offering increasing competition to American industries in the world markets including our own. I call inflation a "strategic" factor because it is our problem and because inflation is most undesirable and should be stopped, even apart from its impact on the balance of payments.

We must realize that the major objectives of economic policy—stable rates of exchange, free convertibility and a high level of employment and growth—cannot be achieved simultaneously unless we check inflation and maintain strict monetary, fiscal, and wage discipline.

The condition for the continued simultaneous achievement of the various policy objectives has not been fulfilled. Inflation has again been allowed to develop. The problem of inflation will be taken up elsewhere in this volume.[9] Here it is enough to stress the fact that the war in Vietnam is not the only cause of inflation. Nondefense government expenditures, too, have expanded by leaps and bounds in the last few years, producing a huge deficit in the federal budget and monetary policy has been extremely expansionary since 1964 apart from a short but dramatic interlude in 1966. In the spring of 1966, the Federal Reserve abruptly stepped on the brakes and tightened money, leading to the famous "credit crunch" in the late summer of 1966. The inevitable consequence was a slowing of the economy, not an outright recession but a period of "pause" of "hesitancy." This induced the Federal Reserve late in 1966 to reverse itself again. It shifted to a policy of rapid expansion, which is still in progress at the time of writing (October 1967). These violent changes are not conducive to economic stability. They reflect a lack of consensus and coordination of fiscal and monetary policies inside the administration.

[9] The present writer has analyzed the inflation problem in some detail in his pamphlet, *Inflation: Its Causes and Cures*, Washington, D.C.: American Enterprise Institute, revised edition 1966.

THE DRIFT TOWARD CONTROLS

It is no wonder that under these conditions it became necessary to retreat more and more from the simultaneous achievement of the policy objectives mentioned above. Since the fixity of the exchange rate is still the law and the level of employment and rate of growth must not be allowed to slip, apart from a short period of hesitance, it has become necessary to compromise more and more with the principle of free convertibility. In other words, there has been a pronounced drift toward more and more controls and hidden restrictions on imports. Duty free tourist allowances have been sharply reduced, foreign aid and loans have been tied, thus reducing the real aid per dollar substantially. "Buy American" policies for government procurement in general and for the needs of the armed forces abroad have been sharply stiffened, which adds substantially to the dollar cost of government purchases. All that is equivalent to a heavy dose of protection. Increasingly stringent restrictions and controls on capital exports have been introduced. An interest equalization tax was imposed on the purchase of foreign securities. Controls of this type always develop leaks after they have been in operation for a while. The interest equalization tax was no exception. In order to prevent evasion and bypassing of the tax the scope of the tax had to be extended. Moreover, the rate of the tax was recently sharply increased. In addition to the interest equalization tax, so-called "voluntary" restraints were imposed on bank loans and direct investment abroad. In reality, the amount to detailed supervision of foreign lending and the scheme is voluntary only in name.

There is great danger that the drift toward controls and restrictions will continue. Protectionist sentiments are rising fast in the country. Leaders of the steel industry have been clamoring for "temporary" import restrictions on steel. For good measure, they have suggested that shipbuilding, textiles, petroleum, "medicinal products" and electrical equipment in dustries, too, would be deserving candidates for higher protection. President Johnson's former Secretary of Commerce, John T. Connor, has publicly called for comprehensive quota import restrictions on all textiles. (*The New York Times,* October 7, 1967) At the urging of the industries concerned, numerous bills have been introduced in Congress which would put a long list of commodities from steel and textiles to mink coats under quota protection.

This upsurge of protectionist sentiment is partly, though by no means entirely, the consequence of the large import volume which is at the root of the weakness of the balance of payments. The adverse balance of payments, in turn, is then used as an argument for import restrictions.

This is a very dangerous development. It violates the letter and spirit of the principles of liberal trade policies which have been embraced by Republican as well as Democratic administrations. Moreover, government interventions in foreign trade, especially those of the quota type, clash with the principles of a free enterprise economy in general; such restrictions sooner or later spread from the foreign trade sector to the domestic area.

How can this drift toward more and more controls of international payments be halted?

The first requirement is to stop inflation. It is not enough to hope for an early end of the war and in the meantime to continue as usual. As a minimum, the steep rise in non-war expenditures ought to be halted and taxes will have to be raised. Above all, the monetary expansion cannot be continued at the present rate.

If we let things drift, trying to give the country more butter and gravy along with the guns, inflation will accelerate, and if other countries do not bail us out by inflating even more than we do, for which they show little inclination at the present time, the balance of payments will further deteriorate and confidence in the dollar will be undermined and eventually shaken.

The point will then be reached when a definite and conscious choice has to be made whether we want to preserve the fixity of the exchange rate or the convertibility of the dollar. If that dilemma has to be faced, it would be far better to give up the fixed exchange. For the alternative is to sink in a morass of controls and restrictions. Not that stable exchanges are unimportant. On the contrary, they are rightly regarded as an important objective, because they facilitate international trade, travel and capital movements; they are especially important for the latter. But if trade, travel and capital flows have to be more and more severely restricted and controlled in order to maintain nominal stability of the exchange rate— then the fixity of the exchange rate has lost its value and *raison d'être*.

This will not be an easy choice. Responsible statesmen and politicians, whether in office or not, do not like to discuss in public the possibility that a major currency may have to be devalued, because public discussion of that possibility may touch off a flight from the dollar. We have not yet reached that stage, but we are rapidly approaching it if inflation is allowed to continue.

A great number of economists have reached the conclusion that we should adopt some system of at least limited flexibility of the exchange rates before we are confronted with a crisis situation. I can do no better than to quote in full a statement by twenty-seven well-known economists of different outlook from eight countries made two years ago:

> "The discussion of possible reform of the present system of international payment has been largely focused on the problem of "international liquidity." More specifically expressed, the discussion has been focused on the temporary financing of imbalances through providing additional reserves and borrowing facilities and on promoting the adjustment process through monetary and fiscal policies. The no less important issue of exchange rates has received little attention in official circles. The fact that, as the present statement shows, many professional economists can agree on a minimum program in that respect, would seem to demonstrate that there is a promising op-

portunity here for improving the international payments system.

Whatever the system of reserves, we believe that more exchange-rate flexibility is needed than exists under the IMF rules now in effect. It has proved impossible, under the present rules, for many countries to maintain stable prices and high employment levels and at the same time avoid the imposition of more and more controls on international payments. To achieve these domestic economic goals simultaneously with equilibrium in external payments requires more leeway for variations in exchange rates than exists now. This is why we favor two modifications in the IMF rules.

Our first proposal is to widen the limits within which countries are obliged to keep the gold value of their currencies. This value should be allowed to vary up to four or five per cent on either side of parity, instead of the present one per cent. A spread of eight or ten per cent would thus be provided between the upper and the lower support points. This first reform would render possible day-to-day fluctuations in exchange rates sufficient to absorb many balance-of-payments disturbances without disrupting foreign trade and investment. The proposed system need not be applied to every country without exception; some could be permitted to peg their currency to another country's or groups of countries could agree to keep the currencies of members of the group fixed in relation to one another.

The second modification we advocate is to allow countries unilaterally to change the par value of their currencies by no more than one or two per cent of the previous year's par value. This seems at first more restrictive than present rules, which allow changes up to ten per cent without prior approval by the IMF; yet since the present permissible changes are based not on last year's but on the originally announced par values which in many cases are now hopelessly out-of-date, our proposal is, in effect, more permissive.

Our two proposals—to widen the range between the support points and to allow gradual adjustments of par values—do not go beyond what most proponents of the Bretton Woods Agreement had in mind. The need for this limited flexibility of exchange rates was generally recognized at the time, but the provisions that were formulated have proved impractical and therefore have not been used by countries even when their exchange rates had become clearly unrealistic.

The undersigned now join in advocating these reforms. While we differ among ourselves on what each of us considers the ideal set of rules and institutions, all of us hold that the alterations we propose would constitute a great improvement over the present situation. We submit that the increased flexibility of exchange rates under these rules would go far in solving the problem of adjusting future imbalances of payments. In addition, some of us believe that this flexibility might also reduce the demand for foreign reserves and would in this way contribute to solving the problem of international liquidity.

The alterations of rules which we propose are designed to deal with the long-run problem of preventing future disequilibria among the industrial countries. They are not suited for the elimination of large imbalances already in existence, nor for the problems of many less developed countries which need stronger medicine."[10]

Spokesmen of the administration have turned a deaf ear to any proposal of that kind. Their response to the challenge of the balance of payments has been almost entirely to introduce more and more controls and to press for international measures designed to increase international liquidity by cre-

[10] This statement was signed by economists ranging from Milton Friedman to Alvin Hansen, thus covering a wide range of views. Some of the signers would go farther and recommend unlimited flexibility, some would prefer the enactment of only one of the two proposals. But they all agree that the measures proposed in the statement would constitute a most desirable reform of the present international payments system.

ating new reserve assets, "paper gold." To the problem of international liquidity I turn now.

INTERNATIONAL LIQUIDITY AND MONETARY REFORM

So far I have discussed the problem of "adjustment," that is, methods, automatic or contrived, of eliminating deficits once they have appeared. However, the larger part of the discussion of the international monetary problem in recent years, official and academic, has been concerned with the "liquidity" problem, that is to say, with the problem of increasing liquid resources ("reserve assets") that permit the temporary financing of deficits.

It cannot be stressed too often and too strongly that adjustment is the more important problem. If the adjustment mechanism works well, little liquidity (reserves) is necessary. If the adjustment mechanism is not allowed to function, if we tolerate inflation while keeping the exchange rate fixed, unlimited amounts of liquidity would be needed; but deficits cannot be financed indefinitely.

Administration officials first denied the need for more international liquidity. Later, *ad hoc* arrangements were made to enable the United States to borrow on a bilateral basis from foreign central banks. Swap agreements were entered into and exchange guaranteed "Roosa bonds" were placed with foreign monetary authorities. But eventually the administration joined the chorus of the world's deficit countries, with Great Britain in the lead, that has been clamoring for the creation of new artificial reserve assets on a global and massive scale.

After long and often difficult negotiations the drive for international action to increase international liquidity, spearheaded by the United States and the United Kingdom, has led to an agreement among the ten leading financial powers —the Group of Ten—to propose a plan for the Creation of New International Reserve Assets. At the Rio de Janeiro annual meeting of the International Monetary Fund in September 1967 the proposal was unanimously accepted. The management of the International Monetary Fund was instructed to draft an amendment to the Fund Charter embodying the provisions outlined in the agreement of the Group of Ten. The new credit facilities to be created are called *Special Drawing Rights*. Since only a fraction of the sums that countries will be able to draw under the new arrangement, if and when it goes into effect, need be repaid ("reconstituted") the new facilities practically constitute reserve assets rather than credits.

The Rio resolution has created a euphoric mood in Washington; it has been acclaimed in glowing terms by officials from the President down; it is called a "major breakthrough" and the "greatest advance in the area of international monetary reform since the adoption of the Bretton Wood Charter."

The European reactions, while on the whole favorable, have been much more restrained. The sober European appraisal comes closer to the truth than the exuberant claims by American and British officials. The Rio agreement is a first step toward a modest reform. Several hurdles have still to be overcome. After the agreement has been put in legal form it has to be ratified. The agreement on the Special Drawing Rights accords the Common Market countries enlarged voting rights which gives them a veto power if they vote as a bloc. This was a major American concession. Some European countries have made it clear that they will ratify the scheme only if the voting rights in the Fund are changed so as to give the Common Market countries that veto power also for other important Fund decisions. The United States and Great Britain oppose the linking of the new drawing rights with the voting arrangements in the Fund. This may delay ratification. After the scheme has been ratified, which may well take two years, the Managing Board of the Fund can decide with an 85 percent majority that Special Drawing Rights be created.

Here is not the place to go into further details. Suffice it to say that if all goes well, in two years the Fund will be ready, if it so decides with an 85 percent majority, to create additional reserve assets or credit facilities. The figure $1–2 billion a year has been mentioned as a reasonable target. This compares with a gold stock for the world as a whole of about $40 billion and total international reserves of about $70 billion. The American share will be a few hundred million dollars, quite small compared with our present deficit.

To be fair, American officials have made it quite clear from the beginning and have stressed repeatedly that they do not regard the new reserve assets as a scheme for making it easier for the United States to finance its deficit. Why is it then, it may well be asked, such a world-shaking event? The plain truth is that it is not world-shaking!

The new scheme is designed to guard against a danger that may arise in the future. The argument is familiar by now. World trade is growing and the growth of international reserves has not kept pace. Gold production is insufficient, private gold hoarding absorbs almost all of the new gold that comes on the market and most countries are reluctant to add to their dollar balances which in the past provided additional reserves.

There is certainly some truth in this argument. Although there does not exist a rigid relationship between the volume of trade and the amount of reserves required at some time in the future, if world trade continues to grow, many countries will want to add to their reserves. But a general scarcity of international liquidity has not yet arisen and it is impossible to foresee when it will arise, because there is no precise mathematical relationship between volume of international transactions and the size of international reserves. On this most experts are agreed. The mere fact that some countries, even though they are reserve currency countries, have balance of payments difficulties, does not constitute a general scarcity of international liquidity.

The new scheme is, thus, directed against a possible future danger that may not arise for quite some time. It is therefore not a very urgent matter.

This does not mean, however, that an acute balance of payments and confidence crisis may not occur soon, long before a general scarcity of liquidity makes itself felt and the agreement on special drawing rights has gone into effect.

Suppose, for example, sterling gets into serious trouble. That it is not yet over the hump was recently highlighted by the critical report of the Brussels Commission on the economic problems involved by Britain's joining the European Common Market. If the pound were devalued, many other countries would follow, there would be additional strain on our balance of payments and a run on the dollar could easily develop.

Or suppose our deficit continues and increases because of inflation at home or adverse developments abroad; confidence in the dollar may be shaken and foreign dollar holders, private and official, may try to get rid of their dollars.

The possibility of an acute confidence crisis cannot be excluded. The new scheme for the creation of Special Drawing Rights, even when ratified and in operation, would not be able and is not designed to cope with such emergencies. An acute crisis would have to be dealt with on an *ad hoc* basis. However, international machinery for that exists in the International Monetary Fund and through the international cooperation of central banks.

That this machinery can be effective was demonstrated when Italy in 1963 and Great Britain in 1964 and 1965 were confronted with acute balance of payments crises and sudden withdrawals of large funds. Billions of dollars were raised almost overnight to prop up the two currencies. The Italian crisis was triggered by ill-advised measures of a leftist government. The electric power industry was nationalized although it had been, according to all competent observers, a highly efficient, well-managed branch of the economy. This shook confidence and led to heavy capital flight from Italy. Furthermore, there was a veritable wage explosion. But when the situation became desperate, the crisis was handled with great energy and skill. The essential part in the rescue operation, without which international credits that were raised would have gone to waste, was that the Italian Central Bank most courageously applied a stiff dose of "classical" monetary medicine. Credit was sharply tightened, confidence was quickly restored and the balance of payments improved almost overnight. True, economic growth slowed down for a while and unemployment increased temporarily. But the pause was mild and did not last very long; in 1965 the Italian economy resumed its expansion with the balance of payments still out of the red.

In view of the great weight of the American economy in world trade, a dollar crisis would, of course, be a much more serious matter than a crisis of the Italian lira or of any other currency. Useful lessons can nevertheless be learned from the successful handling of the Italian crisis.

What must be avoided is a serious recession with heavy unemployment on the one hand and drastic restrictions and regimentations of trade and payments on the other hand. The tiny tail of our deficit must not be allowed to shake violently the huge American economy and through it upset equilibrium in the world economy.

The key to successful balance of payments management is to stop inflation. If that were accomplished or even seriously taken in hand by keeping monetary expansion at a sustainable level, cutting expenditures and raising taxes, we could count on international cooperation. That is to say, foreign countries would not follow France, they would not change their dollars into gold and would probably even be ready to add to their dollar balances.

But can inflation be stopped or slowed sufficiently without causing too much unemployment? Or have wages already risen so high and the push for higher wages which was fostered by inflationary policies become so strong that it will not quickly subside, even if and when inflation is stopped and the cost of living levels out?

A modest transitional rise in unemployment is probably unavoidable when inflation is brought under control. But after seven years of expansion, the longest peacetime cyclical upswing in the annals of the American economy, a mild and short recession would not be a catastrophe; on the contrary, it would have positive salutary effects. It would dampen the wage push; it would induce business to eliminate wastes and extravagances and to tighten labor discipline; it would raise efficiency all-round which has been slipping seriously as it always does in extended prosperity periods. Thus the economy would soon get into a healthier shape ready for a new upsurge. This is the major lesson that can be learned from the Italian example.

CONCLUDING REMARKS

Is there anything else we can do about the balance of payments in addition to controlling inflation and apart from piling up more and more direct controls on international trade, travel, and capital flows?

Let me emphasize once more that some flexibility of the exchange rate would be most helpful; in fact, many experts would put this step first. One further comment. Flexibility does not necessarily mean that the dollar itself, the world's most important currency, would have to be allowed to float. If many lesser currencies were flexible vis-à-vis the dollar and gold, it would greatly ease the payments problems for everybody. One concrete example. Suppose sterling had to be devalued. Under the present system the devaluation would certainly be substantial. For reasons that are well known, it would be only prudent to devalue by *more* than is necessary to restore equilibrium in the British balance of payments. This would be very disturbing for other countries and would put the heat on the dollar. If we had limited flexibility, sterling would gradually reach its equilibrium level and there would be no danger of greatly overshooting the mark. So the impact on the rest of the world, the dollar in particular, would be minimized.

Let me mention one other step we could take. It is to offer a gold guarantee to official foreign dollar holders. There is no logic in our officials declaring and protesting again and again that "the dollar is as good as gold" and at the same time refusing to give a written guarantee. Any risk that such a guarantee might involve in case of a devaluation of the dollar or a general change in the price of gold could and should be eliminated by the proviso that allowance would be made for interest that foreign central banks have earned by holding dollars rather than gold. In other words, we would guarantee that no foreign central bank would be worse off by holding dollars than it would have been if it had held its international reserve in the form of gold.

That would only be fair and should be acceptable to all except those few who change dollars into gold for political rather than for economic reasons. I cannot see any reason why such a guarantee should not be credible and accepted —under one condition, namely, that we avoid serious inflation. By serious inflation, I mean more inflation than other major countries are willing to tolerate. If inflation became serious, other countries might begin to doubt the credibility of the gold guarantee or they may refuse to hold more dollars, not because they are afraid to lose in case of a devaluation of the dollar but simply because they do not want to import inflation and wish to teach the United States a lesson.[11]

POSTSCRIPT—FEBRUARY 1968

Since this was written, the devaluation of the Pound Sterling, hinted at in the concluding remarks above, actually occurred on November 18, 1967, earlier than I expected. The value of the Pound was reduced from \$2.80 to \$2.40, a depreciation of 14.3 percent.

[11] They ought to be told that the only really effective way to avoid importing inflation is to cut oneself loose from the currency of the inflating country by letting the exchange rate go. In other words, a country that really wants to stay out of an inflationary trend abroad must let its currency appreciate. But with the common irrational aversion against any exchange rate changes, which is fully shared by our money managers, they may prefer to maintain the exchange rate unchanged, demand gold for their dollars (get their imported inflation via gold) although it means a loss of interest, in order to show their displeasure.

As expected, the depreciation of the Pound triggered a wave of speculation against the Dollar. Demand for gold by hoarders in the London gold market rose to record proportions. The price of gold was kept close to $35.00 per ounce by sales of gold from the international gold pool to which the United States contributes approximately 60 percent. The United States thus lost over $900 million in December 1967. These dramatic developments together with a sharp deterioration of the current balance in the fourth quarter, which according to preliminary estimates puts the over-all deficit approximately at $3.6 billion for the whole year of 1967, forced the administration to take drastic steps. These steps were announced by the President himself in a New Year's message to the American people and the world at large.

The content of the message can be summarized by saying that it merely offers "more of the same"—new direct controls on capital exports and on current transactions, in particular on expenditures of American tourists abroad. The measures announced and proposed in the President's message constitute a big further step—the biggest yet—into the morass of exchange control, into what used to be called the "Schachtian" system, named after its inventor, the Nazi economic wizard Hjalmar Schacht. The turn in policy was described in the highly respected *Neue Zürcher Zeitung* of Switzerland, undoubtedly the leading continental newspaper noted for its pro-American attitude, as "a complete reversal" of the policy of liberalizing trade and payments "pursued with missionary zeal throughout the postwar period" by successive American administrations.

Two restrictive programs were immediately put into effect, stringent mandatory controls of U.S. direct investments abroad, administered by the Department of Commerce, and a sharp tightening of the restrictions on foreign lending by financial institutions, administered by the Federal Reserve System. These measures were put into effect by Executive Order based on a law passed in 1917 that gives the President sweeping powers in case of war and declared emergency. It was news to most Americans, including many lawyers, that the country has been living under a state of emergency ever since

President Truman declared it in 1950. The Korean War emergency declaration has never been rescinded.

The most sweeping innovation in American foreign economic policy is the proposed tax on tourists traveling outside the Western Hemisphere. This is a violation of the spirit, if not the letter, of the International Monetary Fund Charter, for the Charter forbids controls on current transactions. (Controls on capital movements are permitted.) It is a protectionist measure, because it would provide high protection for the American tourist industry. It thus is in flagrant contradiction to the policy of liberalization of trade which was solemnly reaffirmed last July by administration spokesmen from the President down on the occasion of the conclusion of the Kennedy-round negotiations for reducing import tariffs. It plays in the hand of the rising protectionism. How is it possible to deny import restrictions to the steel, textile, and other industries when the tourist industry receives high protection? These glaring contradictions in the administration's statements and policies have, of course, been noted and pointed up abroad and, as *The New York Times* reported (issue of February 6, 1968), have administered another blow to American prestige all over the world and have undermined the credibility of American policy declarations.

The new restrictions, both on capital and on tourism, discriminate between different countries in a more or less arbitrary manner. What sense does it make to tax tourists going to, say, Israel or Italy or Thailand, but not those going to Argentina or Chile? The investment restrictions that apply to less developed countries and to Great Britain, Australia, Japan and some other countries which depend on capital inflows from the United States are less severe than those put in force for continental European countries and South Africa where a complete moratorium on new capital transfers has been imposed. But a country like Spain, which finds itself in a difficult economic position at the present time and in whose economy receipts from American tourists and from American investment have played an important role, is not in the privileged group. There are bound to be recriminations by countries against which we discriminate. And retaliation either open or concealed by those countries which are hit hardest is unavoidable and will sharply reduce favorable balance of payments effects of the new measures.

The proposed tourist tax is very difficult to enforce. It was aptly described by Professor Henry Wallich of Yale as "financial prohibition." It will have the same corrupting effects as prohibition had in the 1920s.

American prestige and credibility abroad have been dealt a heavy blow. For many years, probably for decades to come, American representatives in international organizations and American negotiators at international and bilateral conferences on economic problems will find themselves in a position of weakness and discomfiture. They will have to listen to embarrassing quotations from the eloquent preachings which they themselves or their predecessors used to address to other countries, which found themselves in balance of payments difficulties, on the desirability and the salutary effects of free convertibility of currencies, freer trade and the disadvantages, inefficiencies or even immorality of direct controls; these pleas will be compared with what the United States is now doing when it got itself into trouble.

It has been pointed out by several observers, among them Professor Samuelson, that many of the measures in protection of the balance of payments that were taken in recent years are equivalent to a partial though disguised devaluation of the Dollar. Thus the proposed tourist tax amounts to a devaluation of the "tourist Dollar"; the interest-equalization tax to a devaluation of the "portfolio investment Dollar," because it takes more Dollars than before to buy foreign securities; similarly, tying of foreign aid can be described as a devaluation of the "foreign aid Dollar" inasmuch as more Dollars are required to give the same amount of effective aid. The "border tax" on all imports and tax refunds on exports proposed in the New Year message would come close to a general devaluation of the Dollar.

Unless something decisive is done soon to put the financial house in order by reducing monetary growth to a sustainable level and bringing the federal budget into better balance, further tightening and extending of controls will be necessary. We rapidly approach the point, if it has not been reached, where a return to free convertibility of the Dollar is not possible without a cut in its international value. But open devaluation would be much less damaging than one concealed by more and more and increasingly constrictive controls.[12]

[12] The President's New Year message has been analyzed in greater detail and suggestions for alternative courses of action have been made by the author and Dr. Thomas Willett of Harvard University in a *Special Analysis* published by the American Enterprise Institute, 1200 17th Street, N.W., Washington, D.C. 20038.

A MONETARY AND FISCAL STRATEGY FOR THE NINETEEN-SEVENTIES

by Raymond J. Saulnier

DR. RAYMOND J. SAULNIER is Professor of Economics at Barnard College, Columbia University, and is a member of the Graduate Department of Economics at Columbia. For eight years (1946–53) he was director of the Financial Research Program of the National Bureau of Economic Research and from 1956 to 1961 he was Chairman of President Eisenhower's Council of Economic Advisers. Four lectures given by Dr. Saulnier at Fordham University in the fall of 1962 under the Millar Foundation have been published under the title of *The Strategy of Economic Policy* (1963). Dr. Saulnier was a contributor to *The Conservative Papers,* published by Doubleday in 1964.

Although the seventies are two years away, it is not too early to be thinking about the economic problems we will face in that decade and shaping a strategy to meet them. Actually, it is already late. As things are developing, we are getting more and more out of the posture we should be in to meet those problems adequately, and it will take time to regain a proper posture. Indeed, it may take as much as two years: thus, the timeliness of the subject.

WHAT THE ECONOMIC PROBLEMS OF THE SEVENTIES WILL BE

There is no need to dwell on what the economic problems of the 1970s will be. They will include all the old, familiar ones plus one new one. The new one arises from the fact that the number of children born in the United States in the five-year period 1946–50 exceeded the number born in the previous five years by 25 percent. A comparison with the thirties is even more striking; on an annual average basis, births in 1946–50 exceeded those in the thirties by 50 percent. As a group, these young people (now aged seventeen to twenty-one) have many interesting features, but the most important may well be their numerousness—the sheer fact of their numbers.

The impact of this generation has been with us for twenty years, taking new forms all the time. Some of its influences are probably too subtle for us as yet fully to understand, but others are quite plain to see. For one thing, it is painfully obvious that it has placed exceptionally heavy demands on the nation's educational facilities—first in the lower grades and now at the university level. The next point of impact will also be plain to see: it will be the job market. It is this impact, which will be felt increasingly as we move into the seventies, and about which there is still time to do something, on which attention must now be focused.

The relevant job requirement figures can be summarized briefly. A recent study by the U. S. Bureau of Labor Statistics (Monthly Labor Review, April 1967, page 13) projects increases in the labor force between 1965 and 1975 that average 1.8 percent a year. If we assume that in the interim (i) the number of persons in the armed forces is reduced to pre-Vietnam size; and (ii) the unemployment rate is reduced to 3 percent, it follows that civilian employment must increase by about 2 percent a year between now and 1975. This means the creation of some 14 million job opportunities. Even on less exacting assumptions—a 4 percent unemployment rate, for example—the decade of the seventies presents an undeniably formidable job-creating challenge.

There are two reasons why we can have confidence in the possibility of meeting the challenge successfully. First, there will be a need not only for vastly increased numbers of jobs but also for a vastly increased output of goods and services.

In the forefront will be the need for housing. In 1975 there will be half again as many people aged twenty-five to twenty-nine in the United States as there were in 1966; and because it is individuals in this age bracket who produce most of the marriages and most of the household formations, and because there is a close relationship between the rate of household formation and the demand for housing, we can therefore expect a very substantial increase in housing demand. No one can be entirely sure what the wishes of this often baffling generation will be with respect to marriage and the family, but the Bureau of the Census—undaunted by this imponderable—has estimated that the number of U.S. households will rise by 1975 to between 68 and 70 million. In other words, in the ten years between 1965 and 1975 the number of families will increase by 20 percent, or more. When this and other factors affecting housing demand are taken into account, it appears that in the first half of the seventies we will need to produce dwelling units at the rate of nearly two million a year, almost half again as many as were built in 1967. Needless to say, the demand for many other goods and services will rise in roughly the same proportion. To an economist, there is comfort in this.

Second, it is also comforting that the task of creating job opportunities at a rapid rate is not a new one for the U.S. economy and that it has been accomplished in the past. Civilian employment grew 2 percent a year between 1900 and 1920. It did it again in most of the twenties. In other words, history is on our side. Given a fair chance, our economy should be able to do it again.

What Was Required to Prepare for the Sixties and What This Tells Us about Preparing for the Seventies

Light can be thrown on the question of what it means to have a fair chance to create jobs by recalling some history. Just as we need to think now about the seventies, we were thinking a good deal in the late fifties about the sixties. And what is especially instructive is that we were affected then, just as we are today, by a number of conditions which, unless corrected, would be impediments to success in meeting the problems we could see shaping up. There are parallels here that suggest a chance to learn from experience.

In my judgment, the crucial similarity between then and now is that in the second half of the fifties the economy was experiencing, as it is today, a serious case of cost inflation. In 1956–57, average hourly compensation in manufacturing industries increased 6.1 percent a year, on the average; output per manhour, on the other hand, rose only about 2 percent a year. The result was a rise in labor cost per unit of output for nonfinancial corporations as a whole that in 1956 through 1958 averaged around 5 percent a year.

With this push from the side of costs and with demand rising strongly, there was price inflation, too. In 1956, wholesale prices of industrial commodities rose 4.4 percent and with some lag this eventually showed up in higher consumer prices. In 1957, the consumer price index rose 3.5 percent. Indeed, price increases were so numerous that it became commonplace to speak of an "Age of Inflation."

Whatever may be the attitude of government toward inflation that proceeds at a lesser rate, cost-of-living increases of 3 percent or more a year cannot be ignored for long. Tolerance to inflation is somewhat higher in Western Europe (though Germany is an exception) and in many Latin American economies it is higher still, but it can be taken as a fact of economic and political life in the United States that a kind of flash point will have been reached when annual cost-of-living increases are at or around the 3 percent level. At that point the question is not whether government will respond, but how it will respond.

Although *a priori* reasoning alone should teach us this, recent experience in the United States, in Britain and throughout Western Europe has shown that the only effective response to cost and price inflation is through monetary and fiscal policy, that is, through the so-called indirect measures of

restraint. There has been a good deal of experimenting recently with direct measures—wage and price guidelines in the
United States and more elaborate and often mandatory incomes policies abroad—but experience has shown that antiinflation programs (*i.e.,* stabilization programs, as they are
nowadays referred to in Western Europe) have had to rely
on monetary and fiscal restraint or face failure. The bankruptcy of wage-price guidelines in the United States is a good
example. And Western Europe abounds in illustrations of the
axiom that no incomes policy can work unless supported by
adequate monetary and fiscal measures.

The argument gets more complicated, however, when one
asks whether the indirect measures should be monetary or
fiscal. The answer is that this depends on the circumstances.
Monetary policy can be the more effective of the two in the
sense that it can frustrate fiscal policy; but fiscal policy can
compromise the monetary authorities; that is, it can put them
in a position in which, as a practical matter, they have no
alternative but to expand money supply at an inflationary
rate. Every now and then the monetary authorities are left
in a position like that of the customers of Mr. Hobson, the
livery stable operator of seventeenth-century England whose
policy it was to permit his clients to take any horse they wanted
from the stable so long as they took the one nearest the door.
That is where the Federal Reserve authorities find themselves
today (November 1967): with only a Hobson's choice. Aside
from this one must draw the conclusion that, whatever the
case may be in other circumstances, the key to inflation
control in the United States today is fiscal policy. More
specifically, it is expenditure policy. But we can return to
current events later.

To return to history, no such dilemma faced the Federal
Reserve authorities in the 1950s. Both monetary and fiscal
policy were used to overcome cost and price inflation. These
policies, particularly as applied in the second half of the fifties,
have been criticized on other grounds, but not on the grounds
that they were working at cross-purposes, or were uncoordinated, or that fiscal policy was expecting monetary policy

do more than its fair share of the job. That they were restrictive is true. Increases in money supply, narrowly defined, averaged 1.3 percent a year in the four years January 1954 through December 1957 and were minus 2 percent in late 1957, several months after the peak of the business cycle had been passed. Although the rate of increase rose to plus 5 percent in early 1958, it was an explicit object of policy to avoid leaving a residue of liquidity that would encourage inflation once recovery was achieved and, with that in mind, the rate of money supply increase fell back to 3.5 percent from spring 1958 to spring 1959.

This might have been the end of monetary restraint had it not been for (i) the emergence in 1958–59 of a large deficit in the U.S. balance of international payments; (ii) a concern abroad about the U.S. dollar which reached its point of greatest intensity in the summer of 1960; and (iii) the fact that the inflationary psychology which had started to build up in 1955 was especially virulent in the early months of 1959. This third factor has not had the attention it deserves, perhaps because of the difficulty of making quantitative measurements of such phenomena as public concern over the outlook for prices, but it has been demonstrated by what is termed "content analysis" applied to representative financial writings that, as a factor in public dialogue, inflation was at its highest early in 1959 and receded only slowly over the rest of that year and in 1960. In fact, it was not until 1964 that public concern over inflation, measured this way, got back to where it had been in 1954. In any case, paralleling a nationwide steel strike that lasted almost six months, money supply increase dropped to minus 3 percent and stayed at that level for six months spanning late 1959 and early 1960.

Summarizing the period as a whole, money supply increases (narrowly defined) averaged just under 1 percent a year from December 1956 to December 1960; on a broad definition, annual increases averaged 3.2 percent. However measured, monetary policy as we approached the '60s gave no encouragement to cost and price inflation.

Nor was there any encouragement from fiscal policy. Fed-

eral cash expenditures were held roughly level from mid
1958 to early 1961. As a result, a cash deficit of $8 billion in
calendar 1959 was transformed in one year into a $3.6 bil
lion surplus. This was, of course, a powerful reinforcement
to monetary policy; moreover, by supplying funds to the
capital market, the federal government helped relieve pres
sure on interest rates and made savings more amply avail
able for nongovernment use, especially for home building.

WHAT WERE THE RESULTS OF THESE POLICIES
IN THE LATE NINETEEN-FIFTIES?

Beginning with the Economic Report of the President in
January 1962, these policies have had nothing but criticism
from official sources and, by and large, the verdict of academic
writers on the period has been adverse. But let us look at the
record.

First, by 1959–60 unit production cost had been stabilized.
There was a brief rise in 1960 but this was followed by a
drop and for seven years thereafter cost per unit of produc
tion was broadly stable. In short, 1958 was the turning point
from cost inflation to cost stability.

It is sometimes argued that less restrictive monetary and
fiscal policies would have favored a higher rate of utilization
of industrial capacity and that higher utilization, by yielding
higher output per manhour, would have stabilized unit cost
at a higher growth rate. There is room for controversy as to
what might have been the effect on productivity, but it can
be said with some certainty that an expansive monetary and
fiscal policy would have accelerated labor cost increases—and
this was the principal economic problem in those years. What
the critics of economic policy in the late 1950s have to an
swer is whether they would prefer to have started the 1960s
with cost per unit of labor input rising 6 percent a year or
at the 4 percent level actually reached.

If preference is for 4 percent—and how could it be other
wise—then the question is how 4 percent might better ha

been achieved. On this point, some critics write as if they believe it should have been brought about by systematic government intervention in wage and price determination. But, as already argued, it is very doubtful that this could have been achieved in the absence of monetary and fiscal policies which, in degree of restraint, were close to those actually pursued. Furthermore, there was absolutely no disposition among policymakers at that time to seek a solution through direct intervention. On the contrary, it was an explicit aim of policy to achieve its purposes without recourse to such measures. It was repeatedly pointed out in official messages that it was a responsibility—shared between labor and management —to keep labor cost increases in line with productivity improvements. But there was no attempt, and this was not an oversight, to try to achieve this result by specifying precise numerical guidelines for wage increases or by direct intervention into the price system. It was the studied purpose of government in this period to play its role under the Employment Act without recourse to direct controls. And there is a good reason for his having been so. Basically, all our freedoms— civil, political, religious, economic and intellectual—depend on power being diffused. So long as power is diffused, no one's freedom is in danger. On the other hand, anything that tends to concentrate power, whether it be in government or elsewhere, threatens freedom in all its parts. Indeed, at the very core of the democratic tradition is an understanding that this is so. Such an understanding has little tolerance for direct government intervention in wages and prices.

The *second* beneficial result was that price levels were stabilized. The implicit GNP price deflator, which is the broadest index of price changes we have, had been rising 3 to 3½ percent a year in 1956–57; in 1959–60 its increases were only 1.6 percent a year and they continued at this low rate until 1965. The index of wholesale prices was stabilized in 1959 and stayed that way for six years. And the index of consumer prices, which had been rising 3½ percent a year in 1956–57, was stable from mid-1958 to mid-1959 and for six years thereafter rose less than 1½ percent a year. Thus, 1959 was the end of one chapter, at least, of the "Age of Inflation."

The *third* result was that the inflationary psychology epitomized in the expression "Age of Inflation" was eliminated. This is clearly visible in the content analysis of financial writing, already referred to.

Fourth, because policy in the late 1950s had an impact on profit margins and, thereby, on investment expenditures, it also had an impact on the rate of economic growth. It is not surprising that this should have been the case, since indirect controls typically retard price increases more quickly than they retard increases in costs. After all, the market power of organized labor is greater than the market power of any one business concern. In manufacturing industries, profit margins dropped from about 10.2 percent of sales in 1955 to 8 percent in 1960. This had the effect not only of dampening the incentive to make capital investments but of limiting the capability of industry to do so. Undistributed corporate profits, which econometric studies tell us are a major factor affecting investment expenditures, were $3.3 billion lower in 1960 than in 1955.

Actually, however, the impact on employment was substantially less than might be thought. The unemployment rate in 1957–60 averaged 5.5 and reached 6.7 in 1961, significantly higher than the 4.2 average for 1953 through 1956, but not much higher than in 1962 through 1966, when it averaged 4.9. Moreover, in making these comparisons, it must be borne in mind that in the first half of the 1950s unemployment rates were affected by war in Korea, which added two million men to the armed forces, and in the 1960s the war in Vietnam has added three-quarters of a million men to the armed forces.

Fifth, and finally—and this is a point only now coming to be acknowledged—the cost and price stability that was established by 1959–60 made it possible, as the decade of the sixties began, to adopt an expansive monetary policy with minimum of inflationary risk. And this is precisely the turn that policy took. In 1961 through 1965, money supply increases on a narrow definition averaged 3.5 percent a year; on a broad definition the annual average was 8 percent. Recall that from December 1956 to December 1960 the comparable figures are 0.8 and 3.2 percent.

There was less difference between the two periods in expenditure policy but, in its total impact, fiscal policy also turned strongly expansive: whereas the cash budget achieved a significant surplus in calendar 1960, there were uninterrupted deficits averaging $5.4 billion annually in 1961 through 1965.

As the decade began, the economy responded to expansionism. On the average, GNP grew in 1961–65 by 4.7 percent a year, in real terms; civilian employment increased by 5.3 million jobs in the five years; unemployment dropped by 500 thousand; and the unemployment ratio was reduced from 5.5 to 4.5.

This was the U.S. growth miracle of the first half of the sixties. Those who term themselves "new economists" have a theory of how it happened. It all happened, so the theory goes, because a policy of restraint was replaced by an immensely imaginative and enormously enlightened policy of expansionism. It is the thesis of this essay, on the other hand, that the U.S. growth miracle of 1961–65 occurred because monetary and fiscal policy in the late 1950s established the conditions of cost and price stability—the preconditions, if you will—that made it possible to turn to expansionism. And here my hat is off: these conditions of cost and price stability were broadly maintained from 1961 to early 1965 as the economy accelerated.

How Economic Balance Was Lost

Unfortunately, the next chapter to the story is a less happy one. It concerns what began to happen in 1965 and continued thereafter. It is a story of expansionism that was pushed too hard and continued too long. Federal cash expenditures in calendar 1966 were 18 percent higher than in the previous year, even though reported expenditures were held down by sales of participation certificates. There was a further significant increase in calendar 1967 and early in the year it was acknowledged officially that a truly massive budget deficit was in prospect.

At the same time, monetary policy became almost unbelievably expansive. By mid-1967, money supply narrowly defined was rising 9 percent a year; broadly defined it was rising at a 13½ percent annual rate.

Naturally, with resource utilization already high, this combination of monetary and fiscal expansionism caused a resumption of cost and price inflation. Labor costs were rising in the first half of 1967 by 6 percent a year, on the average; and in October 1967 a pacesetting labor contract was signed in the auto industry involving annual labor cost increases of at least 6½ percent. Prices, too, were on the move. As 1967 draws to a close, the GNP implicit price deflator is rising 3.6 percent a year and the consumer price index is rising 4 percent, annualized. As a policy, the "new economics" is in total disarray.

How to Regain a Posture Appropriate for Meeting the Problems of the Seventies

What is tragic about all this is that massive budget deficits, inflationary money supply increases, cost and price inflation, century-high interest rates, and an increasing deficit in the balance of international payments are not a posture from which to attack the formidable problems of the seventies. Imagine if we had entered the sixties in such a state of imbalance. Clearly, we must get into a better stance: the question is, how to do it?

Fortunately, the answer is clear. The key to our over-all economic problem is fiscal policy; and the key to fiscal policy is expenditure policy. It is just as simple as that.

RECOMMENDATIONS

What this means for policy is equally clear. To put it succinctly, there is need now for a stabilization program:

(1) At the earliest possible moment the President should lay out a budget under which aggregate cash expenditures would be held through fiscal 1970 to an amount not appreciably more, if more at all, than what is expected for fiscal 1968. If defense considerations permit lower expenditures, the task will be far easier; but what is essential now is a lid on over-all spending.

(2) With a lid on spending, Congress should promptly enact a temporary tax increase in the amount requested by the President.

(3) A joint statement should be made by the President and the leadership of his party in Congress that it is their intention to hold fiscal policy on a line that will bring the federal cash budget to balance not later than fiscal 1970. A ceiling on aggregate expenditures plus the revenue growth that comes automatically with the economy's expansion would close the budget gap by fiscal 1970, at the latest.

(4) On the understanding that a budget-balancing fiscal policy will be pursued, the Federal Reserve authorities should make it clear that they propose gradually to reduce annual money supply increases from the current 9 percent to a level consistent with stable prices. It would help, also, if they made it clear that, with the budget moving to balance, they will not repeat the 1966 performance in which money supply moved abruptly from a 6 percent rate of increase to no increase at all.

(5) Without recourse to the arithmetical illustrations that led to failure in 1965, the Council of Economic Advisers should indicate what can safely be the maximum limit of annual labor cost increases if cost and price stability

is to be re-established. The fact that current labor cost increases are twice as high as what is consistent with cost stability should not deter the Council from making a completely frank statement on this crucial subject.

(6) The President should make it clear that price stability is to be achieved without recourse to direct wage and price controls. He should also disavow the use of direct controls in the markets for capital and credit.

(7) The Secretary of the Treasury should redefine the government's program for eliminating the balance of payments deficit.

THE BENEFICIAL EFFECTS OF A NEW STABILIZATION PROGRAM

The benefits that would accrue from such a program may be summarized as follows:

- It would dispel the spreading fear that federal finances are out of control.
- It would allay the related fear that we stand in risk of financial crisis.
- It would prevent the return of a full-fledged inflationary psychology.
- It would help prevent further escalation of interest rates.
- It would save the U.S. economy from the mischievous effect of direct controls over wages, prices, profits, capital and credit.
- It would assure confidence in the U.S. dollar abroad.
- It would avoid any complication from the side of the United States of Britain's problems with the pound sterling.
- Finally, it would in due course create the precondition that must be established if we are adequately to meet the challenges of the 1970s. Indeed, it is only on the basis of such conditions that we can attack with any hope of success the whole long agenda in the forefront of public concern today: the war on poverty, urban renewal; air and water

pollution; education; health services; urban transportation, *etc., etc.* And it is only on the basis of such conditions that we have even a ghost of a chance of providing comfortable, attractive, convenient homes and interesting and productive jobs for the uncommonly large generation of young men and young women who will shortly be looking for them.

These are not tasks in which we can afford to fail.

THE NEED FOR BALANCE
by Robert H. Michel

ROBERT H. MICHEL is currently serving his sixth term
as a Representative to Congress from the 18th District
of Illinois. A graduate of Bradley University as an Economics major, Mr. Michel was assistant to his predeces-
sor, Congressman Harold Velde, from 1949 through
1956. Mr. Michel is a member of the Appropriations
Committee, serving on the Subcommittees of Labor,
Health, Education and Welfare, and ranking Republican
on Agriculture. He has been a frequent participant in a
variety of Republican Party activities.

There would seem to be two major policy approaches to the
interconnected problems of balance of payments and fiscal-
monetary disturbances. One approach may be called "balance
of payments management" of the kind that is consistent with
our major economic objectives. This is not, however, the balance of payments prescription favored by the Johnson administration. The other approach focuses on economic disturbances which originate in fiscal and monetary policy and
the overriding need to build a base for expansion in the future that rests solidly on real price stability.

BALANCE OF PAYMENTS "MANAGEMENT"

The present administration, to be sure, has been heavily
engaged in a kind of "balance of payments management."
But it involves managing things in the wrong way. It is
wrong because the so-called "management" emphasizes bu-

reaucratic controls rather than tested and powerful adjustment forces of the free market. I submit that we have had enough ineffective controls in the form of back-door dollar devaluation (interest equalization tax) and restrictions on business investment (deceptively packaged as "voluntary" ceilings on the investment decisions of business). These are wrong ways of dealing with our balance of payments problems for the simple reason that once controls are introduced men are encouraged to find leaks, which are plugged by government only with new controls, and so on around an ever-widening circle of restraints on free men. As the relevant historical record clearly shows, the undesirable effects can only be distortions of production, reduced efficiency, a hard-to-recover loss in international competitive standing, and the eventual development of general economic weakness that can be corrected only by way of painful and unpopular measures. Clearly, much is at stake in the current debate over how best to deal with America's balance of payments problems. We had better be sure we take the right route.

Describing such a route is not difficult if we adhere firmly to the widely accepted major objectives of economic policy. In the first place, we all want the American economy to operate at high levels of employment. Second, we want a good rate of economic growth. Third, we seek free and open economic relations among the trading nations of the Free World, which means above all that currencies must be freely convertible rather than exchangeable only under cumbersome, bureaucratic, efficiency-stifling, and competition-debilitating licensing arrangements. And finally, we want as stable a pattern of exchange rates as is consistent with attainment of the three preceding and more basic objectives.

Fortunately, few of us in America differ substantially with respect to our primary economic objectives. But we certainly do differ as to the best means by which they may be achieved.

Consider first my number one economic objective—high or "full" employment. Most of us are committed to this goal, but we are also committed to the avoidance of inflation as we strive to maintain a high job level nationally. For inflation is economic sickness; it represents hidden and haphazard taxation; it impairs economic discipline; and it lowers efficiency by encouraging waste and extravagance.

Now the sad part about our recent conduct of economic policy is that we have adopted all manner of national programs which are inflation-breeding. That we have done so in the name of the very fine objective of high employment, focusing on jobs in part to combat poverty, does not alter the fact that we have been openly flirting with inflation. Concretely, we have tolerated budget-making without adequate safeguards against ballooning, inflation-generating deficits. To proceed in such a way, and then, when inflation stares us in the face, to appeal for higher taxes so as to deflate over-all demand in the country, is to earn the indignation of most Americans. The reason is that our people then suffer in two ways: The government's economic policies hit them with unnecessarily high prices and the government, on top of that, literally soaks them with higher taxes.

Now as to the question of the money supply, the record is abundantly clear on this score. We have expanded the volume of bank credit at a dizzying pace, and done so even as our leaders publicly expressed concern about rapidly rising prices and what might be done to restrain price movements by way of increased taxes. We have continued nondefense spending at extremely high levels while pressing for retrenchment in private expenditure. Why is it that the administration has so often made moves with its right hand without knowing what it was doing with its left?

As a nation we should always fight inflation even if there are no balance of payments problems. Our international payments difficulties, important as they happen to be, are really only an additional reason for wanting to deal vigorously and effectively with the central, dominant inflation danger.

Do we really have to risk inflation in order to maintain high job levels? Certainly not in the foreseeable future and probably never if we first discard the depression day thinking of the administration policymakers and secondly, give really serious thought to inflation-free methods of coping with hardcore unemployment that have been talked about for years by respected men in and out of the Congress.

For example, a number of us in the Congress have introduced the Human Investment Act as the non-inflationary way to full employment. In his book, *87 Million Jobs,* published in 1962, my distinguished colleague from Missouri, Congressman Tom Curtis, was among the first public officials to attach key importance to job training and retraining and in general the upgrading of jobs, as contrasted to unrestrained government spending, as the best way to reach our national employment objectives. It is still not too late to insist that the Curtis variables be allowed to weave their effect on the American economic fabric. By doing so, incidentally, we will do more than anything else simultaneously to solve our balance of payments problem. In this connection, I should remind the reader that a major reason why most foreigners have confidence in the U.S. dollar, and demonstrate this by holding substantial dollar balances instead of converting into gold, is our long-term record of *relative* price stability, and I would underscore the "relative." If we jeopardize such stability by pursuing mistaken policies in Washington, we may wind up having to devalue the dollar as Britain has been forced to do recently. In short, the reasons are legion why it is in our best interest to avoid inflation.

Let me hasten to add that there is highly respected economic authority in support of a Curtis-type approach. I refer to Britain's Sir John Hicks, one of the world's most eminent economists. We in America can profit from his diagnosis of the serious inflation and employment problem in England (which was at the root of last year's devaluation of the pound). The most important point made in his recent work (*After the Boom: Thought on the 1966 Economic Crisis,* London, Institute of Economic Affairs, 1966), is that an economy's "ceiling on growth" represents a limit set not by forces (mainly easy spending) over which the government has much control but by fundamental factors that are hardly responsive to government policy. The first of these basic forces he calls "the rate of improvement in direct labour efficiency," while his second and third are, respectively, the rate of technical progress and the public's willingness to save. Hicks' use of this framework of analysis may well suggest a new approach to economic problems in America.

Suppose an economy is operating below its ceiling. Then a restrained spending approach may help to lift economic activity to the ceiling level. But, Sir John emphasizes, when an economy is bumping against its ceiling, as Britain's was "for years on end" while the government and leading economic advisers thought that "something could still be done by the easy [spending] way," the nation is heading for the worst kind of economic trouble—inflation. The lesson for the United States is obvious, it seems to me. For years now, we have been operating at or very close to our economic ceiling. This has been admitted officially, for example, in terms of the need to avoid "overheating" our economy. Yet the administration has continued to administer spending medicine as if we were well below the ceiling, hoping thereby to beef up employment at least a little more. But our employment problem is not at all one of the deep depression kind. There is not much scope for increasing the employment percentage, which has been very high for years. Our big job, in Hicks' words, is one of increasing the "direct labour efficiency" of those who are least skilled. But this is essentially the Curtis thesis. Is it not high time that we learned our lesson on this score?

It may pay to develop this line of reasoning a bit further to take account of recent intergovernmental (IMF) agreements which promise augmented "international liquidity." This concept, much discussed in high financial circles, is no simple one, to be sure. But disagreement among the experts suggests that the last word on the subject has not yet been pronounced.

As is known, the IMF's conference in Rio in September 1967 set in motion machinery which will generate annually 1 to 2 billion dollars of new international reserve assets ("paper gold") for use by treasuries and central banks the world over. A part of such reserves, admittedly, will be needed to support a growing structure of international trade and investment. But how much will be used in fact to paper over balance of payments deficits, which in a fundamental sense may only reflect the national inflations going on around the world? What are the people in these nations really in for? Are the governments merely trying to find an easier way to "live with" inflation, while people carry the burden of escalating prices? The risk of ballooning international "liquidity" is that problems of inflation may get bigger and tougher rather than smaller and less disturbing to us all.

It is for reasons such as these that I am attracted by the wisdom of Professor Haberler's important rule: if each nation keeps its economy well (i.e., competitively) adjusted in terms of the assortment and prices of the goods and services it sells abroad, there will be no need for greatly augmented international liquidity. Once again, we see that our main goal must be to avoid inflation, for inflation is far and away the principal source of maladjusted economies in today's trading world.

Excess Domestic Liquidity

Could it be that we are in danger of being drowned in liquidity? Our balance of payments focus, developed above, has shown that the world—operating through the IMF—may soon be generating such a large volume of liquid international means of payment that many nations will be running the risk of drowning efficiency, and flooding business management and labor with demands for goods and services which are beyond the capability of normally enterprising businesses to satisfy at stable prices.

There is another, parallel danger—this one of domestic U.S. origin. Professor Saulnier warns us of the risk of a domestically generated "residue of liquidity" that could thwart the realization of a major domestic objective in the years ahead. This is the goal of goals: heavy job creation to satisfy the employment needs of the wave of recruits to our labor force.

I certainly share Professor Saulnier's guarded optimism as

to the nation's ability to generate the necessary jobs. We've done it before, and we can do it again. But can we do it smoothly and in a manner which makes use of our greatest national strengths? Can we do it without impairing our free institutions? Are we sure that we have learned enough about the underlying requirements or preconditions? Cost and price stability in the remaining years of the 1960s are the real preconditions for job-generating monetary expansion with little inflationary risk in the 1970s, as Saulnier sees it. Before the 1960s our money supply in the broad sense increased moderately, setting the stage for impressive economic growth. The contrast with recent years is noteworthy. Instead of expanding moderately, the money supply has grown at over three times the rate which prevailed before the 1960s. No wonder we see inflationary dangers all about us, the threat of so-called "anti-inflation," initiative-stifling controls, and so forth.

Extended booms have a habit of inducing slippage in efficiency. (As an example, the recently negotiated autoworkers' contracts call for a 6 to 7 percent wage increase with only a 3 percent productivity increase.) Labor tends to operate flat-footedly rather than on its toes; managements develop laxity as nearly everything sells easily; governments become bigger and more unwieldy; costs drift upward and upward. The process goes on until the Nation loses out to more vigorous foreign rivals. This is essentially what has been happening for years in Britain, in previously vigorous Continental Europe, and may well happen in a few years' time in Japan. If it happens in the U.S. too, we may well lose the springboard of price stability which is absolutely necessary if we are to be able to employ fruitfully all the newcomers to the labor force that will hit us in the 1970s.

The key to our basic problem is fiscal policy, and within that area the government's expenditure policy. Easy government spending is not the answer to the economic and job challenges of the 1970s, any more than it was the answer to Britain's problems of the 1960s. We must not get bogged down in expensive government programs of all kinds which assume that we are operating our economy well below its ceiling when in fact we are bumping hard against it. If we pursue such programs, we will see our national strengths diverted along the wrong paths; we will see the American economy's productive ceiling caving in rather than being pushed continuously higher. Then, no amount of fiscal or monetary expansion will be able to deliver on job growth for the 1970s, in such a way as to sustain high efficiency and thus an assured competitive posture in tough world markets.

We must hold the line on the federal government's total cash expenditures, so that by fiscal 1970 they will amount to no more than the level attained in fiscal 1968. The stretch-out of non-defense spending seems to be critical if this goal is to be reached. Let me add that stretching out expenditure programs should take precedence over a temporary tax increase.

A second requirement is in the field of money. I favor the Federal Reserve System slowing down the increase in the money supply so that we can stabilize prices.

Thirdly, now that we have had virtually full employment for years on end, neither fiscal policy nor monetary policy should be the main devices for coping with hard-core unemployment. Once high job levels are attained, we should not try to lift ourselves skill-wise by our spending bootstraps. The training and re-training emphasis needs to come to the fore. As Sir John Hicks has so wisely stated, the skill level—as a major element in the "rate of improvement in direct labour efficiency"—is a force which is hardly responsive at all to government spending as such. It follows that U.S. domestic economic policy should get in tune with the times, rather than being mired in thinking born of a depression condition that is a whole generation behind us.

Fourthly, we should assign highest priority to upgrading the skills of our least skilled people by way of on-the-job training in the most flexible and tested environment we possess—private industry. We spur growth-inducing private investment with the "investment credit." Why not try adapting the same device to effect a speedier upgrading of those on the lowest rung of the skill ladder?

Finally, while engaged in the job of upgrading the least skilled should we not review minimum-wage policy? It is now widely agreed among economists that we deny critically important trial jobs to many youths of low skills by establishing wage minima which are above the value of the contributions which beginners could make to employers' output. Is it not time that we eliminated a cause of joblessness, and thus reduced the excessive—inflation-risking—demands made upon fiscal and monetary stimuli?

Chapter 11

OVERSIGHT AND THE NEED
FOR CONGRESSIONAL REFORM

CONGRESS' NEGLECTED FUNCTION
by John F. Bibby

JOHN F. BIBBY is Associate Professor of Political Science
and the Assistant Chairman of the Department of Political
Science at the University of Wisconsin, Milwaukee. Professor Bibby received a B.S. degree with highest honors
from Wisconsin State College, La Crosse in 1956, a M.A.
degree from the University of Illinois in 1957, and his
doctorate from the University of Wisconsin in 1963. Professor Bibby is the co-author of *On Capitol Hill: Studies
in the Legislative Process,* published in 1967 and has recently completed a study of the politics of national convention arrangements and finances. During the summer
of 1967 he was a Research Associate at the House Republican Conference of the U. S. House of Representatives. He served as a Fellow in Government at the
Brookings Institution, Washington, D.C., in 1961–62.

The administration of a statute is, properly speaking,
an extension of the legislative process.

David B. Truman,
The Governmental Process

As never before Congress faces the truth—that its laws
are not self-executing.

Theodore J. Lowi,
Legislative Politics, U.S.A.

Democratic government requires that the governed have a
high degree of control over the governors—that is, political

leaders should exercise power in a responsible manner. The rise of the modern service state accompanied by a vastly expanded role for administrators in the formulation of public policy has created new problems for a nation which wishes to maintain a responsible power relationship between the rulers and the ruled. The problems in which government is involved now are so complicated and the programs and their administrators are so numerous and varied that the task of insuring accountability for administrative acts has become fantastically more complex than it was at the beginning of this century when government's role was much more restricted.

Among the serious problems which the modern service state has created is the danger stemming from excessive reliance on administrator-specialists in the shaping of public policy. Specialists are, of course, indispensable in a complicated and scientific world. However, as Lewis A. Dexter has pointed out, critical decisions are often made by specialists who have "the power of government behind them, and who are easily able to out-argue and overawe those actually affected by their decisions."[1] Often their decisions are the right ones in the long run, but they are also too often clumsily handled and many people are unnecessarily hurt in the process. This occurs because specialists and administrators have not raised such basic questions as: "Is it really necessary to do this thing in the way that hurts these people in this fashion?" or "Have these possible boomerang side-products of the program been adequately considered, and have you figured out how you will deal with them if they occur?"[2] These questions are not asked as often as they should be because the specialist usually acquires a vested interest in his programs. He wants his programs put into operation without outside interference. In addition, specialists are normally "recruited from a rather limited segment of society and have been unconsciously indoctrinated in a whole set of assumptions and values which

[1] Lewis Anthony Dexter, "Check and Balance Today: What Does It Mean For Congress and Congressmen?", in Alfred De-Grazia (ed.) Congress: The First Branch of Government (Washington: American Enterprise Institute, 1966), p. 88.
[2] Ibid.

may not be shared by people affected by their decisions."[3]
If such questions as those noted above go unasked, responsible government is in danger, and the bureaucratic state may take its place.

The modern service state with its constantly expanding array of programs has caused other problems for a nation in the quest for a political order that is not only responsible, but *responsive* to human needs. Recently, thoughtful observers have stressed the need for continuing and intensive evaluations of governmental programs if progress in meeting human needs is to be achieved. For example, Daniel Patrick Moynihan writing in the wake of the urban riots of 1967 made the following comment concerning social welfare programs:

> In our desire to maintain public confidence in such programs, we have tended to avoid evidence of poor results . . . These failings have been accompanied by a formidable capacity for explaining them away.[4]

If the situation which Moynihan describes is allowed to continue, then any hope of either responsible or responsive government is bleak indeed.

There are those who look with dismay upon the modern service state and its manifold activities and functions. But the truth is that the mammoth service state is not going to disappear. Nor is it feasible to suggest (or hope) in a complex and interdependent world that administrators can be stripped or severely restricted in their exercise of discretionary authority. Rather, existing institutions must be adapted to the world of the 1970s if a government which is truly accountable and responsive is to be achieved. To this end, thoughtful students have turned increasingly to the Congress as the institution with the best potential for controlling the Executive and an expanding bureaucracy. Witness the following statements by prominent political scientists:

. . . it may well be that the most abiding role of Congress

[3] *Ibid.*
[4] Daniel P. Moynihan, "White Blindness Lamented," *The Washington Post,* August 6, 1967, pp. B1, B5.

in the years to come will be *its service as a place where
the needs of the bureaucracy are continually being balanced against the prevailing special interests in the community*. We call this our insurance against an irresponsible administration.[5]

. . . Congress must help to supply dissonance or opposition in public decision-making. One of the most important
commodities Congress can provide is an institutional base
for alternative viewpoints and criticisms. Thus, steps
should be taken to increase the probability that Congress
will act independently—that it will possess both the inclination and the influence to function as an autonomous
voice in the affairs of state.[6]

Congress is the central institution of the American
democratic republic. Unless it functions well and powerfully, much more so than it has in the past, the road to
a bureaucratic state . . . will be opened up. Without a
strong Congress the basic structures of voluntary associations, federalism, and autonomous enterprise will tend
to dissolve into centralism. Without a strong Congress,
the major problems of the country will be handled in
ways that will become excessively majoritarian, suppressive of the American ideal of individuality.[7]

Congressional challenges to policy [of the Executive]
. . . at least force the Administration to confront the
issue again and to articulate a defense for its course.[8]

[5] Theodore J. Lowi (ed.), *Legislative Politics U.S.A.*, 2d Ed
(Boston: Little, Brown, 1965), pp. xviii–xix.
[6] Roger H. Davidson, David M. Kovenock, and Michael K
O'Leary, *Congress in Crisis: Politics and Congressional Reform*
(Belmont, Cal., Wadsworth, 1966), p. 175.
[7] Alfred DeGrazia, "The New Model of Congress", in De
Grazia (ed.), *op. cit.*, p. 7.
[8] Samuel F. Huntington, *The Common Defense* (New York
Columbia University Press, 1961), p. 146.

A particularly compelling argument for the point of view that Congress is in the best position to evaluate and control administrators is that of Lewis A. Dexter. He argues that a Member of Congress is in such a position because he is forced as the *"political* man in American society" to be aware of many different concerns and interests. In addition, Congress is the one institution whose Members, as one of their duties, must take "seriously and respectfully the complaints and problems of citizens." Congressmen are also in a position to benefit politically from making an issue of the way policy is being made within the bureaucracy.[9] In addition, as Roland Young has pointed out, the Congressman has an electoral stake in effective administrative policy. Young has written:

> Any Congressman ignores at his own peril the manner in which the government administers, or who administers it, or the costs involved, for there is, in fact, a close inter-relationship between the manner in which the government operates (especially in highly sensitive, politically volatile areas) and the election of members to office.[10]

In its formal declarations of policy, the Congress has not been blind to concerns about insuring responsible and responsive administration. In its two postwar excursions into legislative reform it has stressed the importance of legislative oversight of administration. The 1946 Legislative Re-organization Act prescribed as the duty of each standing committee the "exercise of continuous watchfulness of the execution by administrative agencies concerned of any laws, the subject matter of which is within the jurisdiction of such committees." The 1966 report of the Joint Committee on the Organization of Congress also stressed the importance of effective oversight.[11]

Increasingly and in seeming response to the widely held

[9] Dexter, *op. cit.,* pp. 88–89.
[10] Roland Young, *The American Congress* (New York: Harper and Bros. 1958), p. 167.
[11] U. S. Congress, Joint Committee on the Organization of Congress, 89th Cong., 2d Sess., 1966, Senate Report 1414, pp. 23–25.

views concerning the need for effective legislative oversight of administration, scholars have accorded the oversight activities of Congress a more prominent place. A standard declaration contained in textbooks on American government or the legislative process is to list oversight as one of the primary functions of Congress. Some even go so far as to suggest that it is the principal activity of the Congress.[12]

But what really goes on under the label of legislative oversight? Unfortunately there is no definitive answer because surprisingly little research has been done on this oft mentioned congressional function. Such studies of congressional committees (the principal agents for carrying out the mandate to engage in oversight) as exist point to great variability from committee to committee in their relations with agencies under their respective jurisdictions. Some committees have been aggressive overseers. For example, according to Green and Rosenthal, the Joint Committee on Atomic Energy has evolved into a "co-participant in executive decision-making" that makes its impact on the Atomic Energy Commission mainly by non-legislative means.[13]

Other committees, for example, the Senate Banking and Currency Committee, have been found to be quite inactive in oversight because of the following factors: (1) the chairman and his style of leadership, (2) committee staffing practices, (3) the committee's subcommittee structure, (4) the recruitment patterns of the committee, and (5) the work orientation of committee members.[14] Seymour Scher found in his study of House Education and Labor Committee oversight of the National Labor Relations Board that the Committee members were primarily concerned about Board policy

[12] Samuel P. Huntington, "Congressional Responses to the Twentieth Century," in David B. Truman (ed.), *The Congress and America's Future* (New York: Prentice-Hall, 1965), pp. 22–25.

[13] Harold P. Green and Alan Rosenthal, *Government and the Atom: The Integration of Powers* (New York: Atherton, 1963), p. 268.

[14] John F. Bibby, "Committee Characteristics and Legislative Oversight of Administration," *Midwest Journal of Political Science*, X (February, 1966), pp. 78–98.

as it affected their constituents and that members had little sense of over-all agency policy.[15]

In his comprehensive analysis of the appropriations process, Richard Fenno noted the following tendency on the part of the House Appropriations Committee with regard to oversight:

> The Committee does not, as a rule, probe deeply into well-established programs with well-established bases of support. What it normally does is to check carefully what the agency did with the increase it was given last year and inquire into the purposes for which the current increase is to be used.[16]

Fenno also noted a tendency for the Committee members to question administrative personnel about matters which were familiar and readily comprehensible to the members—though these matters might not be of critical importance.[17]

Another pattern of committee-agency relations is for the committee to act as a protector and guardian of an administrative agency under its jurisdiction. Throughout most of the history of the Small Business Administration, the Senate Small Business Committee has adopted this protector role *vis-à-vis* the SBA.[18]

In an attempt to gain more of a comprehensive picture of the actual state of legislative oversight of administration within the Congress, a survey was conducted in 1967 of standing committees in the House of Representatives. That study

---

[15] Seymour Scher, "Congressional Committee Members as Independent Agency Overseers: A Case Study, *American Political Science Review,* LIV (December, 1960), pp. 911–20.

[16] Richard Fenno, *The Power of the Purse* (Boston: Little, Brown, 1966), p. 318.

[17] *Ibid.*

[18] John F. Bibby, "Legislative Oversight of Administration: A Case Study of Congressional Committee" (unpublished Ph.D. dissertation, University of Wisconsin, Madison, Wisconsin, 1963), Chap. 6.

yielded the following conclusions concerning the extent and nature of House oversight activities.

1. With few exceptions, House committees do not undertake comprehensive, continuing, and systematic reviews of policies and performances of administrative agencies and departments under their jurisdictions in spite of the explicit provisions for "continuing watchfulness" in the Legislative Reorganization Act of 1946. This holds true even on some committees which have established special oversight subcommittees. In one case, such an oversight subcommittee has no staff, holds scant meetings, and its only use in the 90th Congress was a forum for the processing of minor and inconsequential legislation.

2. Such oversight as exists tends to be sporadic, selective and episodic[19] in response to the specific complaints of interest groups, constituents, newsmen, and occasionally administrators. Oversight may also be stimulated by a scandal or tragedy such as the Apollo space disaster which caused the normally passive House Science and Aeronautics Committee to investigate the Apollo program.

3. In a few committees, there is careful surveillance of a particular agency under the committee's jurisdiction while the performance of other agencies is largely ignored. For example, Special Subcommittee on the Federal-Aid Highway Program of the Public Works Committee has overseen federal highway programs in a nonpartisan, continuous, and comprehensive manner. Other programs under the Committee's jurisdiction, however, have not been watched as carefully. This selectivity in committee oversight activities re-

[19] Seymour Scher has also noted that the "typical pattern of committee review of regulatory agencies is . . . one of no review at all for long periods of time. But these occasionally are interrupted." See his, "Conditions for Legislative Control," *Journal of Politics,* XV (August, 1963), p. 540.

flects the extensive jurisdictions which most committees have, the inadequacy of staff resources for oversight purposes, and the natural tendency of Members
of Congress to allocate their scarce resources of time,
energy, good will, and staff on subject matter fields
and activities they deem important. Other particularly
important factors in determining which agencies and
departments will receive oversight attention are the interests and concerns of the respective committee chairmen.

4. Committees normally try at the time they consider
   new legislation proposed by the Executive or renewals
   of existing programs to evaluate administrative performance. The pressures and volume of legislative
   work, however, make it difficult for a committee to
   utilize these opportunities adequately when Congress
   has maximum leverage over the Executive. The House
   Education and Labor Committee, for example, in recent years, has handled a heavy burden of new legislation much of which was initially passed with short
   term authorizations. The continuing pressure to process and renew legislation has made it extremely difficult for either the members or staff to do any sort of
   thorough evaluation of existing programs.

5. Oversight is discouraged because members at times
   believe it would be harmful to their careers, or certainly lacking in political pay-offs. There is, for example, reluctance to investigate and evaluate well-
   established programs, which the members themselves
   have consistently supported for fear of political embarrassment. There is also a reluctance on the part of
   members of the President's party in particular to engage in oversight activities which could prove disquieting to the Administration. This is coupled with
   a fear of reprisal from the Administration.

6. Most committees have insufficient staff to do a
   thorough oversight job. In addition, the zealousness
   of staff personnel is often limited by professional and

friendship ties to their counterparts in the administrative agencies with whom they must constantly work. Staff effectiveness in oversight is also limited by the lack of support Members of Congress often manifest in such staff work.

7. While endorsing the importance of legislative oversight most Members of Congress are not highly motivated to perform the task.[20] One clear manifestation of this is the often superficial treatment given General Accounting Office reports by the various standing committees.[21]

8. The extent and effectiveness of congressional oversight is limited by the fact that committees depend heavily on the various agencies and departments under their respective jurisdictions for information concerning administrative policies and performance. Committee members complain that the Executive divulges voluntarily only that information which it wants made known. This results in situations such as that reported in the summer of 1967 concerning Department of Housing and Urban Development implementation of a major amendment to the urban renewal programs. The administrative implementation rendered the amendment ineffective, but the author of the amendment was not informed of HUD's policy directives by the Department and had to learn of them through third parties.[22]

[20] On this point, see Cornelius P. Cotter, "Legislative Oversight," in DeGrazia (ed.), *op. cit.*, p. 36. On the failure of state legislators to define oversight as a principal legislative role, see John C. Wahlke, Heinz Eulau, William Buchanan, and LeRoy C. Ferguson, *The Legislative System* (New York: Wiley, 1962), p. 136.

[21] For further commentary on the failure of Congress to utilize the GAO, see Robert Ash Wallace, *Congressional Control of Federal Spending* (Detroit: Wayne State University, 1960), pp. 155–60.

[22] Rowland Evans and Robert Novak, "Inside Report: Hedging on Low-Cost Housing," *The Washington Post*, August 7, 1967, p. A5.

These findings concerning House committee oversight would appear to give further substance to the theories of Seymour Scher, who has stated that the decision of Congressmen to become involved in oversight activity is determined by the following strategic considerations.[23]

1. . . . Congressmen tend to see opportunities for greater rewards in things they value in legislative and and constituent-service activity than from participation in oversight activity.
2. Committee members tend to view the agencies as impenetrable mazes and to believe that any serious effort at penetrating them poses hazards for the inexpert Congressman which outweigh any conceivable gain for him.
3. Congressmen who have established mutually rewarding relationships with agency people tend to be reluctant to initiate or become actively engaged in a close review of that agency's affairs.
4. Congressmen tend to view their personal contacts with the agencies as more efficient than committee investigations for serving constituent and group needs.
5. Committee members will tend to avoid agency review if they expect it will provoke costly reprisals from powerful economic interests regulated by the agencies.
6. Congressmen who perceive that gains to themselves can be had by loyalty to the President can be expected to avoid close examination of the performance of agency officials appointed by the Executive.
7. As committee routines become fixed, for all the foregoing reasons, in ways that make no regular provision for agency oversight, in the absence of powerful external stimuli, they tend to resist change.

Much more detailed studies of legislative oversight are needed—particularly comparative studies of different committees—to project a complete picture of oversight behavior in

[23] Scher, "Conditions for Legislative Control," pp. 531–39.

Congress. However, the results of the research of Scher and the survey of the House Committees in 1967 certainly indicate that there is much less oversight being done than would be expected in the light of the official pronouncements of Congress and the scholarly commentaries which assert the pervasiveness of the activity. Indeed, the House survey revealed such a limited amount of oversight that it raises the question of whether legislative oversight is not a phase of legislative behavior where scholarly generalizations have preceded description and analysis.

However, if it is the general consensus that Congress should be an active overseer of the Executive in order to help achieve responsible and responsive administration, and if the existing oversight activities of Congress are neither so extensive or impressive as many have assumed, then it would appear affirmative action must be taken on two levels.

First, Congress must be given the tools and the necessary institutional arrangements to effectively perform the oversight job.

Second, Members of Congress must see more clearly their own and their country's stake in performing the oversight function.

Unless action proceeds along both these levels there is little reason to expect Congress will effectively discharge its oversight responsibilities.

THE NEED FOR REFORM

by Marvin L. Esch

MARVIN L. ESCH in his first elective office (1965–66) represented Ann Arbor in the Michigan State House, where capitol newsmen named him the outstanding Republican Freshman. Elected to Congress in 1966 from Michigan's Second District, he was appointed to the Committee on Education and Labor and the Republican Task Force on Western Alliances. His accomplishments as a Ph.D. from the University of Michigan, a Wayne State University professor, and a consultant for labor and management make him well qualified for his committee assignment. In 1967 he served on the Conference Committee which produced landmark amendments to federal school aid programs. He also is a co-author of *Parallel Steps to Peace in Vietnam* and *Can NATO Survive 1969?*.

The need for Congressional reform has been clearly established by scholars and others including importantly, however belatedly, Members of Congress themselves. It is a need not based on any great fear of rising Presidential power, for while I agree the power of the executive has grown, it has not necessarily grown at the expense of the Congress. Congress has not lost any power; its basic influence remains intact. But it is guilty of neglecting some of its essential functions and is in danger of finding itself structurally unable to cope with the problems of modern America.

If Congress is going to remain a viable force in our federal system, then it must squarely face the need for change. It must fill the void left by its failure to exercise effectively its oversight obligation. It must adopt reforms which make it physically and structurally possible to review what administrators have done with the laws it has passed. It must be willing to withstand the consequences of great public oversight of its own affairs. It must be willing to take a long hard look at its rules and traditions to determine which ones are inconsistent with the times and then be willing to adopt the necessary changes. And it must do all of this in such a way as to insure public confidence and ward off what is rapidly becoming a crisis of neglect.

The last major reform of Congress was accomplished more than 20 years ago. It is clear to every student of the American political scene that, since that time, the federal government and the problems which it must handle have grown tremendously. The structure set up in the 1940s is inadequate to meet the demands of the '60s and '70s.

Republicans in Congress have strongly supported new attempts to reform the Congress. The latest effort is collecting dust in the House Rules Committee where the Democratic leadership has been unwilling to give it a hearing. The Legislative Reorganization Act of 1967, which has the endorsement of the House Republican Policy Committee, represents a big step toward a modern Congress and deserves a better fate than it has so far experienced in the House.

Congressional reform cannot stop with the ultimate passage of this bill. As Minority Leader Gerald R. Ford pointed out

> "The extent to which Congress was willing to clean out its closets was, however, sharply limited by the language of the resolution (setting up the Joint Committee on the Reorganization) 'Provided that nothing in this concurrent resolution shall be construed to authorize the Committee to make any recommendations with respect to the rules, parliamentary procedures, practices and/or precedents of either House.' "[1]

[1] Gerald R. Ford, Introduction to *We Propose: A Modern Congress,* p. xi.

If the Congress is to meet its responsibilities in the years ahead it must take its reforms much further, even to the point of altering its basic structure.

START WITH THE COMMITTEES

"If the Committees are properly structured, if they are adequately staffed and are ably and fairly directed, if the rules of the Committees are so written as to assure full participation by all Members, and if all Members recognize their duty to serve as an effective check upon the Executive Branch and to represent the individual citizen in organized society, then the House will properly serve its historical function as the co-equal branch of government closest to the people."[2]

This ideal, so ably expressed by U. S. Senator Robert P. Griffin, must serve as a guideline for Congressional reform. Effective oversight and legislative processes require power and the most powerful influence in our legislative branch rests in the Committee structure. Thus it is here that reform must begin.

The oversight role, the "duty to serve as an effective check upon the Executive Branch," is probably the most neglected role of the Committee system and one which must be strengthened. If we are to have effective oversight, then Congress must have the professional competence and specialized knowledge needed to analyze the effectiveness of ongoing programs. The establishment of permanent oversight subcommittees in each of the major standing Committees would be an excellent first step in that direction. Such a structure must be developed on a bi-partisan basis and have adequate staffing to carry out the investigations and analyses. While recognizing that the legitimate and ultimate power rests with the Congressmen themselves, the degree to which they can have adequate

[2] Robert P. Griffin, "Rules and Procedure of the Standing Committees" in *We Propose: A Modern Congress*, p. 37.

and effective supporting staff to carry out the investigating inquiries and analyses will be a crucial factor in delivering their effectiveness. Indeed, in comparison with the personnel which departments and agencies utilize to inform Congress of their activities, it seems somewhat inconceivable that Congress has not availed itself of a larger percentage of the personnel in this area.

A parallel need of these subcommittees is to utilize the competence of professionals and specialists on a consultant basis to aid them in their work. Whereas now Committee investigation largely reflects the views of administrative agencies and/or special interest groups, such consultants would tend to identify with the subcommittees and would serve the role of affirmative devil's advocates.

FILL THE INFORMATION GAP

Dr. Philip Donham and Robert J. Fahey in their study of Congress emphasized the need for more and better information.

"Congressional Committees constantly make decisions without having all the relevant facts before them. There is obviously a point at which the line must be drawn in studying a proposed bill, but for lack of staff resources and lack of time, Congress makes its decisions in an absence of hard fact."[3]

Among measures to correct this startling situation would be regular and detailed briefing sessions by administrative agencies regarding their policies. Sufficient notice should be given prior to such sessions so that searching and in-depth questioning can be developed. Administrative agencies must be required to furnish the Committees with complete information on their activities, plans, proposed programs, and proposed

[3] Dr. Philip Donham and Robert J. Fahey, *Congress Needs Help*, p. 117.

administrative ruling before those administrative decisions have the force of law.

Another important avenue to full information and improved oversight is expanded use of the General Accounting Office. This completely nonpartisan and professional organization is exceptionally well qualified to provide the Congress with detailed information regarding administrative actions. The Congress has largely ignored the valuable work this office performs. Further efforts should be made to bring G.A.O. critiques into the decision-making process and to familiarize Members of Congress with their analyses. The loan of G.A.O. specialists to Committees for limited periods of time should also be encouraged.

It is almost unbelievable that the Congress has not taken advantage of the great expansion in computer technology. The need for a comprehensive computer system on Capitol Hill is self-evident. Without a rapid, accurate and independent source of information with which to review administrative claims, the Congress is completely at a loss to judge executive credibility. Computer capability should be established in the Legislative Reference Service of the Library of Congress with the computers available on a priority basis to the Committees in their legislative and oversight functions.

Congress should also begin to employ the blue ribbon study commission approach on specific problems of major national importance. The Executive Branch has long used this device to tap the talents and abilities of experts within government and from the private sector on the most pressing problems of our society.

Unfortunately, the results of the studies conducted by such Executive blue ribbon commissions have frequently been unavailable for Congressional or public scrutiny. An excellent example of this was the Defense Department Commission on the subject of draft inequities appointed by the President in 1964. That study was never released despite repeated requests from Members of the Armed Services Committees of the House and Senate and other Congressmen. Then, in 1966, the President appointed another commission. This commission reported on a small part of its findings but the controversial portions of their study were sent to still another commission —with the conclusions of the first two commissions still unavailable. In the meantime, it was incumbent on the Congress to enact an extension of the Selective Service System during 1967. It was forced to do so without the expert advice of the commissions which had been formed to provide that information.

It is clear that the Congress must take action to prevent future repetitions of this fiasco. First, it must make provisions in the law which require that Presidential Commission findings be made available to Members of Congress—if not on a public basis, at least in executive session. Second, the Congress must make use of blue ribbon commissions of its own which are responsible solely to it and which can provide it with independent information on which to base its judgments.

CLARIFY JURISDICTION AND RIGHTS

These reforms could easily be established without significantly changing the basic structure of the Congress and are thus susceptible to early acceptance. While such changes are essential and would vastly improve the ability of the Congress to fulfill its Constitutional role, attention must also be given to more basic and far-reaching reforms within the Congress, and its committee structure.

Incredibly, there are eight different committees in the House which are vitally concerned with the problems of urban life. Coordination between them is practically non-existent. Not only is it therefore difficult to consider and enact a well balanced and coordinated program and oversee the administration of that program, but frequently one discovers that the Committees, and the agencies which they direct, are working at cross purposes. As Congressman F. Bradford Morse of Massachusetts so accurately pointed out in *We Propose: A Modern Congress,*

". . . while the Public Works Committee is considering legislation to build new highways to bring more cars into the central city, the Housing Subcommittee of the Banking and Currency Committee may be working on legislation to improve mass transit facilities in an effort to keep the cars out."[4]

Similar confusion is caused by the overlapping of the same two committees in regard to water treatment facilities. While Banking and Currency controls programs funded by the Community Facilities Administration of the Department of Housing and Urban Development for new sewage systems, the Public Works Committee controls the Water Pollution Control Administration which funds water treatment facilities.

Clearly, these examples highlight the need for Congress to give careful attention to the reorganization of its Committees along jurisdictional lines. Specific committees should be able to coordinate all the programs dealing with a given problem. Obviously, such basic reorganization would not only simplify the legislative process, but would also increase the ability of the Congress to judge the progress of the administrative agencies guiding those programs.

Attention must also be devoted to the internal operation of the Committees themselves. The arbitrary power of the chairman must be curtailed and the right of a majority of the Committee to consider and report bills must be clarified. The rights of minority party members should be spelled out, including provision for adequate minority staff, the right to call witnesses and adequate time for the preparation of minority reports.

CHANGE THE SENIORITY SYSTEM

"It is a little difficult to say with pride that ours is a government of laws and not of men when power and

[4] F. Bradford Morse, M.C., "Strengthening the Committee Structure: The Problem of Overlapping Jurisdiction" in *We Propose: A Modern Congress*, p. 59.

prestige in Congress are not won, as they should be, through diligent, intelligent achievement, but are rather 'awarded' to the winners of the continuing race against time."[5]

This point, made by Mayor John Lindsay, a former member of the House, is well taken. To make a man a committee chairman simply because he has more years of service than his colleagues does not make sense. Length of service is not necessarily directly proportional to qualification (nor, I hasten to add, does being old disqualify one from leadership). The seniority system is basically antithetical to the democratic system and it should no longer be allowed to encumber the processes of the Congress by placing long-lived but incompetent or senile men in positions of highest power. The Congress should be able freely to elect its chairmen and choose the most able person for that job. Numerous proposals have been put forward as the appropriate method of conducting that election and several are deserving of full consideration. This article is not the proper vehicle for a discussion of those alternatives; it is simply to indicate that those alternatives must be discussed and must be given the attention they deserve.

OPEN THE DOORS

The Congress has devoted much energy to hiding certain facets of its operations from the public eye. This is done not necessarily because they are engaged in dishonest or unethical practices, but more because of a false fear that total disclosure will show an individual and/or a party in something less than a favorable light. This secrecy and planned confusion actually provide more avenues for unscrupulous activities and lead to further public suspicion, distrust and disrespect for the Congress. Congress has everything to gain from opening its doors and should take action to do so.

[5] Honorable John V. Lindsay, "The Seniority System" in *We Propose: A Modern Congress*, p. 32.

Committees, except those of a top security nature, should be open to the public and committee voting and attendance records should be readily available to anyone. Radio and television should be allowed to cover committee and floor proceedings within reasonable limits.

Republicans were influential in the establishment recently of the Committee on Standards of Official Conduct. This Committee should establish a code of ethics for Congressmen which will require disclosure of campaign and personal finances and define the conditions under which travel at public expense can be authorized. Conflicts of interest should be clearly defined and Members who indulge in them should be subject to censure or removal from office. Qualifications for staff, and requirements that staff actually work on the business of the Congress, should be laid out and the "basic rate scale" of employees' pay should be changed so that actual wage figures are readily available to the public.

UNTANGLE THE BUDGET MESS

No greater challenge faces the new legislator than attempting to understand the budgetary process and be conversant enough with appropriations particulars to cast an intelligent vote on money bills and amendments. The challenge becomes greater with the realization that Members with many years of seniority find themselves in the same dilemma.

Cornelius P. Cotter tells us that upward of nine tenths of Congressional consideration is concerned with spending issues. This means, he points out, that "the greatest potential for Congressional oversight of administration lies in the appropriations process."[6]

He also succinctly condemns the antiquated and inefficient structure which the Congress employs in this vital function.

[6] Cornelius P. Cotter, "Legislative Oversight" in *Congress: The First Branch of Government*, p. 46.

"We have gradually come to the realization that the budget document is 'the work plan of the nation.' We must belatedly come to an awareness that the process of reviewing that work plan and putting it on the path to realization, is assigned to a Model-T appropriations process operating in an age of digital computers and space missiles."[7]

No better illustration of the inadequacy of the present budget document can be found than the 90th Congress. On July 1 when the 1968 fiscal year began, only three of the seventeen major appropriations bills had cleared the Congress, and two of those were Supplemental appropriations. Over half (9 out of 17) were passed after November 1, when four months of the fiscal year had already elapsed. Two major appropriations, the Foreign Assistance and Economic Opportunity bills, were still undecided when the final week of the Congressional Session began and were pushed through in the last-minute haste to adjourn the Congress.

Such delay makes for neither a thoughtful legislative process nor efficient program administration. The Congress can hardly expect an agency to show good results when that agency was unable to conduct its business or make concrete plans and commitments for half of the fiscal year because its funds were not approved.

The Legislative Reorganization Act of 1967 contains several major reforms which must be promptly instituted:

"First, it enlarges the scope and functions of the Government Accounting Office to enable it to supply a variety of budgetary and fiscal data to Congress, its Committees and its Members. Second, it attempts to involve Congress in the evolution of the Program-Budgeting System now under way in the Executive Branch. Third, it requires the Executive Branch to supply more detailed fiscal data and forecasts. Fourth, it repeals the moribund fiscal portions of the 1946 Legislative Reorganization Act and sub-

[7] Cotter, *op. cit.* p. 53.

stitutes new appropriations procedures for considering the overall budget and for the review of multi-agency programs. Fifth, it commands the substantive legislative committees to estimate the projected five-year costs of new programs, to review systematically grant-in-aid programs, and wherever possible to authorize new programs on, and transfer old ones to, an annual appropriations basis."[8]

It is also clear that appropriations measures must be considered well in advance of the fiscal year they are to take effect. This must be done to avoid the payless paydays and program suspensions which occurred in 1967.

Dr. Paul McCracken, distinguished economist of the University of Michigan, has urged the establishment of a blue ribbon commission to examine expenditure decision-making and seek ways to coordinate the activities of the Congress and the administration in this important regard. Certainly such a commission would be useful.

RESTORE THE CONGRESS

The oversight function is the key to the revitalization of Congress and the object of most reforms. Recommendations including those I have highlighted propose to arm Congress with more information, more expertise and more time to review the administration of its programs. While the expansive nature of the executive branch makes it increasingly difficult to achieve effective oversight, Congress still has the power. The failure to exercise it constitutes a real threat to the natural and necessary position of the Congress in our form of government.

A realization that modern times deserve a modern Congress is needed to meet this threat. This realization must grow into

[8] Walter Kravitz, *Congressional Reform: Proposed Legislative Reorganization Act of 1967*, The Library of Congress, Legislative Reference Service, pp. 7–8.

J

wideranging reforms. In a practical vein some will take years to enact, but many are realistic immediately. Nothing short of a continuing and intensive introspection will restore and retain Congress as a dynamic force in the progress of our nation.

ANCHOR BOOKS

GOVERNMENT AND POLITICAL SCIENCE

AFRICA AND THE VICTORIANS: The Climax of Imperialism—Ronald Robinson and John Gallagher, A614

AGRARIAN SOCIALISM—Seymour Martin Lipset, A606

AMERICAN STRATEGY: A New Perspective—The Growth of Politico-Military Thinking in the United States—Urs Schwarz, A587

AMERICAN STRATEGY FOR THE NUCLEAR AGE—Walter F. Hahn and John C. Neff, eds., A224

THE ARAB WORLD TODAY—Morroe Berger, A406

BAGEHOT'S HISTORICAL ESSAYS—Norman St. John-Stevas, ed., A451

BASIC WRITINGS ON POLITICS AND PHILOSOPHY—Karl Marx and Friedrich Engels, Lewis S. Feuer, ed., A185

CAN AMERICAN DEMOCRACY SURVIVE COLD WAR?—Harry Howe Ransom, A402

THE CASE OF COMRADE TULAYEV—Victor Serge, A349

CHILDREN AND THE DEATH OF A PRESIDENT—Multi-Disciplinary Studies—ed. by Martha Wolfenstein and Gilbert Kliman, A543

COMMUNITY POWER STRUCTURE—Floyd Hunter, A379

COMPETITION AND MONOPOLY—Mark S. Massel, A386

CONGRESSIONAL CONTROL OF ADMINISTRATION—Joseph P. Harris, A482

THE CONGRESSMAN—Charles L. Clapp, A426

THE DEATH PENALTY IN AMERICA, Revised Edition—Hugo Adam Bedau, ed., A387

DECISIONS IN SYRACUSE—Roscoe C. Martin, Frank J. Munger, et. al., A434

THE DISCOVERY OF INDIA—Jawaharlal Nehru, Robert I. Crane, ed., A200

ECONOMY, LIBERTY AND THE STATE—Calvin B. Hoover, A241

1848: THE REVOLUTION OF THE INTELLECTUALS—Lewis Namier, A385

THE ERA OF TYRANNIES—Elie Halévy, trans. by Robert K. Webb, A463

ESSAYS ON POLITICS AND CULTURE—John Stuart Mill; Gertrude Himmelfarb, ed., A379

THE FEDERALIST PAPERS, Second Edition—ed. by Roy P. Fairfield, A239

THE FIRST NEW NATION—The United States in Historical and Comparative Perspective—Seymour Martin Lipset, A597

FROM RACE RIOT TO SIT-IN—Arthur Waskow, A557

GOVERNMENT AND POLITICS OF INDIA—W. H. Morris-Jones, A561

THE GOOD SAMARITAN AND THE LAW—ed. by James M. Ratcliffe, A541

THE GREAT DEBATE: Theories of Nuclear Strategy—Raymond Aron, trans. by Ernest Pavel, A467

THE HUMAN CONDITION—Hannah Arendt, A182

IMPERIALISM AND SOCIAL REFORM: English Social-Imperial Thought, 1895–1914—Bernard Semmel, A618

INTERNATIONAL POLITICAL COMMUNITIES, A488

LATIN AMERICAN POLITICS—Robert D. Tomasek, ed., A498

LAW AND THE MODERN MIND—Jerome Frank, A350

LIBERAL PAPERS—James Roosevelt, ed., A290

A MAN OF THE PEOPLE—Chinua Achebe, A594

THE MANPOWER REVOLUTION: Its Policy Consequences, Excerpts from the Senate Hearings Before the Clark Committee, ed. by Garth L. Mangum; Foreword by Senator Joseph S. Clark, A522

MARX IN THE MID-TWENTIETH CENTURY: A Yugoslav Philosopher Reconsiders Karl Marx's Writings—Gajo Petrović, A584

MAX WEBER: AN INTELLECTUAL PORTRAIT—Reinhard Bendix, A281

MAY MAN PREVAIL?—Erich Fromm, A275

METROPOLIS 1985—Raymond Vernon, A341

THE METROPOLITAN TRANSPORTATION PROBLEM, Revised edition—Wilfred Owen, A502

THE MIAMI METROPOLITAN EXPERIMENT, Second edition, Expanded—Edward Sofen, A526

MIRAGE OF HEALTH—René Dubos, A258

NECESSITY FOR CHOICE—Henry A. Kissinger, A282

THE NEGRO AND THE AMERICAN LABOR MOVEMENT—Julius Jacobson, ed., A495

A NEW HISTORY OF THE COLD WAR, Third edition, expanded, of A History of the Cold War—John A. Lukacs, A533

THE OLD REGIME AND THE FRENCH REVOLUTION—Alexis de Tocqueville, A60

THE PATH TO DICTATORSHIP, 1918–1933: Ten Essays by German Historians—trans. by John Conway, with an introduction by Fritz Stern, A547

PATTERNS OF ANARCHY—Leonard I. Krimerman and Lewis Perry, eds., A501

PEACE AND WAR IN THE MODERN AGE: Premises, Myths and Realities—ed. by Frank R. Barnett, William C. Mott and John C. Neff, A450

POLITICAL MAN: The Social Bases of Politics—Seymour Martin Lipset, A330

POLITICS IN AMERICA—D. W. Brogan, A198

THE POLITICS OF POPULATION—William Petersen, A452

QUIET CRISIS IN INDIA—John P. Lewis, A383

THE RADICAL PAPERS—ed. with an Introduction by Irving Howe, A532

THE RADICAL RIGHT—Daniel Bell, ed., A376

RED EXECUTIVE—David Granick, A246

THE REFORM OF PARLIAMENT—Bernard Crick, A484

SOCIAL AND POLITICAL PHILOSOPHY: Readings from Plato to Gandhi—John Somerville and Ronald Santoni, eds., A370

SOCIALIST HUMANISM: An International Symposium—ed. by Erich Fromm, A529

SOCIALIST THOUGHT—Albert Fried and Ronald Sanders, eds., A384

STATES AND NATIONS—Benjamin Akzin, A493

THE STUDY OF TOTAL SOCIETIES—Samuel Klausner, ed., A574

TAMING MEGALOPOLIS—What Is and What Could Be: Vol. I— H. Wentworth Eldredge, ed., A593a

TAMING MEGALOPOLIS—How to Manage an Urbanized World: Vol. II—H. Wentworth Eldredge, ed., A593b

TO THE FINLAND STATION—Edmund Wilson, A6

TODAY'S LATIN AMERICA—Robert J. Alexander, A327

TROPICAL AFRICA: Society and Polity, Vol. II, Abridged edition— George H. T. Kimble, A303b

THE TROUBLED PARTNERSHIP—Henry A. Kissinger, A511

UNION DEMOCRACY—S. M. Lipset, M. A. Trow and J. S. Coleman, A296

THE URBAN COMPLEX: Human Values in Urban Life—Robert C. Weaver, A505

URBAN RENEWAL: PEOPLE, POLITICS, AND PLANNING—Jewel Bellush and Murray Hausknecht, eds., A569

WINNING WITHOUT WAR—Amitai Etzioni, A430

WRITINGS OF THE YOUNG MARX ON PHILOSOPHY AND SOCIETY— Loyd D. Easton and Kurt H. Guddat, trans. and eds., A583

ANCHOR BOOKS

ECONOMICS

ANATOMY OF A METROPOLIS—Edgar M. Hoover and Raymond Vernon, A298

COMPETITION AND MONOPOLY—Mark S. Massel, A386

THE CORPORATION TAKE-OVER—Andrew Hacker, ed., A465

CORPORATIONS IN CRISIS—Richard Austin Smith, A475

ECONOMIC PHILOSOPHY—Joan Robinson, A415

THE ECONOMY, LIBERTY AND THE STATE—Calvin B. Hoover, A241

THE ERA OF TYRANNIES—Elie Halévy, Robert K. Webb, trans., A463

THE EXPLODING METROPOLIS—Editors of Fortune, A146

FREE MEN AND FREE MARKETS—Robert Theobald, A447

THE GUARANTEED INCOME—Robert Theobald, A519

INTERNATIONAL POLITICAL COMMUNITIES, A488

INTRODUCTION TO ECONOMIC REASONING, Fourth, Revised Edition —Marshall A. Robinson, Herbert C. Morton, James D. Calderwood, A338

THE MANPOWER REVOLUTION: Its Policy Consequences, Excerpts from the Senate Hearings Before the Clark Committee, ed. by Garth L. Mangum; Foreword by Senator Joseph S. Clark, A522

MARKETS IN AFRICA: Eight Subsistence Economies in Transition —Paul J. Bohannan and George Dalton, eds., N39

METROPOLIS 1985—Raymond Vernon, A341

THE ORGANIZATION MAN—William H. Whyte, Jr., A117

PRIMITIVE, ARCHAIC AND MODERN ECONOMIES—Karl Polanyi, ed. by George Dalton, A605

QUIET CRISIS IN INDIA—John P. Lewis, A383

THE RED EXECUTIVE: A Study of the Organization Man in Russian Industry—David Granick, A246

STRATEGY AND STRUCTURE: Chapters in the History of the Industrial Enterprise—Alfred D. Chandler, Jr., A461

TWO WORLDS OF CHANGE—Otto Feinstein, ed., A396

UNION DEMOCRACY—Seymour Lipset, Martin A. Trow, and James S. Coleman. With a foreword by Clark Kerr, A296

THE URBAN COMPLEX: Human Values in Urban Life—Robert C. Weaver, A505